RECONFIGURATIONS
OF NATIVE
NORTH AMERICA

Reconfigurations of Native North America

AN ANTHOLOGY OF NEW PERSPECTIVES

Edited by

JOHN R. WUNDER AND KURT E. KINBACHER

FOREWORD BY MARKKU HENRIKSSON

Texas Tech University Press

This book is typeset in Adobe Garamond Pro. The paper used in this book meets the minimum requirements of
ANSI/NISO Z39.48-1992 (R1997). ∞

Library of Congress Cataloging-in-Publication Data
Reconfigurations of Native North America : an anthology of new perspectives / edited by John R. Wunder and Kurt E.
Kinbacher ; foreword by Markku Henriksson.
p. cm.
Papers from the Ninth Biennial Maple Leaf and Eagle Conference on North American Studies, held Sept.
2-6, 2002 at the Renvall Institute.
Summary: "Seventeen essays highlight contemporary indigenous studies. Primarily for scholarly audiences,
the essays reflect indigenous voices and consider Native worldviews while confronting issues such as indigenous identity, cultural perseverance, economic development, and urbanization. Discussions examine mainstream policies that
influenced Native peoples in a number of eras and places"—Provided by publisher.
Includes bibliographical references and index.
ISBN 978-0-89672-641-3 (hardcover : alk. paper) 1. Indians of North America—Study and teaching—
Congresses. 2. Indians of North America—Social conditions—Congresses. 3. Indians of North America—Ethnic identity—Congresses. 4. Indians of North America—Government relations—Congresses. 5. North
America—Civilization—Congresses. 6. North America—Ethnic relations—Congresses. I. Wunder, John R. II. Kin-
bacher, Kurt E. III. Maple Leaf and Eagle Conference on North American Studies (9th : 2002 : Renvall-instituutti)
E76.6.R43 2009
970.004'97—dc22 2008044591

Printed in the United States of America
09 10 11 12 13 14 15 16 17 / 9 8 7 6 5 4 3 2 1

Texas Tech University Press | Box 41037 | Lubbock, Texas 79409-1037 USA
800.832.4042 | ttup@ttu.edu | www.ttup.ttu.edu

Contents

Maps and Tables   vii

Acknowledgments   ix

Foreword   MARKKU HENRIKSSON   xi

Introduction   JOHN R. WUNDER and KURT E. KINBACHER   3

I. Comparative Historical and Cultural Perspectives   9

1. Indigenous Colonial Treaties of North America in Comparative Perspective   13
   JOHN R. WUNDER

2. Native Self-Determination Building: The Crees of Northern Québec and
   the Navajos of the American Southwest   32
   DAVID HARDING

3. Bear Ceremonialism and Its Ecological Aspects among Subarctic and
   Plains Indians   54
   RIKU HÄMÄLÄINEN

II. The Literary Indigenous Voice   71

4. The Curious Case of Coyote, or the Tale of the Appropriated Trickster   75
   MARK SHACKLETON

5. "My Cells Will Not Forget": The Writings of Wendy Rose   91
   P. JANE HAFEN

6. Sherman Alexie and Stretching Sexual Boundaries   102
   PATRICE HOLLRAH

III. Challenges Past and Present   109

7. The Image of Indians in the Imagination of the Early Republic   115
   PETER C. MESSER

Contents

8. Perspectives on the Lakota Ghost Dance of 1890   140
   RANI-HENRIK ANDERSSON

9. Force and Possibility: Hopis' Views of the Internet   152
   RITVA LEVO-HENRIKSSON

10. Indian Gaming, Sovereignty, and the Courts: The Case of the
    Miccosukee Tribe of Florida   160
    MIIA HALME

11. Teaching and Learning about Native North America: An Analysis of
    Educational Standards for Schools in the United States and Canada 178
    SUSAN A. WUNDER

IV. Nation and Identity   193

12. Building a Shawnee Nation: Indigenous Identity, Tribal Structure,
    and Sociopolitical Organization, 1400–1770   199
    SAMI LAKOMÄKI

13. "Why Quarrel about Dividing the Hind Quarter When We Are Not
    Going to Hunt?": Seminole Diplomatic Discourse before the Comet 225
    SUSAN A. MILLER

14. Hybridity, Canadian Indian Policy, and the Construction and
    "Extinguishment" of Metis Aboriginal Rights in the Nineteenth Century 236
    GERHARD J. ENS

15. The "Metis Indians" of Ontario   252
    JOE SAWCHUK

V. The People   263

16. Scales of Aboriginal Citizenship in Canada: Postcolonial
    Problems and Progress   269
    PATRICIA BURKE WOOD

17. The Land Remembers the People, the People Remember the Land:
    American Indian History as a Continuing Story   279
    PETER IVERSON

Beginnings   293
    KURT E. KINBACHER

About the Authors   303
Index   309

Maps and Tables

Native North America: Selected Configurations   4

Empowering First Nations: James Bay Crees Confront Provincial
    Hydroelectric Power Schemes, 1970–2000   35

Empowering Native America: Navajo and Hopi Coal Resources   45

Seminole Sovereignty over Two Centuries: Diplomatic Landmarks,
    1820–1845, and Gaming on the Miccosukee Reservations,
    1970–2000   161

Shawnee Culturescapes: The Diaspora, 1670–1725, and the Ohio Valley
    Nation, 1725–1770   202

Metis Country, 1860–2000   237

First Nations Country Today: The Tsuu T'ina Reserve   270

Indian Country Today: The Navajo Reservation   280

States, Provinces, and Territories by Type of Subject Standards   183

States, Provinces, and Territories by Level of Curricular Content   185

Acknowledgments

THIS BOOK would not have been possible without the intellectual curiosity and creativity of the faculty and students of the North American Studies Program of the Renvall Institute of the University of Helsinki, led by Markku Henriksson, McDonnell Douglas Chair of American Studies.

Well-known for its outstanding programming and cutting-edge interdisciplinary excellence, the Renvall Institute is at the forefront of bringing scholars and students together from throughout the world. At Reconfigurations of Native North America, the Ninth Biennial Maple Leaf and Eagle Conference on North American Studies, September 2–6, 2002, more than fifty researchers from four continents traveled to northern Europe to interact and explore important North American Indigenous issues of the day. Professor Henriksson, the North American Studies Committee, and Renvall faculty and students hosted the conference that featured the Indigenous research topics found prominently displayed in this book.

Foreword

FOR A VERY LONG TIME, European and Euro-American history embraced only European kings and bishops, wars, and political events. Even when historians included North America in their narratives they hardly paid attention to the indigenous population of what the Europeans and their descendants called the "New World." Serious research on First Nations and Native American history in North America really only began about thirty years ago, as the former president of the Western History Association, Professor Peter Iverson, writes at the end of this collection.

Since the 1960s, writing on First Nations and Native American history has expanded worldwide, as have anthropology, media studies, sociology, and area and cultural studies. The field of Native North American studies is today pursued by indigenous scholars as well as by Euro-Americans and Europeans. Native scholars have not only enriched the field by their own insights, but also probably forced non-Natives to include new dimensions to their approaches. Today First Nations and Native American studies cover a wide range of topics with great expertise and scholarship.

First Nations and Native American history have been an integral part of the University of Helsinki's North American Studies program ever since its establishment in 1986. All Maple Leaf and Eagle Conferences have included presentations on this theme. However, we were able to dedicate the full venue of the event to Indigenous North America only at the ninth Maple Leaf and Eagle Conference in 2002. The conference theme, "Reconfigurations of Native North America," was both demanding and challenging, resulting in ambitious presentations and a very lively discussion with Natives and non-Natives alike. Selected talks presented at the conference were later turned into articles and essays edited for this book by John R. Wunder and Kurt E. Kinbacher. This collection includes writings by both senior scholars in the field and those who are just about to take their first steps in academia. They include writings from both sides of the Atlantic, and by several indigenous scholars as well as by Europeans and Euro-Americans. I believe this collection is an excellent example of the richness and variety of the field, and it is my hope that you will enjoy reading it.

MARKKU HENRIKSSON
Helsinki, Finland, 2008

RECONFIGURATIONS

OF NATIVE

NORTH AMERICA

Introduction

JOHN R. WUNDER AND KURT E. KINBACHER

*For hundreds of years Aboriginal People in the area now known as Canada were
sovereign and self-sufficient. We are now poised to once again take
charge of our lives and destiny.*[1]

ELIJAH HARPER, Ojibwa-Cree

*Let me be a free man—free to travel, free to stop, free to work, free to trade where I
choose, free to choose my own teachers, free to follow the religion of my fathers, free to
think and talk and act for myself—and I will obey every law, or submit to the
penalty. Whenever the white man treats an Indian as they treat each other, then we
will have no more wars. We shall all be alike—brothers of one father and one
mother, with one sky above us and one country around us, and one government for
all. Then the Great Spirit Chief who rules above will smile upon this land, and send
rain to wash out the bloody spots made by brothers' hands from the face of the earth.*[2]

IN-MUT-TOO-YAH-LAT-LAT (CHIEF JOSEPH), Nez Percé

Reconfigurations of Native North America is a bold title, both for a conference
and a book. It sends strong feelings, messages of re-examination, of redoing, of
revisiting, and then of regaining, what has been lost. Duane Champagne, Turtle
Mountain Chippewa, has written about the pressures inherent from the past facing
indigenous peoples in today's world. Champagne explains,

> The story of the nineteenth century is largely one of Native loss of control
> over land, government, community, and culture. Throughout much of the
> latter half of the twentieth century Native communities sought greater self-
> determination, and by the end of the century many Native groups were
> positioning themselves to regain that authority as well as to promote com-
> munity and cultural presentation. During the twenty-first century increasing

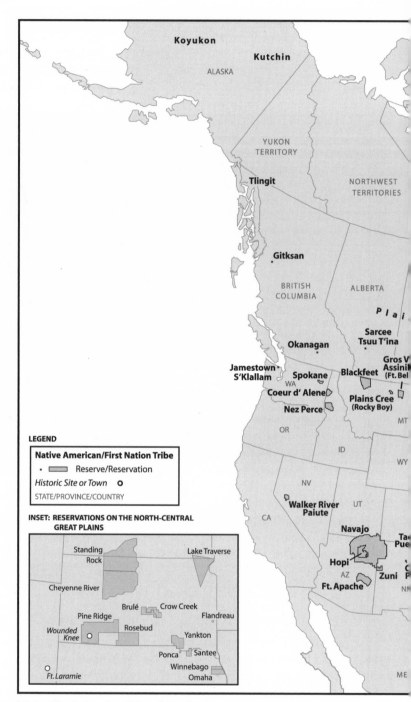

Native North America: Selected Configurations

NUNAVUT

Iqaluit

Naskapi · LABRADOR

NF

QUÉBEC

**Eastern
Cree**

MANITOBA

e e

TCH-
AN

**Sioux
siniboine**

(Ft. Peck)

T.

ND

ONTARIO

NB

NS

PEI

ME

**Kahnawake
Mohawk**

Meech Lake

VT

NH

**Lake Superior
Ojibwa**

MI

MN

NY

MA

CT

RI

SD

Menominee

WI

MI

NJ

PA

IA

OH

MD

DE

NE

ramie

IL

IN

WV

VA

KS

MO

KY

**Eastern
Cherokee**

NC

**Pawnee
Cherokee
Creek**

OK

AR

TN

SC

**Creek
Confederacy**

MS

AL

GA

TX

LA

Seminole

FL

| 500 | 1000 | 1500 km |

| 500 | 1000 mi |

Miccosukee

globalization of cultures, political relations, and economies will continue to challenge Native communities that wish to gain more political and fiscal control over their own affairs.[3]

Reconfigurations take place in reality and also in dreams that can lead to realization. Gord Bruyere, Anishinaabe, gifts us his dreams of reconfigurations that "whisper" in his blood.

> I share a dream with many Aboriginal peoples in Canada. Actually, it is many dreams, but perhaps the most crucial aspects of those dreams involve the well-being and vitality of Aboriginal children and families. I would like to share my own dreams with you, as well as some stark waking moments that intrude upon believing those dreams into reality. My own dreams, I suppose, are somewhat pitiful in comparison to the enormities of the intrusions, but what would happen if enough Aboriginals and non-Aboriginal peoples experienced and followed the same kind of dreams for Aboriginal children and families in Canada? It is a wonderful dream. I have faith in those dreams which, to me, are not simply some kind of chemical process within the human brain. Rather, dreams are aspects of a people's collective memory of past, present, and future. To me, dreams are intuitive lessons that whisper in our blood.[4]

Somewhere after "reconcentration" and "reconciliation," but before "reconnaissance" and "reconquest," one should find "reconfiguration" in *Webster's New Twentieth-Century Dictionary Unabridged* (1983), a truly hefty tome, a second edition promising deluxe color. But it is missing. On the other hand, "configuration" has a variety of meanings. In *Webster's New Twentieth-Century*, it is generally defined as a noun that represents an external shape or form, or even an outline or a contour. In astronomy, configuration is the position of stars in relation to one another; and in astrology, it means a horoscope based on the positions of planets. Moreover, configuration has specific meaning in Gestalt psychology as "an integrated whole with independent properties and functions over and above the sum of the properties and functions of its parts." My, that seems wordy. A "reconfiguration" then of a "configuration" seems somewhat daunting.

In their language, the Omahas explain *Reconfigurations of Native North America* in several ways. "Native North America" is *Níkashi^{n}ga ukéthi^n mó^{n}zho^n thó^n* or "Indian Country." "Reconfigurations" in Omaha can be translated as "revisited," or "remade," or perhaps the closest meaning for this book title as "reconsidered." Thus, *Reconfigurations of Native North America* as "Indian Country considered again" becomes *Níkashi^{n}ga ukéthi^n mó^{n}zho^n thó^n shé theno^n ekítha.* But an even better Omaha expression might serve for the title—*Mîka?e itóⁿthadi wîⁿ Óⁿba téga athîⁿ*, which means in Omaha, "An old star has a new day."[5]

Put another way, reconfigurations are attempts to define new approaches, to "reinvent" or "refine" previous meanings. Of the stars, it might mean a different position of an old celestial body. For this particular book, however, reconfigurations denote new ways to consider scholarship concerning indigenous North Americans. It might mean the reexamination of an old question or the examination of a new question never before pondered. And what it represents is a cutting-edge synthesis for North American studies that combines the best writings of highly regarded scholars with new and promising scholars, all working in the fields of literature, history, religion, anthropology, politics, sociology, and law. These indigenous and nonindigenous scholars come from around the globe. Throughout their work, First Nations and Native American voices ring loud and clear.

Reconfigurations of Native North America is composed of seventeen essays divided into five separate sections. Each section is introduced separately, and most are illustrated with maps by Ezra Zeitler.[6] In concert the sections help illustrate the diversity of cultures north of Mesoamerica.[7] The five sections are titled, Comparative Historical and Cultural Perspectives, The Literary Indigenous Voice, Challenges of the Past and Present, Nation and Identity, and The People. Essays first compare North American indigenous colonial treaties, indigenous responses to environmental crises, and bear ceremonialism. The latter topic is significant because most Native cultures recognize deep connections among "two-leggeds" and "four-leggeds."[8] Additionally, the division between sacred and secular is minimal. While both these concepts are nearly universal, ecological and cultural differences have allowed for a wide array of religious practices to emerge. This variety is evident even in ceremonies that revolve around a single being in adjacent ecosystems. Next, various Native writers are explored and assessed. A third section addresses the meanings of the American Revolution and the Massacre at Wounded Knee along with the problems brought by the Internet, Indian gaming, and modern education. All modern treatments of indigenous studies must dissect sovereignty issues, and the fourth section treats nation-building, indigenous diplomatic discourse, and mixed-blood identity formations. Finally, The People features modern life, its challenges and opportunities, and in particular definitions of indigenous citizenship both in Canada and the United States for Native North Americans.

While modern national boundaries were not conceived in indigenous space, this volume does not include discussions of peoples living in northern Mexico. The lives of Native peoples residing in that nation have certainly been altered by distinct federal policies. Cross-border comparisons would broaden the growing understanding of Native experiences, but that is a story for another day.

These articles are creative and dynamic and stretch traditional boundaries. But they are not the last word. Much more must be read, must be uncovered, and must be shared. It must be reconfigured. Annie Dodge Wauneka, Navajo, perhaps has the proper advice for all who open these pages:

"I'll go and do more."[9]

NOTES

1. Elijah Harper, "Foreword," in *Aboriginal Self-Government in Canada: Current Trends and Issues,* ed. John H. Hutton (Saskatoon, SK: Purich Publishing, Ltd., 1994), 8. Harper represented First Nations interests ably in the Manitoba Parliament at the collapse of the Meech Lake Accords, when Canada attempted to resolve its Québec constitutional crisis without the involvement of indigenous peoples. Harper, former chief of the Red Sucker Lake First Nation, went on to serve in the Canadian Parliament and as Commissioner of the Indian Claims Commission.

2. Chief Joseph, "An Indian's Views of Indian Affairs," reprinted from the *North American Review* (April 1879) in W.C. Vanderwerth, comp., *Indian Oratory: Famous Speeches by Noted Indian Chieftains* (New York: Ballantine Books, 1972), 234.

3. Duane Champagne, "The Crisis for Native Governments in the Twenty-First Century," in *The Future of Indigenous Peoples: Strategies for Survival and Development,* ed. Duane Champagne and Ismael Abu-Saad (Los Angeles: University of California–Los Angeles American Indian Studies Center, 2003), 205.

4. Gord Bruyere, "The Lessons in Our Blood: Reflections on Protecting Aboriginal Children," in *The Future of Indigenous Peoples,* ed. Champagne and Abu-Saad, 133.

5. These translations are courtesy of Kurt E. Kinbacher, who is a student of the Omaha language; Emmaline Walker Sanchez (Omaha), Mark Awakuni-Swetland, and Rory Larson, who are instructors of Omaha; and Alberta Canby (Omaha).

6. Ezra Zeitler earned his doctorate in historical geography at the University of Nebraska–Lincoln in 2008 and is an assistant professor of geography at the University of Wisconsin–Eau Claire.

7. For a definition of Mesoamerica see Carl Waldman, *Atlas of the North American Indian,* revised edition (New York: Checkmark Books, 2000), 50.

8. See, for example, Joseph M. Marshall III, *The Lakota Way: Stories and Lessons for Living* (New York: Penguin Compass, 2001), 20.

9. Carolyn Niethammer, *"I'll Go and Do More": Annie Dodge Wauneka, Navajo Leader and Activist* (Lincoln: University of Nebraska Press, 2001), title quotation.

PART I

Comparative Historical and Cultural Perspectives

*I take off my glove and in giving you my hand I deliver my birthright and lands;
and in taking your hand, I hold fast to all the promises you have made, and I hope
they will last as long as the sun goes round and the water flows.*[1]

MAWEDOPENAIS, Fort Frances Ojibwa

*My dear grandchildren: All of your folks are my relatives, because I am a Sioux, and
so are they. I was glad to hear that the Black Robe had given you this school where
you can learn to read, write, and count the way white people do. You are also being
taught a new religion. You are shown how the white men work and make things.
You are living a new path.*[2]

SITTING BULL, Standing Rock Lakota

RECONFIGURATIONS OF THE INDIGENOUS HISTORY of North America at its most complex require comparative approaches. Few historians and ethnohistorians have learned to grasp these complicated histories beyond one or several First Nations or Native American tribes. Fewer still have mastered an entire region or the indigenous national histories of either all of Canada or the United States. That number becomes more paltry when the stretch of expertise transcends international boundaries and requires the judicious and complex balancing of diverse historical experiences, of separate cultures and separate colonial spheres. Such is the nature of the comparative histories of Native North America.

The following three chapters, however, provide new insight into the historical complexities of divergent Native nations in various eras. They offer a hint of the richness that can be found in the challenging comparative approach to culture and history. First, John R. Wunder explains how nineteenth-century treaty making among indigenous nations in both the United States and Canada have unique twists and turns, and why treaties are taken more seriously in Canada than in the United States today. There are lessons for the colonized and the colonizer, states Wunder, who opens by questioning whether treaty making in today's society can avoid the pitfalls that occurred in the early centuries of negotiation and implementation. In the process of tracing the history of treaty making in North America, Wunder considers the voices of Native American Nez Percés and Lakotas and First Nation Lake Superior Ojibwas and Kahnawake Mohawks. Legal benchmarks, such as the Fort Laramie Treaty of 1868, the Resolution of 1871, the Indian Claims Commission of 1946–1972, and Treaty Four and Five negotiations and renegotiations, are also compared and analyzed. Finally, how American and Canadian treaties fit within the confines of developing international law is carefully sorted out. Wunder suggests that a full understanding of the concept of the "protectorate" is crucial to investigate for modern treaty making.

Next, David Harding compares the building of self-determination in the twentieth century by two disparate indigenous nations: the Crees of Northern Québec and the Navajos of the American Southwest. Both nations were confronted by severe environmental alterations of their homelands by private corporate interests supported by the federal and state/provincial governments of Canada and the United States. The Crees have had to contend with the James Bay Project, which seeks to develop power resources by massive damming of rivers in Cree lands that have traditionally been isolated and not the subject of intervention. That this investment is connected to the politics of Québec autonomy and possible separation further exacerbates tensions among the various parties. Similarly, the Peabody Coal Company has exploited rivalries between the Navajos and their neighbors, the Hopis. Partitioning of the two reservations has occurred at the same time as extensive open-pit coal mining has disrupted the fragile water supplies and landscapes of both peoples. In part, these significant events are occurring because there is so little economic development in these regions, and making agreements that are not in the best long-term interests of indigenous peoples seems like a positive short-run advantage that all too often does not result in overall economic improvement.

Third, Riku Hämäläinen compares the ethnological and ecological aspects of bear ceremonialism among the subarctic Indians of Canada and Plains Indians of the United States. In the past, and continuing into the present, bears are often seen by indigenous peoples as supernatural and human-like. This has resulted in special arrangements, ceremonies, and beliefs celebrated within indigenous cultures. But Hämäläinen, by carefully examining the eastern Crees and a variety of northern Plains Indians, distinguishes between peoples who needed bears to avoid starvation, and those who rarely attempted to kill bears for food supplies. The cosmology of bear ceremonialism thus developed in different ways and contributed to fundamental differences among the Native peoples of North America.

These three chapters then offer diverse comparative analyses of law, environment, and culture that seek greater clarity and highlight the nuances of difference among indigenous North Americans. Just as Sitting Bull foresaw new paths, Mawedopenais retained a careful skepticism of the future.

NOTES

1. Mawedopenais at Treaty Five negotiations (1875), in Olive Patricia Dickason, *Canada's First Nations: A History of Founding Peoples from Earliest Times* (Norman: University of Oklahoma Press, 1992), 280.

2. Sitting Bull to young Indian students at a Catholic school on Standing Rock Reservation, ca. 1889, in *Indian Oratory: Famous Speeches by Noted Indian Chieftains,* comp. W. C. Vanderwerth (New York: Ballantine Books, 1972), 189.

CHAPTER I

Indigenous Colonial Treaties of North America in Comparative Perspective

JOHN R. WUNDER

FUNDAMENTALLY, treaties are legal contracts. Under the common law that influenced North America, as well as international law, these agreements require certain legalistic standards in order to be valid. Basic treaties involve partners making promises, evidence of acceptance by all parties, and what is termed a "consideration," that the subject of the treaty has value. Treaty types range from treaties of friendship and alliance to treaties of land displacement, payments of material goods, and loss of external sovereignty. In North America, initially treaties between indigenous peoples and European Americans documented national equalities. By the mid-nineteenth century, North American treaties had become agreements between the colonized and the colonizer. Vestiges of these treaties are with us today, and while a number of these agreements have proved essential for claiming various fundamental rights of North American indigenous peoples, others have been found wanting.

This essay argues that the treaty experiences of Native Americans and First Nations are multiple and complicated, and that the variety of North American indigenous peoples' relationships with nonindigenous colonial treaty partners may not necessarily offer the models that others may wish to adopt. Today indigenous peoples as diverse as Aborigines, Maoris, and Samis are interested in treaties and sovereignty, but in different ways. How might these interests be expressed? Should they and other indigenous peoples look to the historical and modern experiences of the indigenous peoples of North America for guidance? To answer the above questions, modern treaty issues are described and Native American and First Nation contemporary and historical voices raising concerns about treaties are pondered along with American and Canadian responses and an international law perspective. The chapter concludes with a connection to the United Nations Declaration of Rights of Indigenous Peoples.

CONTEMPORARY INDIGENOUS TREATY CONCERNS

In 1990, the Tjapukai Dancers first recorded the song, "Proud to Be Aborigine." Their album of the same name proved to be a success, crossing the cultural boundaries of Australian music. The lyrics of "Proud to Be Aborigine" mix the past with the present. The song begins with the reflection that for 50,000 years the indigenous peoples of Australia lived in relative peace until the British arrived in Australia, and then the "white man pulled it down under." The singers forcefully remind the world that Aborigines will never die. But there is hope for Australia if blacks and whites learn from each other, respect each other, and treat each other with a mutuality of good faith. After all, "black and white have got to unite or there will be nothing left in the land down under."[1]

"Proud to Be Aborigine" embodies the modern indigenous rights movement in Australia, and a significant part of that movement today urges the federal Australian government to negotiate a treaty with Aborigines and Torres Strait Islanders. The British Crown and the subsequent national and state governments of Australia have never signed a treaty with the Aboriginal peoples, but recent agreements have been made with specific tribes regarding the deeding of fee-simple title to, and shared management of, national parks and public lands. Those who favor a treaty between Australia's indigenous peoples and the federal government want such a document to solidify further land gains and sovereignty with specific land cession as mandated through the *Mabo* and *Wik*[2] High Court decisions; provide reparations for land losses and the Stolen Generation, that is, Aborigine children who were taken from their families and placed in religious institutions and with white families; and guarantee fair treatment in the criminal justice system.[3]

Australia's indigenous peoples have only to look across the Tasman Sea to learn how the Maoris in New Zealand have fared. On February 6, 1840, forty-three indigenous chieftains of New Zealand together with representatives of the English Crown signed the Treaty of Waitangi. Eventually, 540 Maori leaders from throughout the islands signed the treaty. Over the next century, the Crown and New Zealand leaders, Pākehās (non-Maori New Zealanders), abused and corrupted the treaty to steal lands and fishery rights. By the 1970s, Maoris had had enough and protested the treaty violations. In 1975, Maoris organized the Land March on Parliament and began occupying disputed lands. Subsequent events led to public lands, institutions, and buildings being turned over to Maori clans that verified their claims to ownership; reserved representation in Parliament for

Maoris; and the institution of the Waitangi Tribunal, an independent commission that investigates contemporary and historic claims by Maoris of violations of the Treaty of Waitangi by the Crown and subsequent New Zealand governments.

Today indigenous New Zealanders remain vigilant in pursuing land rights and civil rights. Their treaty truly is a "living treaty," a document that retains the basis for Maori sovereignty and nationhood within a nation-state.[4]

The indigenous Samis of Norway, Sweden, Finland, and Russia present a quite different historical and contemporary picture. They have signed no treaties. Perhaps that is because they, like the Native peoples of North America, frequently found themselves the subject of treaties rather than parties to treaties. The first such treaty in 1326, between Dáza (a Sami word for any non-Sami) of Norway, and Novgorod, a Russian city-state, divided Sami lands up between the treaty parties and subjected the Samis residing on the lands to taxation.[5]

After World War II, a Sami civil rights movement emerged that led to greater expressions of self-determination. The Alta Affair in Norway in 1979 galvanized Samis and non-Samis throughout northern Europe. Norway attempted to dam the Alta-Kautokeino waterway, and this construction threatened reindeer grazing and calving lands. Hundreds protested in a level of civil disobedience never before reached in Sapmi, the lands of the Nordic indigenous people. Police arrests further inflamed the situation, so much so that the Samis reached consensus among themselves, stating the Samis held "a right, sanctioned by tradition and by virtue of their being a people, to nurture and develop their own culture, and that state powers are duty-bound to guarantee that these freedoms and rights be fulfilled."[6]

These expressions of sovereignty, however, have been confined to the Nordic nation-states. In 1956, the Samis organized the first of several gatherings that eventually evolved into the Nordic Sami Council. Delegates from Norway, Sweden, and Finland attended. In 1992, Russian Samis attended for the first time; the organization's name was shortened to the Sami Council—Sámiráddi. The Sami Council remains an advisory organization for the Samis in the four nation-states. Sami-elected parliaments also advise Finland (since 1973), Norway (since 1987), and Sweden (since 1992) about Sami concerns.[7]

At the sixteenth annual Sami Conference in October 1996, the Sami peoples, citing the Universal Declaration of Human Rights and the Rio Declaration, issued the Murmansk Declaration establishing that "the Sami are one nation, and interstate borders will not be allowed to break the unity of our peoples, and that the Sami nation has a right to self-determination." Furthermore, the Sami urged Nordic countries to "recognize the rights of the Sami peoples to possess and govern territories" that they traditionally have inhabited.[8] The Sami Council stopped just short of advocating a treaty process. Issues of cultural rights and land rights are handled by national parliaments, and Sami interests in modern treaty making, unlike those of Aborigines, primarily address lobbying the Nordic states to sign international treaty accords that impact the indigenous peoples of the North. Clearly, indigenous peoples as diverse as Aborigines, Maoris, and Samis are interested in treaties, but in different ways. How might these interests be related to the indigenous experience with treaties in North America?

NORTH AMERICAN TREATIES AND INDIGENOUS VOICES

Native Americans and First Nations peoples have commented perceptively and pointedly about treaties. Commentaries vary and reactions run through a range of emotions. Historically, the process of treaty making proved troublesome as fraud and unscrupulous behavior all too often characterized the proceedings. The processes require exacting reconstruction to determine whether in fact a meeting of minds occurred, let alone whether the offer was fair or whether each party actually accepted treaty contents.

In April 1879, *The North American Review* printed what was purported to be a translation of a speech made by Chief Joseph of the Nimiipus or Nez Percés. Entitled "An Indian's Views of Indian Affairs," Joseph told of his reaction over twenty years earlier to the attempts by Washington Territory Governor Isaac I. Stevens to persuade his father Joseph to sign a treaty that would have ceded his people's traditional homelands to the United States. Young Joseph remembered that Stevens argued that there were already hundreds of white people in the Columbia Valley and thousands more going West. The only way Indians and whites could live in peace was for Indians to live in "a country set apart." Joseph recalled with pride that "[m]y father, who represented his band, refused to have anything to do with the council, because he wished to be a free man."[9] He did not sign. But later Lawyer, a chief of another Nez Percé band, did sign a treaty that relinquished nearly all of the Nez Percé homelands. Joseph remembered what his father had told him at the time: "When you go into council with the white man, always remember your country. Do not give it away. The white man will cheat you out of your home. I have taken no pay from the United States. I have never sold our land."[10]

In contrast, Spotted Tail, chief of the Lower Brulé (Sicangu), saw treaty negotiations differently. Already reservation bound, he spoke at a council meeting in 1877 in which he emphasized the similarities between the colonizer and the colonized. Spotted Tail said, "Your people have both intellect and heart; you use these to consider in what way you can do the best to live. My people, who are here before you, are precisely the same." Spotted Tail then offered his perspective: "I see that my friends before me are men of age and dignity, and men of that kind have good judgment and consider well what they do. I infer from that, that you are here to consider what shall be good for my people for a long time to come. I think each of you has selected somewhere a good piece of land for himself with the intention to live on it, that he may there raise his children. My people are not different. We also live upon the earth and upon the things that come to them from above. We have the same thoughts and desires in that respect that the white people have."[11] Spotted Tail had hoped to find common ground in the treaty process, even when a treaty may not have been possible.

First Nations had similar concerns. In 1872, the lieutenant governor of Manitoba and the Northwest Territories, Alexander Morris, opened negotiations with the Lake Superior Ojibwas. As early as 1869, treaty negotiations were proposed, as the Canadians wished to build a road to Red River. The Ojibwas, as was reported by the Canadians, had a keen sense of the treaty process. Mawedopenais, chief of the Ojibwas, began the discussions, restating their position: "The sound of the rustling of the gold is under my feet where I stand; we have a rich country; it is the Great Spirit who gave us this; where we stand upon is the Indians' property, and belongs to them."[12]

Land and trade were twin obsessions of European Americans, particularly with reference to First Nations during the first colonial era of British rule and the second colonial era of the Canadian state in the nineteenth century. Taiaiake Alfred of the Kahnawake Mohawk—or in his language Kanien'kehaka, People of the Flint—wrote *Peace, Power, Righteousness: An Indigenous Manifesto*, wherein he considers the importance of power in various international relationships. Power for the Tlingits, according to Alfred, is called *shagóon*, meaning "ancestors, origins, heritage and destiny/supreme being." Tlingits believed that each of these components were with each party to a treaty during negotiations and throughout the duration of the agreement.[13]

Harry Robinson, an Okanagan elder, chanted his understanding of power:

> See?
> That's another power way.
> He's a powerful man, but
> He can tell what's coming[,] coming to him
> in a certain time.
> But he can't stop it,
> he can't beat it.
> So he [will] die that way,
> by the other power's order.[14]

Robinson's definition of power, like Spotted Tail's, involved mutual respect for the "other power."

Power for First Nations requires the language of recognition and coexistence. For example, the Kanien'kehaka "Kaswentha," or Two-Row Wampum, constituted an agreement with the Dutch in the seventeenth century that did not involve subjugation. The agreement reached embodied "a context of respect for the auton-omy and distinctive nature of each partner."[15] This was a treaty of friendship and alliance. These concepts of power are integral parts of all treaty relationships in current Canadian negotiations involving indigenous sovereignty.

Thus, the voice of North America's indigenous peoples suggests several approaches to treaty conceptualization. These involve historical definitions of power, respect, homelands, and sovereignty.

AMERICAN TREATY MAKING

The U.S. federal government made over 350 treaties with Native American nations between 1776 and 1871. The Congress along with President Ulysses S. Grant abolished all future treaty making with Indian nations through an amend-ment to an Indian appropriations act called the Resolution of 1871. Straightfor-ward and direct, it provided an important guarantee: "[N]o Indian nation or tribe within the territory of the United States shall be acknowledged or recognized as an independent nation, tribe or power with whom the United States may contract by treaty: Provided further, [t]hat nothing herein contained shall be construed to invalidate or impair the obligation of any treaty heretofore lawfully made and rati-fied with any such Indian nation or tribe."[16]

This statute had astounding implications. First, it made the treaty experience between indigenous peoples and the U.S. government a near static and finite dimension, as it lasted for ninety-five years, encompassing much of the nineteenth century. Second, it did not expressly recognize prior or concurrent treaties made between the states and colonies with Native nations or those made by European colonial powers with North American Indian nations pertaining to the lands com-prising the United States. It remained for future U.S. Supreme Court decisions to give full faith and credit to those diplomatic agreements. Third, an important guarantee within the law placed treaties made between 1776 and 1871 at the apex of the U.S. legal system. No American governments could ignore these treaties.

The guarantee emphasizing the importance of legally concluded treaties has been a useful tool for various groups seeking the verification of rights and various forms of tribal sovereignty. Even the investigation into treaty violations by the Indian Claims Commission from 1946 to 1972 and its weak attempts at satisfying long-standing indigenous complaints of U.S. government treaty violations did not weaken the power of the 1871 Resolution. The strength of this legal caveat has also held against the greatest assault on treaties and indigenous sovereignty, the termi-nation movement of the 1950s to the 1970s. The U.S. Supreme Court in *Menom-inee Tribe of Indians v. United States* (1968) held that all treaties unless expressly abolished retained their applicability, and Indian nations kept their treaty-guaranteed powers, such as hunting, fishing, and water rights, over and against congressional termination statutes.[17]

Why was this rather unusual step, that of abolishing future treaty-making powers, taken by the U.S. government? A number of explanations have been postulated by scholars. The resolution has been interpreted as the result of (1) a desire by the House of Representatives to infringe upon the traditional foreign policy powers of the Senate; (2) congressional melding of fiscal conservative sentiment, anti-Indian settler attitudes, and reformer conversion to the idea that the treaty system took unfair advantage of Indian parties; and (3) a representation of Congress's willingness to follow the recommendations of the Indian Peace Commission of 1867–1868 and reports of the Board of Indian Commissioners.[18] These reasons are certainly plausible factors for the immediacy of the treaty abolition decision, but the status of Indian diplomacy with the United States and with other tribes during the 1860s was also crucial to any understanding of this massive rupture in diplomatic relations.

Throughout the decade of the 1860s, the United States accelerated its treaty-making initiatives with Indian nations. Countless councils were held, and fifty-nine treaties were ratified by the U.S. Senate. The 1860s constituted the most intense era of Native American–United States treaty making ever. Great Plains peoples were extensively involved, accounting for over one-third of all treaties made in the 1860s. The largest number of treaties were made with the Lakotas, Nakotas, and Dakotas, peoples often collectively known as "Sioux."

During the 1860s, the United States concluded eleven treaties with the various groups of the Sioux, the most significant being the 1868 Treaty of Fort Laramie with the Sicangu (Brulé), Oglala, Miniconjou, Hunkpapa, Sihaspa (Blackfeet), Oohenunpa (Two Kettle), and Itazipacola (Sans Arcs) Lakotas; Pa Ksa (Cuthead) and Yanktonai Nakotas; and Santee Dakotas. Red Cloud, the Hunkpapa chief, helped lead negotiations.[19]

Red Cloud assumed a position of national leadership in the early 1860s at a time when large numbers of miners and settlers were traveling the Bozeman Trail, violating a previous 1851 Fort Laramie agreement. The Trail ran through some of the best Sioux hunting grounds in the Medicine Hat and Yellowstone River valleys of Wyoming and Montana. Lakotas objected to travelers with such steadfast determination that in June 1866, American leaders arranged for a council at Fort Laramie. Red Cloud and other Sioux leaders attended the gathering.

At the outset of the talks, it appeared that peaceful travel on the Bozeman Trail might be negotiated if travelers would agree to avoid disturbing the game. This potential agreement was scuttled because the United States sent troops to Fort Laramie with orders to build forts in Lakota country. This direct aggression on the part of the United States infuriated Red Cloud and other Lakota leaders. Red

Cloud said that the peace council had treated the chiefs like fools, and he left the council. This marked the initial stage of over twenty years of sporadic United States–Lakota warfare.[20]

The December 21, 1866, incident, when a young army lieutenant stupidly led his troops into an ambush by the Lakotas on the Bozeman Trail, highlighted the failure of the U.S. government's Indian policy. It also showed the U.S. Army the power of the Lakotas over the northern Plains. In response, a commission arrived at Fort Laramie with a treaty in hand that they believed would be acceptable to the Sioux and their allies.

In brief, the Fort Laramie proposals provided for a permanent peace between the United States and all signatory nations. It also stipulated that all whites who committed wrongs or depredations upon the Indians would be punished, and it set apart the Great Sioux Reservation, an area covering all of South Dakota west of the Missouri River. There were also clauses in this 1868 treaty that dealt with establishment and operation of the reservation. The treaty further stipulated that the country north of the North Platte River and east of the Big Horn Mountains was unceded Indian territory. No one could settle there without Lakota and their allies' permission. The United States agreed that within ninety days after the signing of the treaty, all military posts currently established in the territory would be abandoned. The Indians in return would withdraw all opposition to railroads and roads south of the North Platte. Spotted Tail and other chiefs signed the treaty on April 29, 1868; Red Cloud refused. Finally, on November 6, 1868, Red Cloud signed and the ratification process began.[21]

The Treaty of Fort Laramie and Red Cloud were instrumental in the decision of the United States to change its treaty-making process. The government and military had already begun to have serious doubts about dealing with Red Cloud and the Lakotas. In contrast to the usual U.S. policy of opposition to Indian resistance, they conceded to Red Cloud everything for which he had been fighting. It was a retreat for the United States and a victory for the Lakotas.

In 1870, Red Cloud traveled to Washington, DC, and it became evident during his conversations with government officials that his understanding of the Fort Laramie Treaty was completely different from contents of the actual document. Red Cloud remonstrated:

> When you send goods to me they are stolen all along the road, so when they reach me there is only a handful. They held out a paper for me to sign and that is all I got for my land. I know the people you send out there are liars. Look at me, I am poor and naked, I do not war with my government; the railroad is passing through my country now; I have received no pay for the land, not even a brass ring. You might grant my people the powder we ask.

We are but a handful and you are a great and powerful nation. You make all the ammunition; all I ask is enough for my people to kill game. . . .[22]

When the treaty provisions were explained to him, he learned that the Sioux were not to be supplied with ammunition and horses. The Lakotas believed that Red Cloud had been deceived.

Although in July 1871, Red Cloud and his people finally attained a new agency located on the Platte River near Laramie, it was becoming increasingly clear to all that the old treaties would not satisfy miner and settler demands for access to the Great Sioux Reservation. Reductions in the collective Sioux homelands would follow only after violent confrontation.[23]

Red Cloud and the Lakota nation had a direct impact on the prevailing colonial policy. So did other Plains Indian nations who rejected American overtures. These troubles caused the U.S. government to lose faith in its own abilities to practice Indian diplomacy. Moreover, many in Congress became convinced that involvement with treaties simply was not worth the price paid. This malaise was a key element in the abolition of the treaty-making process.

CANADIAN TREATY MAKING

While the year 1871 represented the formal end of treaty making in the United States, it marked the beginning of what Canadian historian Jill St. Germain calls Canada's treaty binge, "the most ambitious ever undertaken in British North American Indian relations."[24] The British gave control of Indian affairs to Canada in 1860, and with the passage of the British North America Act of 1867, the Canadian Parliament assumed all responsibilities and powers over "Indians and lands reserved for Indians."[25] The first accord in the Numbered Treaties was reached in 1871, but it was Treaty 4—concluded between Canadian authorities and the Plains Crees—that seems to have prompted the greatest First Nation commentary at the time.

By 1871, settlers in northern Saskatchewan petitioned the government to pay them for losses resulting from the 1867 creation of the Dominion of Canada and the recognition of their land titles. The power in the region continued to be the Hudson's Bay Company, which garnered $300,000 for its Rupert's Land claims in high-level negotiations. Plains Crees also noted these happenings. Chief Sweetgrass, an apparent master of understatement, told the lieutenant governor of Manitoba and the Northwest Territories, Adam G. Archibald, "We heard our lands were sold, and we did not like it."[26] During negotiations for Treaty 4, the Crees claimed the payment given to Hudson's Bay Company and demanded agricultural aid. They also put pressure on Saskatchewan settlers and disrupted survey and telegraph linesmen.[27]

Treaties 4 and 5 were concluded with various bands of Plains Crees in 1874 and 1876. The Canadian negotiators' primary goal was simply to clear First Nations land titles, a requirement of common law land traditions, and thus the treaty authors were content to promise a variety of payments to the Crees for agricultural assistance. In Treaty 4, Plains Crees agreed to relinquish their homeland claims and to settle on reserves selected by government officers after consultation with Cree band leaders. Each family was to receive 160 acres on the reserve prorated for larger or smaller families. In addition, gifts worth $12 per man, woman, and child were to be distributed. Chiefs received $25, a Queen's silver medal, a flag, and a coat. Interestingly, the Crees succeeded in obtaining powder, shot, blankets, and calico cloth for those at the treaty proceedings. No other Numbered Treaty negotiations promised ammunition for participants, although Treaty 4 and other treaties did allocate certain amounts for powder, shots, and balls in good faith payments every year. Annuities guaranteed per year included $5 per man, woman, and child, $25 per chief, and $15 per clan headman. Each chief and headman received a suit of clothing every three years.

For every Plains Cree family who agreed to farm, the Canadian government pledged in Treaty 4 to supply two hoes, one spade, one scythe, and one axe; and for every ten farm families, one plough and two harrows. Each Cree band chief received for the band's use one crosscut saw, five handsaws, one pitsaw, a number of files, one grindstone, five augers, and one chest of ordinary carpenter's tools. The government pledged sufficient oat, wheat, barley, and potato seed to plant land "actually broken up." Moreover, each band chief received a yoke of oxen, a bull, and four cows. These materials constituted a one-time-only foreign aid package.

In return, Crees could not sell or alienate reserve lands. Liquor was prohibited on the reserves, and schools were to be built on the reserves. Crees had to consent to a census as soon as possible. Crees also were to be loyal subjects of the Crown, obey Canadian laws, and keep the peace. They pledged not to bother people on nearby ceded tracts of Cree land or persons traveling through former Cree homelands. Finally, the Crees agreed to assist in bringing to justice other indigenous peoples who violated laws or the treaty.[28]

Treaty 4 constituted a permanent settlement strategy by the Canadian government. The problem that would continue into the twentieth and twenty-first centuries is that government after government failed to live up to numerous promises. These failures have led to recent legal challenges in Canadian courts that have mandated reconstituting the treaties and ordering governments to adhere to treaties, and the promise of provincial and national governments to renegotiate treaties. Indeed, unlike that of the United States, the Canadian treaty-making experience is not static. It is ongoing and subject to numerous political and emotional highs and lows for all participants. Today the Numbered Treaties are being renegotiated as are other treaties.

INTERNATIONAL LAW AND AMERICAN AND
CANADIAN TREATIES

International law during the nineteenth century was in flux. At the beginning of the era, four types prevailed: classical natural law; historical jurisprudence; analytical legal science, which was popular with English-speaking peoples; and analytical thought. The first type dealt with abstractions. Classicists quoted Plato and Cicero in order to deduce rules of conduct from rational behavior. The nineteenth century marked the decline of the school of classical natural law, and by 1900, it had been reduced to providing critiques rather than promoting or creating policy concepts. Subsequently, the other three schools vied for control of the dynamics of international law practice, each seeking to translate the law of "oughts" into the law of verifiable codifications.[29] The last half of the twentieth century has seen the United Nations enter this debate and establish international law and order on a scale never previously practiced.

Despite the diversity that characterized international legal jurisprudence as it moved toward a worldwide enforced format, most scholars agreed on the crucial issues concerning the status of relationships between North America's indigenous peoples and European Americans. Legal scholar Emmerich de Vattel's 1834 edition of his work, *The Law of Nations,* issued immediately after the U.S. Supreme Court Cherokee cases, defined a state as "a body politic, or a society of men united together for the purpose of promoting their mutual safety and advantage by their combined strength."[30] This very general definition depended on the teachings of Cicero. Henry Wheaton disagreed with Vattel, if only in specificity. Wheaton, in his treatises that were revised throughout the nineteenth and early twentieth centuries, accepted Vattel's definition subject to limitations. Wheaton defined a state as necessarily one race or one people, and negatively—nation-states excluded corporations, voluntary associations of pirates, [and] unsettled hordes "of wandering savages not yet formed into a civil society."[31]

By 1906, the definition of a state had been codified. According to John Bassett Moore, a state was

> a people permanently occupying a fixed territory, bound together by common laws, habits, and customs into one body politic, exercising through the medium of an organized government, independent sovereignty and control over all persons and things within its boundaries, capable of making war and peace, and of entering into all international relations with the other communities of the globe.[32]

Moore attacked Wheaton's limitations of a state with his definition, but he misunderstood Wheaton's own specific placement of indigenous peoples within an international law framework. Moore wrote, "Hence he [Wheaton] excludes from the category of the state . . . the North American Indians, although the United States has allowed them, on grounds of expediency, a certain national existence."[33] In fact, Wheaton wrote in 1863 that Native American tribes, even those residing east of the Mississippi River, constituted nation-states. These were not "unsettled hordes." Those nations, as Wheaton termed them, were "semi-sovereign states, under the exclusive protectorate of another power."[34]

Wheaton recognized the diversity of status among Indians within the United States. Some Native Americans had extinguished their national fires, while others held absolute power over their lands. But most importantly, "[a] weak power does not surrender its independence and right to self-government by associating with a stronger and taking its protection." To Wheaton, "[t]his was the settled doctrine of the Law of Nations. . . ."[35]

Thus, by 1900 under international law, the American and Canadian governments had signed hundreds of treaties with numerous indigenous nations. These treaties comprised a wide variety of diverse documents, as the party nations themselves underwent considerable change. Many Native nations originally signed documents when they were strong, sovereign states; then subsequent documents or other circumstances altered their status into semisovereign states on a permanent land base. Under international law, North American indigenous nations by the twentieth century still held limited forms of sovereignty as a protectorate of a stronger nation-state.[36]

What then were the rights of a nineteenth-century protectorate? International legal scholars have agreed that two forms of semisovereign states existed then and exist today: the protectorate and the suzerainty. A suzerainty depends on a protector state or suzerain for all grants of power. It has no international status. A protectorate gave or lost limited portions of its sovereignty to its protector. Thus, a protectorate can achieve nearly complete independence or total dependence, but these characteristics require consent. Typically, protectorates control their own internal affairs, but not their external affairs.[37] The vast majority of Native Americans and First Nations comprise nations that evolved under protectorate status.

A semisovereign nation protected by a sovereign nation retained certain guaranteed rights. The peoples of a protectorate could not be forced to give up fundamental rights even by treaty or statute. If a protectorate chooses to submit completely to the will of the protector, then the peoples of the protector must guarantee the peoples of the protectorate equality. The responsibilities of the protector are great; above all, the protector state guarantees to the peoples of the protectorate economic, social, and political liberty. Failure to do so is to participate in an "uncivilized protectorate."[38]

Given that many indigenous peoples were semisovereign nations at the time of their entering into treaty relationships, did this reduce the power of the treaty? The overwhelming evidence suggests a resounding answer of "no" to this question. Henry Wheaton wrote that all states were equal "in the eye of international law, whatever may be their relative power."[39] The equality was, however, only legal, a significant distinction from a declaration of moral equality or an enforced legal equality.

John Pomeroy explained in 1896 that a protected state never lost its potential for legal independence and sovereignty. The ability to carry on external relations in the future existed. Pomeroy wrote that "no mere inequality of alliance is destructive of the personality of a state among nations."[40] Protectorates retain their international personality. "The effect of this personality," insisted Pomeroy, "is to clothe the political society with its own international rights, and to subject it to its own international duties."[41] Moreover, if the protectorate forfeited its external rights to the protector, and some Native American nations did so by treaty, its peoples were placed in a situation like "that of colonists to the mother country."[42]

In order to break the treaties of the past, the protectorate had to be destroyed, and the only way to destroy a protectorate was to deny somehow the existence of Native peoples as semisovereign states. Change in political status does not change treaty rights. Only by attacking the economic, social, and cultural fabric could a protectorate be altered, and this required the suspension of most fundamental rights.

Thus, the treaty seems indestructible as a legal instrument. The degree of sovereignty held by American Indians or First Nations at the time of an agreement could not distort the legal equality inherent within the treaty. American courts recognized this notion as early as the mid-nineteenth century. "It is contended that a treaty with Indian tribes, has not the same dignity or effect as a treaty with a foreign and independent nation," an 1852 U.S. federal circuit court in *Turner v. American Baptist Missionary Union* summarized. "The distinction is not authorized by the Constitution."[43] Consequently, other legal means, and more often than not illegal means, had to be employed in order for the protectorate to be dismembered, both literally in the form of lands taken out of the hands of indigenous peoples and figuratively with reduction of the legal power residing in the treaty. This circumstance, of course, characterizes the history of treaties in Canada and the United States, especially from the 1880s to World War II.

CONCLUSION

Elizabeth Cook-Lynn, Crow Creek Dakota, articulate advocate for Native rights, writer and poet, in her recent work argues that the mere telling of their own stories is a constant struggle for the colonized indigenous peoples of North America. Whether it be through literature or politics or revolutionary movements, or for that matter telling the history of treaty making, Cook-Lynn sees "[t]he denial of this basic human right through the development of nationalistic, legal, social, and intellectual systems that make it impossible for a domestic people, or a domestic nation of Indians, to express itself collectively and historically in terms of continued self-determination. . . ." This is "a kind of genocide that is perhaps even more immoral than the physical genocide of war and torture" that her people and others have endured.[44] Control over the story, for Cook-Lynn, constitutes a crime in international law, and for indigenous peoples, this has been a part of their ongoing colonial experience.

The pursuit of those rights stipulated in North American treaties remains for many an exercise in control over the story. Since the 1960s, Native Americans and First Nations have had a greater hand in telling the story, and the world audience has been sympathetic up to certain decibel levels. It seems fairly well-established that in the early twenty-first century, the U.S. Indian Claims Commission (ICC) proceedings (1946–1972) were exercises closely related to and determined by the termination movement, and while they constituted legal decisions, courts are now reluctant to give them full credence. The mere fact that the ICC investigated most U.S. treaties, however, has kept most Native American tribal governments and indigenous legal activists from resurrecting the reinterpretation of Commission findings. More time and legal energy, led in part by the Native American Rights Fund, has been invested in solidifying the kinds of indigenous sovereignties and strengthening of Indian identities than in revisiting the treaty process. No Native American leader or tribal government today is calling for a new round of treaty negotiations, although this could change depending on developments farther to the north.

Conversely, First Nations are embarking on a revisiting of the treaty process in hopes of achieving greater self-determination. Elijah Harper writes: "For hundreds of years Aboriginal Peoples in the area now known as Canada were sovereign and self-sufficient. We are now poised to once again take charge of our lives and destiny."[45] It was Harper, after all, who represented Aboriginal interests ably after the collapse of the Meech Lake Accords when Canada attempted to resolve its constitutional crisis without the involvement of its indigenous peoples.

First Nations in Canada are considering any number of approaches to self-determination. The Mohawks have endorsed the goal of absolute sovereignty and complete independence and territorial autonomy in statehood. Inuits in parts of the previous Northwest Territory negotiated a home-rule institutional accommodation within the Dominion, creating the indigenous government of Nunavut. British Columbia and Plains First Nations are renegotiating treaties, among them the Numbered Treaties.[46]

In many ways these recent developments have been spurred by United Nations efforts in the past two decades to strengthen human rights and to examine the relationships between indigenous peoples and colonial powers. Here indigenous representatives have been accorded a common ground on which to discuss with nation-states self-determination and sovereignty issues, "the stuff of treaties." New Zealander Dr. Augie Fleras summarizes in reference to New Zealand, Canada, and Australia:

> Nationally and internationally, there is an expanding awareness both of indigenous rights and of a need to restore these rights as set out in the recently completed United Nations Universal Declaration of the Rights of Indigenous Peoples. With rights as their *trump cards,* indigenous ethno-politics have looked to the courts for reparations or justice. Indigenous protests in the 1970s helped to stir the consciences both of politicians and of the general public; they also paved the way for judicial enhancement of indigenous rights. The judiciary has proven more malleable than elected officials in endorsing the principle of indigenous rights, thanks to its relative freedom from the constraints of political pragmatism or electoral expediency.[47]

While certainly true for these three Commonwealth colonials, the reverse has occurred during the last decade in the United States. It should be noted that despite Canadian court attempts to interpret treaties in ways that open the dialogue, negotiations have been sluggish and difficult, and indigenous-colonial relations in Australia and New Zealand are not harmonious despite judicial recognition of indigenous land rights.

Although the Universal Declaration of the Rights of Indigenous Peoples was not approved by all nonindigenous nations, the dialogue among indigenous leaders and between established nation-states and Native "state" representatives nevertheless brought with it revelations and certain understandings. Helen Corbett, of the Ingrada, Bardi, and Noongar Peoples of Western Australia, and United Nations advocate for the Declaration, observed that for indigenous peoples, international agreements are their safety net and help to strengthen domestic political engagement. Because of these discussions, treaties are "living" and for many indigenous peoples are under evaluation. Corbett writes, "Indigenous people have come from out of the dark and dangerous shadows of history and are moving towards the light of recognition. Just like the kangaroo, they can only go forward, not backward."[48]

NOTES

1. Tjapukai Dancers, "Proud to Be Aborigine," Larrikin Records, Sydney, Australia, 1990.

2. See *Mabo & Ors v. State of Queensland,* 83 ALR 14, 63 ALJR 84 (HC) (1988) [*Mabo*

no. 1] and *Mabo & Ors v. State of Queensland,* 107 ALR 1 (HC) (1992) [*Mabo no. 2*]. The *Mabo* cases in effect ended the legal notion in Australia that the continent at the time of the British invasion was *terra nullius,* a land unoccupied and unclaimed. See *Wik People v. State of Queensland, Thayoree People v. State of Queensland,* 141 ALR 129 (HC) (1996) wherein Australia's High Court ruled that long-term pastoral leases did not extinguish Native title and encouraged formal land negotiations.

3. See Paul Havemann, "Native Title in Australia: Denial, Recognition, and Dispossession," 408–27, and David McConald, "Australia: The Royal Commission into Aboriginal Deaths in Custody," 283–301, in *Indigenous Peoples' Rights in Australia, Canada, and New Zealand,* ed. Paul Havemann (New York: Oxford University Press, 1999).

4. Alan Ward and Janine Haywood, "Tina Rangatiratanga: Maori in the Political and Administrative System," 93–96; and Ranginui J. Walker, "Maori Sovereignty, Colonial and Post-Colonial Discourses," 116–20, in *Indigenous Peoples' Rights,* ed. Paul Havemann.

5. Samuli Aikio, Ulla Aikio-Puoskari, and Johannes Helander, *The Sami Culture in Finland* (Helsinki: Lapin Sivistysseura, 1994), 16, 23; Harald Eidheim, "Ethno-Political Development among the Sami after World War II: The Invention of Selfhood," in *Sami Culture in a New Era: The Norwegian Sami Experience,* ed. Harald Gaski (Kárásjohka, Norway: Davvi Girji OS, 1997), 34.

6. Eidheim, "Ethno-Political Development," 47.

7. Aikio et al., *Sami Culture,* 131–43; Steinar Pedersen, "Saami Rights: A Historical and Contemporary Outlook," in *Essays on Indigenous Identity and Rights,* ed. Irja Seurujärvi-Kari and Ulla-Maija Kulonen (Helsinki: Helsinki University Press, 1996), 67–75.

8. Declaration of Murmansk, October, 1996, 1–2, www.saamicouncil.org/english /murmanskdek.htm. See also Remarks of Anne Nuorgam, President of Saami Council, June 2001, to 10th meeting of Arctic Environmental Protection Strategy, 1–4, www.saamicouncil.org /english/statements.php?statements'&readmore'2&lang' for further expressions of Sami sovereignty issues.

9. Chief Joseph, "An Indian's Views of Indian Affairs," in *Indian Oratory: Famous Speeches by Noted Indian Chieftains,* comp. W.C. Vanderwerth (New York: Ballantine Books, 1972), 213–14.

10. Ibid., 214.

11. Spotted Tail, "I See That My Friends before Me Are Men of Age and Dignity (1877)," in *Indian Oratory,* comp. Vanderwerth, 178.

12. Alexander Morris, *The Treaties of Canada with the Indians of Manitoba and the North-West Territories including the Negotiations on which they were based* (1880), 62, quoted in Jill St. Germain, *Indian Treaty-Making Policy in the United States and Canada, 1867–1877* (Lincoln: University of Nebraska Press, 2001), 38.

13. Taiaiake Alfred, *Peace, Power, Righteousness: An Indigenous Manifesto* (New York: Oxford University Press, 1999), 49.

14. Ibid., 49–50.

15. Ibid., 52.

16. "An Act making Appropriations for the current and contingent Expenses of the Indian Department, and for fulfilling Treaty Stipulations with various Indian tribes, for the

Year ending June thirty, eighteen hundred and seventy-two, and for other Purposes," *Statutes at Large* 16 (March 3, 1871), 544–71 at 566.

17. *Menominee Tribe of Indians v. United States*, 391 U.S. 404 (1968). See also John R. Wunder, *"Retained by The People": A History of American Indians and the Bill of Rights* (New York: Oxford University Press, 1994), 130–31, 233–34.

18. Wilcomb Washburn, *The Indian in America* (New York: Harper & Row, 1975), 97–98; Francis Paul Prucha, *The Great Father: The United States Government and the American Indians,* 2 vols. (Lincoln: University of Nebraska Press, 1984), 1:527–33; and John R. Wunder, "No More Treaties: The Resolution of 1871 and the Alteration of Indian Rights to Their Homelands," in *Working the Range: Essays on the History of Western Land Management and the Environment,* ed. Wunder (Westport, CT: Greenwood Press, 1985), 39–56.

19. Robert W. Larson, *Red Cloud: Warrior-Statesman of the Lakota Sioux* (Norman: University of Oklahoma Press, 1997), 123–39, 285–302.

20. See generally William T. Hagan, *American Indians,* 2nd ed. (Chicago: University of Chicago Press, 1979), 108–10. For a cogent analysis of Sioux geopolitics prior to the Treaty of Fort Laramie (1868), see Richard White, "The Winning of the West: The Eighteenth and Nineteenth Centuries," *Journal of American History* 65 (September 1978), 319–43. See also "Fort Laramie Treaty of 1868," in *The Great Sioux Nation: Sitting in Judgment on America,* ed. Roxanne Dunbar Ortiz (Berkeley, CA: Moon Books, 1977), 94–99, and Peter John Powell, "The Sacred Treaty," in *The Great Sioux Nation,* ed. Dunbar Ortiz, 105–9.

21. "Treaty between the United States of America and different tribes of Sioux Indians (Brulé, Oglala, Miniconjou, Yanktonai, Hunkpapa, Blackfeet, Cuthead, Two Kettle, Sans Arc, and Santee) and Arapaho, 1868," *Statutes at Large* 15 (February 16, 1869), 635–47. See also K. Kirke Kickingbird, ed., *Treaties and Agreements and the Proceedings of the Treaties and Agreements of the Tribes of the Sioux Nation* (Washington, DC: Institute for the Development of Indian Law, 1974), 74–100.

22. Quoted in Doane Robinson, *A History of the Dakota or Sioux Indians* (Minneapolis, MN: Ross and Haines, Inc., 1956), 397.

23. Larson, *Red Cloud,* 185–216.

24. St. Germain, *Indian Treaty-Making Policy,* 13.

25. Robert J. Surtees, *Canadian Indian Policy: A Critical Bibliography* (Bloomington: Indiana University Press, 1982), 41.

26. Sweetgrass to Adams Archibald, 1871, in *Treaties of Canada with the Indians of Manitoba and the North-West Territories including the Negotiations on which they were based, 1880,* ed. Alexander Morris (Saskatoon, SK: Fifth House, 1991), 170–71, quoted in Surtees, *Canadian Indian Policy,* 39.

27. St. Germain, *Indian Treaty-Making Policy,* 39–40. See also Olive Patricia Dickason, *Canada's First Nations: A History of Founding Peoples from Earliest Times* (Norman: University of Oklahoma Press, 1992), 276, 279, 298–301, 320–21.

28. St. Germain, *Indian Treaty-Making Policy,* "Appendix 2: Comparison of Terms in the Numbered Treaties," 178–84.

29. Roscoe Pound, "Philosophical Theory and International Law," in *Bibliotheca Visseriana,* ed. Thomas Primus (London: E.J. Brill, 1923), 82–85.

30. Emmerich de Vattel, *The Law of Nations,* edited by Joseph Chitty, 2nd ed. (London: Stevens & Sons, 1834), 1.

31. Henry Wheaton, *Elements of International Law,* edited by William Beach Lawrence, 2nd ed. (Boston: Little, Brown & Co., 1863), 32–34. See also *Wheaton's Elements of International Law,* considerably enlarged and rewritten by Coleman Phillipson, 5th English ed. (London: Stevens and Sons, Ltd.; New York: Baker, Boorhis & Co., 1916), 50–51; and Theodore S. Woolsey, *Introduction to the Study of International Law,* 6th ed. (New York: Charles Scribner's Sons, 1891), 34–36.

32. John Bassett Moore, *A Digest of International Law,* 2 vols. (Washington, DC: Government Printing Office, 1906), 1:14–15.

33. Ibid., 16.

34. Wheaton, *International Law,* 2nd ed., 68.

35. Ibid., 69.

36. See Rennard Strickland and Charles F. Wilkinson, eds., *Felix S. Cohen's Handbook of Federal Indian Law* (Charlottesville, VA: Michie Bobbs-Merrill, 1982), 62–127.

37. See Charles G. Fenwick, *Cases on International Law* (Chicago: Callaghan and Company, 1935), 37. In 1922, Charles C. Hyde wrote in his treatise that "The American Indians have never been regarded as constituting persons or states of international law." He then misquoted from John Marshall's *Cherokee Nation v. State of Georgia* (1831) decision. The evidence overwhelmingly contradicts Hyde's position. Instead, Native Americans constituted various forms of nation-states under international law before the twentieth century. If anything, their claims to protectorate status have been enhanced by twentieth-century legal developments. Charles Cheney Hyde, *International Law,* 2 vols. (Boston: Little, Brown and Company, 1922), 1:19.

See also George Grafton Wilson, *Handbook of International Law* (St. Paul, MN: West Publishing Co., 1910), 35–39. An English court noted in 1910 that "[t]he one common element in Protectorates is the prohibition of all foreign relations except those permitted by protecting the State." From *The King v. The Earl of Crewe* (1910), 2 King's Bench 576, excerpted in Lawrence B. Evans, ed., *Leading Cases on International Law* (Chicago: Callaghan and Company, 1917), 29.

38. Moore, *A Digest of International Law,* 30.

39. Wheaton, *Elements of International Law,* 3rd ed. (London: Stevens and Sons, Ltd., 1889), 49.

40. John Norton Pomeroy, *Lectures on International Law in Times of Peace,* edited by Theodore Salisbury Woolsey (Indianapolis: Bobbs-Merrill Company, 1886), 50.

41. Ibid., 63.

42. Ibid., 64.

43. *Turner v. American Baptist Missionary Union,* 24 Fed. Cas. 344 (1852).

44. Elizabeth Cook-Lynn, *Anti-Indianism in Modern America: A Voice from Tatekeya's Earth* (Urbana: University of Illinois Press, 2001), 203–4. This paragraph in the original is italicized, but the italics have been removed because of the split quotation within the essay narrative.

45. Elijah Harper, "Foreword," in *Aboriginal Self-Government in Canada: Current Trends and Issues,* ed. John H. Hylton (Saskatoon, SK: Purich Publishing, 1994), 8.

46. Augie Fleras, "Politicising Indigeneity: Ethno-politics in White Settler Dominions," in *Indigenous Peoples' Rights,* ed. Paul Havemann, 197–99.

47. Ibid., 222.

48. Helen Corbett, "The Rights of Indigenous Peoples: A Comparison of the Rights of Saami and Aboriginal Peoples in Australia," in *Essays on Indigenous Identity and Rights,* ed. Seurujärvi-Kari and Kulonen, 61. See also David Maybury-Lewis, *Indigenous Peoples, Ethnic Groups, and the State* (Boston: Allyn and Bacon, 1997); and Antonio Cassese, *Self-Determination of Peoples: A Legal Reappraisal* (New York: Cambridge University Press, 1995).

CHAPTER 2

Native Self-Determination Building: The Crees of Northern Québec and the Navajos of the American Southwest

DAVID HARDING

SINCE THE 1960s and the emergence of the Native rights movement in North America, the impetus toward Native self-determination has been accelerating in both Canada and the United States. Increased interest in cultural identity and awareness of legal rights on the part of aboriginal peoples, coupled with the growing willingness of significant elements of society at large to acknowledge and accept these identities, led to the gradual re-empowerment of Native peoples in both countries. This process, however, has not occurred without controversy and problems. Such an undertaking is bound to result in conflicts. This essay is an attempt to examine some of the issues behind the more salient conflicts that have arisen.

At the heart of questions that are generating conflict in the self-determination building process, three issues are central—the efficacy, viability, and legitimacy of the mechanisms of Native self-determination. Efficacy involves whether newly established forms of tribal government are adequate to the task of truly providing Native peoples with an effective means to manage their own affairs. Having established such means, are they truly viable? In other words, are the resources necessary for sustaining these means available? Finally, do such mechanisms function in a manner truly representative of the Native peoples in question, that is, do they view these mechanisms as legitimate organs for the expression of their will?

Jeanette Wolfley has attempted to define the essentials of Native sovereignty. She lists four fundamental requirements for sovereignty: a "secure land base, functioning economies, self-governance, and cultural vitality."[1] She sees these four elements as inextricably interdependent, with land being the linchpin. Writes Wolfley, "A tribal land base or homeland is the *sine qua non* of sovereignty."[2] These two statements taken together constitute a dilemma for many Native peoples. If sovereignty requires economic self-sufficiency, then how to achieve it? A number of individual Natives, as well as many non-Natives, propose to do so through the exploitation of natural resources on Native lands. However, this is problematic for a number of reasons. Native lands are also essential to the maintenance of traditional ways of life. There are fears that exploitation of Native lands will render them unfit for traditional cultural practices. What are the implications for cultural vitality? Should this term be defined as maintenance of traditional ways of life, or should it also allow for Native adaptation and participation in an industrialized society?

In order to illuminate the importance of these issues to the self-determination building process, two cases will be examined. The Crees (Eeyouch) of northern Québec and the Navajos (Diné) of the southwestern United States provide excellent opportunities to set these questions in relief. Both are among the largest Native groups in their respective countries. In terms of language, a critical element of culture, they also represent the two most important indigenous language groups in North America. The Cree language has an estimated 64,000 speakers (including groups not residing in northern Québec), and 130,000 people speak Navajo. The smaller the language group, the smaller the chances for linguistic survival. Cree and Navajo have relatively strong chances of survival compared to other Native languages in North America.[3]

Additionally, both peoples possess considerable natural resources. The Crees reside in a region with prime hydroelectric power sites, and Navajo territory is rich in deposits of uranium and low-sulfur coal. Due to land-base size and resource potential, their prospects for creating economically viable mechanisms of self-government seem high. The question of developing these resources is, however, generating fault lines on the issues of efficacy and legitimacy. The development of resources, although promising to generate substantial revenue, is seen by many as threatening the existence of tribal ways of life. Furthermore, the mechanisms of self-determination are based on models drawn from the dominant Euro-Canadian and European American societies. Many tribal members in both instances question whether these mechanisms are truly adequate to represent tribal wishes and aspirations. There is also concern that they may allow for coopting tribal governments for the benefit of outside interests, such as energy and construction firms, as well as provincial/state and federal governments.

In his work on co-cultural theory, Mark P. Orbe defines co-cultures as social groups that are less privileged in society. He posits that such groups have three options vis-à-vis dominant groups: assimilation, separation, or accommodation.[4] As co-cultures then, Native peoples are faced with these options. They can choose to abandon their own cultural identity and adopt that of the dominant culture in order to fit in. They also have the option of turning their backs on the dominant culture in an attempt to remove themselves from mainstream influences of the dominant society. A third option is to attempt negotiating a middle approach in the hope of maintaining elements of one's own culture while interacting with, and perhaps modifying, the dominant culture, resulting in a multicultural compromise. In the cases of the Crees and Navajos, all three impulses are evident as they attempt to negotiate their relationship with the dominant society.

THE CREES AND THE JAMES BAY PROJECT

Turning first to Canada and the Crees of northern Québec, it is useful initially to place their situation in its proper historical context. The Cree people residing in the eastern James Bay region are regarded as having been permanent residents in the area for over 1,000 years. Anthropologists believe that this region has been continuously occupied by humans for 6,000 or 7,000 years, and that the Crees are directly descended from these earlier inhabitants.[5] There is little argument then that the Crees are the original inhabitants of the region. Cree title to the land is further solidified by virtue of the fact that until recent decades, they never entered into any agreements or treaties concerning their lands.[6] Arctic location and climate limited intrusions by Europeans into Cree territory before the second half of the twentieth century, when interest in mineral deposits led to increased incursions.

Since World War II, the region's minerals, forests, and game have attracted the interest of numerous outsiders. The extraction of minerals and timber as well as the taking of game such as moose have impacted traditional Cree culture. The impact of these activities, although not to be underestimated, is not, however, the focus of this essay. Instead, it is the influence of hydroelectric projects that is of prime concern. As will be demonstrated, these projects pose a threat to the Crees of a magnitude far greater than the other types of resource exploitation.

Specifically, the Crees are dealing with the "largest hydroelectric complex in North America"—the James Bay Project.[7] Initially proposed in 1971, the first phase of Hydro-Québec's undertaking impounded the La Grande River and flooded an area thirty times larger than Prince Edward Island.[8] Its huge electricity output has subsequently been sold to New York City. Additional dams are envisioned on the Eastmain, Great Whale, Nottaway, Broadback, and Rupert Rivers. All of these areas are within the traditional homelands of the northern Crees.

The development of hydroelectric potential in the eastern James Bay region sheds light on the tensions experienced by Native people who are trying to cope within the context of an outside dominant culture, and also illuminates core fault lines running through Canada as a whole. The question of hydroelectric develop-

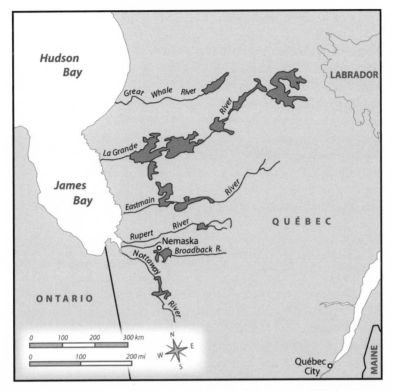

Empowering First Nations: James Bay Crees Confront Provincial Hydroelectric
Power Schemes, 1970–2000

ment in northern Québec is inextricably tied to questions of Canadian federalism
and Québec nationalism. It is a case of two co-cultures, the Crees and the
Québéquois, both grappling with questions of cultural identity and self-
determination. The energy resources of northern Québec are a factor in the political calculus of both groups.

The James Bay Project moved to the forefront of Québec politics in the spring
of 1971 when Liberal Premier Robert Bourassa proposed the $6 billion water proj-
ect. Bourassa attempted to sell the project as necessary to Québec's economic
development:

> The development of James Bay is a project without precedent in the
> economic history of Québec. It is a turning point in our history. James
> Bay is the key to the economic and social progress of Québec, the key
> to the political stability of Québec, the key to the future of Québec. It
> will no longer be that we live poorly on such a rich land. We will get

out of our situation of economic inferiority.[9]

The James Bay Project was clearly intended to be a monumental undertaking, lifting Québec from its second-class economic status. It is interesting to note that Bourassa, at the time, regarded the James Bay Project as a force for unity in Canada. By placing Québec on a more equal economic footing with the rest of Canada, it was hoped that the province would lose its inferior status, thereby mitigating pressures for separation. At the time, Québec separatists tended to oppose the project, recoiling from the immense amount of outside capital required, as they were fearful of its cultural impact. However, separatists, driven by the same concern for viability in their self-determination enterprise as Native peoples, eventually came to view hydroelectric power as a potential source of economic viability for an independent Québec.

Environmental groups were less sanguine about the project and Bourassa's motives when the project was first announced. They regarded it as a cynical attempt to rescue Bourassa's political reputation, which had been seriously damaged in the previous year. He had been perceived as weak and ineffective during the FLQ (Front de Liberation du Québec) crisis in 1970. He proposed the project even though two previous feasibility studies in 1964 and 1967 had indicated that the proposed energy development should not proceed.[10] In short, Bourassa needed to do something on a grand scale in order to bolster his status as a leader. And there is no questioning the grandness of the James Bay Project as proposed by Bourassa. Estimates as to the size of the watershed that would be affected by the project range from 144,000 to 174,000 square miles.[11] This amounts to about one-quarter of the total area of Québec, or an area much larger than the entire United Kingdom and approximately the same size as the state of California.[12]

The initial project was made public in 1971 without prior consultation with the Crees nor a proper environmental review.[13] In fact, during seven years of reviews by various authorities, the Crees had never been contacted for their input.[14] Boyce Richardson claims that had this project been proposed for more populous parts of Canada, inhabited by non-Natives, it probably would not have been given serious consideration. "The James Bay Project is on a colossal scale and involves an intervention in natural systems that would immediately be recognized as unacceptable if anybody other than a small number of Indians were living in the territory."[15] It was not an auspicious start to the relationship between Québec and the Crees to come to some type of cooperation on the project.

The first response by the Crees was to seek a court injunction against the project. A Québec judge, after nearly a year of hearings, issued an injunction blocking the project over concerns for Native hunting rights.[16] This injunction was subsequently overturned. A year to the day after the injunction, an agreement in principle was signed between the Crees and Québec, the James Bay and Northern Québec Agreement, providing monetary compensation and a framework for dealing with future disputes over the project.[17] This was ratified a year later. The agreement provided recognition for Cree hunting, fishing, and trapping rights, as well as a cash compensation of $225 million. Bourassa emphasized that "[m]oney . . . was not the central issue. What was at issue for the Cree and Inuit was their concern about the potential disruption of their way of life."[18]

Some Native groups were less sanguine about Bourassa's seeming concern for their rights. Grand Chief Matthew Coon Come accused the government of Québec of practicing institutionalized racism by placing the world's largest hydroelectric project on their lands without prior consultation. He claimed that the agreement was approved only "with a gun at (the leaders) heads."[19] Others have termed provincial interaction with Natives as "slightly colonialist," as it was only concerned with getting Indians to adjust successfully to the project, and not truly with engaging Native concerns over culture.[20] With the courts ultimately overturning the initial injunction, the Crees felt compelled to accept a less-than-perfect deal rather than no deal at all. In essence, they exchanged a land base that they had never previously ceded for firm title to scattered areas that are about one-fifth the size of their previous territory.

This agreement initially approved by the Crees concerned only a portion of the overall project envisioned by Bourassa and Hydro-Québec. The first phase of the project involved the more northerly La Grande River. Subsequent plans to develop the more southerly sites involving the Eastmain and Rupert Rivers renewed the controversy. Having experienced the consequences of the La Grande project, many Crees became reluctant to see a similar project repeated to the south. A number of consequences result from the completed and proposed projects. These hydroelectric projects not only involve the damming of particular rivers, but also require the wholesale diversion of parallel rivers to increase the flow of water at the power generating sites. In some areas then, prime hunting grounds are lost to the massive reservoirs behind the dams. On other rivers, the downstream flow of water is lost, having been diverted upstream into the reservoirs, essentially killing these rivers. Also, by holding back water in reservoirs, there is increased leaching of heavy metals into the water, and by altering the hydraulic systems of the watersheds, groundwater is adversely impacted.

The James Bay Project has created significant environmental issues, but it has even broader implications for Québec and the rest of Canada. It has been a major cause for the Crees to be mistrustful of Québec and any potential separation of Québec from Canada. In fact, this issue was probably the deciding factor in the most recent referenda on Québec sovereignty. Indigenous peoples are in the majority in the northern half of Québec. These people voted overwhelmingly against the separation of Québec from Canada.[21] The referendum was supported by a majority only in the Francophone south, and there it was concentrated mainly in rural areas, with cosmopolitan Montreal also in opposition.[22] If Natives had been supportive in 1995, the Péquistes—members of Parti Québécois, a political group that champions provincial sovereignty—would have received a "yes" vote on separation.[23] The Crees then represent the swing vote in Québec, and their position pivots heavily on the James Bay Project question.

There is a fundamental issue underlying the controversy—just who holds sovereignty in the northern regions of Québec? The Québec government would certainly assert that its control over this territory is obvious, but history demonstrates that this is questionable. Québec's control over its northern regions is in fact due to relatively recent and arbitrary legislation, rather than deliberate cessions of rights on the part of First Nations to Québec. The eastern watershed of James Bay was only annexed by Québec in 1898 and 1912 under agreements and legislation negotiated with Ottawa, "rather than actual occupation or consent of aboriginal nations."[24] Therefore, the status of these lands in a postseparation Québec is questionable.

There is also a feeling among Native leaders that their status would be diminished under an independent Québec. This is something Pierre Trudeau asserted in 1981 when he stated to Native leaders that under an independent Québec, "their goose would be cooked."[25] Although one would expect the Québécois, seeing themselves as an oppressed minority in Canada, to be more attuned to the situation of other minority groups, most Natives do not expect this. This is evidenced by the stand taken by Cree Grand Chief Matthew Coon Come in the run-up to the most recent referendum on separation. He claimed that an independent Québec was not entitled to retain control of northern hydroelectric facilities.[26] This was not an entirely new position. The Crees have been active at United Nations conferences on aboriginal peoples since the 1980s. A main objective of this presence has been to assert their right to self-determination against domination by Québec and to ensure that Canada upholds their rights.[27] The Crees feel safer under Canadian federal control than they do under possible Québec rule, in part because of their status under the Constitution Act. Claims agreements have the same status as treaties under Section 35.[28] As a consequence of this status, agreements cannot be amended without Cree assent or constitutional amendment. The status of these agreements under an independent Québec would be uncertain, and Québec's cavalier attitude toward the Crees during the early phases of the James Bay Project has left Québécois leery of testing this status.

Northern hydroelectric resources have also been elemental in shaping Québec's view of indigenous peoples. Québec is just as dependent on the export of raw materials and energy as the rest of Canada, where together they account for a little less than half of all exports.[29] The hydroelectric power potential of the James Bay Project constitutes a significant chunk of this resource base, the exploitation of which is an essential requirement for the feasibility of Québec sovereignty. Native peoples are seen as obstacles to the development of such resources, and hence to sovereignty, resulting in less sympathy for Native rights in Québec than in the rest of Canada. The Péquistes are torn between trying to accommodate Natives or to exploit this lack of sympathy for political gain.[30] They have been able to agree, however, on the question of Québec's territorial integrity—they have made it clear that they are unwilling to negotiate any changes in Québec's dimensions. An advisor to the Péquistes, Daniel Turp, had to retract an opinion that Natives have the same status under international law as the Québéquois, as such a stance would ultimately strengthen the position of Natives wishing to separate from Québec.[31]

Carving a sovereign Cree territory from an independent Québec might be argued for under international law. Russel Lawrence Barsh makes the case for Cree sovereignty over their lands as follows:

> Unlike the contiguous U.S., where indigenous people live in small enclaves surrounded by nonindigenous majorities, Canada is characterized by a sharp ethnic and linguistic frontier. . . . The northern half of Canada has an indigenous majority. . . . The North therefore meets the basic condition of a claim to self-determination: a contiguous territory that is distinct geographically and ethnically from the society administering it.[32]

This is further bolstered by the fact that Crees have continuously occupied the lands of the James Bay Project since well before the first European contact in North America.[33] This territory is also not historically French nor was it a part of Québec until the late 1800s. It was originally claimed by the Hudson's Bay Company and was part of Rupert's Land, which was ceded to the Crown in 1870. The southern border with Québec was not clear, and Québec only advanced its claims by degrees over time, moving north to the Eastmain River in 1898, and then to its present configuration under the Québec Boundary Act of 1912. All of this was accomplished without Cree approval. The Dorian Commission in 1971 declared that Natives have "incontestable" rights over much of Québec in terms of subsistence hunting and fishing. All in all, Québec's claim to sovereignty over the territory is tenuous.[34]

Despite such past disagreements over the issue of sovereignty, the Crees and Québec have finally been able to come to an agreement, after more than twenty years of discussion, regarding the Eastmain and Rupert River components of the James Bay Project. On October 23, 2001, Bernard Landry, prime minister of Québec, and the grand chief of the Council of the Crees, Ted Moses, signed an agreement in principle that would allow for the development of the Eastmain hydroelectric project and the diversion of the Rupert River to proceed. This phase of the James Bay Project will cost $3.8 billion and produce 200 megawatts of power. In exchange for their approval, the Crees will receive payments of $23 million annually, increasing to $70 million after several years, for a period of forty years. Additionally, there are provisions that deal with forestry and land use that are intended to ensure that development in these areas is compatible with traditional Cree culture.[35]

Matthew Coon Come is pleased with the new agreement negotiated with Québec:

> Most important for us will be the positive impact that this agreement will have in improving the prospects for our youth and children in the future. To be strong the Crees must continue to occupy and be involved in the whole of the James Bay territory through the pursuit of both traditional and non-traditional activities. We must continue to work together as the Cree nation and to build the institutions we need to further our political, economic and social interests. We must and will build this future with the people of Québec. This was what was intended in 1975 in the James Bay and Northern Québec Agreement. . . . It will give form and life to the Cree rights in the Treaty.[36]

Chief Coon Come clearly prefers accommodation as the way for the Crees to come to grips with their minority status within both Québec and Canada. He does not wish to abandon the Cree way of life entirely, but he sees both necessity and advantage in cooperating with Québec. He believes that the project promises long-term economic benefits to his nation. He does not state it directly here, but underlying this willingness is the knowledge that the force of Québec's will in this matter may ultimately prove irresistible in any case, and perhaps it is better to strike a deal now rather than to have one imposed at some later point.

This viewpoint has been questioned by Deputy Grand Chief Matthew Mukash. He claims that "[t]he land is part of creation. We don't have the right to sell it." He sees the James Bay Project as neocolonialism:

> [U]nless we concentrate on the big picture, that what we are faced with is the on-going process of "colonization" and the effect of "oppression" that comes with it—we are going to destroy ourselves. Oppression is intergenerational and plays a huge role in our reactions to the actions of governments, our leaders, and it's very damaging. The most overpowering effect is fear. Fear is the greatest tool of the colonizer. Its effect is the following: you get a sense of worthlessness, helplessness, depression, paranoia, distrust, sleeplessness, unable to focus at home, in the workplace, harassment, anger, breaking up friendships, relationships, divisions within families, churches, leadership and so on. It is very damaging, and we are its victims. Québec

must be laughing really hard now. Well, there is a saying that goes something like this: "The greatest tool of a colonizer is the mind of the colonized."[37]

He essentially portrays the ratification process as one of divide and conquer. By sowing fear of the potentially negative consequences of not supporting the project, Québec has succeeded in convincing enough Crees to abandon their cultural heritage. He paints a picture of Native cooptation where Natives have become mere dupes, rather than one of self-determination. He does not find the argument that accommodation will allow the Crees to retain the core of their culture as plausible. He sees it rather as an act of erosion that will eventually undermine the basis for maintenance of Cree culture.

On its surface, the ratification of the most recent agreement on the James Bay Project seems to be accepted overwhelmingly by the Crees. The agreement was approved by secret ballot by 70 percent of those voting. To all appearances, this is a democratic expression of the true will of the Cree people. But opponents claim that a closer look must be taken at the process. Approximately 50 percent of those eligible to vote abstained. This would not seem overly problematic to many North Americans, who readily accept the notion that elections should be determined by the results of those who bother to turn out on election day, and not by any percentage of those eligible to vote. Opponents see the question differently, however. They prefer the word "boycott" to that of "abstain." They believe that nonparticipation is not merely a sign of apathy, disinterest, or laziness, but rather a conscious choice of symbolic value. In most Native societies, the Cree among them, consensus is valued. By choosing not to participate in the process, these tribal members are actively voicing disapproval of the process. Based on this interpretation, the vote cannot be viewed as legitimate.

If this viewpoint is adopted, it calls into question the legitimacy of the process of building Cree self-determination. Accepting Jeanette Wolfley's assertion that cultural vitality is fundamental to sovereignty, the imposition of a decision-making process based on a simple majority of those choosing to participate seems to run counter to this requirement. Rather than sustaining Native culture, an element of which is decision making based on consensus, it divides the Crees, alienating those who choose to show displeasure through the traditional method of nonparticipation.

The legitimacy of the election has also been questioned on other grounds. There have been claims that the referendum was not uniformly worded to all voters, but that the text varied by locale. Also, the referendum was not held on the same day at all polling places. This is problematic because results from some areas were prematurely released, potentially affecting results in those areas voting later. And due to the fact that many Crees live in remote settlements they often leave to hunt and trap, it was difficult or impossible to poll them on their views. Robert Taylor, editor of *The Nation,* a publication dealing with Cree issues, has also alleged manipulation by tribal leadership: "The Agreement-In-Principle was one of the most closely guarded secrets in Québec."[38] He portrayed the agreement as a deal made behind closed doors and sprung on the population, and not openly debated in the spirit of consensus building. The result of this process has not been the resolution of the question of the James Bay Project, but the creation of an intratribal schism at a deeper level than the project itself.

Why is there such strong opposition among Crees, considering the large monetary settlement they have achieved? First, many have a strong desire to maintain their traditions, and the massive hydroelectric power projects threaten them. At the heart of Cree culture are the moose and the beaver. Both species will be severely reduced in numbers if not wiped out entirely. Furthermore, geese will also be affected, primarily through water diversion. Rupert Bay, located at the southern end of James Bay, is one of the three most important resting and feeding places for geese during migration. The diversion of rivers flowing into Rupert Bay will have an adverse impact.[39] Second, there are doubts as to the long-term direct economic benefits of the project. The agreement does not guarantee jobs for Crees, and even if it did they would not be permanent. The experience of the first stage of James Bay shows that most jobs created by hydroelectric projects are in the construction phases, with very little manpower required to run and maintain the projects once they are in place.

Another opponent to the project, Bob Orr from Nemaska, synthesizes Cree concerns in his argument against the project. "We don't want to see another river dammed because it is our provider. We believe it's a gateway to our own economy, through eco-tourism. We can share our values of the land, the animals, the universe and the Creator. We can do it ourselves. We believe Government funding is a spirit killer."[40] Orr strongly asserts that Cree culture and the land are inextricably linked. One of the fundamental determinants of culture has always been the means of subsistence. But Orr is clearly not suggesting cultural separation. His approach involves accommodation, recognizing the potential of the eastern James Bay region for ecotourism. This optimism is not unfounded. The region is the last significant wilderness in the eastern half of North America.[41] This fact is recognized by others besides the Crees. These same environmental concerns primarily caused New York State to cancel plans to buy power from the Great Whale segment of the project during the 1990s. Orr sees traditional Cree culture coupled with ecotourism as a more viable use for the region economically. He also believes that it would be a more empowering and spiritual path to self-determination.

Controversy over exploitation of the James Bay watershed is far from over. It was not settled by Cree government acceptance of the most recent agreement. Only a portion of Bourassa's grand vision for development has been realized to date. In *Power from the North,* Bourassa details a grand ambition, not just for the generation of hydroelectric power, but for the exportation of fresh water from the region. The GRAND (Great Recycling and Northern Development) Canal is a proposal to build a dike across James Bay, cutting it off from Hudson Bay, making it a freshwater collection basin. From this basin, water that "has already served its useful purpose in Canada and would otherwise be lost to the sea" would be available for export to the Great Lakes–St. Lawrence system as well as the western United States and Canada.[42] With growing pressure on water use in both countries, coupled with a less than environmentally friendly administration in Washington that has already shown willingness to put diplomatic pressure on Canada for the exploitation of its resources for the benefit of the United States, as well as enormous potential for construction profits, this idea is likely to achieve some momentum in the near future. Such a colossal modification of nature affecting Cree lands is bound to be a source of controversy, not just among Natives, but among non-Natives as well.

THE NAVAJOS AND BLACK MESA COAL MINING

The Navajos are faced with issues similar to those of the Crees. For many Navajos, the exploitation of natural resources also presents an opportunity to create a viable economic base for tribal self-determination. Jeanette Wolfley notes, "Approximately one-third of the low-sulfur coal in the western states, more than half of all uranium deposits, and 20% of all known U.S. reserves in oil and natural gas are located on tribal homelands. More recently, tribal lands also have been viewed as sites for waste disposal."[43]

The Navajo tribal land base is approximately 15 million acres, the largest reservation in the United States. A substantial proportion of tribal natural resources are located on their lands, particularly coal and uranium. Additionally, due to the Navajos' remote location on land regarded by many Americans as nothing but desert wasteland, it makes an attractive site for potential storage of toxic and nuclear wastes. There are therefore pressures, both from certain tribal elements and American society in general, to exploit this potential. This issue then has been an ongoing source of tension and conflict among Navajos.

The Navajos are the largest Indian nation in the United States. In 1995, they numbered over 240,000, with a 4 percent annual growth rate, substantially higher than the American population as a whole. The size of the Navajo population is an element of strength, but also the cause of a dilemma. Although the reservation encompasses approximately 2,500 square miles, it is located in an arid region that supports little food production besides sheep and goat herding. The reservation economically provides for only 35,000 people.[44] In fact, it is ironic that for a people so rich in energy resources, over 30 percent of all Navajos lack access to electricity. The problem for Navajos is how to support as many of its members as possible from its tribal land base, while maintaining the ability of that land base to support its culture. This problem has been officially recognized by Navajo courts:

There are valuable and tangible assets which produce wealth. They provide food, income and the support of the Navajo People. The most valuable tangible asset of the Navajo Nation is its land, without which the Navajo Nation would [not] exist and without which the Navajo People would be caused to disperse. . . . Land is basic to the survival of the Navajo People.[45]

The case of the Navajos is more complex because of the peculiar nature of its reservation lands. Lying smack in the middle of the Navajo Reservation is the Hopi Reservation, created by President Chester Arthur in 1882. The Hopi Reservation was not based on a treaty, as Congress had decided to stop making treaties with Native Americans in 1871.[46] It hardly reflected the true use and settlement patterns of either people; the president dictated that the reservation would be a perfect rectangle, one degree of latitude by one degree of longitude. Some Natives alleged that the true motive of this designation was to prevent homesteading on this particular site by Mormon settlers. Others believed that the land, which contained valuable recognized deposits of coal and oil, if kept in the hands of Indians could be more easily manipulated through the Bureau of Indian Affairs (BIA). Thus, it would be easier and cheaper for large energy interests to obtain access to the land.[47] Still other Indians regard this peculiar allotment of reservation land between the Navajos and the Hopis as a perfect setup for playing the two tribes off against each other for the benefit of outsiders. Detailing the land dispute between Navajos and Hopis in any depth is far beyond the scope of this article, but the exploitation of natural resources has been at its core.

There has been interest in Navajo mineral rights almost since the foundation of their reservation. Coal was first discovered there in 1909. Interest in the reservation really took off in the 1920s with the discovery of oil. Standard Oil of California wanted to lease tracts from the Navajos. Since the federal government was legally the trustee for the Navajos, Standard Oil attempted to negotiate with federal officials. As trustee, the government could not negotiate without the consent of the Navajos, and this was problematic since there was no tribal entity recognized by the federal government that could act on the Navajos' behalf. The BIA first called together leaders at the San Juan Agency in May 1922. The leaders, however, rejected all lease applications. To overcome this hurdle, Secretary of the Interior Albert Fall created a Navajo "business council" with the authority to sign leases.[48] This was not the first case of whites defining Native leadership on white terms in order to obtain more pliable leaders. The Navajos, like many Native peo-

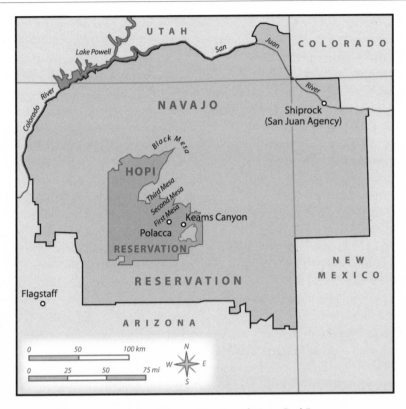

Empowering Native America: Navajo and Hopi Coal Resources

ples, did not have one grand chief with authority over the entire tribe. Numerous head men of smaller groups were better equipped to handle leadership on a day-to-day basis. All too often, Indian chiefs have been a fiction of whites looking for someone to give legitimacy to sham agreements. There is abundant historical justification for Native suspicion of Native leaders, who were either chosen by whites or through so-called tribal elections.

During the 1930s under John Collier's leadership, reforms were proposed and implemented. Collier wanted to preserve tribal integrity and to reverse the effects of the General Allotment Act, which broke up collectively owned reservation land into parcels privately owned by individual Indians. He managed to get the Indian Reform Act (IRA) passed in 1934, which called for some degree of tribal self-determination while imposing specific structures for tribal government. The Navajos defeated the IRA by a slim margin due to suspicions they held regarding the federal government's true intentions. Despite this defeat, a Navajo Tribal Council was approved by the BIA. Some Navajos alleged that the council was put together on the advice of a Catholic priest who spoke Navajo and who toured the reservation and compiled a list of head men. He then submitted a shortened list to the BIA, which adopted it as the Navajo Tribal Council.[49]

The development of energy resources on tribal lands in northeastern Arizona has been an issue for the Hopis as well, whose tribal territory is completely surrounded by Navajo land. The exploitation of coal and uranium resources has pitted the two peoples against each other in a protracted legal struggle. Some claim that the federal government has purposely fueled this controversy, playing the two tribes off against each other, using their so-called range war as a pretext for legislative intervention designed more for the benefit of outside energy concerns than the Natives involved. Members of both peoples complained publicly that the primary causes of the dispute were tribal attorneys, quasi-outsiders manipulating the situation for their own benefit.[50]

The Hopis have also experienced manipulations from outsiders. The Hopi Tribal Council ceased to function in 1939 when elders refused to attend meetings, ensuring that there never was a quorum. This situation was exploited by two Mormon lawyers, John Boyden and his law partner, Ernest Wilkinson. As an employee of the Department of the Interior, Wilkinson helped draft legislation that restricted Natives to receiving monetary compensation only for surface land claims, and not for subterranean mineral and water rights. Furthermore, it required the Interior Department to pay legal fees amounting to 7 to 10 percent of the value of claims paid. Boyden managed to convince the BIA to reconstitute the moribund Hopi Tribal Council, which then appointed Boyden tribal claims counsel. Boyden maintained a thirty-year relationship with the Hopis.[51] He is also alleged to have secretly represented Peabody Coal Company at the time.[52] David M. Brugge, author of *The Navajo-Hopi Land Dispute: An American Tragedy*, states that Boydon's law firm was on retainer with a number of energy companies, but Brugge expresses uncertainty over who manipulated whom in the matter.[53] In any case, Boydon's leadership led to a lease agreement between the Hopis and Peabody Coal in 1966, although Hopi elders disagree. For many members of both the Navajo and the Hopi nations, tribal governments and their dealings with energy concerns seems fraught with cooptation and corruption.

The discovery of the richest known deposit of coal in the United States in 1951 brought the question of ownership of the land to the forefront of Navajo-Hopi relations. Although the coal was located on the Hopi Reservation, Navajos believed that they had a claim to the land due to prior occupancy. The Navajo Nation filed a friendly suit to clarify mineral rights. This led to creation of a joint-use area shared by both tribes.[54] Peabody Coal proceeded to negotiate contracts with the Department of the Interior and both tribes to mine coal at Black Mesa, with payments divided 50-50 between the tribes. These payments were substantially below standard market prices. The lease agreements were disputed in federal court by Hopi elders. They wished to stop the mining, as Black Mesa is sacred to both the Hopis and Navajos. The Hopis based their case on alleged violations of the tribe's BIA-approved constitution. In a curious decision, the court ruled that the federal government would not interfere with the Hopi tribal government as the issue had a political dimension that affected the Hopis' sovereign status under U.S. law.

The joint-use area obviously made it more difficult for energy concerns to negotiate leases with the tribes. Minor local disputes over issues such as grazing rights were blown out of proportion by the mainstream press. They depicted the situation as an outright range war.[55] This eventually led to the Navajo-Hopi Settlement Act, passed by Congress in 1974. This act facilitated partition of the joint-use area.[56] It was followed by the Navajo-Hopi Land Dispute Settlement Act of 1996. This act resulted in the forced relocation of 12,000 Navajos living on what was now designated Hopi land, and 400 Hopis who found themselves residing on designated Navajo land. The relocation of 12,000 Navajos sparked the interest of the United Nations. After an investigation, the UN Commission on Human Rights, on April 1, 1997, urged the United States not to pursue relocation. This position was reinforced the following year by expert testimony from relocation expert Professor Thayer Scudder from the California Institute of Technology. In a letter to the UN, Scudder stated:

> Frankly, the situation as it has developed over the years appalls me for it is one of the worst resettlement efforts that I have observed during a research career of over 40 years. Certainly no further forced removal should be required which I sincerely hope will be the position that results from your investigation.[57]

In the end, an inter-tribal dispute over natural resources has culminated in a massive human tragedy for the displaced Navajos and Hopis. The dispute has been exacerbated by tribal lawyers who were appointed by governments of questionable legitimacy and dubious loyalties. For the Navajos, it has also been a contest conducted on a foreign premise. With great respect for individual opinion and consensus, the Navajo tribal government has been reluctant to take up the cause of those being relocated before those people expressed themselves. The tribal government has also been reluctant to pursue causes unless they seem to affect all Navajos.[58] The Navajos have been at a decided disadvantage when doing battle with a more aggressively individualistic nonindigenous society.

Tribal sovereignty has also proven to be a double-edged sword in terms of the fiduciary responsibility of the federal government vis-à-vis Native peoples. On March 4, 2003, the U.S. Supreme Court ruled against the Navajos in a case filed by the tribe against the Department of the Interior (DOI). The tribe sued because it felt the DOI had not properly represented tribal interests in approving the lease agreement with Peabody Coal. The tribe signed an agreement calling for 12.5 percent royalty payments, even though the DOI approved the contract, knowing that the BIA, without Navajo knowledge, had recommended 20 percent. Although a federal court of appeals had earlier concluded that the DOI had failed to live up to its fiduciary duty to protect tribal interests, the U.S. Supreme Court ruled that the DOI did not have "managerial supervision" over the contract. Navajo Nation President Joe Shirley, Jr., indicated that this decision illuminated a major risk for Native peoples in asserting self-determination. Shirley observed "that the government will remain an accountable trustee only if tribes remain wholly dependent."[59] Native sovereignty is seen by the highest federal court as obviating any need for a federal fiduciary relationship with tribes.

THE HUMAN RIGHTS FRAMEWORK

Both Navajos and Crees have grappled with self-determination issues within a human rights framework. Attempts to protect Native rights at the supranational level have sought to define more clearly and protect indigenous rights in the Americas through several hemispheric agreements, both approved and proposed. The American Convention of Human Rights, produced by the Inter-American Conference on Human Rights, held in San José, Costa Rica, on November 22, 1969, was ratified on July 18, 1978. Article 21 of this document contains the provision that "[e]veryone has the right to the use and enjoyment of his property."[60]

This builds on the 1948 American Declaration on the Rights and Duties of Man passed by the Organization of American States during its Ninth International Conference. Article XXIII states that every person has the right "to own such private property as meets the essential needs of decent living and helps to maintain the dignity of the individual and the home."[61] Legal scholars James Anaya and Robert Williams, Jr., argue that these documents must be interpreted as meaning that the property forms they protect "attach to the property regimes that derive from indigenous peoples' own customary or traditional systems of land tenure independently of whatever property regimes derive from or are recognized by official state enactments." The Inter-American Commission on Human Rights agrees with this, having declared the following:

1. Indigenous peoples have the right to the legal recognition of their varied and specific forms and modalities of their control, ownership, use and enjoyment of territories and property.
2. Indigenous peoples have the right to the recognition of their property and ownership rights with respect to lands, territories and resources they

have historically occupied, as well as to the use of those to which they have historically had access for their traditional activities and livelihood.[62]

This clearly supports the right of Native peoples in the Americas to maintain traditional, communal-based forms of land ownership.

Concomitant with support for indigenous land ownership is the need to preserve the integrity of tribal forms of political organization. Under the proposed American Declaration on the Rights of Indigenous Peoples, the need to protect aboriginal forms of political organization is recognized. Section 3 of Article VII (Right to Cultural Integrity), states: "The states shall recognize and respect indigenous ways of life, customs, traditions, forms of social, economic and political organization, institutions, practices, beliefs and values, use of dress, and languages."[63]

This declaration recognizes that the retention of indigenous political practices is integral to cultural preservation. By instituting tribal governments that rely on the election system prevalent in the United States and Canada, where a simple plurality of votes is all that is necessary to govern, rather than the broad consensus required in most traditional Native approaches, there is a strong risk of alienating a significant proportion of tribal members, and thus threatening the efficacy of such systems. Delmer Lenowski enumerates several specific consequences of plurality voting on tribes. He claims that it engenders both a sense of political alienation and a lack of faith in the efficiency of tribal governments, defined as the ability to have one's concerns addressed. The cumulative results of these consequences are low rates of participation in tribal government and elections.[64] It would appear then that many of the indigenous political systems prevalent in Canada and the United States are in contravention of the intent of the declarations of the Organization of American States.

There are those who claim that among the motivations of the United States for promoting Native self-determination has been the desire to circumvent any possible intrusion from the United Nations in the matter of aboriginal rights within its territory. Others suggest this is part of an international lack of interest in Native issues. In 1970, the United Nations Sub-Commission on the Prevention of Discrimination and the Protection of Minorities recommended that the question of abuses against indigenous peoples be studied. This eventually led to the launching of Human Rights Day in 1992, declaring 1993 the International Year of the World's Indigenous People, and to the United Nations draft Declaration on the Rights of Indigenous Peoples in 1994. It is curious to note that few UN delegates attended Native elders' speeches that inaugurated 1993.[65] Additionally, though many indigenous groups are specifically named by the United Nations in a fact sheet issued on the self-determination question, there is no direct mention of Native peoples specifically located in the United States.[66] Ultimately, it would appear the United States government would prefer to regard the issue of Native sovereignty as a strictly internal matter. This is consistent with Supreme Court Chief Justice John Marshall's notion of "domestic dependent nations." It is interesting to note that under principles of common law, Canadian legal interpretations of indigenous rights have been much influenced by Marshall and United States Supreme Court decisions.[67]

CONCLUSION

The process of building institutions of self-determination among Native peoples in Canada and the United States, while seemingly a worthwhile effort, and "the right thing to do," is not the simple and straightforward process that some might regard it to be. This process has to be considered within the broader context in which it occurs. Self-determination building takes place under the aegis of dominant political systems and societies that do not share heritages with Native peoples regarding notions of governance and law. As noted above, there are forces driving dominant societies to engage in this process beyond simply showing respect for Native peoples—forces such as the wish to avoid international censure, the desire to exploit valuable indigenous resources, and an ethnocentric belief in the primacy of democratic/majority rule systems of government. All of these forces are evident in the Crees' approaches to the James Bay Project and the Navajos' responses to the Black Mesa coal mining and reservation partition.

Accepting that forms of governance serve to underpin, reflect, and maintain the cultural values of a society, the imposition of European-based, "democratic" systems of governance on Native peoples carries with it the risk of the destruction of Native cultures. If cultural vitality is as critical an element of Native sovereignty, as Wolfley claims, then such self-determination building efforts might be viewed as counterproductive. And yet there is also the need to avoid viewing Native peoples as frozen in time. There are those who romanticize about a purer and nobler Native past, viewing any cultural adaptations as contamination. Such a view, where Native peoples can only exist as primitive relics, or else vanish through assimilation, has been a part-and-parcel assumption of Native ethnocide of the past several centuries. A closer and more honest examination of history makes clear that the Native peoples of North America have always engaged actively in cultural exchange and development. The present is no exception. The forces of European conquest in North America have stripped Native peoples of their sovereignty, leaving them bereft of modern experiences in self-determination. Contact has also shaped Native peoples, and for most there is little hope or desire of returning to some mythical pristine past. The keyword here should be "process." There is an ongoing process of building Native self-determination, and all issues are not likely to be settled quickly. It will require a continuous process of negotiation among Native peoples themselves, as well as between Natives and the society at large.

NOTES

1. Jeanette Wolfley, "Ecological Risk Assessment and Management: The Failure to Value Indigenous Traditional Economic Knowledge and Protect Tribal Homelands," *American Indian Culture and Research Journal* 22, no. 2 (1998), 151.

2. Ibid.

3. Phillip Wearne, *Return of the Indian* (Philadelphia: Temple University Press, 1996), 8.

4. William B. Gudykunst and Young Yun Kim, *Communicating with Strangers* (Boston: McGraw Hill, 2003), 122; and Mark P. Orbe, *Constructing Co-Cultural Theory: An Explanation of Culture, Power and Communication* (Thousand Oaks, CA: Sage Publications, 1998), 86–93.

5. Boyce Richardson, *James Bay: The Plot to Drown the North Woods* (San Francisco: Sierra Club, 1972), 28.

6. Ibid., 52.

7. Ronald Niezen, *Defending the Land: Sovereignty and Forest Life in James Bay Cree Society* (Boston: Allyn and Bacon, 1998), 64.

8. "First Power Surges from the Dam," *The National,* broadcast October 27, 1979, in CBC Archives, http://archives.cbc.ca/400i?asp.

9. Richardson, *James Bay,* 9.

10. Ibid., 13.

11. Ibid., 38.

12. Ibid., 15.

13. Ibid., 46.

14. Ibid.

15. Ibid., 37.

16. Russel Lawrence Barsh, "Aboriginal Peoples and Québec: Competing for Legitimacy as Emerging Nations," *American Indian Culture and Research Journal* 21, no. 1 (1997), 4.

17. Robert Bourassa, *Power from the North* (Scarborough, Ontario: Prentice-Hall Canada, 1985), 34.

18. Ibid.

19. Sally Farrar, "Structural Racism Pushing Canada's Indigenous to the Edge," *Indian Country Today,* October 8, 2001, http://www.indiancountry.com.

20. Richardson, *James Bay,* 79.

21. Barsh, "Aboriginal Peoples," 1.

22. Ibid., 7–8.

23. Ibid., 14.

24. Ibid., 11.

25. Ibid., 13.

26. Ibid., 10.

27. Ibid., 18.

28. Ibid., 4.

29. Ibid., 10.

30. Ibid., 12.

31. Ibid., 14.

32. Ibid., 2–3.

33. Richardson, *James Bay,* 51.

34. Ibid., 55.

35. Secrétariat aux affaires autochones Québec, "Signature of an Agreement in Principle Between the Grand Council of the Crees and the Quebéc Government," http://www.mce.gouv.qc.ca/w/html/w1474002.html.

36. Secrétariat aux affaires autochones Quebéc, "Speaking Notes Grand Chief Ted Moses Signing of the Agreement in Principle," http://www.mce.gouv.qc.ca/w/html /w1480001.html.

37. Will Nichols, "Interview: Deputy Grand Chief Matthew Mukash Breaks Ranks," *The Nation,* online, http://www.ottertooth.com/Reports/Ruper/News/Nation-mukash.htm.

38. Robert Taylor, "Cree Vote Yes on Québec Deal," *Indian Country Today,* February 8, 2002, http://www.indiancountry.com.

39. Richardson, *James Bay,* 98.

40. Taylor, "Cree Vote Yes."

41. Richardson, *James Bay,* 23.

42. Bourassa, *Power from the North,* 147.

43. Wolfley, "Ecological Risk Assessment and Management," 155.

44. Sioux Harvey, "Two Models to Sovereignty: A Comparative History of the Mashantucket Pequot Tribal Nation and the Navajo Nation," *American Indian Culture and Research Journal* 20, no. 1 (1996), 153.

45. S. James Anaya and Robert A. Williams, Jr., "Protection of Indigenous Peoples' Rights over Lands and Natural Resources under the Inter-American Human Rights System," *Harvard Human Rights Journal* 14 (Spring 2001), 43–45.

46. Jill St. Germain, *Indian Treaty-Making Policy in the United States and Canada, 1867–1877* (Lincoln: University of Nebraska Press, 2001).

47. Navajo Timeline, http://www.lapahie.com/Timeline_USA_1869_1927.cfm.

48. Ibid.

49. Navajo Timeline, http://www.lapahie.com/Timeline_USA_1928_1940.cfm.

50. David M. Brugge, *The Navajo-Hopi Land Dispute: An American Tragedy* (Albuquerque: University of New Mexico Press, 1994), 116.

51. Navajo Timeline, http://www.lapahie.com/Timeline_USA_1941_1969.cfm.

52. Duane A. Beyal, "Echoes of Old Political Controversies and Battles," *The Navajo Times,* http://www.navajotimes.com.

53. Brugge, *The Navajo-Hopi Land Dispute,* 251.

54. Ibid., 97–118.

55. Ibid., 210.

56. Ibid., 239.

57. Letter, Thayer Scudder, Professor of Anthropology, California Institute of Technology, to Abdelfattah Amor, Special Rapporteur of the United Nations Commission on Human Rights, January 31, 1998, http://www.aics.org/BM/scudder.html.

58. Brugge, *The Navajo-Hopi Land Dispute,* 243.

59. Bill Donovan, "Tribal Leaders Disappointed, Mull Next Legal Move Against Peabody," *Navajo Times,* March 6, 2003, http://www.navajotimes.com.

60. American Convention on Human Rights, "Pact of San José, Costa Rica, November 22, 1969," Part 1, Chapter 1, Article 21, http://nethics.net/nethics_neu/n3/quellen /voelkerrechtsverg_texte/american-convention-on-human-right-1969.pdf.

61. Organization of American States, "American Declaration of the Rights and Duties of Man," Res. XXX Ninth International Conference of American States (1948).

62. Anaya and Williams, "Protection of Indigenous Peoples' Rights," 43–45.

63. Organization of American States, Inter-American Commission on Human Rights, "Proposed American Declaration on the Rights of Indigenous Peoples," Inter-American Commission on Human Rights, February 26, 1997, 133rd session, 95th regular session.

64. Delmer Lenowski, "A Return to Tradition: Proportional Representation in Tribal Government," *American Indian Culture and Research Journal* 18, no. 1 (1994), 148.

65. Alexander Ewen, ed., "Introduction: An Indigenous Worldview," *Voice of Indigenous Peoples: Native People Address the United Nations* (Santa Fe, NM: Clear Light Publishers, 1993), 25.

66. Fact Sheet No. 9 (Rev.), The Rights of Indigenous Peoples, Programme of Activities for the International Decade of the World's Indigenous People (1995–2004) (para. 4), General Assembly resolution 50/157, December 21, 1995, annex.

67. Leonard Ian Rotman, *Parallel Paths, Fiduciary Doctrine and the Crown-Native Relationship in Canada* (Toronto: University of Toronto Press, 1996), 248.

CHAPTER 3

Bear Ceremonialism and Its Ecological Aspects among Subarctic and Plains Indians

RIKU HÄMÄLÄINEN

IN CULTURES where the principal source of livelihood is hunting, relations between humans and animals are particularly important. Animals are the source of food and material culture, and they are also an essential part of the indigenous worldviews and religions. They outline the position of humans among other forms of life, all of which comprise the natural world.

The relationships among human culture, religion, and nature have been examined particularly from the viewpoints of cultural ecology and the ecology of religion.[1] Among Native North Americans, hunting has traditionally been an important way of life, especially in northern regions. As elsewhere in the world, hunting is an ancient way of obtaining food, and thus animals retain a central role in Native American religions.

The worldviews of Native Americans differs from a Western, or Judeo-Christian worldview. In traditional Native American religions, humans and other animals are intricately connected. Humans, and especially "medicine men"—that could be defined as individuals who practiced "spiritual and healing ceremonies"[2]—might appear in the form of animals, and animals usually appear in human form in stories. In legends and visions, the borders between humans and other animals are practically nonexistent. The transformation between humans and bears, for example, can be found in many indigenous stories.[3]

In Native North American worldviews, humans and animals are often seen as equal, and since animals were created before humans, they are superior to humans in terms of the ability to create power. According to Joseph Epes Brown, in the creation beliefs of Plains Indians,

[54]

[T]he animals were created before human beings, so that in their anteriority and divine origin they have a certain proximity to the Great Spirit . . . , which demands respect and veneration. In them the Indian sees actual reflections of the qualities of the Great Spirit, which serve the same function as revealed scriptures in other religions. They are intermediaries or links between human beings and God. This explains not only why religious devotions may be directed to the deity *through* the animals, but it also helps us to understand why contact with, or from, the Great Spirit, comes to the Indian almost exclusively through visions involving animal or other natural forms.[4]

In Native North America, beliefs concerning animals have traditionally included views equating animals to humans. Animals even had tribes like humans, and animals and humans were thought by nature to possess similar kinds of souls. Especially among the northern Algonquins, it also is common to believe that animal species were protected and ruled by a supernatural master, or guardian spirit. Regina Flannery and Mary Elizabeth Chambers have written that the eastern Crees and northern Algonquins conceptualized the animal world as tripartite, composed of creatures of earth, water, and sky. Caribou constituted a fourth category of food animals. Each of these realms was presided over by a guardian spirit, or *o:či:ma:w.* The four named guardian spirits, or caretakers, include *Meme:kwe:ši:w,* the one who presides over all of the "clawed" animals. The bear, known as *Meme:kwe:ši's,* "little dog" or "pup," is his primary charge. A second spirit is *O:ki:čiko,* responsible for everything that flies in the air; a third is *Misče:na:ku,* overseer of the fish and all life in the water. Finally, *Či:če:na:pe:w,* "smart man" (i.e., the one with great ability), is in charge of caribou.[5]

If a hunter respected the animals he killed, the supernatural master, or the guardian spirit, was pleased and provided him with more animals. But, if the hunter did not respect the animals enough, he would not obtain game, and his family would starve. Relations between humans and animals are thus revealed clearly in hunting rites and animal ceremonies. According to Åke Hultkrantz, the animal ceremonialism of American Indians has centered on the bear, and bear ceremonialism was the most developed form of animal ceremonialism.[6] The Naskapis, subarctic Indians in northeastern North America, consider bear ceremonialism the most important of animal ceremonies even though bear ranked as a food source after caribou.[7]

This essay discusses bear ceremonialism among Native North Americans in two surroundings, among subarctic First Nations, especially the eastern Cree, and in the northern Plains, focusing particularly on the Blackfeet and Lakota. When surveying bear ceremonialism in these two diverse regions, differences in form and function are stark. Why they are so different, even though the peoples in both of these regions have primarily been hunters, and thus the relations between humans and animals have been central in their worldview, has perplexed scholars. The contrasts cannot be explained only by cultural differences. What contributes to a greater understanding is considering culture within the ecological features of each region and the environmental influences on the cultures. This study does not seek to discover the origins of bear ceremonialism; rather, it investigates the ecological integration between Native North American cultures, religions, and nature.[8]

BEAR—THE AWESOME NORTHERN PREDATOR

Bears, the largest carnivores on earth, have been respected for thousands of years by all inhabitants of the Northern Hemisphere. In Eurasia, prepared bear skulls have been found in caves that had been placed in certain positions during the Paleolithic era, and some scholars believe Neanderthal humans may have worshiped the bear.[9] Bear ceremonialism of Native Americans derives from ancient times, and bear symbolism can be seen in very early rock art. For example, a cave-like petroglyph site in northernmost Nebraska along the Missouri River revealed first by Garrick Mallery includes several bear paws and a whole bear drawn in an upright position. This site has recently been associated with the Great Cave of the Bears, one of the animal lodges that had never before been located in Pawnee sacred geography.[10]

According to E.O. James, the bear's great strength caused it to become such a cult object.[11] Bears are the largest and most dangerous predators in North America. Washington Irving wrote in the early nineteenth century that "the grizzly bear alone of all the animals of our Western wilds is prone to unprovoked hostility. His prodigious size and strength make him a formidable opponent, and his great tenacity of life often baffles the skill of the hunter." Regarding the American Indians, he also stated that a bear's "enormous claws are worn around the neck of an Indian brave, as a trophy more honorable than a human scalp."[12] Trader Edwin Thompson Denig, in turn, mentions in his mid-nineteenth-century memoir that among the Upper Missouri tribes, the killing of a grizzly bear by a single man deservedly ranked next to killing an enemy,[13] and in earlier days at the Cochiti Pueblo anyone who killed a bear was eligible to join the Warrior Society, just as if he had killed a human enemy.[14] In the late nineteenth century, George Bird Grinnell observed that the "reverence for the bear appears to be common to all North American tribes, and is based on the fact that it is the largest carnivorous mammal of the continent, the most difficult to kill and extremely keen in all its senses."[15] Moreover, immediately after killing a bear, hunters of some northern Athapaskan Indians even cut off the forepaws of the bear and poked out its eyes so the dead animal could not hurt them or see who killed it. All of these cultural responses reflect a kind of fear of the bear.

Fear alone, however, does not account for the rich and varied traditions linked to bears among Native North Americans. Indians have felt a kinship with bears, for humans and bears share many characteristics. It could be said that both people and bears have lived in the same regions, fished salmon in the same streams, dug the same roots, and harvested the same berries. Physically, bears resemble humans. Bears are built somewhat like people. Unlike other animals, bears can stand on their hind legs and sometimes walk upright, and sometimes bears use their forepaws as humans use their hands. A bear's skinned body looks human, and the bear's skeleton resembles the human skeleton.

Northern Plains peoples have special relationships with bears. The Blackfoot, for example, believe that a bear is part animal and part human.[16] Indians have also considered bears to have the same kind of souls as humans.[17] One Shoshone medicine man even told Hultkrantz that he had seen some bears performing the Sun Dance at a place called Sweetwater Gap. According to the medicine man, the bears were praying. "They act just like a person. They are smart."[18] Thus, Indians cannot be sure if the bear confronted is a man in bear form, or vice versa.[19] These similarities have undoubtedly given the bear its unique status. The Lakotas call the bear *matho,* but they also have a name for a spirit bear, *Hunonpa,* meaning "Two-Legged." Bears to the Lakotas retain a special position among all other animals, or four-legged creatures, as well as a similarity to humans.[20]

Ceremonialism in honor of the bear has been practiced throughout the northlands, both in Eurasia and in North America. In his 1926 classic study, "Bear Ceremonialism in the Northern Hemisphere," A. Irving Hallowell collected data in both the Old and the New Worlds. He then offered an overview of bear ceremonialism and identified its common practices among indigenous peoples. These elements included: (1) hunting bears at a preferred time in the spring while bears were still in their dens; (2) referring to bears by metaphorical expressions, such as "Grandfather," "Cousin," "Short Tail," or "Honey Eater"; (3) calling the bears out of their dens; (4) killing bears using special ancient weapons; (5) making speeches to bear spirits after their death and paying attention to bear carcasses as the foci of elaborate ceremonies in which they were dressed up in borrowed finery and offered food, tobacco, and decorated objects; (6) organizing a communal feast, often called an eat-all, of bear meat; and finally, (7) handling respectfully the disposition of bear bones, especially skulls.[21] The purpose of this ritualism was to make the rebirth of bears possible, so that people could hunt more bears in the future.

CREE BEAR CEREMONIALISM

Bear ceremonialism of the eastern Cree, the subarctic people in northeastern North America, closely follows Hallowell's elements of bear ceremonialism. Cree practices are representative of bear ceremonialism in the North American subarctic.[22] In the northernmost regions, agriculture is not possible and gathering food plants is also limited. The principal and practically the only way to obtain food has been by hunting. The amount of game varies. Especially in winter, game is often scarce, resulting in springtime starvation. Among subarctic people, starvation has been considered a natural part of life.[23] During extremely hard times, even cannibalism has been known to occur. In the early twentieth century, Alanson Skinner claimed that there still were "individuals at nearly every post who have tasted human flesh under these conditions."[24]

In the subarctic regions, bears have been hunted following certain rules and rites. Cree bear hunts began with divination rites, with which the hunter tries to connect with the guardian spirit of bears, *Meme:kwe:ši:w,* to determine whether the hunt will be successful. Included are Shaking Lodge rites,[25] with the divination of a bear patella.[26] Hunters also used their own dreams to predict the outcome of their hunts, which was considered to be the best way to achieve a divine outcome. Some Cree men would not hunt without first divining the outcome.

According to Adrian Tanner, the hunt normally had two separate time phases, the first being at winter time when the bear is discovered in a den where it is killed. The second more dangerous kind of hunt happens in summertime when bears can be found in the paths they use year after year.[27] Winter hunting seems to have been more common among Crees and other subarctic people.

Discovering the bear in its den usually happened at the end of winter. Hunters first cleansed themselves in a sweat lodge. Spiritual purity is important in ceremonialism,[28] and the bear hunt was considered a ceremony in which hunters communicated with the spiritual world and *Meme:kwe:ši:w,* the guardian spirit of bears. The Crees never said the word "bear" when preparing for the hunt; instead the animal was called by metaphorical expressions, such as "The Angry One," "The One Who Owns the Chin," or "Black Food," or even as a kinsman, such as "Grandfather/Grandmother" or "Cousin."[29]

In the evening before the hunt, the hunter offered tobacco for *Meme:kwe:ši:w.* In the morning of the hunt, the hunter put on his very best clean hunting clothes. All of the equipment used in the bear hunt had to be clean and in good condition. *Meme:kwe:ši:w* was not happy and the bear could not be killed if the equipment and the camp of the hunter were dirty. The hunter took his *ta:piska:ka:n,* a richly decorated piece of animal skin or cloth, and strung it across his chest. After all these preparations, the hunter traveled to the den that had been discovered beforehand. When the hunter reached the den, he called the bear until it came out. When the bear appeared, the hunter killed it. Crees thought that it was proper to kill the bear only with a traditional weapon, such as a club, axe, or spear. The bow and arrow was not considered a strong enough weapon.[30]

Once the hunter was sure that the bear was dead, he turned the body on its back and put some tobacco on its chest. He removed his chest-hanging cloth, the *ta:piska:ka:n,* and tied it around the bear's neck. He sat down and spoke solemnly to the bear. He asked that "Black Food" and other spirits would not be angry. He explained that he killed the bear only because he is poor and hungry, and that he needs the skin for his coat and the meat so that his family could eat. He then smoked his pipe and put the pipe into the bear's mouth to let him smoke, too. The hunter did not dress the carcass in the forest, he just removed the stomach, small intestines, and some fat. He also cut off the middle toe and claw of the right forepaw and returned with it to his camp.

When the hunter reached the camp, he first smoked for a while saying nothing of what he had done. Finally, he asked someone to bring the bear to the camp and butcher it. Usually, if he were a married man, the person chosen would be his wife. He asked the person to do this by giving her the bear claw taken from the carcass. This claw was wrapped in a beaded or painted cloth, and kept as a memento of the occasion.[31] When the bear was brought to camp, women were not allowed to look at it, and the hunter gave the carcass to the oldest man. After the hunter and other men had smoked, the bear was butchered. Certain parts of the bear's flesh were at once burned as an offering, so that *Meme:kwe:ši:w* would provide more bears in the future. Under an elder's direction, men set up a special lodge outside the camp for a bear feast.

Just after sunset, people dressed in their best clothes and gathered at the feast lodge. When everyone had arrived, the feast-keeper sealed the lodge, and no one could open the lodge until dawn. The feast-keeper sang and made offerings to *Meme:kwe:ši:w* by dropping pieces of meat into the fire. He asked for more bears to be hunted. He drank some of the bear's grease and smeared a bit on his forehead. He passed the container of grease clockwise around the lodge, and the others did the same. David Rockwell has noted that Crees considered the nutritious grease the most important part of the bear.[32] Bear meat had been prepared in two parts, the head and front legs together and the hind legs with the rest of the meat. Women were not allowed to eat the head and the front legs of the bear. According to some accounts, only men were able to eat the bear feast, and in some feasts women partook at a second sitting.[33]

The first part of the bear to be eaten was the head. The oldest men ate first, the youngest last. After the head was eaten, the front legs were then consumed. Once the men had eaten these sacred parts, the rest of the meat was passed in a clockwise direction, and everyone was allowed to eat. At this point the mood lightened, and people talked and laughed. Men smoked, the feast-keeper sang and drummed, and later others drummed and sang as well. In the early morning hours, after most of the meat had been eaten, people danced. The feast had to end before the sun rose.

All bear ceremonialism also involved the ritual handling of the bones and especially the skull. Bones were not allowed to be thrown away, and dogs were not allowed to take them. The skull was not to be broken, not even when killing the bear. After the feast, a tree of five or six meters was cut down and stripped of most of its bark and branches, so that only a small tuft was left at the very top. The tree was painted and stuck in the ground at the edge of the camp. The bear skull was painted, tobacco put in the jaw, and ribbons of hide or cloth tied to it. Then the skull was lashed to the pole about three meters above the ground, and the other bones were bundled and hung below the skull. The Crees did this for every bear they killed so the bear would return to life and come back to be hunted again. The skin of the bear was dried, and not until after a year or so was it used for clothing. Claws and the chin served as medicine objects or trophies of the hunt.[34]

PLAINS INDIAN BEAR CEREMONIALISM

On the Great Plains, another kind of bear ceremonialism existed among several Plains tribes, especially in the northern Plains. In the early 1880s, Alice Fletcher called attention to what she termed "animal cults" among the Siouan tribes on the Plains. She noticed that each cult was composed of individuals who had obtained supernatural power from the same animal species through a vision, and each of these groups possessed certain rituals and ceremonial regalia symbolic of the animal from which the power was obtained.[35] Members highly valued the medicine derived from the animal and the special relationship formed among them. George Sword told James Walker that among the Lakotas, the bear medicine men resembled a brotherhood.[36]

Although Plains Indians hunted the bear, information concerning bear ceremonialism in the Plains does not tell us much about bear hunting rites and bear feasts. In the 1830s, George Catlin described a bear dance the Lakotas held before a bear hunt. The leader wore a full bearskin mask, and others had smaller bear masks. Catlin painted a scene of this ceremony.[37] Bear dances also existed among other tribes, but these have not been connected with hunting bears.[38] In the 1850s, Denig wrote a Cree-like description of a bear hunt conducted by the Assiniboines.

"When a den is discovered, six or eight Indians go to attack it, approaching the hole so close as to see the foremost bear, when three of them fire, the others reserve their shots," he explained. "When a bear is killed he is skinned, all except the head, which is covered with scarlet cloth, the hair smeared over with vermilion, handsome feathers stuck around it, and new kettles and tobacco laid before it. It is presented with the pipe to smoke and a long ceremony of invocations takes place, purporting that they give him property and pay this attention to have pity upon their wives and children and not tear them when they are hunting after fruit and berries. They say if this is not done the bear will certainly sooner or later devour some of them or their children."[39]

Unfortunately, Denig does not describe the ceremony after the hunt.

Even though Plains Indians also hunted bears, the focus of their bear ceremonialism was not in the hunting rites and rebirth of the bear as among the Crees. During his fieldwork among the Assiniboines in the summer of 1953, John Ewers collected information about their bear cult. Henry Black Tail recalled three major functions of the Assiniboine bear cult: ceremonies in honor of the bear, aggressive participation in war expeditions, and doctoring the sick.[40] Since the bear cult seemed to be similar throughout the Plains area, it can be suggested that these functions comprised the bear cult of Plains Indians in general.[41] The bear ceremonialism of the Plains Indians was especially focused on warfare and healing.[42]

When the Assiniboine bear cult members gathered for the bear feast, they sang their bear songs, and each member was served a large bowl of berry soup since the "bears love berries, their favorite food." No meat was served at the bear feast since the members observed a strict taboo against eating bear. The ceremonial bear hunt was re-enacted by an individual cult member at the Sun Dance encampment. The cult member himself represented the bear, which was symbolically hunted by young boys.[43] Samuel Pond describes similar mock bear hunts among the Santee Dakotas in the 1830s.[44]

The legend of the bear knife of the Blackfoot, one of the more powerful tribes of the northern Plains, shows the close connection of bear ceremonialism to warfare. In this legend, of which different versions have been offered by Clark Wissler and David Duvall, Ted Brasser, John Ewers, and Walter McClintock, the bear knife was given to the people with two other medicine objects, the bear lance and the bear tipi design. Men were also taught how to use the knife in warfare. The Blackfoot bear cult and the medicine objects related to it, the bear knife, the bear spear, and the tipi painted with a "Hugging Bear" design,[45] were an important part of Blackfoot cultural and spiritual life.

Warfare was an essential part of traditional Plains Indian society. A man's social status was dependent on his success in warfare.[46] The members of the bear cult were generally known as fierce fighters. They obtained their powers from bears, and bears served as their guardian spirit in battle. When bear cult members went into action against the enemy, they wore their distinctive outfits, painted their faces in a peculiar way, and usually carried bear knives. When the bear men charged the enemy, they acted like bears and made noises like a bear.

The Assiniboine bear cult members' attire impressed their opponents. The top of each member's head was shaved, and some of the hair was rolled at each side into a ball representing bear ears. Each painted his face red and made vertical scratches on his face by scraping away some of the paint. A black circle was painted around each eye and mouth. The member wore a bear-claw necklace and a yellow skin shirt perforated with several cut holes. A small rectangular flap cut from the shirt itself was hanging at the center of the chest. When going to war or participating in cult ceremonies, each member carried a special bear knife, and in battle a member might also carry a shield with bear symbolism. According to Black Tail, one member also had a bear-painted tipi.[47] Prince Maximilian of Wied saw and described such a tipi in the Assiniboine camp in the early 1830s, and artist Karl Bodmer made a painting based on this description.[48]

A bear is a dangerous antagonist and comparable to a warrior. Indigenous men who had obtained their power from the bear were respected warriors who terrified opponents. Many Assiniboines feared both bears and the warriors who had bear power, and the cult members often acted as bears and made noises like bears.[49] When carrying his ceremonial regalia, a bear cult member was assured that his bear power was with him and would help him in battle. With such regalia, he made clear to his enemies who was challenging them, and thus he also might gain the psychological upper hand over his enemies.[50]

Plains Indians also had a high regard for the bear as a curing agent. Among the Lakotas, for example, the bear was regarded as the only animal that in a dream could offer herbs for healing purposes. Two Shields, in a conversation with anthropologist Frances Densmore, stated that the Lakotas considered the bear the chief of all animals in regard to herbs, and therefore if a man dreamed of the bear he would be expert in the use of herbs for curing illness. Bear medicine was the most sought after because bear medicine men could treat all ordinary diseases, and only they were allowed to treat wounded warriors.[51]

The best-known description of the curing rites of bear medicine men is George Catlin's vivid testimony of such a rite that he observed in the early 1830s. A Blackfoot medicine man, wearing a "skin of the yellow bear" decorated with the skins of dozens of smaller animals and various animal parts from "almost everything that swims, flies, or runs, in this part of the wide world," tried to cure a fatally wounded warrior who was shot through his stomach. The medicine man grunted and growled like a bear and prayed to his guardian spirit. The rite continued for some half an hour, until the patient died.[52] A Lakota medicine man, Eagle Shield, told Densmore that he treated a man who had attempted suicide by shooting himself. The bullet had passed through his body and broke the edge of his shoulder blade. His arm was paralyzed and European American doctors said that his arm must be amputated, but Eagle Shield cured the man using his bear medicine. When involved in healing, Eagle Shield used a bear claw, among other medicine objects.[53] According to Lame Deer, the Lakota bear medicine men were especially successful when fixing broken bones. They used a special bear medicine, *huhuwenhanhan pejuta,* which was mixed with fat and applied to a broken arm or leg.[54]

Among Plains Indians, then, the healing power of bear medicine men was closely linked to warfare, and bear medicine seems to have been practiced especially to heal wounds. According to Thomas Lewis, the bear medicine men of the Lakotas have almost disappeared since the battles and wounds ended once they were forced to reside on reservations.[55]

CONCLUSIONS ON COMPARING BEAR CEREMONIALISM

The major function of bear ceremonialism among arctic and subarctic peoples has been to ensure game in the future. Returning the bones, and particularly the skull where the spirit of the animal lived, back to the woods hanging from a special tree allowed the spirit to go back to the supernatural master of the species and made rebirth of the animal possible. According to some Ojibwas, the killed bear was reborn with exactly the same bones it had in its previous life.[56]

Ivar Paulson, who has examined the rites concerning the bear skull and its return to the woods, noticed that the area where these rites existed in North America includes the areas from the Columbia Plateau in the west to the north, and from the eastern Woodlands and the Great Lakes in the east to the north. He does not mention Plains tribes. The area he describes encircles the northern Plains.[57] Hallowell, in turn, mentions that although Plains Indians have had great respect for the bear, there is no evidence that any rites were performed in connection with the killing of that animal, except by the Plains Crees, the Plains Ojibwas, and the Assiniboines.[58]

Some Crees and Ojibwas moved into the Plains area relatively late[59] and preserved many features of their subarctic culture. Killing the bear ceremonially and the rites connected to it belong to cultural artifacts that survived in the new environment. David Mandelbaum, however, states that among the Plains Crees, "there is some indication that a lapse of bear observances had occurred, perhaps due to the Plains influence on Cree culture."[60] Denig's description cited previously clearly shows that the Assiniboines had certain rites after the killing of a bear, including decorating the head of the animal and offerings in its honor.[61]

In the North, where game sometimes was scarce, subarctic people could not depend on a single source of food. Toby Morantz states that starving and disease were common enough to explain why the eastern Crees could not afford to depend on just a single resource.[62] Subsistence depended on the quantity of game and, thus, the people made use of all available food sources. The only large food animal besides the caribou and moose was the bear. Adrian Tanner states that display of the meat of these large animals has been of greatest importance to the eastern Crees. Alanson Skinner, in turn, noticed that the bear actually was an important part of the diet among eastern Crees, and, according to Frank Speck, the Naskapis, another subarctic people in eastern Canada, considered the bear second in rank as a food source.[63]

Hallowell's study of human relationships to animals can be approached from two standpoints. "First is the utilitarian, that is, the exploitation of animals for their flesh, skins, or other substances," as he put it. Second, he says, one can study this relationship as the people themselves viewed it. This is what he calls the psychological aspect, which may include all folk beliefs and customs connected with animals.[64] In reality, the latter comprises the religious and cultural aspects. But, especially among subarctic peoples, are these foci mutually exclusive?

Since religion is not separate from culture but a part of it, religion also shares some of the effects that the environment has on the culture. Using his method of cultural ecology, Julian Steward[65] has demonstrated an ecological integration between nature and culture in which nature not only constrains but also promotes cultural development. Hultkrantz has further developed this method, comparing the relationship between religion and the natural environment, especially among circumpolar hunting peoples.[66] The ecology of religion then is "the study of the environmental integration of a religion and its implications," as Hultkrantz has put it.[67] His model shows that there is an explicit environmental influence on religion that stands in close relation to a cultural dependence on nature. Germans and Nordic peoples have also addressed the cultures of "nature peoples," that is *Naturvölker* in German, *naturfolk* in Swedish, and *luonnonkansat* in Finnish, to distinguish these people from "culture peoples."

According to Toby Morantz, no discussion of the environmental factors impinging on the lives of subarctic hunters would be complete without examining starvation.[68] In Hultkrantz's religio-ecological model, animal ceremonies belong to the primary integration, as he calls it, which includes environmental adaptation to basic cultural features, like subsistence and technology and the religious features associated with them.[69] In the Canadian north, the bear has sometimes been a very important source of food, especially in the late spring when game is scarce, and this is when bears were primarily hunted. As a large animal, the bear could offer a feast to the entire community.[70]

Hallowell has stated that even among tribes that had no special ceremonies when a bear was killed and eaten, the animal may, nevertheless, have been greatly respected or even revered. Here, Hallowell mentioned especially the Plains Indians.[71] It seems that the bear was not frequently eaten in the Plains area,[72] and thus bear hunting rites and the disposal of bones and the skull were not required among Plains Indians. While game in the Plains area might have been scarce in the late spring, huge herds of buffalo and other game animals as well as plants offered more plentiful food sources than in the subarctic regions. Since the bear did not have the same significance as a game animal among Plains tribes, bear ceremonialism does not belong in the religio-ecological model of primary integration as among subarctic peoples. For Plains peoples, a secondary integration, the indirect adaptation of religious beliefs and rituals that "are organized into a framework that takes its forms from the social structure, which is, in its turn, a model suggested by the economic and technological adaptation to environment," is practiced.[73] In addition, among the Plains tribes, the concept of the supernatural master, or the guardian spirit, of the animal species was replaced by the idea of individual guardian spirits.[74] Among Plains Indians, the bear was the symbol of power and wisdom, and the medicine obtained from the bear helped warriors succeed in warfare and enabled medicine men to act for the communal welfare.

NOTES

1. Julian H. Steward, *Theory of Culture Change: The Methodology of Multilinear Evolution* (Urbana: University of Illinois Press, [1955] 1963); Åke Hultkrantz, "Type of Religion in the Arctic Hunting Cultures: A Religio-Ecological Approach," in *Hunting and Fishing*, ed. Harald Hvarfner (Luleå: Norrbottens Museum, 1965), 265–318; Åke Hultkrantz, "Ecology of Religion: Its Scope and Methodology," in *Science of Religion: Studies in Methodology* (The Hague: Mouton Publishers, 1979), ed. Lauri Honko, 221–36; and Åke Hultkrantz, "Some Critical Reflections on the Ecology of Religions," *Temenos* 21 (1985), 83–90.

2. Joseph M. Marshall III (Lakota), *The Journey of Crazy Horse: A Lakota History* (New York: Penguin, 2004), 50. "Medicine men" was a term originally assigned by Jesuits in New France to both "wise men" and individuals with "supernatural gifts." It maintains currency in Native American societies in the twenty-first century. It is notable that men have dominated the role of sacred people, or medicine people, throughout Native North America, even though medicine women have existed almost everywhere. See Åke Hultkrantz, *The Religions of the American Indians* (Berkeley: University of California Press, [1979] 1980), 84–102; Åke Hultkrantz, *Shamanic Healing and Ritual Drama: Health and Medicine in Native North American Religious Tradition* (New York: Crossroad, 1992), 1–4; Åke Hultkrantz, "On the History of Research in Shamanism," in *Shamans*, ed. Juha Pentikäinen, Toimi Jaatinen, Ildikó Lehtinen, and Marjo-Riitta Saloniemi (Tampere, Finland: Tampere Museums, 1998), 60.

3. See George A. Dorsey, *Traditions of the Arikara* (Washington, DC: Carnegie Institute, 1904), 126–27; George A. Dorsey, *Traditions of the Caddo* (Washington, DC: Carnegie Institute, 1905), 14; Robert H. Lowie, "Myths and Traditions of the Crow Indians," *Anthropological Papers of the American Museum of Natural History*, 25 (1918), part 1, 205–11; Catharine McClellan, "The Girl Who Married the Bear," *Publications in Ethnology*, no. 2 (1970); Alice Marriot and Carol K. Rachlin, *Plains Indian Mythology* (New York: Mentor, 1975), 93–96; Daniel J. Gelo, "The Bear," in *American Wildlife in Symbol and Story*, ed. Angus K. Gillespie and Jay Mechling (Knoxville: University of Tennessee Press, 1987), 140–51; Lewis Spence, *The Myths of the North American Indians* (New York: Dover Publications, [1914] 1989), 308–11; Douglas R. Parks, *Myths and Traditions of the Arikara Indians* (Lincoln: University of Nebraska Press, 1996), 146–52; Karl Kroeber, *Artistry in Native*

American Myths (Lincoln: University of Nebraska Press, 1998), 95–173; and Keith Cunningham, *American Indians: Folk Tales and Legends* (Ware, England: Wordsworth Editions, 2001), 118–19, 168–69, 282–84, and 399–403.

4. Joseph Epes Brown, *The Spiritual Legacy of the American Indian* (New York: Crossroad, [1982] 1993), 38.

5. Regina Flannery and Mary Elizabeth Chambers, "Each Man Has His Own Friends: The Role of Dream Visitors in Traditional East Cree Belief and Practice," *Arctic Anthropology* 22, no. 1 (1985), 3–4.

6. Åke Hultkrantz, *Native Religions of North America: The Power of Visions and Fertility* (San Francisco: Harper, 1987), 137.

7. Frank G. Speck, *Naskapi: The Savage Hunters of the Labrador Peninsula* (Norman: University of Oklahoma Press, 1935), 79.

8. I have previously discussed this question in Finnish. See Riku Hämäläinen, "Mustaa roukaa ja kaksijalkaisia: karhukultti subarktisen alueen intiaanien ja tasankointiaanien parissa," in *Kojootteja sulkapäähineitä uraanikaivoksia: Pohjois-Amerikan intiaanien kirjallisuuksia ja kulttareja*, ed. Sami Lakomäki and Matti Savolainen (Oulun yliopiston Taideaineiden ja antropologian laitoksen julkaisuja A. Kirjallisuus 11) (Oulu: Oulun Yliopisto, 2002), 54–86.

9. Sam D. Gill, *Beyond "The Primitive": The Religions of the Nonliterate Peoples* (Englewoods Cliffs, NJ: Prentice-Hall, Inc., 1982), 40; Matti Sarmela, "Karhu ihmisen ympäristössä," in Pekka Laaksonen and Sirkka-Liisa Mettomäki, eds, *Kolme on kovaa sanaa: Kirjoituksia kansanperinteestä* (Helsinki: Suomalaisen Kirjallisuuden Seura, 1991), 209.

10. Garrick Mallery, *Picture-Writing of the American Indians*, vol. 1 (New York: Dover Publications, [1893] 1972), 90–92, plate XIII; Patricia O'Brien, "'Great Cave of Bears,' a Pawnee Animal Lodge," a paper presented at the conference "Furs, Faith, and the French: Colonial and Post-Colonial Encounters," Bordeaux, France, April 25–28, 2001; Riku Hämäläinen, "Indians, French, and the Multi-faceted Encounter," *European Review of Native American Studies* 15, no. 2 (2001), 54.

11. E.O. James, *Prehistoric Religion: A Study in Prehistoric Archaeology* (London: Thames and Hudson, 1957), 21.

12. Washington Irving, *A Tour on the Prairies*, ed. John Francis McDermott (Norman: University of Oklahoma Press, [1859] 1956), 158–59.

13. Edwin Thompson Denig, "Indian Tribes of the Upper Missouri," ed. J.N.B. Hewitt, *Forty-sixth Annual Report of the Bureau of American Ethnology, 1928–1929* (1930), 499.

14. Mark Bahti, *Spirit in the Stone: A Handbook of Southwest Indian Animal Carvings and Beliefs* (Tucson: Treasure Chest Books, 1999), 46; Hamilton A. Tyler, *Pueblo Animals and Myths* (Norman: University of Oklahoma Press, 1975), 184.

15. George Bird Grinnell, *Blackfoot Lodge Tales: The Story of a Prairie People* (Lincoln: University of Nebraska Press, [1892] 1962), 260.

16. Ibid.

17. Åke Hultkrantz, "Religion and Experience of Nature among North American Hunting Indians," in *The Hunters: Their Culture and Way of Life*, ed. Åke Hultkrantz and Ørnult Vorren (Tromsø: Universitetsforlaget, 1982), 167.

18. Åke Hultkrantz, *Belief and Worship in Native North America*, ed. Christopher Vecsey

(Syracuse, NY: Syracuse University Press, 1981), 149–50.

19. Joseph Epes Brown, *Animals of the Soul: Sacred Animals of the Oglala Sioux* (Rockport, MA: Element, 1992), 33.

20. James R. Walker, "The Sun Dance and Other Ceremonies of the Oglala Division of the Teton Dakota," *Anthropological Papers of the American Museum of Natural History* 19 (Part 2, 1917), 80, 84; James R. Walker, *Lakota Belief and Ritual,* ed. Raymond J. DeMallie and Elaine A. Jahner (Lincoln: University of Nebraska Press, 1980), 128; James R. Walker, *Lakota Myth,* ed. Elaine A. Jahner (Lincoln: University of Nebraska Press, [1983] 1989), 28–29. This dualism of the bear can be found among other tribes as well. See Bahti, *Spirit in the Stone,* 47; Tyler, *Pueblo Animals and Myths,* 206; and Adrian Tanner, *Bringing Home Animals: Religious Ideology and Mode of Production of the Mistassini Cree Hunters* (London: C. Hurst & Company, 1979), 136–37.

21. A. Irving Hallowell, "Bear Ceremonialism in the Northern Hemisphere," *American Anthropologist* 39 (1926). Because of the similarities of bear ceremonialism in both the Old and the New World, Hallowell sees their common origin. Bear ceremonialism is just one of those cultural and religious features common throughout the Northern Hemisphere; the others include shamanism and bathing traditions. For example, the roots of Native American sweat lodges have sometimes been sought as far as in Northern Europe and Finland (Riku Hämäläinen, "The Sweat Lodge of the North American Indigenous People," in *The Finnish Sauna, the Japanese Furo, the Indian Inipi: Bathing on Three Continents,* ed. Juha Pentikäinen [Helsinki: Building Information, Ltd., 2001], 122).

22. Alanson Skinner, "Notes on the Eastern Cree and Northern Salteaux," *Anthropological Papers of the American Museum of Natural History* 9 (Part 1, 1911), 68–73, 162–64; Speck, *Naskapi,* 94–110; Edward S. Rogers, "The Quest for Food and Furs: The Mistassini Cree, 1953–1954," *Publications in Ethnology,* no. 5 (1973), 39–44; Tanner, *Bringing Home Animals,* 145–46; Mareile Kohn, *Das Bärenzeremoniell in Nordamerika: Der Bär im Jagdritual und Vorstellungswelt der Montagnais-Naskapi-East Cree und der Chippewa-Ojibwa* (Hohenschäftlarn: Klaus Renner Verlag, 1986), 141–51; David Rockwell, *Giving Voice to Bear: North American Myths, Rituals, and Images of the Bear* (Niwot: Robert Rinehart Publishers, 1991), 26–40.

23. See Toby Morantz, "An Ethnohistoric Study of Eastern James Bay Cree Social Organization, 1700–1850," *Mercury Series, Canadian Ethnology Service Paper* 88 (1983), 35–37.

24. Skinner, "Notes on the Eastern Cree and Northern Salteaux," 25.

25. Flannery and Chambers, "Each Man Has His Own Friends," 14–15; Richard J. Preston, "Cree Narrative: Expressing the Personal Meanings of Events," *Mercury Series, Canadian Ethnology Service Paper* 30 (1975), 80–81; Tanner, *Bringing Home Animals,* 138; Kohn, *Das Bärenzeremoniell in Nordamerika,* 137–40.

26. Rogers, "The Quest for Food and Furs," 11.

27. Tanner, *Bringing Home Animals,* 145.

28. See Hämäläinen, "The Sweat Lodge," 42.

29. Skinner, "Notes on the Eastern Cree and Northern Salteaux," 71–72; Hallowell, "Bear Ceremonialism in the Northern Hemisphere," 44–45.

30. Skinner, "Notes on the Eastern Cree and Northern Salteaux," 26, 72–73.

31. Ibid., 69.

32. Rockwell, *Giving Voice to Bear,* 38.

33. Tanner, *Bringing Home Animals,* 164.

34. Skinner, "Notes on the Eastern Cree and Northern Salteaux," 68, 72.

35. Alice C. Fletcher, "The Elk Mystery or Festival: Ogallala Sioux," *Sixteenth and Seventeenth Annual Reports of Peabody Museum of American Archaeology and Ethnology* 3 (1884), 276–82.

36. Walker, *Lakota Belief and Ritual,* 91.

37. George Catlin, *Letters and Notes on the Manners, Customs, and Conditions of the North American Indians,* vol. 1 (New York: Dover Publications, [1841] 1973), 245.

38. David G. Mandelbaum, *The Plains Cree: An Ethnographic, Historical, and Comparative Study* (Regina: Canadian Plains Research Center, University of Regina, [1979] 1996), 210; Robert H. Lowie, *The Crow Indians* (Lincoln: University of Nebraska Press, [1935] 1983), 264–68. For the Great Basin area, see Verner Z. Reed, "The Ute Bear Dance," *American Anthropologist* 9 (1896), 237–44; Joseph G. Jorgensen, "Ghost Dance, Bear Dance, and Sun Dance," in *Great Basin,* Vol. 11 of *Handbook of North American Indians,* ed. Warren L. d'Azevedo (Washington, DC: Smithsonian Institution, 1986), 662–65.

39. Denig, "Indian Tribes of the Upper Missouri," 537–38.

40. John C. Ewers, *Indian Life on the Upper Missouri* (Norman: University of Oklahoma Press, [1968] 1988), 134.

41. Riku Hämäläinen, "Pohjois-Amerikan tasankointiaanien karhukultti" [including English summary of "The Bear Cult of the North American Plains Indians"], *Suomen Museo 2001* (2002), 82.

42. See John G. Neihardt, *Black Elk Speaks: Being the Life Story of a Holy Man of the Oglala Sioux* (New York: Washington Square Press, [1932] 1972), 89–90; Åke Hultkrantz, *Prairie and Plains Indians* (Leiden: E.J. Brill, 1973), 27; Ted J. Brasser, "The Pedigree of the Hugging Bear Tipi in the Blackfoot Camp," *American Indian Art Magazine* 5 ([1977] Winter 1979), 37; William K. Powers, *Oglala Religion* (Lincoln: University of Nebraska Press, [1977] 1982), 45; Alfred W. Bowers, *Mandan Social and Ceremonial Organization* (Moscow: University of Idaho Press, [1950] 1991), 108; Walter McClintock, *The Old North Trail: Life, Legends and Religion of the Blackfeet Indians* (Lincoln: University of Nebraska Press, [1910] 1992), 358–59; and Mandelbaum, *The Plains Cree,* 210.

43. Ewers, *Indian Life on the Upper Missouri,* 134–35.

44. Samuel W. Pond, *The Dakota or Sioux in Minnesota as They Were in 1834* (St. Paul: Minnesota Historical Society, [1908] 1986), 103.

45. For these legends, see Clark Wissler and D.C. Duvall, "Mythology of the Blackfoot Indians," *Anthropological Papers of the American Museum of Natural History* 2 (Part 1, 1908), 92–94; Brasser, "The Pedigree of the Hugging Bear Tipi," 33: John C. Ewers, *The Blackfeet: Raiders in the Northwestern Plains* (Norman: University of Oklahoma Press, [1958] 1988), 165–66; McClintock, *The Old North Trail,* 354–61. For bear knives, see Horst Hartmann, *Die Plains—und Prärieindianer Nordamerikas* (Berlin: Museum für Völkerkunde, [1973] 1979), fig. 100. For the Blackfoot bear knife medicine bundle, see Clark Wissler, "Ceremonial Bundles of the Blackfoot Indians," *Anthropological Papers of the American Museum of Natural History* 7 (Part 2, 1912), 131–34.

46. Not infrequently, social status was presented by certain public symbols like feathers or other marks of rank. See Riku Hämäläinen, "Etnografiset esineet kulttuurisina dokumentteina" (including English summary "Ethnographic objects as cultural documents"), *Suomen Museo 1999* (2000), 92–98.

47. Ewers, *Indian Life on the Upper Missouri,* 132–33. Bear medicine symbolism has generally existed among other tribes as well. See John C. Ewers, "The Awesome Bear in Plains Indian Art," *American Indian Art Magazine* 7 (Summer 1982), 36–45.

48. Maximilian Prince of Wied, *Travels in the Interior of North America,* vols. 22–24, in *Early Western Travels, 1748–1846,* ed. Reuben G. Thwaities (New York: AMS Press, [1906] 1966), 19; William H. Goetzman, David C. Hunt, Marsha V. Gallagher, and William J. Orr, *Karl Bodmer's America* (Omaha and Lincoln: Joslyn Art Museum and University of Nebraska Press, 1984), 195.

49. Denig, "Indian Tribes of the Upper Missouri," 537–38; Ewers, *Indian Life on the Upper Missouri,* 135.

50. McClintock, *The Old North Trail,* 353.

51. Francis Densmore, *Teton Sioux Music and Culture* (Lincoln: University of Nebraska Press, [1918] 1992), 195; Walker, *Lakota Belief and Ritual,* 105.

52. Catlin, *Letters and Notes,* 39–40.

53. Densmore, *Teton Sioux Music and Culture,* 253–54.

54. John (Fire) Lame Deer and Richard Erdoes, *Lame Deer: Seeker of Visions* (New York: Washington Square Press, [1972] 1976), 154.

55. Thomas H. Lewis, *The Medicine Men: Oglala Sioux Ceremony and Healing* (Lincoln: University of Nebraska Press, [1990] 1992), 183.

56. Hultkrantz, "Religion and Experience," 173.

57. Ivar Paulson, "Die rituelle Erhebung des Bärenschädels bei arktischen und subarktischen Völkern," *Temenos* 1 (1965), 162–66.

58. Hallowell, "Bear Ceremonialism in the Northern Hemisphere," 73.

59. Koozma J. Tarasoff, "Persistent Ceremonialism: The Plains Cree and Salteaux," *Mercury Series, Canadian Ethnology Service Paper* 69 (1980), 2–3.

60. Mandelbaum, *The Plains Cree,* 219–20.

61. In his study of the Siouan Cults, James Owen Dorsey describes Assiniboine bear rites, and his description closely resembles Denig's description. See J. Owen Dorsey, "A Study of Siouan Cults," *Eleventh Annual Report of the Bureau of Ethnology, 1889–1890* (1894), 477.

62. Morantz, "An Ethnohistoric Study," 37.

63. Tanner, *Bringing Home Animals,* 157; Skinner, "Notes on the Eastern Cree and Northern Salteaux," 26; Speck, *Naskapi,* 79.

64. Hallowell, "Bear Ceremonialism in the Northern Hemisphere," 3.

65. See Steward, *Theory of Culture Change.*

66. See Åke Hultkrantz, "The Indians and the Wonders of Yellowstone: A Study of the Interrelations of Religion, Nature and Culture," *Ethnos* 19 (1954); Åke Hultkrantz, "Accommodation and Persistence: Ecological Analysis of the Religion of the Sheepeater Indians in Wyoming, USA," *Temenos* 17 (1981); Hultkrantz, "Type of Religion in the Arctic

Hunting Cultures"; Hultkrantz, "Ecology of Religion"; Hultkrantz, Religion and Experience"; and Hultkrantz, "Some Critical Reflections."

67. Hultkrantz, "Ecology of Religion," 221; cp. Svein Bjerke, "Ecology of Religion, Evolutionism and Comparative Religion," in *Science of Religion. Studies in Methodology*, ed. Lauri Honko (The Hague: Mouton Publishers, 1979), 238.

68. Morantz, "An Ethnohistoric Study," 35.

69. Hultkrantz, "Religion and Experience," 176–77; Hultkrantz, "Ecology of Religion," 227–28.

70. It is also interesting to note that among the Navajos, the bear was not eaten under ordinary conditions. During winter, if faced with starvation, the Navajos were permitted to hunt a bear. See W.W. Hill, "The Agricultural and Hunting Methods of the Navaho Indians," *Yale University Publications in Anthropology* 18 (1938), 157.

71. Hallowell, "Bear Ceremonialism in the Northern Hemisphere," 151.

72. Catlin, *Letters and Notes*, 245. However, he mentions that the Lakota and other Plains tribes were fond of bear meat.

73. Hultkrantz, "Ecology of Religion," 228.

74. Hultkrantz, "Religion and Experience," 166–68.

PART II

The Literary Indigenous Voice

INDIAN BLOOD

the teacher's voice was loud:
"From the land of the Midnight Sun!"
All of them stared at me
for the first time I felt
their flowing force
did she ask me to speak
or did I crouch there like a rabbit
in the curious quiet . . .
In time I got away
and toward night I crept
into a closet
and bit my hand
till it was pierced
with moons of dark
Indian blood[1]

MARY TALLMOUNTAIN, Koyukon

SQUASH BLOSSOM SHIT AND HEISHI HORRORS

Once quietly beautifying
brown chests and wrists as the
yucca and cactus upon a summer's desert
now made quite common and ugly
to be seen from new york's poshest
to the santa fe opera
milled out by factories japanese
and miss sarah coventry[2]

LUCI ABEITA, Kutchin

IN THE PAST QUARTER CENTURY, indigenous literature has expanded expo-
nentially. The fiction of Native Americans and First Nations in North America
moved beyond the exceptional and unusual to become commonplace within literary canons. This development brings to literature the powerful commentary of
Native writers who not only assert their voices but reclaim that which has been culturally stolen and misshapen by non-Natives. Complex social issues are central to
the most recent indigenous novelists and poets. They seek not only to reclaim their
Native voice but to re-appropriate Native culture and stories and reassert their
agency within the indigenous literary world.

This section features three chapters. First, Mark Shackleton documents and discusses the appropriation of Coyote in modern popular literature. This appropriation of the Trickster from indigenous storytelling is not only a matter where the
indigenous voice has been adopted and profited upon by non-Native writers. They
have willingly or perhaps innocently redefined Coyote so radically that the Trickster's indigenous purpose is unrecognizable. Thus, this appropriation is beyond
mere cultural theft; it has taken a familiar indigenous story form and recast it into
something unrecognizable to Native North Americans. In severe appropriations,
Coyote becomes something to fear or a symbol of utter horror rather than the
irreverent and self-absorbed Trickster that makes one smile and reflect knowingly.

The next two chapters assess the literary reconfigurations inherent within the
writings of Wendy Rose, Hopi poet, and Sherman Alexie, Spokane novelist and
short story writer. P. Jane Hafen (Taos Pueblo) analyzes the poems of Wendy Rose
and highlights her recent search for the meaning of indigenous life from outside
her tribe looking in. Rose originally believed when she started writing that she had
a Hopi father and a mixed-blood Miwok mother. In the course of her poetry
career, she learned that her father might not be the man she had believed but
instead may be a non-Native. Rose had been raised Hopi and spoke Hopi, but this
revelation created greater distances between her and her "people." That the Hopis
are matrilineal and thus do not recognize her as Hopi made her indigenous attach-
ments even more difficult to practice. Hafen explores the problems of belonging
and identity in her assessment of Rose's poetry. As Hafen allows, Rose is perhaps
one of the very best living indigenous poets, and part of her emotional appeal is
due to her struggle to achieve agency and identity within the Hopi world. Moreover, Hafen recognizes that the meaning of Rose's work changes if she can no

longer be Hopi, and this unique development underscores the modern challenge of identity and its impact on the words and interpretations of indigenous writers.

Patrice Hollrah explains how the work of Sherman Alexie, one of the most celebrated of recent Native American writers, stretches and alters the sexual boundaries of Native peoples. Her chapter draws upon Alexie interviews and a textual analysis of several Alexie short stories that consider indigenous homophobia and how Indian peoples deal with homosexuality within the family. Alexie is quite clear about his political agenda for both Natives and non-Natives alike. As Hollrah quotes Alexie, "Find me a country of gay men that's invaded another country. Find me a lumberjack who's been straight-bashed by a group of raving lesbians."[3] Indigenous homophobia, to Alexie, is an appropriation by Indian people that they need to avoid or culturally expunge.

These three chapters, then, provide a small sample of the rich literary analysis of modern indigenous writing. Identity, appropriation, and agency are common themes in modern Native fiction, and they lead the way to new places. They are found in Mary Tallmountain, who as a child drew strength and solace from her Indian identity while suffering humiliations in boarding school; and in Luci Abeita, who observed and excoriated the shame of the commodification of indigenous culture by the outside world. No more can these offenses be only silently suffered; instead, they can be read by the world.

NOTES

1. Mary Tallmountain, "Indian Blood," in *The Remembered Earth: An Anthology of Contemporary Native American Literature,* ed. Geary Hobson (Albuquerque: University of New Mexico Press, [1979] 1981), 404.

2. Luci Abeita, "Squash Blossom Shit and Heishi Horrors," in *The Remembered Earth,* ed. Hobson, 405.

3. Sherman Alexie, "Chats and Events," October 14, 2000, http://www.barnesandnoble.com/co/transcript.asp?userid+24L2DFWCYO&eventId'218.

CHAPTER 4

The Curious Case of Coyote, or the Tale of the Appropriated Trickster

MARK SHACKLETON

COYOTE, the Trickster of many Native North American nations—indeed a figure who has been said to have become pan-Indian, is also an indigenous anti-hero who is best known to and most appropriated by non-Natives.[1] This chapter will discuss some of the issues raised by the appropriation debate, and then contrast the portrayal of Coyote found in recent works by both Native and non-Native writers. Most non-Native writers studied here provide a one-dimensional view of Trickster and present a figure that is divorced from the social and cultural matrix in which the Trickster has meaning.

ISSUES OF APPROPRIATION

The appropriation of Native voice reached a peak in the United States in the 1970s with the raising of the issue of "white shamanism." Gary Snyder, a non-Native writer, wrote of "shaman songs" in *Myths and Texts* (1960) and won the 1975 Pulitzer Prize for *Turtle Island* (1974), a collection of poems that relies to some extent on Amerindian lore.[2] Geary Hobson (Cherokee-Quapaw/Chicksaw) in "The Rise of the White Shaman as a New Version of Cultural Imperialism" (1979), has rightly pointed out that Snyder does not actually refer to himself as a "shaman," and that stronger criticism should be attached to those "bastard children of Snyder" who have set themselves up as self-styled shamans—among them such Western writers and poets as Gene Fowler, Jim Cody, Norman Moser, and Barry Gifford. Hobson also mentions Carlos Castaneda, Hyemeyohsts Storm, Tony

Shearer, and Doug Boyd as other neoromantic writers who have posed as Indians or as Indian spokesmen.[3] Leslie Marmon Silko's (Laguna Pueblo) critique of Snyder's *Turtle Island* in "An Old-Time Indian Attack Conducted in Two Parts" (1979), on the other hand, is directed at his selective vision of America, which, she argues, attempts to leap-frog the harsh details of what white settlers did to the land and to indigenous peoples and seeks naively to return to an unspoiled continent. Silko advises Snyder to come to terms with his own (white) ancestors rather than borrow them from Native peoples.[4]

It is, of course, a common phenomenon that non-Natives have sought release from Western angst by returning to a supposedly purer time and society—one need only think of the works of D.H. Lawrence or Paul Gauguin.[5] But wider issues beyond the personal are also involved in cultural appropriation. Many Native writers, for example, feel that they should be allowed to speak for themselves. In effect, it is argued, appropriators gain money and prestige at the expense of those for whom they would claim to speak. And indeed, large sums of money are to be made and have been made by New Age authors, such as Carlos Castaneda, Ruth Beebe Hill, and Lynn Andrews, not to mention the popularity of such films as *Dances with Wolves*. Appropriation can also be seen as what Geary Hobson calls "a new version of cultural imperialism."[6] The history of post-contact America for Native peoples is one of dispossession—of rights, land, and life; the subsequent theft of Native cultural materials by ethnologists and ethnopoets (the "museumification" of Native peoples, if you will) can be seen as imperialism in another guise.

Appropriators may well be insensitive to the value placed on cultural materials by Native peoples. Native oral tales, for example, often pass down closely guarded truths that define the identity of the people, and there are often strict taboos about the transmission of such materials to communities beyond the tribe. Careless or ignorant handling of what Hobson has called these "cultural lifeways" may actually mean the destruction of indigenous values that have survived for centuries or millennia.[7] Part of the problem lies in different notions of "art." As Hartmut Lutz has pointed out, Europeans tend to see art as an individual practice and as a resource that any individual can use (as long as copyright is not infringed), whereas to Native peoples art belongs to the community and is therefore circumscribed by communal rules that the traditional tribal person willingly acknowledges.[8]

In brief, these are some of the cultural appropriation issues most frequently raised, particularly in recent years by First Nations writers. The appropriations of Coyote represent a specific example of this process.

THE FEARED COYOTE

The most obvious example of the appropriation of Coyote, of course, is the Warner Brothers cartoon character Wile E. Coyote, which at least maintains an essential element of Coyote tales—the Trickster is often (in Wile's case, always) outsmarted. But in recent literature in which non-Native authors have adopted Native American Trickster figures, it would appear that only Coyote, out of all the possible Native Trickster figures—Nanabush, Glooscap, Weesageechak, Hare, Raven, and so on—has been appropriated. This is no doubt because the form and characteristics of the animal are instantly identifiable, and the wily characteristics of Coyote are akin to such European Tricksters as Reynard the Fox. The problem in this modern appropriation, however, is that fear, not trickery, is evoked by Coyote. Coyote becomes the demon "other," a malevolent and revengeful Indian spirit, and as such the representation of this complex figure is all too often one-dimensional and disrespectful.

Tony Hillerman's *Coyote Waits* appeared in 1990, the tenth in a series of fifteen bestselling crime novels featuring Lieutenant Joe Leaphorn and Sergeant Jim Chee of the Navajo Tribal Police. Credited by some as the father of the American Indian detective novel, Hillerman is white. He gained early experiences with Native peoples when as a child he was enrolled by his farmer parents in a boarding school for Native American girls at Sacred Heart, Oklahoma, a town near the Benedictine mission to the Citizen Band Potowatomie Tribe. The title of the book alludes to a malevolent force that haunts the snake-infested hills of the Navajo Reservation, and we are continually reminded that Coyote (representing fear, death, evil, disorder, and chaos) is there: "You don't have to go looking for Coyote. Coyote's always out there waiting." "Coyote is always out there waiting, and Coyote is always hungry." "Coyote was waiting for Nez." (Nez is a Navajo policeman shot by a drunken Indian.) "Coyote ate Redd." (Redd is the main criminal killed by a snake.)[9]

One of Hillerman's professed aims, in addition to telling a good yarn, is to provide non-Native readers with a certain insight into Navajo culture. Consequently, we are told that Coyote stories can be funny: "They say Coyote is funny, some of those people, say that." "The children are told the funny stories about Coyote." However, the darker side of Coyote is always foregrounded.[10] The comic story of Coyote's vanity, "Coyote Juggles His Eyes," is related, as well as the legend that tells how Coyote flings a blanket full of stars up into the sky to form the Milky Way, though we are told that "[e]ven then, what Coyote did was evil." Through the mouthpiece of Hosteen Pinto, a Navajo elder, we are given an ethnographical explanation that Coyote was originally known in the Navajo Fourth World as *atse'hashkke,* or "First Angry," and that he is "the metaphor for chaos among a hungry people who would die without order."[11] Still, although a fuller picture of

Coyote is suggested, the dominant image, reinforced by the title and by the action, is of Coyote as the malevolent destroyer.

Hillerman's evil Coyote is clearly not the same Coyote described by recent Native North American writers. One criticism, therefore, of Hillerman is that in overtly speaking about Navajo culture, he is not only speaking for the "other," but he is not doing a very thorough job of it. Interestingly, Hillerman was one of the appropriators singled out by Beth Brant (Mohawk) in a 1991 symposium. Said Brant, "The truth is not told in the books of Lynn Andrews, Tony Hillerman, W.P. Kinsella, and the many white writers who use their hundreds of years of colonial supremacy to speak for us. . . . *No one can speak for us but us.*"[12]

In 1996, six years after *Coyote Waits* was published, the first novel by Canadian writer Gail Anderson-Dargatz, *The Cure for Death by Lightning,* appeared. It received much critical acclaim, and is indeed a well-written novel, developing in striking ways such themes as the madness and hysteria that war can bring. As in Hillerman, however, Coyote is primarily evoked as a figure of terror. In the novel, it is 1941, with war raging in Europe; the settlers in Turtle Valley, a remote part of British Columbia, are plagued by deaths and insanity. A fourteen-year-old girl is mauled to death, apparently by a bear, and the father of the house, John Weeks, becomes erratic and violent in his behavior, the obvious cause being a head wound received in the Great War. Some whisper, however, that the spirit of Coyote has entered into him; meanwhile Coyote Jack, a possible rapist and murderer "ridden" by the malevolent Trickster, lurks in the bush.

Bertha Moses, an Indian woman who is a friend to the Weeks family and lives on the nearby reservation, provides a relatively rounded depiction of Coyote. She explains to her daughter and her teenage friend Beth Weeks that Coyote is "not all bad," that "Coyote gave us good things" such as salmon, night and day, and the seasons.[13] In other words, Coyote is what anthropologists would call a culture hero, as well as being the anarchic, chaotic, and even devilish principle in the universe.[14] Bertha further links Coyote to white people: their greed, noisy assertiveness, frantic and futile energy, and lies show, she says to Beth, that "[y]ou are his children." But Bertha also compares Coyote to Hitler, that "scary little clown," suggesting that it is the spirit of Coyote that expresses itself in the ludicrous megalomania and lust to dominate that seems almost intrinsic in a European psyche and is endemic in Western history.[15]

This section of the novel, where Bertha explains the ambivalence of Coyote—an ambivalence in which simplistic notions of goodness and badness dissolve—is essentially static and descriptive. Where Coyote is most dynamically felt and embodied in the novel is in the simple and naked sense of fear and terror that stalks Beth. She hears footsteps behind her, or suddenly a path appears in the grass that aims at speed straight for her, carrying with it "the overpowering stench of wet dog."[16] The strength of this writing is that the fear is suggested rather than objectified, so that the novel's conclusion, where Coyote Jack transforms into a coyote before Beth's eyes, is disappointing. The ending where Beth faces up to Coyote Jack and similarly confronts her sexually abusive father, taming and shaming both beasts, is also a little too neat. It is a simplification and reduction of the figure of Coyote.

Anderson-Dargatz's novel in fact harkens back to one of the classics of Canadian modernism, Sheila Watson's *The Double Hook* (1959).[17] Both novels are set in small-town rural British Columbia, a place where, as in many Canadian novels, the regional and the gothic meet. Both novelists' brand of Pacific Northwest gothic draws on Coyote to provide the spirit of the malevolent "other." In his 1972 essay, "Coyote as Trickster in *The Double Hook*," Leslie Monkman sees Coyote as functioning in "Satanic opposition to Old Testament Jehovah," as "the Satanic tempter," "the mystical force which can drive the passions of men . . . to . . . desperate heights," a spirit of "malevolence" that like "the cruel justice of the Old Testament Jehovah" will be superseded by "the promise of a benevolent deity."[18] A recent essay, Margaret Morriss's "'No Short Cuts': The Evolution of *The Double Hook*," confirms Monkman's analysis. Working from canceled drafts of Watson's novel, Morriss points out that Draft II at one point portrays Coyote as part of a creation myth ("[T]he country was Coyote's. He had opened the ground . . ."). However, this more complex presentation that implied Coyote is both creator and destroyer was sacrificed "to maintain consistency in the presentation of Coyote." Watson confirmed this one-sided portrayal in her unpublished "Commentary on *The Double Hook*," writing that Coyote is "[f]ear incarnate, both cause and response."[19]

Watson's novel is clearly a work of literary sophistication in terms of its poetic concision, allusions, and implications, but its appropriation of Coyote is more schematic than Anderson-Dargatz's or even Hillerman's. Nowhere in the text is the Indian village, the reservation, or a tribal community presented, so that Coyote appears as if from a vacuum, a malevolent deus ex machina. Nor is the ambivalent nature of Coyote, his role as "creator and destroyer, giver and negator," fully acknowledged or developed.

THE LE GUIN EXCEPTION

Watson's Coyote is very much the settlers' Trickster, expressing the fear of reprisals from the avenging aboriginal gods. There is an enormous difference between this Trickster and the role the Trickster plays in the work of contemporary Native North American writers, where Trickster figures are far more likely to be seen as avatars of resistance and cultural survival. Tomson Highway (Cree), for example, has prefaced two of his published plays with "A Note on Nanabush," which reads:

Some say that Nanabush [the Ojibway Trickster] left this continent when the white man came. We believe she/he is still here among us—albeit a little the worse for wear and tear—having assumed other guises. Without the continued presence of this extraordinary figure, the core of Indian culture would be gone forever.[20]

Sometimes a non-Native writer properly understands the role Coyote plays. Lee Maracle (Metis/Salish) in a 2002 interview cited Ursula K. Le Guin's short story, "Buffalo Gals, Won't You Come Out Tonight,"[21] as an example of a non-Native writer whose style is similar to the way many Native writers layer language.[22] Le Guin's family put her in contact with Native culture in her childhood. She was the daughter of anthropologist Alfred L. Kroeber and writer Theodora Kroeber, who took care of and wrote about Ishi, the last surviving member of the Yahis.

In "Buffalo Gals," a female Coyote takes care of a child, Myra, who has fallen from the sky after an air crash. Myra has lost an eye in the accident and the Coyote promises to help her look for it, recounting at the same time the legend of "Coyote Juggles His Eyes" in which the boastful Coyote learns the trick of throwing his eyes up only to suffer for his hubris and have his eyes stolen by a passing bluejay.[23] Later, Jay makes Myra a new eye, which alters her view of the world so that things become "blurry and yellowish, but deep."[24] Vision is very much the theme of this story, which attempts to present the world from the perspective of the other—the animal other and the Native other. We are invited, as Denise Levertov put it, to "[c]ome into animal presence." Here the other is not a threat or a source of fear. Instead Le Guin's Coyote introduces a humorous, nonidealized world in which animals and humans coexist. Myra wonders about the clothes-wearing animals she meets: "I don't understand why you all look like people," to which Coyote replies, "We are people." The story returns in essence to the earliest times when there was no distinction between Natives and animals. In the end, Myra returns to white civilization, a place of terror, "blanknesses, invisible walls, terrible smells and pressures," although she returns with new knowledge. She is allowed to keep the eye Jay made, she has her memories of Coyote, and Grandmother Spider will be with her in her dreams and ideas.[25]

Of the non-Native writers discussed, Le Guin's Coyote tale would seem to be the closest in tone and spirit to traditional Coyote stories as well as to the kind of reworkings of Coyote tales found in the work of such Native writers as Simon Ortiz or Leslie Marmon Silko. Radical Natives might well argue, however, that Le Guin's skillful cultural ventriloquism does not relieve her of the charge of appropriation of voice. Hartmut Lutz, in his essay, "Cultural Appropriation as a Repression of Peoples and Histories," persuasively argues that where appropriation takes place within a colonial structure, characteristically all traces of origin or authorship are repressed and disavowed. In particular, the history of Native and non-Native relations is erased.[26] For reasons of guilt or expediency, the unpleasant facts of colonial history are conveniently ignored. This is largely the case with Hillerman, Anderson-Dargatz, and Watson, but it is less true of Le Guin. In "Buffalo Gals," Le Guin contrasts a timeless Native world with a non-Native world obsessed with time, an obsession that expresses itself in terms of violence, possession, and conquest. This lust to possess and destroy is satirized by Coyote, who characterizes Myra's white "kith and kin" as a tribe of hunters and killers:

> "But they're your folks," Coyote said [to Myra]. "All yours. Your kith and kin and cousins and kind. Bang! Pow! There's Coyote! Bang! There's my wife's ass! Pow! There's anything—BOOOOM! Blow it away, man! BOOOOOOM!"[27]

The destruction of anything that represents difference expresses itself in terms of sexism ("There's my wife's ass! Pow!") and racism (Coyote's "BOOOOOOM!" surely evokes Hiroshima and the destruction of others considered less than human). When Myra, who now sees things with Native eyes, returns to small-town White America, she immediately finds herself in an "overwhelming rush of Time straight forward rolling her helpless as a twig in the race above a waterfall."[28] Manifest Destiny, the conflicts between indigenous peoples and settlers in U.S. history, and the appalling consequences of dominant and often racist ideologies are all suggested here.

COYOTE STORIES AND INDIGENOUS COMMUNITIES

What is foregrounded in Native writers like Silko and Ortiz, and what is usually ignored by non-Native writers, is that traditional tales are told within a community and have a communal role or function. Such tales consolidate and define the wisdom and values of the people. This is not, it hardly needs saying, the same for non-Native communities in the Western world, where stories are primarily marketed for entertainment. In the introduction to Silko's novel *Ceremony,* she includes a poem which begins:

CEREMONY
I will tell you something about stories
[he said]
They aren't just entertainment.
Don't be fooled.
They are all we have, you see,
all we have to fight off

illness and death.

You don't have anything
if you don't have the stories.[29]

The link between stories and cultural survival and resistance is clear. The life of the people is carried on through rituals, ceremonies, and stories, which are continually attacked from the outside:

Their evil is mighty
but it can't stand up to our stories.
So they try to destroy the stories.[30]

This view of the resistant nature of Native culture is close to Edward Said's, who in *Culture and Imperialism* argues that folktales, heroes, poetry, novels, and drama, as well as political agit-prop, resist the official discourses of colonizers. Through these means, as he puts it, the "imprisoned nation" is restored to itself.[31]

What is also foregrounded by Native writers, again like Ortiz and Silko, is the role of the poet as the voice of the community rather than as an individual. Simon Ortiz prefaces his collection, *Woven Stone,* with these words:

The stories and poems come forth,
and I am only a voice telling them.
They are the true source themselves.[32]

Storytelling as a community activity means that one story leads to another. Ortiz's poem, "And there is always one more story," has a long explanatory title to this effect.

My mother was telling this one. It must be an old story but this time she heard a woman telling it at one of those Sunday meetings. The woman was telling about her grandson who was telling the story which was told to him by somebody else. All these voices telling the story, including the voices in the story—yes, it must be an old one.[33]

The story is then told of Coyote Lady being left on a pinnacle by Quail Woman. In the telling, many contexts, such as language, society, and geography, are provided. The voices of the audience, including the voice of Ortiz's own daughter, Rainy Dawn, are heard. The typography is a score of the teller's voice:

The basket began to descend,

down

and

down[34]

The Keresan language is heard: Coyote Lady is called Tsuushki and *u-uuhshtyah* is defined as "juniper berries" in the glossary so that the reader is aware that the story was probably told in Keresan, or in a mixture of English and Keresan. The Acoma Pueblo mesa landscape is also precisely located:

> The water was in a little cistern
> at the top of a tall rock pinnacle
> which stands southeast of Aacqu.[35]

Aacqu or "Acu," as it is often spelled, names the place, the mesa. Ortiz refers to himself as an Aacqumeh, someone who comes from Ácoma: the ending "ma" or as Ortiz spells it "meh," means "people of," often in the sense of "their village." The language thus preserves the difference between the land and what the people do to, with, or on it. The Ácomas have lived on the same 350-foot mesa sixty miles west of the Rio Grande in west-central New Mexico for over eight hundred years. Language, history, and geography are intertwined; time and again, the listener is referred back to an actuality and context in which cultural materials have meaning.[36]

Silko and Ortiz speak within a community in which family relations are of great importance.[37] Silko's *Storyteller* contains photographs of her family as well as other Laguna Pueblo people. Aunts and grandparents are lovingly remembered, and there is an attempt to retell their tales with the same tone and phrases they used:

> This is the way Aunt Susie told the story.
> She had certain phrases, certain distinctive words
> she used in her telling.
> I write when I still hear
> her voice as she tells the story.[38]

Parts of the extended family are fellow storytellers. In *Storyteller,* we are told that "Uncle Tony's Goat" is derived "from a story Simon [Ortiz] told me when he called one morning about 4 a.m. and we had a long discussion about goats."[39] Later on in *Storyteller,* as if to return the gift, Silko dedicates "Toe'osh: A Laguna Coyote Story" to Ortiz. Again, the specificity is remarkable, a specificity that is, as we noted above, absent from most appropriated material. The date ("July 1973") when the poem is written is given. Before the tale is told, we learn that Coyote tales are winter and nighttime stories, and during the telling Spañada (a cheap wine) is drunk by the stove. The reader can imagine Silko and Ortiz swapping Laguna and Ácoma Coyote stories, Silko telling the Laguna ones and Ortiz the Ácoma, but who precisely the teller might be is left deliberately open, emphasizing the shared nature of the telling.

One story tells how Coyote lost his fur in a poker game and how he reclaimed his fur when sparrows stick on bits of old fur. This, of course, is a story familiar to Ortiz; in fact, it is told in greater detail in his poem, "Telling about Coyote." Part of the delight of storytelling is to tell familiar tales. Silko's Laguna story, like Ortiz's Ácoma version, leads from one Coyote story to another, and in both poems there is an interweaving of the traditional and the contemporary. In Silko's poem, the story of how Coyote got his patchy fur leads on to a Navajo story about Coyote tricking Chipmunk, Badger, and Skunk in a competition to see who could sleep outside longest during a snowstorm. This tale in turn gives way to an account of how Coyote-like white men (or alternatively, Coyote in the form of white men) came to Ácoma and Laguna country to fight for land and women, and how tricky politicians such as Charlie Coyote act in pretty much the same way today. The Trickster politicians are out-tricked, however, when their ham and turkey bribes are eaten but no votes are given in exchange. Here Trickster strategies are admired, adopted, and adapted as a way of resisting the wiles of would-be exploiters. Similarly, a Trickster ruse is used to subvert the power of big business, out-coyoteing the Coyotes:

> The Trans-Western pipeline vice president came
> to discuss right-of-way.
> The Lagunas let him wait all day long
> because he is a busy and important man.
> And late in the afternoon they told him
> to come back tomorrow.[40]

Immediately after this story, Silko returns to a shortened version of "Coyotes and the Stro'ro'ka Dancers," a tale told at length ten pages earlier. This is a typical scatological tale of the foolishness of Coyote. A group of coyotes are hanging over a cliff, each coyote gripping the tail of the one in front, in order to steal some picnic food at the base of the cliff. The chain crashes to the ground when one of coyotes farts and the one behind him opens his mouth to say, "What stinks?" We are a long way here from Watson's or Hillerman's terrible Coyote, but it is totally in keeping with Native views of Tricksters that this figure can at one and the same time be seen as a resistance hero and as a buffoon. Silko's poem ends, however, with Coyote as the culture hero and resistance leader:

> Howling and roaring
> Toe'osh scattered white people
> out of bars all over Wisconsin.
> He bumped into them at the door
> until they said
> > "Excuse me"
> And the way Simon meant it
> was for 300 or maybe 400 years.[41]

Robert M. Nelson (in an e-mail to me on March 13, 2003) explains the real-life events behind this mythic tale. In the version of the story that he heard in July 1973, Ortiz along with seven other Native American writers had been invited to a conference on Indian literature at the University of Wisconsin. Feeling that there was an enormous gap between what the writers wished to say and what the conference audience members were willing to hear, Ortiz decided to shock the attendees out of their complacency and ignorance by means of a Coyote trick. In a Madison bar crammed with conference attendees, Ortiz acted out the stereotypical role of the drunken Indian by announcing loudly that he felt sick, scattering white people in all directions as he headed for the door, where outside he made violent retching noises. This buffoonish pantomime, very much in keeping with traditional Coyote tales, was greatly appreciated by all Native writers who subsequently heard about it. The polite "excuse me's" of the offended whites in the bar no doubt were a source of much mirth. In Silko's poem, it is implied that the apologies Ortiz extorts are also intended to remind complacent whites of the effects of 300 to 400 years of colonial history in the United States. Ortiz's Coyote prank is a joke that he and Silko share, a joke whose serious implications Silko acknowledges at the end of her poem.

Another Coyote tale (this time a traditional one) that Silko and Ortiz share is the story of Skeleton Fixer putting together the scattered bones of Old Coyote Woman/Coyote Lady. Ortiz's aptly named poem, "And there is always one more story," tells of Coyote Lady's abandonment by Quail Women on a rock pinnacle on which she is marooned, the rescue by Spider Grandmother who lets Coyote Lady down in a basket with the warning that she should not look up Grandmother's skirts in the process, and the inevitable violation of the warning.[42] When Coyote does look up, Spider Grandmother drops the basket and Coyote crashes to the ground, scattering her bones everywhere. The benevolent Skeleton Fixer, Coyote's brother, comes along and not knowing who the bones belong to starts putting them together. When the jigsaw is complete, Skeleton Fixer is less than enthused to find that it is Coyote, and as the ungrateful Coyote runs away, Skeleton Fixer calls out that he hopes she may get crushed by a falling rock somewhere. In Silko's companion poem, "Skeleton Fixer," which is acknowledged at the end to be "A Version Told by Simon Ortiz," Old Man Badger Man (another name for Skeleton Fixer) sets about lovingly organizing some scattered bones he finds.[43] When the bones are finally put together to form an ungrateful Old Coyote Woman, Skeleton Fixer doesn't curse her, but instead muses, "It is surprising sometimes . . . how these things turn out," and the poem ends:

> But he never has stopped fixing
> the poor scattered bones he finds.[44]

CONCLUDING RE-APPROPRIATIONS

What is important here, especially in Silko's poem, is the notion that for a Native storyteller to retell traditional Native tales is an act of re-appropriation. This is made clear in the opening of Silko's poems, where bones are compared to words "scattered all over the place," it being the duty of someone who knows how the bones (words) should be placed to repatriate them.[45] Robert M. Nelson, in his excellent essay, "Rewriting Ethnography: The Embedded Texts in Leslie Silko's *Ceremony*," shows how Silko in both *Storyteller* and *Ceremony* is repatriating Laguna "artifacts" (poems, legends, tales), rescuing them from their death as ethnographic museum pieces and returning them to circulation.[46] In particular, Silko is reassembling the stories published in Franz Boas's *Keresan Texts*, liberating them from Boas's stilted ethnographic prose and scientific classifications.[47] Silko (and Ortiz) return the individual voice to the stories, reasserting what Nelson calls the "anatomical relationship between stories and their tellers."[48]

The final poem, and the penultimate text of *Storyteller*, indexed as "In 1918 Franz Boas, ethnologist and linguist," is about the transmission of a Coyote story among white people.[49] It thus touches on the theme of appropriation. The poem begins with Boas, who came to Laguna with the intention of constructing a Laguna grammar. Laguna is a tonal language and as, according to Silko, Boas was tone-deaf, the job of collecting Laguna texts is left to his assistant, Elsie Clews Parsons. Robert Marmon, Silko's white great-grandfather, told Parsons a simple Coyote story in the Laguna language.[50] Coyote is carrying water back to her pups, but is distracted by a teasing meadowlark until in exasperation she spits the water out. This happens four times so that when Coyote finally gets back to her pups they have died of thirst. Before giving the motivation for her great-grandfather's choice of story, Silko sketches the controversy surrounding the Marmon brothers, who married Laguna women, and along with a Baptist preacher named Gorman did their best to eliminate "pagan" Laguna ceremonialism.

Looking at the old photographs of great-grandpa Marmon, Silko sees in his eyes that "he had come to understand this world / differently."[51] The implication is that it is possible for non-Natives to learn from Native culture, just as in Le Guin's "Buffalo Gals" when Myra comes to see the world through Native eyes. Robert Marmon had possibly learned that:

> No matter what is said to you by anyone
> you must take care of those most dear to you.[52]

Silko and Ortiz are taking care of what is most dear to them by passing down cultural values and memories of their families through their words. Coyote tales in both their cultural specificity as well as their disturbing ambivalence—portraying the Trickster as both creator and destroyer, culture hero, resistance leader, survivor extraordinaire, and selfish buffoon, winner, and loser—are central to that task.

ACKNOWLEDGMENT

I would like to thank Hartmut Lutz and Robert M. Nelson for their very valuable comments on an earlier draft. For any remaining distortions or errors I am, of course, solely responsible.

NOTES

1. The Trickster figure is called Coyote among Native peoples in an area covering California, Oregon, the inland plateau, the Great Basin, the Southwest, and the southern Plains. It would appear that Coyote is fast becoming a pan-Indian figure in art and literature. Similarly, William Bright's anthology, *A Coyote Reader* (Berkeley: University of California Press, 1993), is divided into sections devoted to particular features of Coyote's character, such as Coyote the lecher, the loser, or the survivor, as though Coyote were a pan-Indian figure.

2. Gary Snyder, *Myths and Texts* (New York: New Directions, [1960] 1978), and *Turtle Island* (New York: New Directions, 1974).

3. Geary Hobson, "The Rise of the White Shaman as a New Version of Cultural Imperialism," in *The Remembered Earth: An Anthology of Contemporary Native American Literature,* ed. Geary Hobson (Albuquerque: University of New Mexico Press, 1979), 103. Hobson recently provided a useful update on the appropriation issue in "The Rise of the White Shaman: Twenty-Five Years Later," *Studies in American Indian Literatures* 14 (Summer/Fall 2002), 1–11. In both his first essay on white shamanism and in his reprise twenty-five years later, he makes the same point that his criticism of "white shaman" American poets in the

1970s is directed more at second-rate poets who capitalized on Snyder's "Shaman Songs" than on Snyder himself.

4. Leslie Marmon Silko, "An Old-Time Indian Attack Conducted in Two Parts," in ed. Hobson, *Remembered Earth,* 211–16.

5. The by now classic study of appropriatory ideological constructions and uses of the American Indian by Europeans and European Americans is Robert F. Berkhofer's *The White Man's Indian: Images of the American Indian from Columbus to the Present* (New York: Alfred A. Knopf, 1978). A study of Canadian popular cultural appropriations of the Indian icon is Daniel Francis's *The Imaginary Indian: The Image of the Indian in Canadian Culture* (Vancouver, BC: Arsenal Pulp Press, 1992). The most thorough historical analysis of European Americans' needs and desires to construct themselves as Natives is Philip J. Deloria, *Playing Indian* (New Haven, CT: Yale University Press, 1998). For examples of the commercial appropriation of American Indian cultures, see Carter Jones Meyer and Diana Royer, eds., *Selling the Indian: Commercializing and Appropriating American Indian Cultures* (Tucson: University of Arizona Press, 2001).

6. Hobson, *Remembered Earth,* 100.

7. Ibid., 101.

8. Hartmut Lutz, "Confronting Cultural Imperialism: First Nations People Are Combating Continued Cultural Theft," in *Approaches: Essays in Native North American Studies and Literatures,* ed. Harmut Lutz (Augsburg, Germany: Wissner, 2002), 88–89.

9. Tony Hillerman, *Coyote Waits* (Baytown, TX: Harper Torch, 1992), 64, 220, 248.

10. Ibid., 50, 165.

11. Ibid., 51, 166, 181

12. Beth Brant, "Whose Voice Is It, Anyway?" *Books in Canada* 20 (January/February 1991), 12.

13. Gail Anderson-Dargatz, *The Cure for Death by Lightning* (London: Virago, [1996] 1998), 171, 170.

14. See Andrew Wiget, ed., *Native American Literature* (Boston: Twayne Publishers, 1985), 15–21, for a useful overview of the ambiguous nature of the Trickster. One paradigm is to see this figure as an unpredictable combination of anarchy and creativity, a "Trickster/Transformer." Wiget (p. 16) also characterizes the three distinct roles of this figure as "the aggressive Culture Hero like Monster-Slayer, the cunning Promethean Culture Hero, and the bumbling, overreaching Trickster."

15. Anderson-Dargetz, *Cure for Death.*, 170.

16. Ibid., 201.

17. Sheila Watson, *The Double Hook* (Toronto, Canada: McClelland and Stewart, [1959] 1966).

18. Leslie Monkman, "Coyote as Trickster in *The Double Hook,"* *Canadian Literature* 52 (Spring 1972), 71, 76.

19. Margaret Morriss, "'No Short Cuts': The Evolution of *The Double Hook*," *Canadian Literature* 173 (Summer 2002), 61.

20. Tomson Highway, *Dry Lips Oughta Move to Kapuskasing* (Saskatoon, SK: Fifth House, 1989), 13. See also how Tomson Highway's novel, *Kiss of the Fur Queen* (1998), has "A Note on the Trickster" rather than "A Note on Nanabush," and substitutes the Cree

Trickster Weesageechak for the Ojibway Nanabush: "Some say that Weesaceechak [sic] left this continent . . ." (*Kiss,* n.p.). It is interesting to speculate why Highway should choose Nanabush as his central Trickster figure in his plays rather than Weesageechak, as Highway is himself Cree. One explanation for this is that the setting of his two published plays is the fictional Indian Reserve of Wasaychigan Hill on Manitoulin Island, Ontario, which, Highway explains in his Production Notes, "has a mixture of both Cree and Ojibway residents" (*Dry Lips,* 11). *Kiss* by contrast is more autobiographical, which might have motivated the choice of the Cree Trickster in the novel's introductory "A Note on the Trickster." Robert M. Nelson has suggested (in an e-mail to me on March 13, 2003) that citing Weesageechak rather than Nanabush in the later novel could indicate an increasingly clan-centered rather than pan-Indian (or pan-woodlands Indian) basis of authority, a change that is symptomatic of much post-1992 Native writing.

21. Ursula K. Le Guin, "Buffalo Gals, Won't You Come Out Tonight," in *Buffalo Gals and Other Animal Presences* (New York: ROC, 1990).

22. Mark Shackleton, "'We Keep Telling Each Other Stories. It Never Ends': An Interview with Lee Maracle," *The Atlantic Literary Review* 5, nos. 1 and 2 (January–March and April–June 2004), 201–02.

23. The most easily available versions of "Coyote Juggles His Eyes" are in Mourning Dove's *Coyote Stories* (New York: Brompton Books, [1933] 1990); and "Doing Tricks with Eyeballs" told by Rachel Strange Owl, a Northern Cheyenne, in *American Indian Myths and Legends,* ed. Richard Erdoes and Alfonso Ortiz (New York: Pantheon Books, 1984). The two versions differ in detail but the basic plot line is similar; that is, Coyote boasting about his trick of throwing up his eyeballs and then getting them stolen by a bird or birds.

24. Le Guin, "Buffalo Gals," 31.

25. Ibid., 35, 54.

26. Hartmut Lutz, "Cultural Appropriation as a Repression of Peoples and Histories," in *Approaches,* ed. Lutz, 75.

27. Le Guin, "Buffalo Gals," 55.

28. Ibid., 54.

29. Leslie Marmon Silko, *Ceremony* (New York: Penguin, [1977] 1986), 2.

30. Ibid.

31. Edward W. Said, *Culture and Imperialism* (New York: Alfred A. Knopf, 1993), 215.

32. Simon J. Ortiz, *Woven Stone* (Tucson: University of Arizona Press, 1998), v.

33. Ibid., 177.

34. Ibid., 179.

35. Ibid., 177.

36. For a profound pioneering study of the intricate and literal relatedness among language, contemporary Native American literature, and specific locations, see Robert M. Nelson, *Place and Vision: The Function of Landscape in Native American Fiction* (New York: Peter Lang, 1993). The Arizona rancher and anthropologist Keith H. Basso went even a step further and (field) studied the way in which specific stories are tied to specific locales on the Fort Apache Reservation, thus conveying history as chronotopic rather than chronological. Keith H. Basso, *Wisdom Sits in Places: Landscape and Language among the Western Apache* (Albuquerque: University of New Mexico Press, 1996).

37. One of Silko's criticisms of Snyder in her review of *Turtle Island* is that he seldom reveals his family roots and does not wish to acknowledge that side of his identity. See Silko, "Old-Time Indian," in *Remembered Earth,* ed. Hobson, 211–16.

38. Leslie Marmon Silko, *Storyteller* (New York: Arcade Publishing, 1981), 7.

39. Ibid., 170.

40. Ibid., 238.

41. Ibid., 239.

42. Ibid., 245.

43. Ibid.

44. Ibid.

45. Ibid., 242.

46. Robert M. Nelson, "Rewriting Ethnography: The Embedded Texts in Leslie Silko's *Ceremony,*" in *Telling the Stories: Essays on American Indian Literature and Cultures,* ed. Elizabeth Hoffman Nelson and Malcolm Nelson (New York: Peter Lang, 2001), 47–58.

47. Silko opens "Imitation 'Indian' Poems," which is part one of her essay, "An Old-Time Indian Attack Conducted in Two Parts," in *Remembered Earth,* ed. Hobson, 211–13, with a scathing reference to white ethnologists. To her, people like Franz Boas and J.R. Swanson typify the racist assumption that whites, through some imagined superiority, are able to comprehend fully the values and emotions of Native American communities.

48. Nelson, "Rewriting Ethnography," 47–58.

49. Silko, *Storyteller,* 254.

50. It is not certain that Boas was in fact tone deaf. Again, the source of my information is Robert M. Nelson (e-mail to M. Shackleton, March 13, 2003).

51. Silko, *Storyteller,* 256.

52. Ibid.

CHAPTER 5

"My Cells Will Not Forget": The Writings of Wendy Rose

P. JANE HAFEN

W ENDY ROSE and her poetry stand at the forefront of American Indian literatures. From her earliest work of student protest in the late 1960s and her
involvement in the Alcatraz takeover in the 1970s, she has been recognized as an
outstanding Native poet. Darryl Babe Wilson (Pit River) has described her writing
as "a special combination of . . . ancient wisdom . . . *unique* and *powerful.*"[1] She
has been widely anthologized as an American Indian poet and listed in major publications, such as the Gale series of literary biography and literary criticism, Harold
Bloom's *Native American Women Writers,* and Andrew Wiget's *Dictionary of Native
American Literature.*[2] Indeed, Rose's primary identification is with her Hopi father
and with a limited Miwok heritage through her mother's line. However, her latest
collection, *Itch Like Crazy* (2002),[3] adds a major complication when she confesses
that she is not sure whether her biological father is Charles Loloma (Hopi) or Dick
Edwards.[4]

BEING HOPI

Regardless of who Rose's birth father may be, she has lived most of her life believ-
ing and acting as if she were Hopi. She has directly confronted the detribalizing
factors in her life. With her essays, interviews, poetry, and titles like *The Halfbreed
Chronicles* (1985) and *Long Division: A Tribal History* (1976), she has forthrightly
admitted to a complicated background. She has said:

My father is full-blood Hopi from Arizona. He lives on the reservation. My mother is mostly Scots and Irish, but also Miwok, which is an Indian tribe from the area near Yosemite National Park here in California.[5]

Because of the social omnipresence of race, Rose's Indian half seems to consume her. The "white part of [her] family wanted nothing to do [with her]."[6] Being Indian plays on her consciousness in several distinct ways: as a Hopi with those tribal-specific and biological connections, as an Indian object in mainstream society, and as a part of a larger indigenous community. Yet, Hopi ties are tenuous for Rose. The insular Hopis have tribal barriers of history, place, and culture.

Historically, the Hopis have been one of the most isolated and definitive communities. The eleven villages (thousands of years old) on mesas in north-central Arizona resisted European colonization. When the Spanish returned to the Southwest after the Pueblo Revolt of 1680, the Hopis denied their pervasive influence and rejected them. Only one village on the far east side of the mesas accepted the return of the Catholic friars. Unlike other southwestern tribes who have mediated for hundreds of years with Europeans and Americans, Hopis have only relatively recently engaged with the mainstream, first trading with Mormon missionary Jacob Hamblin in 1858. They also have been more accommodating to anthropologists, missionaries, and tourists than many of the other Pueblo nations, while still maintaining a sharply defined sense of tribal community. The cohesiveness of the Hopi peoples makes Wendy Rose's detribalization even more acute. As the child of a Hopi father, she would have no standing in the matrilineal society. She grew up in California. She is not a legal Indian according to definitions imposed by the U.S. government because she is without documentation—she lacks a certificate of degree of Indian blood. Such an absurdity tells us more about those legal definitions than Rose's own Indianness.

POETRY AND IDENTITY

To the mainstream world and the literary world, Rose has been unquestionably Indian. She is not what Sherman Alexie describes as a "newly discovered Indian," an adult who has been raised with all the privileges of being white and could pass for white but uncovers an Indian somewhere in family genealogy. Neither is she a dissociated Indian who "fell from the sky," or a "lost bird" without any tribal knowledge. That she speaks directly and truthfully to the complex nature of her background gives veracity to her voice. She has said,

It would certainly be better for my image as an Indian poet to manufacture something and let you believe in my traditional, loving spiritual childhood

where every winter evening was spent immersed in storytelling and ceremony, where the actions of every day continually told me I was valued.[7]

She honestly tells of a troubled childhood, of rejection, of pain and anger, saying,
"I hate it when other people write about my alienation and anger. Even if it's true,
I'm not proud of it. It has crippled me, made me sick, made me out of balance. It
has also been the source of my poetry."[8]

The result is a powerful and lyrical art. She has been published for nearly thirty
years, is widely recognized, and continues to explore her life through her writing.
Her work demonstrates the multifaceted ontology of Indians. Apart from her Hopi
identifying markers, Rose's consciousness is Indian and she is treated as such. Being
detribalized does not spare an Indian from discrimination and prejudice, and Rose
writes of those experiences on personal and institutional levels. In her retrospective
collection, *Bone Dance: New and Selected Poems, 1965–1993,*[9] one of her earliest
poems, "For My People," was written at Berkeley in 1965: "I was myself blown /
two leafs apart / seeing the ground swim within / sliding and slipping together /
and apart."[10] In a later poem, "Incident at a Hamburger Stand: Iowa City," a construction worker confronts her:

> "Girl, you are in the midwest now;
> keep your place—eyes down—while
> I get a good long look
> at your fat Indian body
> before I go."

She responds to the blatant racism:

> One last swallow
> of creamed coffee
> and I tip my head back
> to defy him, square up
> my own shoulders
> and refuse the white man's burden.
> I am not angry you know
> but wonder:
> what kind of man
> can be like that
> so early in the morning?[11]

The man who challenges her does not distinguish her tribal identity; he sees her as a brown woman and presumes to tell the girl her place. Although she resists, she responds not with anger, but with questioning.

Racial prejudice from strangers is an issue that many people of color must cope with and adds a dimension to definitions of Indianness even without tribal specificity. More subtle and insidious are the institutional manifestations of being ignored or appropriated. In "Literary Luncheon: Iowa City," she feels the chilly atmosphere and writes:

> The great ones gather
> at the university buffet
> like cattle around
> alfalfa and barley.
> I maintain
> without willing it
> an Indian invisibility.[12]

To not be seen or to be ignored on a personal level reflects the statistical insignificance of Indians in the general population. Yet, the Indian of the imagination permeates American culture while individuals and tribes remain unseen.

ROSE AND CULTURAL APPROPRIATION

Another element of institutional racism is cultural appropriation. This theft occurs on a variety of levels, including the academy. Rose protests by situating this trend in a literary and spiritual context. As a poetic counterpart to her essay on "White-shamanism," Rose writes in "For the White Poets Who Would Be Indian":

> just once
> just long enough
> to snap up the words
> fish-hooked
> from our tongues.
> You think of us now
> when you kneel
> on the earth,
> turn holy
> in a temporary tourism
> of our souls.
>
> . . .
>
> You think of us only when your voice
> wants for roots,

when you have sat back
on your heels
and become primitive.
You finish your poem
and go back[13]

Rose identifies those whose romantic ideas of Indians somehow give license to assume Indian voices and practices. Yet these "temporary tourists" or New Agers can always return to their mainstream privilege and power.

In addition to the tensions that Rose feels with mainstream society, her familial ties are strained. In a statement that could be the definition of detribalization, she says, "I have heard Indians joke about those who act as if they had no relatives. I wince, because I have no relatives. They live, but they threw me away—so, I do not have them. I am without relations."[14] Yet, she is not. She does not examine specific Hopi relations, but she turns her sharp eye and ear on her non-Indian family. In a play on the Sioux expression, "mitakuye oyasin," her 1993 collection is titled, *Going to War with All My Relations*.[15] She admits to a complicated genealogy, knowing that certain of her non-Indian ancestors behaved poorly and inhumanely. In one of her most compelling poems, "Margaret Neumann," she gives the history of her great-great-grandmother who emigrated from Germany to San Francisco. Yet while offering a narrative journey of this woman, Rose parallels and acknowledges the terrible history of California and indigenous peoples:

The dangerous dreams of a wild girl,
they said, who goes to meet her husband
beneath the twisting serpent and eagle
of Mexico's flag
who mounts the wagon bound for California
where the very streets are gold, gold on which
stolen kisses fall not gently at all and the
sun glimmers
from a thousand Spanish swords, ankle-deep
already
in Miwok bones.[16]

By acknowledging the horrid price of colonialism, Rose removes the colored glasses of California history. She also acknowledges her maternal indigenous heritage.

COMMUNITY AND HISTORY

One of the characteristics that marks traditional tribal writers is their sense of community. The individual is subordinated to the needs of the communal whole. For example, in James Welch's *Fools Crow*, the main character sacrifices individual desire for service to the tribal Pikuni well-being, while his foil, Fast Horse, acts in self-interest and eventually disappears from Blackfeet awareness.[17] For Wendy Rose, disenfranchisement from traditional Hopi tribal practices manifests itself in several prominent ways.

The first is communal history, what Gerald Vizenor calls "genetic memory." Although Rose was not socialized through Hopi ceremonial rituals, or ritual re-enactments of historical events, like the expulsion of the Catholic priests in 1680, she certainly must know about them. Even if she learned Hopi information from books, she identifies with that history and communal sense. She knows that the blood in her veins carries the genes of survival. This tribal knowledge is part of her history in the poem, "To Some Few Hopi Ancestors":

> You have engraved yourself
> with holy signs, encased yourself
> in pumice, hammered on my bones
> till you could no longer hear
> the howl of the missions
> slipping screams through your silence,
> dropping dreams from your wings.
> Is this why
> you made me
> sing and weep
> for you?[18]

The images of bones, mesas, and red sandstone, interspersed in poetry with a variety of themes, consistently remind the reader that Rose is Hopi.

In addition to communal Hopi signifiers, Rose writes beyond the tribal specific to consider hemispheric indigenous issues. Only a small group of Arawaks met Christopher Columbus over 512 years ago, yet that singular incident impacted all Natives. Numerous epic gestures exceed tribally specific concerns, as those actions pierce the hearts of all indigenous peoples. Rose addresses some of these gestures: the Massacre at Wounded Knee in "I Expected My Skin and Blood to Ripen"; the decapitation of a Seminole leader in "Retrieving Osceola's Head"; international terrorism in "The Day They Cleaned Up the Border: El Salvador"; and in the environmental violation and stealing of sacred Sioux lands in "Mount Rushmore." Rose challenges the sacrilegious display and commodification of indigenous peoples in "Three Thousand Dollar Death Song" about displays of skeletal remains; in "Truganinny" about the display of stuffed and mounted Australia Aborigines; and in "Julia" about the public display of a deformed Mexican Indian woman. In the refrain from "Excavation at Santa Barbara Mission," she laments:

> They built the mission with dead Indians.
> They built the mission with dead Indians.
> They built the mission with dead Indians.
> They built the mission with dead Indians.[19]

While the specifics of these poems refer to particular Indian nations and particular historical events, Rose's indignation stands for all indigenous peoples.

Rose also enters the pan-Indian community of Native scholars and writers, of urbanized Indians who share common concerns and issues. Her collaboration with Mohawk poet Maurice Kenny emerges in the 1993 collection, *What the Mohawk Made the Hopi Say.*[20] While some themes are common, each writer remains tribally distinct, as Rose observes: "[T]o be Pan-Indian is not to become less tribal. To be tribal and to be Pan-Indian exist side by side, and in fact Pan-Indianism is intended to protect those tribal identities, not to replace them."[21] Rose exemplifies this paradox in the title poem: "Somewhere in the Adirondacks, January 1985":

> . . .
> Bless this tongue
> in your special way
>
> . . .
> I finally agree
> turning into a rock
> that these are mountains
> noble as any
> and all of Arizona
> must wait
> for spring thaw.[22]

Her own sense of place as home and self-definition spill over into an empathy for Kenny's identification with his own mountains.

One of the tribal ties that continually brings Rose back to Hopi topics is connection to place. As mentioned previously, the bones, mesas, and sandstones for Rose are persistent images. Yet when Rose travels from place to place, from California to New York, her language is interspersed with comparative references to Hopis, even when far from California or Arizona as in "Corn-Grinding Song to Send Me Home: New Hampshire":

> The mountains of the east
> are softened and claimed by snow
> not angry or chastised
> like the temper of the Sierras.
>
> . . .
>
> My hands are still Hopi
> and will keep me home
> moving back and forth
> palms down, fingers curled
> on cool stone, dreaming
> the metate and maize within.[23]

With the imagery of traditional Hopi tasks, Rose is inextricably connected with place and tribal identity.

RETURNING TO IDENTITY

Wendy Rose is not a resident of the Hopi tribal community, yet she has represented herself as undeniably Hopi. She does not write from the inside out but from the outside in. In the multiple ways society approaches race and Indian peoples, Rose is treated like an Indian on both personal and institutional levels. She is sensitized to issues of larger indigenous communities. Though detribalized, she identifies as a Hopi Indian:

> My father told me . . . that Hopi earth does contain my roots and I am, indeed, from that land. Because the roots are there, I will find them. But when I find them, he said, I must rebuild myself as a Hopi. I am not merely a conduit, but a participant.
> I am not a victim, but a woman.
> I am building myself.
> There are many roots.
> I plant, I pick, I prune.
> I consume.[24]

Rose meets Craig Womack's (Muscogee Creek) charge "that emphasizes Native resistance movements against colonialism, confronts racism, discusses sovereignty and Native nationalism, seeks connections between literature and liberation struggles, and, finally, roots literature in land and culture."[25]

After the revelations in *Itch Like Crazy,* the question is how Rose's work changes if she is not genetically Hopi. Certainly she has opened herself to critics and self-appointed arbiters of Indian authenticity and identity. However, rather than a constructed fraud, like Asa "Little Tree" Carter or Gregory Markopoulos/J. Marks/Jamake Highwater,[26] Rose has conducted her life with legitimate assumptions about her Hopi identity, not unlike the late Michael Dorris and his claims of Modoc heritage.[27] Rose has established ties with the Hopi community while documenting urban and academic American Indian experiences with her writings.

In a recent interview in *News from Native California*, Rose says *Itch Like Crazy* began as a genealogical search that unearthed information she did not "like at all."[28] The last three pieces of *Itch Like Crazy* are accompanied by photographs of the important men in Rose's life. The third from the end is of Dick Edwards by himself, whom Rose identifies as "one of the two men who may or may not be my father." The penultimate is a photo and narrative about Rose's husband, Arthur Murata, and his parents. The last section is a photo of Rose and "Charles Loloma, the man who is most likely my father and whom I have always regarded as such." She recapitulates his family and clan history at the village of Hotevilla and her disenfranchisement because of Hopi matrilineal social structure. Because of his prominence as an artist and because she did not want to appear as "just a 'wannabe,'" she regrettably kept their relationship secret until after his death in 1991. She concludes: "It really was not until I learned that there was a possibility that he was not my father that I decided to 'come out' and just state the facts as I knew them."[29]

In the interview, Rose adds: "I finally got to a point where I couldn't agonize about it any more. And the other thing is, in Indian Country, if you start saying you're not sure about your background, things get political."[30] Nevertheless, through the encouragement of Simon Ortiz (Acoma Pueblo) and Leslie Marmon Silko (Laguna Pueblo), she boldly "just states the facts."

As for the political nature of Indian identity, contemporary definitions are tied to tribal enrollment, blood quantum, and perceived economic advantages associated with casinos.[31] As Kathryn Shanley (Nakota/Assiniboine) observes:

> Any definition of American Indian identity obviously must begin with Indians themselves, and . . . this is not a simple matter given tribal diversity, the ruins of colonialism, intermarriage, language extinction, and the like. Definitions of any human community can never adequately contain the multiplicities, the inexhaustible readings of a collective of individual lives—yet each needs to accommodate the other, the individual, and the community, and vice versa.[32]

Clearly, Rose's identity questions as mixed-blood Hopi, as urban and academic reflect that multiplicity. As Robert Allen Warrior (Osage) says of her writing, "Rose brings to the . . . conversation a stark reminder of the need for healing in Indian communities and presents a profound challenge for American Indian intellectuals to be more honest, more inclusive, and to recognize the profound challenges we face."[33] Her personal honesty in addressing these matters, unlike some Native writers who enhance and exaggerate their own American Indian backgrounds, adds to the uniqueness and the power of her poetry.

NOTES

1. Daryl Babe Wilson (Pit River), Review of *Bone Dance: New and Selected Poems, 1965–1993, American Indian Culture and Research Journal* 18, no. 3 (1994), 278.

2. The Gale Series that features an entry on this author include *Contemporary Authors,* vols. 53–56; *Contemporary Authors New Revision Series,* vols. 5 and 51; *Contemporary Literary Criticism,* vol. 85; *Contemporary Women Poets* (St. James Press, an imprint of Gale); *Dictionary of Literary Biography,* vol. 175; *Discovering Authors Modules,* multiple editions; *Native North American Literature; Poetry Criticism,* vol. 13; *Poetry for Students,* vol. 13; *Reference Guide to American Literature* (St. James Press, a Gale imprint), four editions; *Something about the Author,* vol. 12; Harold Bloom, ed., *Native American Women Writers* (Philadelphia: Chelsea House, 1998); and Andrew Wiget, *Dictionary of Native American Literature* (New York: Garland, 1994). (Note: The Gale Series is a proprietary master index of literature and literary criticism commonly employed by researchers in the humanities. They exist in multivolume hardcopy encyclopedias and on-line forms.)

3. Wendy Rose, *Itch Like Crazy* (Tucson: University of Arizona Press, 2002).

4. Ibid., "Part Three: Listen for the Voices."

5. Laura Coltelli, *Winged Words: American Writers Speak* (Lincoln: University of Nebraska Press, 1990), 122.

6. Ibid.

7. Wendy Rose, "Neon Scars," in *I Tell You Now: Autobiographical Essays by Native American Writers,* ed. Brian Swann and Arnold Krupat (Lincoln: University of Nebraska Press, 1989), 261.

8. Ibid., 253.

9. Wendy Rose, *Bone Dance: New and Selected Poems, 1965–1993* (Tucson: University of Arizona Press, 1994).

10. Ibid., "For My People," 3.

11. Ibid., "Incident at a Hamburger Stand: Iowa City," 23–24.

12. Ibid., "Literary Luncheon: Iowa City," 37.

13. Ibid., "For the White Poets Who Would Be Indian," 22.

14. Rose, "Neon Scars," 255.

15. Wendy Rose, *Going to War with My Relations: New and Selected Poems* (Flagstaff, AZ: Entrada Books, 1993), 73.

16. Ibid., "Margaret Neumann," 77.

17. See James Welch, *Fools Crow* (New York: Viking, 1986).

18. Wendy Rose, "To Some Few Hopi Ancestors," in *Bone Dance,* 16.

19. Wendy Rose, "Excavation at Santa Barbara Mission," in *Bone Dance,* 85.

20. Maurice Kenny, "What the Mohawk Made the Hopi Say," in *Bone Dance,* 63.

21. Coltelli, *Winged Words,* 129. Although Karen Tongson-McCall offers a good close

reading of several of Rose's poems, the title of her essay, "The Nether World of Neither World: Hybridization in the Literature of Wendy Rose," *American Indian Culture and Research Journal* 20, no. 4 (1996), 1–40, falls into several critical traps. "Hybridization" is a postcolonial critical term that masks assimilation and authenticity questions; it fails to acknowledge paradox and complexity. Additionally, the teleological caught-between-worlds polarization can only result in tragedy and the vanishing American rather than seeking modes of survival.

22. Wendy Rose, "Somewhere in the Adirondacks," in *Bone Dance,* 68–69.

23. Wendy Rose, "Corn-Grinding Song to Send Me Home: New Hampshire," in *Bone Dance,* 41.

24. Rose, "Neon Scars," 261.

25. Craig Womack, *Red on Red: Native American Literary Separatism* (Minneapolis: University of Minnesota Press, 1999), 11.

26. See Kathryn Shanley, "The Indians America Loves to Love and Read: American Indian Identity and Cultural Appropriation," *American Indian Quarterly* 21 (Fall 1997): 675–703. Shanley discusses Indian identity, including Highwater. She says, "[T]he problem is that he has appropriated Indianness for his own gain and peddles it as an artifact. He has little if any relationship to living Indian communities or nations" (p. 683).

27. Elizabeth Cook-Lynn (Crow Creek Dakota) has excoriated Michael Dorris for his representations of mixed-blood identity in "American Indian Intellectualism and the New Indian Story," in *Native and Academics: Researching and Writing about American Indians,* ed. Devon A. Mihesuah (Choctaw) (Lincoln: University of Nebraska Press, 1998), 111–38; and "Letter to Michael Dorris," 69–71; and "A Mixed-Blood, Tribeless Voice in American Indian Literatures: Michael Dorris," 72–90, in *Anti-Indianism in America: A Voice from Tatekeya's Earth* (Urbana: University of Illinois Press, 2001). Dorris has said, "I think when you're a mixed blood who certainly doesn't look like anybody's stereotype of the Indian, you either get comfortable with who you are very early on in life, or you spend your whole life schizophrenic and defensive." http://www.wooster.edu/ArtfulDodge /Dorris.html, October 1, 2000.

28. "An Interview with Wendy Rose," *News from Native California* 17 (Fall 2003): 30.

29. Rose, "Part Three."

30. "Interview with Wendy Rose," 30.

31. For thorough discussions of identity issues, see Devon Mihesuah (Choctaw), "American Indian Identities: Issues of Individual Choices and Development," in *Contemporary Native American Cultural Issues,* ed. Duane Champagne (Walnut Creek, CA: Sage Publications, 1999), 13–38; and Eva Marie Garroutte, *Real Indians: Identity and the Survival of Native America* (Berkeley: University of California Press, 2003). The current attacks on Indian identity and authenticity have become more virulent with the rise of Indian gaming. See Jeff Benedict, *Without Reservation: How a Controversial Indian Tribe Rose to Power and Built the World's Largest Casino* (New York: Perennial, 2001).

32. Shanley, "The Indians America Loves to Love and Read," 692–93.

33. Robert Allen Warrior, *Tribal Secrets: Recovering American Indian Intellectual Traditions* (Minneapolis: University of Minnesota Press, 1995), 121.

CHAPTER 6

Sherman Alexie and Stretching Sexual Boundaries

PATRICE HOLLRAH

SHERMAN ALEXIE, noted Spokane/Coeur d'Alene novelist and storyteller, writes strong women into his works. In an interview with brothers John and Carl Bellante, Alexie presents his views on the importance of the role of women in culture when asked, "[W]hat precisely about white culture makes [him] so angry?"

> Pretty much everything patriarchal. . . . There used to be a sense of matriarchal power [among Indian societies]. That's not the case anymore. Not in my tribe anyway. We've resisted assimilation in many ways, but I know we've assimilated into sexism and misogyny. . . . As with anything else, women always have power. Women are the creators. We get into trouble when we try to deny that. So I'm angry toward this patriarchal country that creates an environment totally hostile toward women. If we can't love our own mothers and sisters, how can we start loving?[1]

By critiquing a U.S. patriarchal culture that subordinates and devalues women, Alexie privileges the inherent power in women's roles as creators. His attitude of valuing the role of women and their power contrasts with the negative consequences of ignoring their contributions to the culture and the indigenous ideology of gender complementarity, in which there is no hierarchy between the genders but rather an equal regard for the roles and work of each other. Alexie further states, "Indian women are the reason Indian cultures have survived,"[2] and he openly acknowledges his political position with regard to how women are treated in the United States. This chapter examines how Alexie portrays strong Native female characters in his work and specifically those beyond the boundaries of stereotypical heterosexual roles.

ALEXIE AND INDIAN HOMOSEXUALITY

In his short story, "Indian Country," from the collection *The Toughest Indian in the World,*[3] Alexie does not deal with the same kinds of female characters that have filled the pages of his previous works. Instead, he introduces lesbian characters. When asked in an on-line chat if he was making a political statement with the addition of homosexuality in his writing, Alexie had the following to say:

> It's a personal and political statement. As my life has become more urban and more diverse, so have my friends become more urban and diverse. I think the hatred I am most upset with in the world is homophobia. It's the only hatred that has absolutely no basis in reality. Every other group of people has oppressed every other group of people—except the gays and lesbians. Find me a country of gay men that's invaded another country. Find me a lumberjack who's been straight-bashed by a group of raving lesbians.[4]

Alexie takes a strong position about the discrimination that gays and lesbians have suffered. Claiming that his position is both political and personal, he critiques the dominant culture's attitudes and treatment of gays and lesbians because he argues that there is no rational basis for that kind of hatred. Noting that there would not be nearly as much art produced were it not for gays and lesbians, Alexie points out the hypocrisy of homophobia: "You get rid of all the gay art in the world, and you'd have two auto-repair manuals and three albums by John Tesh, and do you really want to live in that world?"[5] In the same way that Alexie critiques the illogical bias of people who discriminate against lesbians, he examines how painful and damaging that attitude can be for both the lesbian characters and their families and friends in the short story "Indian Country."

Low Man Smith, a Coeur d'Alene Indian writer, travels to Missoula, Montana, from his hometown of Seattle, Washington, at the invitation of Carlotta, a Navajo poet who teaches English at Flathead Indian College. Going with the intention of asking Carlotta to marry him, he learns upon his arrival that Carlotta has already married an old flame, Chuck, and left for Flagstaff, Arizona. Broken-hearted, confused, and at a loss for what he should do next, Low Man looks for a used bookstore where he can read a good book and drink coffee. Through a series of misunderstandings, he lands in jail. In his disoriented condition, the police officers want to release him to someone who can look after him. Low Man then learns that an old college lesbian friend, Tracy Johnson, works at the local Barnes and Noble bookstore and is earning her MFA at the University of Montana, and he calls her. She agrees to pick him up at the police station on her way to meet her Spokane Indian partner and law school student, Sara Polatkin, whom she plans to marry.

Riding in Tracy's 1972 half-ton Chevrolet pickup, Low Man appraises her physical looks since he last saw her: "Forty pounds overweight, she was beautiful, wearing a loose T-shirt and tight blue jeans. Her translucent skin bled light into her dark hair. . . . 'You're lovely,' he said."[6] Even some of Alexie's white women, who are drawn as large and beautiful physical presences, go against the dominant culture's standards of Barbie Doll beauty: thin and blond. Tracy's partner, Sara, is the opposite, or complement, of her in stature: "She was short, thin, very pretty, even with her bad teeth and eccentric clothes—a black dress with red stockings, and Chuck Taylor basketball shoes with Cat in the Hat socks. . . . Her black hair hung down past her waist."[7] What Sara lacks in height and weight, she makes up for in her personality. She immediately third-degrees Low Man about his feelings for Tracy and their past relationship, wanting to know if he still loves her and if he ever had sexual relations with her.[8] As the jealous and protective partner, she lives up to her family name, much like Marie Polatkin does in Alexie's novel *Indian Killer,* and she resembles the warrior wife of Qualchan who attacks her husband's enemies in the short story "The Trial of Thomas Builds-the-Fire" from the collection *The Lone Ranger and Tonto Fistfight in Heaven.*[9] In this case, however, Sara is a lesbian protecting her interests in her soon-to-be wife.

INDIANS, MORMONISM, AND HOMOPHOBIA

The conflict in "Indian Country" is not that Carlotta has jilted Low Man but that Sara's parents, Sid and Estelle Polatkin, object to her plans to marry Tracy. They are coming from the Spokane Reservation with the intent to change their daughter's mind. Alexie characterizes them with histories that might belong to any number of people living on a reservation:

> [Sid] was president of the Spokane Indian Reservation VFW. . . . [His] hair was pulled back in a gray ponytail. So was Estelle's. Both of their faces told stories. Sid's: the recovering alcoholic; the wronged son of a wronged son; the Hamlet of his reservation. Estelle's: the tragic beauty; the woman who stopped drinking because her husband did; the woman who woke in the middle of the night to wash her hands ten times in a row. Now they were Mormons.[10]

Between them, this couple has survived military service, alcoholism, and obsessive-compulsive disorder, a lot to be said for the gender complementarity within their own marriage. Alexie uses the shorthand of Mormonism for the parents' homophobia because of the Mormons' well-known role as a primary political force behind anti-homosexual issues and their position supporting what they term a traditional family structure. The parent's anti-lesbian stance stems mainly from their

Mormon conviction that homosexuality is a sin and their fear of losing their daughter's presence in their heavenly family for committing such acts.[11] Concerning the general attitude toward gays and lesbians on Indian reservations, Alexie states, "Tragically, I think the homophobia in minority communities is greater than in the dominant culture. That whole lateral violence thing."[12] To make this point, Alexie resorts to using the Mormons' stance associated with homosexuality. The parents come in the spirit of love with intentions of forgiving Sara, but things do not work out as they had hoped.[13]

Over a salmon dinner at the Holiday Inn, tempers flare as the five characters argue over Christianity, lesbianism, and who has the right to sit at the table. With Estelle in tears, Sara begging her mother not to cry, Tracy telling Low Man to go for a ride, and Sid becoming angrier by the minute, things quickly deteriorate. When Tracy suggests that maybe she should be the one to leave, Sara takes charge of the situation:

> "No," said Sara. "Nobody's going anywhere." In Sara's voice, the others heard something new: an adulthood ceremony taking place between syllables.
> "What's wrong with you?" Low asked Sid. "She's your daughter. You should love her no matter what."[14]

The authority with which Sara speaks lets everyone know that she is not just the daughter in this situation but also an adult. Her strength in trying to calm her parents and restore some kind of emotional order to what has transpired indicates that she is acting as an autonomous woman who knows how to deal with a volatile situation. This adulthood ceremony then signifies that Sara has made the break from her parents, an act requiring maturity and emotional strength, an act that empowers her.

As Sara announces that she's leaving, she tells her parents that she loves them and steps away from the table toward Tracy. Sid warns his daughter that if she leaves, she should plan on never speaking to them again.[15] Low Man tries to explain to Sid how useless that kind of threat is: "'These women don't need us. They never did'."[16] Low Man's name accurately reflects the position of not only him but also all men in the lives of these two women: Men are not in a privileged position. Unable to accept that his daughter chooses to disregard his parental and patriarchal authority, Sid resorts to physical intimidation. He chases after the two women, pushes Tracy into a wall, and takes Sara by the elbow, saying, "'You're coming with us.'"[17] Estelle asks Low Man to help them, one of only two times that she speaks in the whole story, an example of how her voice is subsumed in the patriarchal marriage. Just as Low Man runs to their aid, Sid slaps his daughter twice, shouting, "'She's my daughter, she's mine.'"[18] Sid then punches Low Man, who falls to the floor, and Sid continues yelling about his ownership of his daughter until Tracy slaps him: "Surprised, defeated, Sid dropped to the floor beside Low."[19] Low Man's final question to the parents emphasizes what should be important: "'What are you going to do when she's gone?'"[20]

Indeed, how will Sid and Estelle feel when they can never see their daughter again? Focusing on the love that families and friends have for one another, Alexie makes the point that the pain of not seeing loved ones ever again *should* be far greater than the discomfort of tolerating lifestyles different than their own. Tracy and Sara feel no guilt about their sexual orientation or their love for each other. Instead, they are proud of each other's accomplishments and do not hide in the closet. Both of these women demonstrate strength and power in confronting the discrimination that they encounter, and their openness about their lifestyle and love for each other is a political statement about the rights of individuals to live their own lives. Alexie's critique asks those who would shun gays and lesbians to examine the damage inflicted on families and friends when there is a lack of understanding, consideration, respect, and tolerance for those who are different.

Alexie presents a contemporary version of a peace party between warring factions: Indian/White, Christian/pagan, and heterosexual/homosexual. The parties meet at the dinner table, talk, fight, and depart; however, there is no reconciliation, no treaty is signed. The peace party, in one sense, is a failure. Alexie makes a case against those who would try to control a woman and her sexual orientation. He also challenges the hero/coward opposition and makes a case for an antihero, Low Man, a Coeur d'Alene who does not meet the usual stereotype of the Indian warrior. In this story, women are the contemporary warriors who win in a context of complementing each other.[21]

CONCLUSION

When asked what people should know about Indians, Alexie answers by focusing on the political:

> I think the primary thing that people need to know about Indians is that our identity is much less cultural now and much more political. That we really do exist as political entities and sovereign political nations. That's the most important thing for people to understand, that we are separate politically and economically. And should be.

Alexie discusses the political aspect of tribal nations as sovereign entities. The same could be said on a micro level about his strong female characters. They, too, are political sovereign entities who are strong, powerful, autonomous, contemporary female warriors, whether they are matriarchal mythic figures like Big Mom in his novel *Reservation Blues*,[22] college students and political activists like Marie Polatkin in *Indian Killer*,[23] teachers and wives like Grace Atwater in the short story "St. Junior,"[24] fry bread–making experts and nurturers-to-dying-people like Norma Many Horses in the short story, "The Approximate Size of My Favorite Tumor,"[25] or lesbians like Tracy Johnson and Sara Polatkin. The value of these women's roles and work grows out of a context of gender complementarity; they are valued for who they are and what they bring to relationships and the community within the context of specific tribal and intellectual sovereignties.

Alexie takes a political position outside of his writing and makes it his agenda within his writing. That Alexie, a male author, is the one who offers public anti-patriarchal statements, when usually women are perceived as the ones doing this kind of criticizing, points out how men can comfortably critique patriarchy when they are securely grounded in a worldview of gender complementarity. This kind of behavior does not make men appear to be less masculine or more effeminate, but merely men who are comfortable with both sexes equally contributing to the community in a balanced way. Just as women can perform what might seem to non-Natives as male-gendered behaviors, men also can perform what might appear as female-gendered behaviors.

Alexie's statements regarding the Spokane nation's acculturation of sexism, misogyny, and homophobia, characteristics of U.S. patriarchal culture, are a way of critiquing the effects of colonization on Spokane Indians, but his writing constructs strong female characters as if the dynamics of gender complementarity have never vanished. His conscious construction of autonomous Native female characters, particularly in "Indian Country," is a political act of resistance and recovery of traditional tribal gender relations, a reconfiguration resulting in powerful women for all of Indian country.

NOTES

1. John and Carl Bellante, "Sherman Alexie: Literary Rebel," *Bloomsbury Review* 14 (May/June 1994): 15.

2. Bernadette Chato, "Book-of-the-Month: *Reservation Blues*," *Native America Calling*, interview, KUNM 89.9 FM, Albuquerque, New Mexico, June 26, 1995, rebroadcast on American Indian Radio on Satellite (AIROS), June 2, 2001, http://www.airos.org.

3. Sherman Alexie, "Indian Country," in *The Toughest Indian in the World* (New York: Atlantic Monthly Press, 2000), 121–49.

4. Sherman Alexie, "Chats and Events," October 14, 2000, http://www.barnesandnoble .com/co.../transcript.asp?userid+24L2DFWCYO&eventId'218, 3.

5. Ibid.

6. Alexie, "Indian Country," 136–37.

7. Ibid., 138.

8. Ibid., 138–39.

9. Sherman Alexie, *Indian Killer* (New York: Warner Books, 1996), and Sherman Alexie, *The Lone Ranger and Tonto Fistfight in Heaven* (New York: Harper Perennial, 1994).

10. Alexie, "Indian Country," 142.

11. Ibid., 145.

12. Alexie, "Chats and Events."

13. Alexie, "Indian Country," 142.

14. Ibid., 146.

15. Ibid., 147.

16. Ibid., 148.

17. Ibid.

18. Ibid.

19. Ibid.

20. Ibid., 149.

21. Sherman Alexie, "A Dialogue on Race with President [William] Clinton," *Online NewsHour,* aired July 9, 1998 on PBS, transcript May 31, 2001, http://www.pbs.org/newshour/bb/race_relations/OneAmerica/transcript.html.

22. Sherman Alexie, *Reservation Blues* (New York: Warner Books, 1995).

23. See Alexie, *Indian Killer.*

24. Sherman Alexie, "St. Junior," in *Toughest Indian,* 150–88.

25. Sherman Alexie, "The Approximate Size of My Favorite Tumor," in *Lone Ranger and Tonto,* 154–70.

PART III

Challenges Past and Present

For us, the ownership of territory is a marriage of the Chief and the land. Each chief has an ancestor who encountered and acknowledged the life of the land. From such encounters come power. The land, the plants, the animals and the people all have spirits—they all must be shown respect. That is the basis of our law.[1]

DELGAM UUKW, Gitxsan

We live with our ancestors in our hearts. Their voices speak of the trees, the water and all of the earth's riches. We have the foundation of our Indian livelihood, culture, and spiritual strengths that have existed for centuries.[2]

TRINA BRIDGES AND KATHY DUNCAN, Jamestown S'Klallam

WHAT HAS SO OFTEN been missed by scholar observers of the indigenous present and past are the connections between the two. While it may sound hackneyed and even stereotypical, Native Americans and First Nations today are a part of a culture that celebrates the "living past." These connections are vital and vibrant, and they are a fundamental aspect of the cultural renewal that on a daily basis attempts to decolonize indigenous life.

The five chapters in this section explore a wide variety of past and present challenges for Native peoples. Two contributions consider two watershed events that continue to reverberate throughout Indian country: the American Revolution and the Massacre at Wounded Knee. Three others take up current issues that include the use of the Internet in Native worlds, the legal issues surrounding gaming, and educational standards and indigenous contributions to curricula reform in Canada and the United States. Broad perceptions of sovereignty for Native Americans and First Nations permeate each chapter both directly and indirectly. Diverse questions abound: How do indigenous peoples fit within the framework of revolutionary democracy? Can a massacre continue to impact a culture? What are the ramifications of technology in traditional Native life? Must a people who seek self-governance embrace the legal battlefield as well as the economic opportunities and dangers inherent in gambling in order to protect their rights? And how best to educate Canadians and Americans, indigenous and nonindigenous, about First Nations and Native American history and culture, from both the past and current perspectives?

Reflections from the past are documented by Peter C. Messer and Rani Andersson. Messer takes us through the labyrinth of discussions and writings that occurred among historians and other intellectuals immediately after the conclusion of the American Revolution. The inconsistencies of the revolutionary ardor and rhetoric upon relations with American Indians were not lost upon these chroniclers of the new American nation. How might they be reconciled? Some believed that the new nation had to confront this dilemma in order for it to realize its own potential. That confrontation needed to embrace policy adjustments. Others rationalized ways to excuse the taking of indigenous lands and sovereignty and killings of Indians in the face of pious revolutionary goals. In the end, only Mercy Otis Warren, the United States' revolutionary conscience, warned that the callousness of breaking the bonds of a moral democratic revolution in U.S.–Native

American relations would paralyze the achievement of the highest order of nationhood.

Rani Andersson explains how a revitalization movement in the 1880s, the Ghost Dance, spread across the American West. It assumed several different forms and developed various kinds of meanings for a variety of constituencies. Andersson identifies five different groups who each had separate responses to not only the messianic religious fervor, but the violence that eventually resulted in the Massacre at Wounded Knee in December 1890. These groups include the U.S. Army, the Congress, Indian agents, the American press, and Lakotas. What is particularly insightful about this essay is Andersson's placement of the Ghost Dance within Lakota cultural frameworks. That has not been done before, and those who have sought to explain Lakota responses have often taken the tack that the Ghost Dance could only be viewed outside traditional Lakota experiences. This, it seems, is most definitely not the case, and it helps explain why so many Lakotas willingly embraced this movement even though they intuited that it could lead to violence with the American colonial presence.

After looking at past challenges, modern issues confront indigenous peoples of North America, and these are explained in three diverse chapters dealing with technology, gaming, and education. First, Ritva Levo-Henriksson describes how many North American tribal nations, particularly in the Arctic regions, have embraced the Internet and found ways to reach out to the world community. She specifically refers to her case study of the Hopis of Arizona who are known for their adherence to traditional culture practices, and she finds that even among the Hopis, there is a strong interest and careful and cautious usage of electronic technology. Troubling to older Hopis is the lack of control of the Internet and what it might mean for tribal sovereignty and the transfer of Hopi traditions to the young. A salient feature of Levo-Henriksson's essay is extensive interviews of a diverse range of Hopis.

Miia Halme offers a similar kind of modern case study, this time among the Miccosukees of Florida and their successful adoption of gaming. She finds that this economic success for the Miccosukees—in a context where gambling is not always a positive experience for indigenous peoples—has led to increasing hostility from their non-Indian neighbors and particularly the State of Florida. That opposition has taken the form of threats to tribal sovereignty in the courts, but the Miccosukees have been able to retain their self-sufficiency in part because of gaming revenues. The legal playing field of the late twentieth and early twenty-first centuries is much more level than it was in the past.

Finally, Susan A. Wunder surveys recent requirements of educational standards in both the United States and Canada, and she does so with reference to Native American and First Nation historical content. In both nations, educational reform has favored specific learning content in the schools, which means that at state, provincial, and territorial levels, standards have been developed for the teaching of national histories. How indigenous peoples are portrayed in history has been the subject of considerable debate, and she finds that local entities have chosen to construct at least three kinds of standards that treat Native people from vague to specific forms of content. This is an important development for Native Americans and First Nations in how they pursue sovereignty issues.

These five chapters, therefore, stretch the connections between the past and present. As Trina Bridges and Kathy Duncan tell how indigenous peoples today live with their ancestors close to their hearts, the past informs the present. Delgam Uukw sees indigenous people's relatives in their land, and just as one respects one's relatives, one respects one's territory. All must center dynamically on remembering and recognizing the totality of sovereignty rights.

NOTES

1. Gisday Wa and Delgam Uukw, *The Spirit in the Land,* The Opening Statement of the Gitxsan and Wet'sewet'en Hereditary Chiefs in the Supreme Court of British Columbia, May 11, 1987 (Gabriola, BC: Reflections, 1989), 7.

2. Trina Bridges and Kathy Duncan, "Jamestown S'Klallam," in *Native Peoples of the Olympic Peninsula: Who We Are,* ed. Jacilee Wray (Norman: University of Oklahoma Press, 2002), 35.

CHAPTER 7

The Image of Indians in the Imagination of the Early Republic

PETER C. MESSER

T HE IMAGE OF Native Americans played a vital role in attempts of nationalis-
tically minded citizens of the United States to place their newly created nation
on the world stage, and to define the rights, responsibilities, and characteristics of
its citizens. This chapter analyzes how historians manipulated that image in the
early national period in order to define the boundaries and goals of the American
Revolution. When viewed from this perspective, the history of Indian-white relations and what they meant to the new republic underscores a dramatic shift in how
nationalistic Americans understood their revolution. On the one hand, the evolution of how Native Americans were depicted and their relationship with whites
points to the emergence of a more democratic form of politics in the United States.
On the other, it highlights how this shift in political ideas was accompanied by a
retreat from a view of the Revolution as the start of a greater reworking of American society toward a more modest call for individual reform. Americans continued
to remember their struggle for independence as a call for change; but, as the evolution of the image of Indians underscores, this impulse was directed outside the
boundaries of the United States, and the Revolution became the justification for
external empire rather than internal change.

The image of Native Americans in the historical imagination of the early republic offers a particularly useful window through which to view changing attitudes
toward the Revolution. Authors and audiences both viewed understanding the history of the colonies and the Revolution as a vital prerequisite to establishing and
securing a viable republic in the United States.[1] Native Americans played an
important part in these accounts because they offered Americans what literary

scholars would describe as a convenient Other, or group that embodied the opposite of the ideals around which an author believes a community should construct itself.[2] The volatile atmosphere of the first years of the nation's existence magnified both the importance of history and the role the Other would play in recounting it. Many Americans believed that the Revolution would allow the people of the United States to secure their own future, and potentially to redeem all of humankind.

These same people, however, were also concerned that Americans were squandering their opportunity. The result of this combination of conviction and concern was a stream of didactic writing intended to awaken the people of the United States to both the opportunity that lay before them and the very real possibility that they were squandering their chances.[3] In this environment, situating the white Self in relationship to the Indian Other in time became an essential first step to defining what it meant to be an American and to protect the recently established republic.[4] Multiple definitions of what constituted the Indian Other and its relationship to the white Self emerged, and they evolved to reflect the new realities created by ongoing attempts to fashion an effective national identity. This evolving image offers us, in Eve Kornfeld's words, a window into "hidden or forgotten contests of meaning and power, suppressed possibilities and internal contradictions, unforeseen twists and surprising legacies" produced by the new nation's attempt to define itself.[5]

To uncover these lost contests over power, the suppressed possibilities surrounding them, and the surprising legacies they produced, this essay also explores the degree to which historians extended agency to Native Americans. *Agency*, for the purposes of this chapter, is the ability for historical actors to act rationally to shape their world when that rationality is the product of a fundamental similarity between peoples. The degree to which authors granted agency to the Indian Other reveals the degree to which they sought to destabilize the national Self and to raise questions about the people and communities that made up the United States. If Native American actions were incomprehensible, or comprehensible only as the actions of an Other, then descriptions of Indian cultures and their relationships with whites offer either negative examples that readers should avoid or a spectacle of savagery intended to titillate, shock, and amuse.

In all these cases, the ultimate reference point was back toward the readers' own cultures, portraying them as clearly superior and not in need of any fundamental change.

Alternatively, if those same actions reflected a fundamental similarity between the cultures and could be explained as the Indians' rational attempt to shape their worlds, they take on a radically different meaning. Now those actions illustrate the weaknesses of the readers' civilizations and call on them to reconsider the institutions and assumptions around which they have constructed their communities.

Thus, a history of the emergence of the American nation that grants to Native Americans both a degree of similarity and agency would necessarily serve as a call for a radical reconsideration of the meaning of the nation. On the other hand, a history that reinforced the separation between the white Self and the Indian Other would necessarily discourage an extensive reconsideration of the form and goals of the nation as it existed.[6]

JEREMY BELKNAP, DAVID RAMSAY, AND DEFINING
THE REVOLUTION

When two of the first historians of the United States recognized Indian agency, a potentially significant moment occurred in the contest to define the American Revolution. In truth, Jeremy Belknap and David Ramsay were no friends of Native Americans, but they were captivated by the possibility of the Revolution and particularly fearful that the actions of the people would undermine its potential. Their histories, consequently, were intended to direct readers to complete the larger project of reformation and improvement that they believed lay at the heart of the American Revolution.[7] An essential element of that project was to ask their readers to rethink the history of the relationships between Native Americans and whites, and to consider what obligations this revised account placed on the reader as a citizen of the new republic.

Belknap was quite direct in his use of Native Americans to set the tone for his history of the Revolution and the vision it offered. His conscious effort reflected a use of Indian history to tweak white sensibilities.[8] He stated bluntly on the fourth page of his *History of New Hampshire* (1791) that "however fond we may have been of accusing the Indians of treachery and infidelity, it must be confessed that the example was first set them by the Europeans. Had we always treated them with that justice and humanity which our religion inculcates, and our true interest at all times required, we might have lived in as much harmony with them, as with any other people on the globe."[9] In these few sentences, Belknap collapsed the gulf that supposedly separated the white colonists and their Indian neighbors. If they had proven cruel and treacherous, it was not because of an inherent character flaw, but because they learned such behavior from the Europeans. If Indian actions lay in an irrational savagery, it was no different than the colonists' abandonment of their own rational interests and religion in their treatment of the Indians. Both sides, in short, shared the same fundamental flaws, and thus even if the Indians had proven particularly egregious in manifesting those flaws, they ultimately pointed to the similarities rather than the differences between the cultures.

Once Belknap established that Indian wars highlighted the similarity between the two peoples, it was a short step to interpreting their actions as rational efforts to control and shape their world. Belknap began his discussion of New Hampshire's Indian wars with the observation that "it must be acknowledged that human depravity appeared in these unhappy creatures in a most shocking view. . . . Yet, as bad as they were, it will be difficult to find them guilty of any crime which cannot be paralleled among civilized nations." He concluded his discussion of this subject with the observation that "their jealousy and hatred of their English neighbors may easily be accounted for, if we allow them to have the same feelings with ourselves."[10] From there he noted that while "the greater part of the English settlers came hither with religious views, and fairly purchased their lands of the Indians, yet it cannot be denied that some, especially in the eastern parts of New-England, had lucrative views only; and from the beginning used fraudulent methods in trade with them." This combination of "encroachments on their lands, and fraud committed in trade afforded sufficient grounds for a quarrel . . . and kept alive a perpetual jealousy of the like treatment again" and served as a reoccurring justification for conflict.[11] The Indians, Belknap made clear, could not be dismissed as savages because their actions could be explained as the product of rational attempts to order and control their world. Their actions were no worse than those of white Europeans in general, and their hostility toward the colonists arose from recognizable and acceptable motives, a point he underscored by cataloging their very real grievances against the settlers.

When viewed in this context, this account set the stage for a thorough rethinking of American society. If these actions of the Indians had unfortunate consequences for whites, which Belknap's lurid descriptions of the wars made clear, it was as much an indictment of white society as it was of Native Americans. The flaws he identified were not specific to the Indians or their culture, but applied more generally to human nature. If in particular instances he identified particular groups responsible for triggering the conflict, his blanket condemnations made sure that blame could not be so neatly apportioned. Similarly, his acceptance of Indian complaints put readers in the odd position of sympathizing with their reaction, if not their actions, and forcing them to reconsider their own attitudes toward Indians and themselves. He emphasized this point by observing that "it ill becomes us to cherish an inveterate hatred of the unhappy natives. Religion teaches us a better temper, and providence has now put an end to the controversy, by their almost total extirpation."[12] The Indians, at least those in New Hampshire, would not benefit from this broader reconsideration, but that did not absolve Americans of the responsibility to do so. The history of Indian-white relations, as a result, underscored the need for the people of the United States to reconsider themselves and their nation, if they sought truly to reflect their religion and advance their own interests.

David Ramsay also extended to the Indians both similarity and agency as a means of disrupting Americans' conception of themselves and their world and as a call for a continuing revolution.[13] He introduced the topic of Indian-white relations in *The History of the American Revolution* (1789) as part of a broader consideration of whether the discovery of America had been helpful or hurtful to humankind. As a counterpoint to the possibility that Christopher Columbus be considered "among the greatest benefactors of the human race," he proposed that "when we consider the injustice done to the natives . . . the havoc among the first settlers—the slavery of the Africans . . . and the long and bloody wars which [the discovery of America] has occasioned, we behold such a crowd of woes, as excites the apprehension, that the evil has outweighed the good."[14] That Ramsay posed the question as unanswered clearly implied that the American people had considerable work in front of them to prove the legitimacy of their communities despite the successful completion of their revolution against England. That he did so by equating the suffering of the Indians with that of the whites in bloody imperial wars, many of whom, his readers knew, died at the hands of Indians, implied that answering the question would require more than just embracing the assumptions of the past.[15]

Ramsay's subsequent discussions of Indian affairs emphasized two essential points: that white American society was far from virtuous, and that the Revolution demanded a reconsideration of it. As with Belknap, Ramsay extended agency to the Indians to transform the history of hostility between the two peoples into an indictment of white American society. The origins of the bloody conflict on the frontier lay in

> the Europeans [in their] avidity for land, the possession of which is the ultimate objective of human avarice, were prone to encroach on the territories of the Indians, while the Indians from obvious principles of human nature, beheld with concern the descendants of the ancient proprietors circumscribed in their territory by the descendants of those strangers, whom their fathers permitted to reside among them. From these causes and especially the licentious conduct of disorderly individuals of both Indians and white people, there were frequent interruptions of the peace in their contiguous settlements.[16]

Ramsay's emphasis on the obvious principles of human nature as the cause of the Indians' hostile reaction to whites and his assertion that they had chosen to allow Europeans to settle in America bridged the cultural gap between the two peoples and raised questions about white actions. The two were equals, more or less, in contending for control of the continent, and the motives of both needed to be examined before either was condemned. The fact that he singled out European avarice and the disorderly conduct of whites as well as Indians for the particular attention of readers suggests that he wanted his readers to reform their own society rather than simply condemn the Indians.[17] This is a powerful comment in light of his earlier observation that it was exactly these bloody wars that had raised questions about the discovery of America and its subsequent revolution.

Ramsay closed his book with a not-too-subtle blurring of the line between the Indian Other and American Self to make a powerful statement about the unfinished nature of the Revolution. The project of completing the Revolution, he informed readers, required them to

> give over wishing for the extermination of the ancient proprietors of this land. . . . The most enlarged happiness of one people does not require the extermination of another. . . . It would be far more glorious to civilize one tribe of savages than to exterminate or expel a score. . . . Instead of invading their rights, promote their happiness, and give them no reason to curse the folly of their fathers who suffered yours to sit down on a soil which the common Parent of us both had previously assigned to them.[18]

Ramsay's cataloging of the failures of whites with regard to Indians effectively precluded the existence of a fully developed white American Self. The agency he extended to the Indians by arguing that they were endowed by their creator with the same right to property and happiness enjoyed by whites effectively reduced both parties to the same level. That white Americans had not recognized these facts meant that, at the present time, any meaningful distinction between the two peoples, and hence clear definition of what the Revolution had created, was impossible. Ramsay's call to civilize the Indians made it clear that he believed such a distinction should and could exist, and a definitive interpretation of the Revolution thus produced. Since the clearly defined distinctions between the white Self and Indian Other had not yet emerged, however, the process remained very incomplete. Only the emergence of a new society that established and justified those boundaries would legitimate the American Self and complete the Revolution. The 1780s, in other words, was a time to reject the status quo and embark on a larger project of change. Only then, he informed readers, would "the Almighty Ruler of the Universe make the American Revolution an Era in the history of the world, remarkable for the progressive increase of human happiness."[19]

THE JEFFERSONIAN OVERVIEW

Not all authors embraced Belknap's and Ramsay's attitudes toward Indians and their relationship with whites. Other authors used their histories and accounts of Native American culture to reestablish firmly the line between the Self and Other that Belknap and Ramsay had sought to blur. The most influential of these interpretations of Indians and their relationship to whites was Thomas Jefferson's *Notes on the State of Virginia* (1782). Jefferson's primary intent in his discussion of Native

Americans was to rebut European authors who believed that animal and vegetable life was imperfectly formed in America and would corrupt any Europeans who migrated there.[20] With this goal in mind, he defended Indians from suggestions of innate inferiority by arguing that Native American understandings of honor, love, sex, and war were products of their environment rather than indications of inferiority. He also praised their native intelligence and political institutions as a way of comparing Native Americans to the ancients and as an indication of the potential of the New World to improve humankind.[21]

Jefferson filled his account with qualifiers, however, that asked readers to take into account the influence of "nature" on Indians. He compared Native Americans to "the white reduced to the same diet and exercise," and "other barbarous people," and asked that "great allowance be made for those circumstances of their situation."[22] These qualifications, because they accepted the premise that Indian culture was prima facie irreconcilable with Old World ideals, created a gap between the reader and the Indian subject. In Jefferson's interpretation, both the strengths and weaknesses of Indian civilizations marked their essential difference from white civilizations. Moreover, since the decisive influence on Indian culture was nature rather than their own choices, they were transformed into components of a fixed natural system and possessed neither the agency to shape their own lives nor the essential similarities to critique white culture.

It is the fixed nature of the gap between the American Self and Indian Other that distinguishes Jefferson's view of Indians from that of Ramsay and Belknap and, ultimately, indicates the author's desire to contain rather than expand the meaning of the Revolution. The argument that Belknap and Ramsay offered that Indian actions reflected their rational response to their interactions with Europeans created a dynamic history that subjected both cultures to scrutiny and called for change from both. In Jefferson's narrative, and those authors who embraced his style, this possibility was effectively removed. Instead readers were left with a sense of permanent difference that absolved them from thinking of Indians as anything but a static inferior society in contrast to their own equally static superior society. Thus, Indian society in general and its interactions with whites in particular tended to confirm the integrity of the status quo rather than open the call for a reconsideration of society, and in this case, the Revolution that brought it about.

This approach overlapped with Jefferson's political vision in the 1780s. Where Belknap and Ramsay saw a nation in crisis needing drastic reform, Jefferson saw a country with its most important institution, the agrarian character necessary to preserve its civic virtue, intact. His larger aim as a result was not simply to defend America from aspersions from abroad, but to encourage its people to remain true to the principles he believed it already possessed. Consequently, he sought to confine the Revolution to a fairly narrow political scope that discouraged people from rethinking the social and economic institutions of their communities.[23]

Jefferson's account of the transfer of land from the Indians to the whites illustrates the way in which his view of Indian culture promoted continuity rather than change in white culture. Land was central to Jefferson's idea of an agrarian republic. Only if new lands could be acquired could he justify a nation of farmers rather than of shopkeepers, manufacturers, and workers. Thus, to preserve the agricultural character of the nation, he needed a history of land acquisition that naturalized and organized that process. He informed his readers "that the lands of this country were taken from them [Indians] by conquest, is not so general a truth as is supposed. I find in our histories and records repeated proofs of purchase, which cover a considerable part of the lower country; and many more would doubtless be found on further search. The upper country we know has been acquired altogether by purchase made in the most unexceptional form."[24]

Although there is an implied similarity and agency in the process of sale, it is undercut by the absence of any Indians from the account. Unlike in Ramsay, Jefferson's Indians did not choose to sell the land or possess the capability to regret that sale nor, as in Belknap, was the possibility entertained that the sale might not have established the grounds for truly harmonious relations. The result is a picture of harmonious Indian-white relations emerging from a process that does not actually involve any thought about the Indians or the whites. The process of territorial acquisition was reduced to an unproblematic exercise in the transfer of title from one people to another that excused the reader from any responsibility to reconsider the historical processes of territorial expansion or the struggles that had accompanied it. The drive to gain new lands upon which Jefferson built his agrarian vision of the republic was thus a natural and unproblematic element of the past that the present generation could and should embrace.[25]

Jefferson did not abandon the idea that whites had on occasion mistreated Indians, but rather than pointing to the systemic failures identified by Ramsay and Belknap, he apportioned blame to both parties in a way that minimized white culpability.[26] He acknowledged that the Indians of Virginia "were, in the space of 62 years, reduced to about one-third of their former numbers. Spirituous liquors, the small-pox, war, and an abridgement of territory, to a people who lived principally on the spontaneous productions of nature, had committed terrible havock among them."[27] Even though whites played a role in corrupting Indians, the devastation was primarily a product of the weakness of Native American civilization, specifically their dependence on nature. In direct contrast to Belknap and Ramsay, the demise of Indians did not indicate that Americans should reconsider their past and implicitly their present. Instead, this argument reconfirmed the superiority of white civilization even as it offered a clear criticism of those who introduced liquor to Indians and encroached on their land.[28]

THE EMERGING CONSERVATIVE CONSENSUS

In the years following the adoption of the Constitution, a gradual consensus emerged around the Jeffersonian vision of Indians and their relationship with whites, with its clearly defined lines between Self and Other and its conservative interpretation of the Revolution.[29] The emergence of this consensus parallels a larger pattern of change in American society and politics. The political tumult of the 1790s, both in America and in Europe, the perceived spread of deism, growing unrest among servants and slaves, and the actions of land rioters and whiskey rebels convinced many in the new nation of the need to disassociate the struggle for independence with dramatic change.

While concern over the fate of the republic and the quality of its citizens remained, nationalist authors now sought to achieve these ends through a process of reform that focused on bringing particular groups in line with a national consensus.[30] Not surprisingly, the encouragement for drastically rethinking society produced by stressing the similarities between the white Self and Indian Other that granted the latter agency did not sit well with this more conservative agenda. A clearly drawn line between the two, however, could point to specific deficiencies that needed to be addressed when particular groups were identified whose behavior needed to be changed. As a result, the view of the Revolution that emerged in the 1790s stressed not the need to change the nation, but to embrace the economic and social patterns that were deemed most beneficial to the nation. This point could be easily and subtly made by identifying those patterns as the qualities that defined the differences between whites and Indians.

Samuel Williams's *The Natural and Civil History of Vermont* (1794) offers a typical illustration of the approach taken by historians after 1790, and illustrates the potential usefulness of a clearly defined Other to promote reform rather than revolution. While Williams offered a superficially sympathetic interpretation of Indian life, he nonetheless preserved the distance between the two cultures. He praised Indian government, but only because it reflected "the dictates of nature" and was "well adapted to the state and situation of the savage" rather than any of its intrinsically useful meritorious components.[31] With regard to Native American culture as a whole, he found that they had achieved no "intellectual attainment," their "ideas of religion . . . were extremely weak," professed no "reverence and respect to the Deity," and were "very little employed in relieving the distresses, supplying the wants, or gratifying the desires of others." They had developed no "arts," their lifestyle "tended much to retard population growth," they lacked any "fixed settlements," and were engaged in perpetual wars, and Indians "opposed all improvements" proposed by whites. In short, Williams concluded, the "disadvantages far exceeded the advantages" associated with the Indians' way of living, as they "operated with a certain and fatal tendency, to continue man in a state of infancy, weakness, and the greatest imperfection."[32]

Williams's account posited the existence of two different civilizations, one defined by education, art, fixed settlement, the production of surpluses, Christianity, and a reluctance to go to war, and the other by the opposite of these qualities. Those members of white society who had drifted toward the "savage lifestyle" that Williams roundly condemned were called on to recognize its defects and embrace the ideals that defined its "civilized" alternative. The detached description of Indian life only, unlike Ramsay and Belknap who had placed their criticism of Indian culture in the context of its interaction with white culture, made the problem of slippage on the boundaries between the two relatively minor in scope. The United States as a whole, Williams's account made clear, was securely established as the opposite of the Indian Other. A few wayward souls might need to reform, but for the rest little change was needed.

Authors still found fault with white settlers and their treatment of Indians, but more often than not, these criticisms were constructed to cast aspersions on specific groups rather than the population as a whole. John Lendrum's *Concise History of North America* (1795), for example, recounted that "the greatest part of the first adventurers bought of the natives the lands on which they settled," but he cautioned that while some did so "from the purest motives," others bought land "merely from motives of personal security . . . , [an] inference . . . justly drawn from their subsequent quarrels with the natives and encroachment on their grounds."[33] The settlers were composed of two groups, those who purchased the lands out of pure motives and those who did so only out of baser desires. It was on this latter group, rather than on settlers as a whole, upon whom blame for conflict and unsettled relations fell.

Ramsay and Belknap had made similar distinctions, but they offered a slightly different focus. Ramsay, for example, pointed out that "policy as well as justice led the colonists to purchase and pay for what they occupied. This was done in almost every settlement, and they prospered most, who by justice and kindness took the greatest pains to cultivate the good will of the natives."[34] The presumption in Lendrum's case is that past relations offered examples drawn from specific groups that the reader should avoid, whereas in Ramsay's description the past offered a model to which readers should aspire. Ramsay's conclusions also made it clear that it was a model the present generation had abandoned. He underscored this last point by encouraging readers to cultivate the goodwill of Indians, a process that required readers to consider how to modify their aspirations to achieve this end. Lendrum's portrayal of Indians as vendors without feelings or as the victims of disingenuous legal transactions merely admonished readers to remain true to their ideal of contractual stipulations.

Lendrum further discouraged readers from reading about these events and the damage they implicitly caused to Indians as a criticism of American society by absolving whites from the responsibility for the demise of the Native population as a whole. Echoing Jefferson, Lendrum, on the page following his account of the squabbles over land, observed that

> notwithstanding the frequent ruptures of the Indians with the colonies very few, comparatively, have perished by war. Famine, and its companion the pestilence, frequently destroy whole tribes. Their dominant passion for spirituous liquors, in which they have been initiated by whites, proves likewise repugnant to population.[35]

Once again it was the position of the Indians with regard to nature, their inability to provide adequate food, their susceptibility to disease, and their inability to control their passion for drink that explained their demise as a people. To be sure, this last vice had been encouraged by whites, but the fault lay primarily with the Indians' lack of self-control. Lendrum did not ask his readers to consider that they had failed as Christians or that this state of affairs had raised questions about the desirability of the Revolution. Instead, he pointed to the intrinsic weaknesses of Indian civilization and the deficiencies of some members of the white community, and he made no effort to systematically critique the dominant white culture. Indians, and a few whites, were in need of reform, but white civilization itself was sound.[36]

A similar pattern emerged in the work of Hannah Adams, who through her *Summary History of New England* (1794), sought to reawaken the religious sensibilities of the Puritan founders among her readers. Not surprisingly, she focused on the way in which Native American culture, and its interactions with whites, highlighted the centrality of religion to the success of the American project. She recalled that "the interposition of Divine Providence was visible in restraining the savages from destroying their infant settlements."[37] Later, she observed that "when the European adventurers first settled in New England, the [N]atives were a wild and savage people. Their mental powers were wholly uncultivated; their passions strong, impetuous and ungoverned; and they were immersed in the thickest gloom of ignorance and superstition."[38] Where Ramsay and Belknap saw the disappearance of the Indians as evidence of the problematic origins of the colonies, Adams embraced it as evidence of their divinely allotted role in history. Where Ramsay and Belknap had used the supposed savagery of the Indians to raise questions about the civilized qualities of the colonists, she used it to underscore the courage and piety of the founding generation. The Indians had become signposts reminding the colonists of their debts to Divine Providence and of their responsibility to honor the Puritan past.

Adams's borrowings from Belknap's history of the wars in New Hampshire and Maine underscore the degree to which she preferred to use Indians to validate the

American past. She appropriately cited Belknap as the source for her observations that "the fraudulent methods of trading with the [N]atives, and some other injuries, were alleged as the grounds of this war," and that in 1688 "as a pretense for commencing hostilities," the Indians pointed to abuse in trade and refusal to honor agreements relating to trade. In the first passage, however, she substituted "were alleged" for "it cannot be denied." In the second passage, she replaced "pretenses for which were not wanting on their part" with "as a pretense," and she left out entirely Belknap's later observation that "some of these complaints were doubtless well founded." Where Belknap called on his readers to confront the inherent justice of the Indians' complaints, Adams blunted that possibility by altering Belknap's words as to the legitimacy of their grievances. The settlers, of course, were not entirely let off the hook, as she left intact Belknap's admonitions concerning their greed and lack of religion, but having undercut the legitimacy of Indian grievances these descriptions merely drew attention to the behavior of a select group of whites within the confines of traditional assumptions about white superiority and Indian savagery. As with Williams, some Americans might need to reform, but the people as a whole could rest secure in their assumptions about their nation and their culture.[39]

DAVID RAMSAY'S CAPITULATION

The best indication of the triumph of the Jeffersonian view of Indians appears in the evolution of David Ramsay's view of Indian-white relations in his *History of the United States* (1818). Immediately following the war, he had embraced the Revolution as an opportunity to remake America and its people, but as he observed the political turbulence of the 1790s he gradually retreated from this early position. His later work emphasized the need to embrace the peculiarities of the various regions, and he tended to venerate the Revolution and those who brought it about. His readers' attention was gradually directed away from political involvement and toward improving their moral character and economic opportunities. The republican citizen of the nineteenth century, from Ramsay's perspective, should confine his actions to preserving rather than changing his world.[40]

His view of history and Indians, as a result, underwent the same transformation. He retained the passages from his earlier work urging whites to reconsider their treatment of Indians, but now he placed them in the context of a history that made the conduct of the white population much less problematic. Ramsay's first descriptions of Native Americans seemed calculated to alleviate rather than accentuate any worries his readers might have over the disastrous effects of European contact: "With respect to morals, they were miserably depraved. They were liars, thieves, and murderers. They were insidious and revengeful. They in general kept many concubines. . . . They imposed all the drudgery on their women. The men declined labor, of every kind," and they were governed by "an absolute monarchy." Ramsay still lamented the disappearance of the Indians in a later part of the book, but after such descriptions of the Indians, the stigma that originally fell on European settlers lessened considerably. The disappearance of an immoral, sexually incontinent, violent, unchivalrous, lazy, and tyrannous people could hardly be lamented, let alone used to encourage readers to reflect on their own civilizations. No better evidence exists of this revised interpretation than Ramsay's decision to conclude his discussion of the massacre of the Pequots by militia from Plymouth Colony with the observation that "reprehensible as this conduct of the whites must be deemed, beneficial consequences resulted from it."[41]

Ramsay removed all doubts about whether the history of the relationship between whites and Indians was in any way problematic in his description of the changes brought by the Constitution. His conclusion of the section on Indian wars observed that the Indians

> such of them, as are acquainted with past transactions, and can reason on them, must be doubly gratified, in tracing the wars of European nations, for the partition of their country, to their termination in the ejection of them all, and the establishment of an American government, friendly to the best interests of the aborigines, by a new people, who like themselves are natives of the soil.

Whatever defects he had found in the behavior of whites toward Indians in the past, they had been removed by the framers of the new government. The sense of ambiguity that had ended his account of the American Revolution was gone, to be replaced with a certainty about both the specifics of white-Indian relations and that they did not warrant a larger reconsideration of American society.[42]

POPULAR POLITICS AND THE JEFFERSONIAN CONSENSUS

The triumph of the Jeffersonian view of Indians and of white-Indian relations coincided not only with a gradual retreat from the possibilities of Revolution, but also with the rise of popular politics in the United States. The retreat from the radical implications of the Revolution, as a result, cannot simply represent a backlash of the elites against the people at large. The experiences of the 1790s and early 1800s had made it clear that although elites could set the terms of debate, they could not control the direction it took or its outcome. As a result, a complex process of negotiation emerged between the people and their rulers, in which the latter attempted to legitimize their claim to authority by extending certain privileges to the former. The emergence of the Jeffersonian consensus on white-Indian relations highlights this process at work. In particular, it reveals the ways in which racial and cultural differences were used as substitutes for political activism as the defining quality of American citizenship. As a result, more people could be included in the political process, but their ability to alter fundamentally that process and the structure of American society would be limited. In short, the people could become subsumed within the tradition of the Revolution, without embracing a truly revolutionary tradition.[43]

James Sullivan's *History of the District of Maine* (1795) provides an illustration of how this process could unfold from the perspective of a prominent Democratic-Republican politician. Post-Revolutionary Maine was the scene of an increasingly bitter contest between frontier settlers and metropolitan proprietors. Federalist landowners, such as Henry Knox, who claimed to own the land through grants that the land colony and state of Massachusetts had purchased from the Indians, sought to impose their claims on lands occupied by settlers who lacked legal title to it. Knox and others hoped both to derive personal profit from these claims and to improve the moral quality of the nation and frontier by transforming the settlers into industrious farmers, or replacing them with those who were. Not surprisingly, these efforts provoked a running, and occasionally violent contest between the landowners and the self-styled "Liberty Men." These settlers claimed the land by right of occupancy and improvement, and pointed to the tradition of the Revolution to justify their violent resistance to the legally valid claims of proprietors. The controversy gradually ended when, after Jefferson's election, Democratic-Republicans forged a compromise with the settlers in which they paid a nominal fee for legal title to the land and were forced to settle their disagreements with proprietors in court.[44]

When viewed in this light, Sullivan's treatment of Indian-white relations illustrates an early step in the ultimately successful strategy of simultaneously including people in a political system while limiting their power. On the sticky question of who owned the land in North America, he argued that "neither the Europeans nor the Savages had a right to sell the land." Instead he appealed to the "divine precept that man shall cultivate the soil, and carry the mass of matter over which dominion is given to him, to the highest pitch of usefulness to which his powers can raise it."[45] Sullivan's interpretation of the origins of land title in the New World potentially confirmed the Liberty Men's claim to own their land in the face of claims by Federalist proprietors by denying the validity of Indian sale.

This rhetoric, however, also represented a subtle shift away from the discourse of the frontier protestors. Instead of arguing that their grounds for resistance emerged from the principles of the Revolution, he instead proposed that it lay in the cultural gap between the Indian Other and the white American Self. The defining characteristic of the new nation was its members' shared commitment to improving the land as members of an agricultural community, not their commitment to the revolutionary principle that individuals had a right to challenge unjust authority. In addition, he placed a burden on the frontier settlers to continue to replicate the cultural gap between whites and Indians, ensuring that full and equal citizenship would only be granted to those who improved the land and, by extension, themselves. Sullivan, in other words, extended to the Liberty Men equality with their Federalist betters, while limiting their ability to shape their world to meet their expectations by substituting racial and cultural bonds for political activism as the defining characteristic of American citizenship.[46]

Federalist politicians embraced the same strategy in their attempts to define membership in the national community. By the 1790s, despite their reluctance to appeal to the people, the Federalists found themselves needing to build popular support for unpopular policies, such as John Jay's commercial treaty with England and later in the 1790s war with France. In order to accomplish this rather difficult task, they set out to create a greater sense of union among the people that would generate popular support for Federalist policies.[47] The effect was essentially the same as the strategy proposed by Sullivan, to offer a vision of national community that replaced class lines and revolutionary principles with cultural homogeneity as the defining features of American citizenship.

The account of Indian-white relations in Federalist historian George Minot's *A Continuation of the History of the Province of Massachusetts* (1798, 1803) offers a useful illustration of this approach. As other authors had done, Minot started from the assumption that a vast gulf separated whites from their Indian neighbors, and he used that gulf to define his vision of citizenship. As an illustration of this idea, he offered the case of King Philip's War, which had erupted when the Indians realized that

> the combined state of their [European] society, so unlike the loose incorporation of his own national family; their exclusive mode of occupying lands, and enjoying moveable property, so different from the common use made of the one by the savages, and from their furtive ideas concerning the other; their power in war so destructive to their enemies; the rapid increase of their numbers, and their spirit of enterprise and encroachment, exceeding even their increase, must have driven him, from speculative conjectures of such a nature, to a realizing view of the effects which was about to follow their success.[48]

In this account, two distinct communities faced each other across a vast cultural divide and were in competition with one another for control of the continent. The qualities that ensured the eventual triumph of the white community, of course, could have come directly from an editorial in a Federalist newspaper: a strong central government, a vigorous defense of the rights of property holders, a strong military capability, a readily expanding population, and a vigorous spirit of enterprise. Federalism, in Minot's hands, had gone from a set of political ideas to a cultural institution. As such they theoretically became more democratic, that is to say, they were qualities that everyone shared rather than only being appreciated by a natural aristocracy. However, they were also more rigid and less subject to debate; to deny them would be to identify oneself with the savage Other.

Ultimately, Federalism may have failed as a political philosophy and cultural institution, but the fact that both Minot and Sullivan embraced the same approach to accommodating the political aspirations of the populace is a telling commentary on politics in the early republic. Both authors were implicitly expanding the body politic to include a broader cross-section of people and to diminish the gaps between them. Both stressed that most white Americans could make a claim to membership in the national community. At the same time, both authors sought to make dissent more difficult. That is to say, membership in the national community, because it was defined by accepting the stark lines that differentiated the civilized white Self from the savage Indian Other, precluded the possibility of alternative worldviews or even political systems. Of course, neither the Federalists nor the Democratic-Republicans succeeded in establishing complete control over the people and the political system that these accounts imply they sought. They, however, created a powerful hegemonic discourse that shaped nineteenth-century politics by grounding political views in a set of unifying cultural norms that drew clear boundaries between a republican Self and the tyrannical and corrupt Other. It proved a polarizing view of politics that eventually produced the Civil War.[49]

The revolutionary message of dramatic transformation did not disappear entirely from the history of white-Indian relations in the 1790s, but it was dramatically redirected. The complicated relationship between the Native American Other and the white Self that had originally served as a justification for a critical interpretation of white society became a justification for encroaching on the land and culture of Indians. Samuel Williams argued that "in two or three centuries the race must become extinct," but that "it would add to the glory of the United States to make a serious attempt to prevent it." Williams explained that "Cortez and Pizarro performed the most accursed transactions that ever were done by man. And everywhere the Europeans have settled, misery, calamity, and destruction have been entailed on this unhappy race of men." He was also careful to add that the "bitterness of their wars," their "frequent hardships and sufferings," and "a defective population" were to blame. Williams concluded by proposing that white Americans should seek "to impart the blessings of the civil state to Indians whose greatest miseries and misfortunes" came from the "power of civilized nations."[50] The narrative starts from Belknap's and Ramsay's original assumption that white civilization has, in very real ways, failed the Indians. The similarity, however, ends there. Where Belknap and Ramsay had used the tragedy of Indian mistreatment to highlight the similarities between the two people, Williams carefully included references that underscored the persistent differences between the peoples. Rather than being participants in the historical process—agents who learned from whites, reacted to them, and initiated events—Native Americans had become objects of it, hapless victims dependent on whites for their salvation.[51]

Williams's call for conversion echoed the conclusions of both Ramsay and Belknap, but pointed the nation in a very different direction. If "saving the Indians" remained a benchmark to measure the success of the Revolution, it would be measured in the transformation of Others rather than Americans themselves.[52] Paradoxically, the literary device that had begun as a means of encouraging Americans to transform themselves had become a requirement to transform others. In a relatively short time, the history of Indian-white relations had gone from a means to create a revolution committed to remaking America, to a means to create a revolution committed to the expansion of America.[53]

MERCY OTIS WARREN, CONSENSUS DISSENTER

The lone dissenting voice among those historians who chronicled the evolving relationships between Indians and whites was that of Mercy Otis Warren. In *History of the Rise, Progress, and Termination of the American Revolution* (1805), she retained much of the tone and style of Belknap and Ramsay in their original works. She described the early history of conflict between the two peoples as the result of the common human desire to protect their property:

> It is an undoubted truth that both the rude savage and the polished citizen are equally tenacious of their pecuniary acquisitions. . . . Thus the purchase of their commodities, the furs of the forest, and the alienation of their lands for trivial considerations; the assumed superiority of the Europeans; their knowledge of arts and war, and perhaps their supercilious deportment towards the aborigines might awaken in them just fears of extermination. Nor is it strange that the natural principle of self-defense operated strongly in their minds, and urged them to hostilities that often reduced the young colonies to the utmost danger and distress.[54]

When Warren turned her attention to those who justified harsh treatment for the Indians based on their cruelty, she remarked that Native Americans acted "from the same impulse that in human nature prompts all mankind, whether civilized or savage, to resist the invaders of his territory." She cautioned western settlers that "the voice of heaven, and their natural boundaries forbid these encroachments on the naked forester, content with the produce of nature in his own grounds, and the game that plays in his own wild woods, which his ancestors have possessed from time immemorial." Finally, Warren concluded that since

> there is no difference in the moral or intellectual capacity of nations, but what arises from adventitious circumstances . . . it is to be hoped that humanity will teach Americans of a fairer complexion to use the most strenuous efforts to instruct them in arts, manufactures, morals, and religion, instead of aiming to their extermination.[55]

In Warren's hands the dominant narrative of white-Indian relations lay in tatters. The Indians were no more to blame for the early wars than the colonists who cheated them. Moreover, their actions arose from their essential humanity, and if settlers found fault with Indians, then they also found it with themselves. The movement westward was a violation of divine precepts, rather than the completion of a divine mandate. As a partial concession to conventional wisdom, she urged the people of the United States to lift Indians from their own weaknesses, but she carefully reminded readers that these arose from "adventitious" rather than inherent circumstances. Her fellow citizens, it seems, were not so much better than Native Americans as they were luckier. The Revolution, at least as it related to the human character, was far from complete, and judging by her account of Indian-white relations, the people of the United States needed to embark on a protracted journey of self-examination and even policy reconsideration to complete it.

It is important to note that these observations came from an author who was particularly dissatisfied with the Revolution and its outcome. Warren saw the ratification of the Constitution and the emergence of the Society of the Cincinnati as signs of the imminent destruction of the republic. These fears were coupled with a persistent belief in a natural aristocracy that was being subverted by the will of a feckless people, a sentiment compounded by her own family's loss of political power. Contrary to most Americans, she did not accept the power of law to preserve the republic in the absence of a virtuous population, which she identified in decidedly moral and pious terms. She was, in her private correspondence, quite hopeful about the ultimate fate of the Revolution, but her public declarations were intended to ensure that the project of reformation in manners and character that had begun would be completed.[56]

CONCLUSION

For those who had a truly revolutionary interpretation of American history, it seems, a problematic presentation of Native Americans was integral to their attempt to create an active citizenry and enshrine a legacy of continued improvement. For these authors, Indians were rational actors who were often wronged by the unbecoming behaviors of European colonists. Their ferocious attacks on the settlers were learned responses and perhaps even justified considering the circumstances. While Native societies and governments may have been inherently flawed, they were not innately savage or inferior. The Revolution, if extended throughout American social structures, could atone for colonial indiscretions by protecting Indian rights and including Natives within the body politic. Such graciousness would also strengthen the character of the young republic and its citizens as spreading the principles of equality and justice across the land should be the true purpose of any revolution.

That so few echoed the words of Belknap, Ramsay, and Warren underscores the degree to which, by the nineteenth century, Americans, both elite and nonelite, were willing to put that revolutionary vision aside. Recasting Indians as objects rather than actors was an important step in the movement toward a stable, conservative republic. The backbone of this system was a body politic that agreed on the essential mission of the nation and celebrated its heritage. Native American resistance to colonial occupation was cast as a series of savage acts. Strengthening the otherness of Indians reified the shared history and common future of white Americans. The national consensus, then, became a story of common cause in spreading a perfect republican order rather than restructuring social relationships through revolutionary and inclusive principles.

NOTES

1. A considerable historiography exists on the use of history both to promote nationalism in general and particular political agendas in the period following the Revolution. Ralph N. Miller, "American Nationalism as a Theory of Nature," *William and Mary Quarterly* 3d ser., 12 (January 1955), 74–95; Sidney Kaplan, "*The History of New Hampshire:* Jeremy Belknap as Literary Craftsman," *William and Mary Quarterly* 3d ser., 21 (January 1964), 18–39; Arthur Shaffer, *The Politics of History: Writing the History of the American Revolution, 1783–1815* (Chicago: Precedent Publishing, 1975); William Raymond Smith, *History as Argument: Three Patriot Historians of the American Revolution* (The Hague: Mouton, 1966); Charles E. Modlin, "The Loyalists Reply," in *American Literature, 1764–1789: The Revolutionary Years,* ed. Everett Emerson (Madison: University of Wisconsin Press, 1977), 59–71; Cecilia Tichi, "Worried Celebrants of the American Revolution," in *American Literature, 1764–1789: The Revolutionary Years,* ed. Everett Emerson, 275–91; Lester Cohen, *The Revolutionary Histories: Contemporary Narratives of the American Revolution* (Ithaca: Cornell University Press, 1980); Lawrence Leder, ed., *Colonial Legacy,* 4 vols. (New York: Harper & Row, [1971] 1973).

2. Jill Lepore, *In the Name of War: King Philip's War and the Origins of American Identity*

(New York: Alfred Knopf, 1998); Robert F. Berkhofer, Jr., *The White Man's Indian: Images of the American Indian from Columbus to the Present* (New York: Alfred Knopf, 1978); Eve Kornfeld, "Encountering 'The Other': American Intellectuals and Indians in the 1790s," *The William and Mary Quarterly* 3d ser., 52 (July 1995), 287–314; Gary B. Nash, "The Image of the Indian in the Southern Colonial Mind," *William and Mary Quarterly* 3d ser., 29 (April 1972), 197–230; Roy Harvey Pearce, *The Savages of America: A Study of the Indian and the Idea of Civilization,* rev. ed. (Baltimore: Johns Hopkins University Press, 1965); Bernard W. Sheehan, *Seeds of Extinction: Jeffersonian Philanthropy and the American Indians* (Chapel Hill: University of North Carolina Press, 1973); Richard Slotkin, *Regeneration through Violence: The Mythology of the American Frontier, 1600–1860* (Middletown, CT: Wesleyan University Press, 1973); Carroll Smith-Rosenberg, "Dis-Covering the Subject of the 'Great Constitutional Discussion, 1786–1789,'" *Journal of American History* 79 (December 1992), 841–73, have all argued, to various degrees, that the images of Native Americans recorded by eighteenth-century authors offer a useful window into how these Americans saw their own society. For a discussion of how nationalism rests on a common identity among citizens, see Benedict Anderson, *Imagined Communities: Reflections on the Origin and Spread of Nationalism,* rev. ext. ed. (New York: Verso, 1991). For discussions of how a dominant culture manipulates images of subordinate or less powerful groups in order to enhance its own stature and solidify its authority, see Edward Said, *Culture and Imperialism* (New York: Alfred Knopf, 1993); Homi K. Bhabha, ed., *Nation and Narration* (London: Routledge, 1990); and James Clifford, *Writing Culture: The Poetics and Politics of Ethnography* (Berkeley: University of California Press, 1986).

3. Jack P. Greene, *The Intellectual Construction of America: Exceptionalism and Identity from 1492 to 1800* (Chapel Hill: University of North Carolina Press, 1993); Tichi, "Worried Celebrants of the American Revolution," 275–91; Lawrence J. Friedman, *Inventors of the Promised Land* (New York: Knopf, 1975); Robert Lawson-Peebles, *Landscape and Written Expression in Revolutionary America: The World Turned Upside Down* (Cambridge: Cambridge University Press, 1988); Ruth Bloch, *Visionary Republic: Millennial Themes in American Thought, 1756–1800* (Cambridge: Cambridge University Press, 1985); Peter Messer, "From Revolutionary History to a History of Revolution: David Ramsay and the American Revolution," *Journal of the Early Republic* 22 (Summer 2002), 205–33.

4. Kornfeld, "Encountering 'The Other,'" 287.

5. Ibid.

6. In literary theory, this process is referred to as negation, in which the author attempts to persuade a reader by placing critical ideas in a familiar context. In the absence of the familiar context or identification, the critique loses its meaning and the author the power to persuade. Wolfgang Iser, *The Act of Reading: A Theory of Response* (Baltimore: Johns Hopkins University Press, 1978); Wolfgang Iser, *The Implied Reader: Patterns of Communication in Prose Fiction from Bunyan to Beckett* (Baltimore: Johns Hopkins University Press, 1974); and Roland Barthes, *Writing Degree Zero,* trans. Annette Lawyers and Colin Smith, with a preface by Susan Sontag (New York: Hill and Wang, 1968). In the context of the role of the self and other, in this case, the relationship between whites and Indians within the histories, it is the proposition that Indians share attributes with whites, and that they possess agency even

while possessing the characteristics of the other that creates the clash between familiar and unfamiliar around which a critique of society can emerge. S.P. Monhaty, "Us and Them: On the Philosophical Bases of Political Criticism," *Yale Journal of Criticism* 2 (Spring 1989), 1–31; Michel Foucault, "Nietzsche, Genealogy and History," in *Language, Counter-Memory, Practice: Selected Essays and Interviews,* trans. Donald F. Bouchard and Sherry Simon, with an introduction by Donald F. Bouchard (Ithaca, NY: Cornell University Press, 1977), 139–64.

7. Kaplan, *"The History of New Hampshire,"* 18–39; Arthur Shaffer, *To Be an American: David Ramsay and the Making of the American Consciousness* (Columbia: University of South Carolina Press, 1991), 71–104; Friedman, *Inventors of the Promised Land,* 17–30.

8. Kaplan, *"The History of New Hampshire,"* 33.

9. Jeremy Belknap, *History of New Hampshire,* 3 vols. (New York: Arno Press, [1791] 1972), 1:4.

10. Ibid., 1:125, 127.

11. Ibid., 1:128. See also 1:33, 2:47.

12. Ibid., 1:124.

13. Ramsay's unusually generous treatment of Indians is discussed by Jack P. Greene, *The Intellectual Construction of America: Exceptionalism and Identity from 1492 to 1800* (Chapel Hill: University of North Carolina Press, 1993), 190.

14. David Ramsay, *The History of the American Revolution,* 2 vols., ed. Lester Cohen (Indianapolis: Liberty Classics, [1789] 1990), 1:14.

15. Despite a trend among historians to revise their understanding of Indian culture that began in the early eighteenth century when the question turned to the demise of Native Americans, the general assumption remained that it was, at best, a lamentable inevitability and no cause for concern. On the reconsideration of Indian culture, see Berkhofer, *The White Man's Indian,* 35; Sheehan, *Seeds of Extinction,* 5, 121; Slotkin, *Regeneration through Violence,* 217; and Nash, "The Image of the Indian," 197–230. On the persistence of the view of Indians as deserving their fate, see Nash, "The Image of the Indian," 224, 229; and Lepore, *In the Name of War,* 173–90.

16. Ramsay, *History of the American Revolution,* 2:464.

17. Ramsay was extremely skeptical of the quality of life on the frontier, complaining to Thomas Jefferson in 1786 that "our backcountry people are as much savage as the Cherokees. I believe in opposition to Dr. Robertson that were it not for the commercial cities on the sea coast even the use of the plough far to the westward would be forgotten." Ramsay to Jefferson, May 3, 1786, "David Ramsay, 1749–1815, Selections from His Writings," in *Transactions of the American Philosophical Society* (Philadelphia: The Society, 1965), 55:4.

18. Ramsay, *History of the American Revolution,* 2:666.

19. Ibid., 2:267.

20. Anthony F.C. Wallace, *Jefferson and the Indians: The Tragic Fate of the First Americans* (Cambridge: Belknap Press of Harvard University Press, 1999), 76; and Miller, "American Nationalism," 83; On the importance of this debate for American intellectuals as a whole, see Miller, "American Nationalism," 74–95; Berkhofer, *The White Man's Indian,* 42–43; Sheehan, *Seeds of Extinction,* 66–88; Pearce, *Savages of America,* 77; Slotkin, *Regeneration*

through Violence, 205; and Lawson-Peebles, *Landscape and Written Expression,* 32.

21. Thomas Jefferson, *Notes on the State of Virginia: Edited with an Introduction by William Peden* (Chapel Hill and Williamsburg: Institute for Early American History and Culture, 1955), 59–60, 93.

22. Ibid., 59, 60, 62.

23. Significantly, Jefferson's most unqualified praise of the Indians referred to their political institutions, the effectiveness of which raised the real possibility that it was European government that "submits man to the greatest evil." Ibid., 93. On Jefferson's desire to preserve the distinctive agrarian nature of the American republic as the *sine qua non* of the Revolution, see Drew McCoy, *The Elusive Republic: Political Economy in Jeffersonian America* (Chapel Hill: University of North Carolina Press, 1980); Myra Jehlen, *American Incarnation: The Individual, the Nation, and the Continent* (Cambridge, MA: Harvard University Press, 1986).

24. Jefferson, *Notes on the State of Virginia,* 96.

25. On Jefferson's desire to use Indian land to fix permanently the agrarian nature of the republic, see Wallace, *Jefferson and the Indians,* 206–7.

26. On Jefferson's reluctance to condemn white treatment of Indians except in the most egregious cases, see ibid., 191–205.

27. Jefferson, *Notes on the State of Virginia,* 96.

28. This interpretation reflects Jefferson's belief that those Native peoples who resisted American expansion were destined for extinction. Wallace, *Jefferson and the Indians,* 79.

29. Two works in particular, John Lendrum, *A Concise and Impartial History of the American Revolution, to which is Prefixed a General History of North and South America,* 2 vols. (Boston: I. Thomas and E.T. Andrews, 1795), and Jedidiah Morse, *History of America in Two Books,* 2nd ed. (Philadelphia: Thomas Dobson, 1795), relied heavily on Jefferson and reprinted several passages verbatim; Miller, "American Nationalism," 86. Samuel Williams's *Natural and Civil History of Vermont* (Walpole, NH: Isiah Thomas and David Carlisle Jun, 1794) was also deeply influenced by Jefferson's work. Ralph Miller, "Samuel Williams' 'History of Vermont,'" *New England Quarterly* 22 (March 1949), 78.

30. On the general conservative drift of American attitudes toward citizenship, see McCoy, *The Elusive Republic*; Fawn M. Brodie, *Thomas Jefferson: An Intimate Biography* (New York: Norton, 1974); Joseph Ellis, *American Sphinx: The Character of Thomas Jefferson* (New York: Alfred Knopf, 1997); Leonard W. Levy, *Jefferson and Civil Liberties: The Darker Side* (Cambridge: Belknap Press of Harvard University Press, 1963); Steven Watts, *The Republic Reborn: War and the Making of Liberal America, 1790–1820* (Baltimore: Johns Hopkins University Press, 1987); Sean Wilentz, "Society, Politics, and the Market Revolution," in *The New American History,* ed. Eric Foner (Philadelphia: Temple University Press, 1990), 51–73; and Joyce Appleby, "New Cultural Heroes in the Early National Period," in *The Culture of the Market; Historical Essays,* ed. Thomas L. Haskell and Richard Teichgraeber III (New York: Cambridge University Press, 1993), 163–88. See also Ruth Bloch, "Religion, Literary Sentimentalism, and Popular Revolutionary Ideology," in *Religion in a Revo-*

lutionary Age, ed. Ronald Hoffman and Peter Albert (Charlottesville: University of Virginia Press, 1994), 308–32; and Paul E. Johnson, *Shopkeepers' Millennium: Society and Revivals in Rochester, New York, 1815–1837* (New York: Hill and Wang, 1978).

31. Williams, *Natural and Civil History of Vermont,* 141. More generally, see ibid., 133–70.

32. Ibid., 172, 173, 175, 176–77, 179, 180, 181, 184–85, 186. A similar summary of Indian life can be found in Lendrum, *A Concise and Impartial History,* 1:18–46; Morse, *History of America,* 1:18–110; and James Sullivan, *History of the District of Maine* (Boston: I. Thomas and E.T. Andrews, 1795), 81–101.

33. Lendrum, *A Concise and Impartial History,* 1:219.

34. Ramsay, *History of the American Revolution,* 1:17.

35. Lendrum, *A Concise and Impartial History,* 1:220.

36. In this context, Lendrum could even recapitulate Belknap's account of the origins of King Philip's War without implying any systematic critique of American life. Lendrum, *A Concise and Impartial History,* 1:161.

37. Hannah Adams, *Summary History of New England from the First Settlement at Plymouth to the Acceptance of the Federal Constitution* (Dedham, MA: H. Mann and J.H. Adams, 1799), 68.

38. Ibid., 81.

39. Ibid., 128, 150, 153, 173; Belknap, *History of New Hampshire,* 1:128; 1:243–44.

40. Shaffer, *Politics of History,* 194, 205, 231.

41. David Ramsay, *History of the United States from Their First Settlement as English Colonies in 1607 to the Year 1808,* 3 vols. (Philadelphia: M. Carey & Son, 1818), 1:42, 1:85. Ramsay used almost identical language following his account of the war of extirpation that followed the 1622 Indian attack in Virginia. Ibid., 1:56.

42. Ibid., 1:319.

43. The idea of the emergence of popular politics as part of a process of negotiation in which neither elite nor popular forces triumphed, but forged a compromise represents a growing trend in the historiography of the early republic. Particularly useful articulations of this thesis appear in Christopher Grasso, *A Speaking Aristocracy: Transforming Public Discourse in Eighteenth-Century Connecticut* (Chapel Hill, NC, and Williamsburg, VA: Institute for Early American History and Culture, 1999); Alan Taylor, *Liberty Men and Great Proprietors: The Revolutionary Settlement on the Maine Frontier, 1760–1820* (Chapel Hill, NC, and Williamsburg, VA: Institute for Early American History and Culture, 1990); and Alfred F. Young, ed., "Afterword: How Radical Was the American Revolution," *Beyond the American Revolution: Explorations in the History of America* (DeKalb: Northern Illinois University Press, 1991), 317–64.

44. This abbreviated summary of the controversy in Maine comes from Taylor, *Liberty Men and Great Proprietors.*

45. Sullivan, *History of the District of Maine,* 129–30.

46. Sullivan was an adamant opponent of organized opposition to duly constituted authority. He warned protesters in Middlesex County, Massachusetts, sympathetic to the Shays Rebellion in 1786, that they should "be assured that by your turbulence and sedition

you are preparing a yoke for your own necks, and heaping millions of burdens upon those you now think to grievous to be bourne." Similarly, he wrote to Samuel Adams in October 1786 that "I wish the idea of a county convention being a legal body could be exploded." At the same time, he preached moderation toward protestors, suggesting in the wake of Shays Rebellion that "the late unhappy commotions do not fix the people as ungovernable. They arose from an unfortunate concurrence of circumstances . . . which under free institutions, are attended by consequences peculiarly disagreeable." Thomas C. Amory, *The Life of James Sullivan with Selections from His Writings,* 2 vols. (Boston: Phillips, Sampson and Co., 1859), 1:194, 197, 206.

47. David Waldstreicher, *In the Midst of Perpetual Fetes: The Making of American Nationalism, 1776–1820* (Chapel Hill, NC, and Williamsburg, VA: Institute for Early American History and Culture, 1997), 144, 165. Jedidiah Morse, author of *The History of America in Two Books,* was also closely affiliated with the Federalist Party.

48. George Richards Minot, *A Continuation of the History of the Province of Massachusetts Bay from the Year 1748,* 2 vols. (Boston: Manning and Loring, 1798), 1:67–68.

49. A brief summary of the assumptions of the dominant political parties of the nineteenth century illustrates this point. Jacksonians defined legitimate political discussion as the conflict between agrarian and industrial interests to the exclusion of any consideration of sectional interests such as slavery. Republicans reduced political debate to a discussion of the need to combat the slave power and create an expanding economy that provided ample opportunity for wage labor and the eventual ownership of land. Southern Democrats understood political competence as the defense of hierarchies that defended an ideal of individual autonomy and self-sufficiency. In all of these cases, all who embraced these views were welcome to participate, while those who rejected them were deemed enemies of the republic and a threat to the good order of the community. See Harry L. Watson, *Liberty and Power: The Politics of Jacksonian America* (New York: Hill and Wang, 1990); Eric Foner, *Free Soil, Free Labor, Free Men: The Ideology of the Republican Party before the Civil War* (New York: Oxford University Press, 1970); and Stephanie McCurry, *Masters of Small Worlds: Yeoman Households, Gender Relations, and the Political Culture of the Antebellum South Carolina Low Country* (New York: Oxford University Press, 1995).

50. Williams, *Natural and Civil History of Vermont,* 209.

51. Williams, for example, included European examples of cruelty, but never suggested, as Belknap did, that the Indians had learned from these examples. Ibid., 161–62.

52. Sheehan, *Seeds of Extinction,* 121; Berkhofer, *The White Man's Indian,* 144.

53. Lepore, *In the Name of War,* 8–12; Gregory H. Nobles, *American Frontiers: Cultural Encounters and Continental Conquest* (New York: Hill & Wang, 1997), 115–18; James E. Lewis, Jr., *The American Union and the Problem of Neighborhood: The United States and the Collapse of the Spanish Empire, 1783–1829* (Chapel Hill: University of North Carolina Press, 1998), 12–40.

54. Mercy Otis Warren, *History of the Rise, Progress, and Termination of the American Revolution,* 3 vols. (Boston: Manning and Loring, 1805), 1:19.

55. Ibid., 2:120–23.

56. These views are summarized from Lester Cohen, "Explaining the Revolution: Ideology and Ethics in Mercy Otis Warren's Historical Theory," *William and Mary Quarterly* 3rd ser., 37, no. 2 (April 1980), 200–218; and Rosemarie Zagarri, *A Woman's Dilemma: Mercy Otis Warren and the American Revolution* (Wheeling, IL: Harlan Davidson, 1995).

CHAPTER 8

Perspectives on the Lakota Ghost Dance of 1890

RANI-HENRIK ANDERSSON

In THE 1880s, a revitalization movement known as the "ghost dance" swept across the North American Plains and galvanized more than thirty Indian nations. The ghost dance was basically a religious movement that took many forms as it passed from one tribe to another, yet its core message of a return to the old ways and a future of peace and happiness remained the same. The doctrine of the ghost dance gave new hope to Indians who had been forced to relinquish both their lands and traditional ways of living. Unfortunately, the U.S. Army opened fire on Lakotas who had left their reservation and were participating in the ghost dance in December 1890, resulting in what would become known as the Wounded Knee Massacre.[1]

The Lakota ghost dance can be understood from several perspectives. A growing number of studies in the United States suggest multidimensional interpretations.[2] This discussion will focus on five groups: the U.S. Army, the Congress, Indian agents, the press, and the Lakotas. In order to demonstrate how differently these groups perceived of the ghost dance, several examples are presented here in this brief chapter.[3] By describing how each group exercised its own voice and viewpoint, the ghost dance is then placed in a larger perspective, and it is also more fully understood through a multi-ethnohistorical approach.

LAKOTA RESPONSES TO THE GHOST DANCE

Understanding the ghost dance from a Lakota point of view requires a careful look at what was familiar to Lakotas at that time. The ghost dance must be viewed within the context of Lakota culture. In most ways, Lakota society and culture, including the Lakota ghost dance, constitute a continuation of old Lakota traditions in slightly different forms. The ghost dance then should not be considered a completely new religion or doctrine.[4] Many historians have failed to see the Lakota ghost dance as a cultural phenomenon or within old Lakota traditions, treating it instead as a new political, military, or perhaps "religious-political" movement.[5] Professor Raymond J. DeMallie, however, has noted that every attempt to understand the history of the Lakota people must start with an understanding of their culture. He states further that "[i]f we are to understand history as lived reality, it is essential to understand the perspectives of the actors involved. It is equally important to understand the distinctive features of historical narrative from the perspective of the groups whose past we are investigating."[6] These words are guidelines fundamental to the construction of this essay.

During the year of 1889, the Lakotas as well as many other Indian nations sent delegates to meet with an Indian Messiah in Nevada, a Paiute called Wovoka. The Messiah told the delegates about many miracles and the coming of a new world where no whites would exist. Wovoka explained to his visitors that they could meet the spirits of their dead and that eventually all dead Indians would be resurrected. He also foretold that the buffalo, which had almost been killed to extinction by 1890, would return. Lakota delegates were excited by this news, and in the spring of 1890 they brought this message of hope back to their people.[7]

Contemporary white commentary about the Lakota ghost dance started in April 1890 when newspapers reported that the Lakotas were planning an outbreak, holding large conferences, and dancing war dances. Whites also heard that Indians were expecting to meet with some terrible ghosts of the dead and thus called the new religion by the name "Ghost Dance."[8] Lakotas, however, called it by the name *wanagi wachipi kin,* which is best translated as "spirit dance," since the word *wanagi* refers specifically to a spirit that had once been in a living human. For Lakotas, spirits were normal things, a part of their everyday life. A person could meet the spirits of the dead, for example, in a vision or in the spirit world. Although *wanagi* could also be translated as "ghost," in the *wanagi wachipi* it probably referred to the spirits of those dead relatives you could meet in a vision during a ceremony. In the context of the ghost dance, a special word, *wanagiyatapi,* was used to describe visits to the spirit world. So here is the first confusion. The basic idea of meeting the spirits of the departed was a natural part of Lakota life, and meeting the spirits in the ceremony of *wanagi wachipi kin* was equally natural. For whites, these ideas were unnatural and frightening and perhaps best expressed in an English word—"barbarism."[9]

Understanding this then and even now has been difficult. People who do not believe one can meet with spirits or resurrect the dead perceived of the ghost dance as something strange that had to be explained. James Mooney, for example, in his classical study of the ghost dance, maintained that the Lakota delegates had to be under "an unexplained psychological influence" when they told these strange stories of Wovoka and his beliefs to their people. Some historians, even in recent years, have tried to explain the stories by discussing the delegates' personal ambitions. According to these historians, delegates told these stories in order to gain more influence among their people.[10] This argument, however, is not insightful. How could these men gain more influence among their people, if the stories really were so strange or unbelievable to the Lakotas? Would not the people have rather considered them to be liars or crazy men as the whites did?

The stories, of course, were not strange to the Lakotas at all. For example, there is in Lakota culture a story about the resurrection of a buffalo. For whites, historians as well as contemporaries, the idea of the resurrection of a dead buffalo was absurd. Lakotas, however, believed that buffalos and human beings were relatives. Both originated from beneath the earth and would eventually go back under the earth. It was only natural then that the buffalo could once again resurface, maybe even with the help of a new messiah.[11]

The ghost dance among the Lakotas, therefore, was very much compatible with their traditional system of beliefs; and for people who did not share the same viewpoints, the power of the ghost dance is difficult to comprehend. Furthermore, when changes in the ghost dance are analyzed, it must be taken into account that there was never any single doctrinal form of religion in the traditional Lakota belief system. As anthropologist Raymond J. DeMallie has noted,

> Each individual man formulated a system of belief by and for himself. There was no standardized theology, no dogmatic body of belief. Basic and fundamental concepts were universally shared, but specific knowledge of the spirits was not shared beyond a small number of holy men. Through individual experience every man had the opportunity to contribute to and resynthesize the general body of knowledge that constituted Lakota belief.[12]

The traditional Lakota system of belief, thus, was constantly changing and adapting to new circumstances, and the Lakota ghost dance followed this same pattern. There also was no single universal doctrinal teaching in the Lakota ghost dance. It too was constantly changing through personal experiences. This can already be seen in the first messages the delegates visiting Wovoka brought back with them; but it is even more obvious in later phases, when individual trances and visions started to influence and alter the original ghost dance ceremony.[13] The actual ghost dance as taught by Wovoka was quite simple. People holding each other by hands danced in a circle and sang. The Lakotas, however, made the ceremony somewhat more complicated. They danced around a pole and purified themselves in a sweat lodge. These, of course, were modifications, which helped the Lakotas to associate the ghost dance with their old traditions. The sacred pole for the ghost dance was the same as used in the Sun Dance, and the sweat lodge was one of the most sacred of Lakota traditions.[14]

Wovoka's message of hope, then, was neatly inserted into the Lakota worldview, and many Lakotas enthusiastically participated in ghost dances. The return of buffalos through ceremony was in perfect harmony with their conceptions of supernatural forces, and their dire circumstances in the 1880s made Indian resurrection extremely attractive. While ghost dancing was a peaceful activity, it appeared strange to most non-Indians and was, therefore, considered threatening.

WHITE RESPONSES TO THE LAKOTA GHOST DANCE

Few white Americans in the 1880s understood the nature of the ghost dance. Those who shaped public opinion and public policy did little to discover what the Lakotas were actually doing and why they were doing it. Reporters, congressmen, and some military officers were equally shrouded in ignorance.

White newspapers reported the ghost dance quite differently. One paper wrote that Indians were dancing around a pole, which was covered with blood, and there were pieces of human flesh hanging off the tree. Black Elk, one of the medicine men very much involved with the ghost dance, however, explains that the sacred tree was often painted with red paint, which was the sacred color of the sun and also the sacred color of the ghost dance. The things hanging off the tree were probably offerings like tobacco bags or stuffed animals. Another newspaper wrote that an eyewitness had seen how Indians thought one man had been transformed into a buffalo and then Indians ate the man-buffalo. It was quite common that a human could act the role of a buffalo, or some other animal, in traditional Lakota religious ceremonies. It was therefore, not strange if a person was believed to be a buffalo during the ghost dance either. Clearly, newspaper publishers played an important role in miseducating their readers about the ghost dance.[15]

These newspaper accounts as well as other rumors about the Lakotas who were engaging in a "wild dance" caused several responses in the U.S. Congress. Two congressmen believed that Indians were starving and should be fed and clothed. The Indians were dancing a dance of starvation and death, voiced Senator Daniel W. Voorhees from Indiana. The most notable reactions in the Congress came from Senator Henry L. Dawes, who at the time chaired the Senate Committee on Indian Affairs and was considered an expert on Indian policy. Senator Dawes condemned the ghost dance fiercely. He thought that Indians were planning an outbreak. According to him, the Lakotas were doing well on their reservations. Only those who followed their fanatical leaders, Sitting Bull and Red Cloud, to the "warpath" were suffering from the want of food. The senator demanded that ghost dancing be stopped and order restored. Senator Dawes believed that altogether more that 6,000 well-armed Lakota warriors were ready to launch a major attack against white settlements. This comment came a few days after Senator Dawes himself had pointed out that the Lakotas did not even have more than 5,000 grown-up males, including old men and teenage boys. Senator Gilbert A. Pierce from the new state of North Dakota supported Senator Dawes. Senator Pierce also claimed that Indians who danced were at war with the United States. These comments are remarkable, since at the time these men were speaking, Indians interested in the ghost dance had not fired a single shot toward whites even though they had been suffering from famine for at least two years.[16]

These senators basically shared the same opinion about the ghost dance, but from different perspectives. Senator Dawes had been formulating the current Indian policy pursued by the U.S. government since 1887 when he authored the General Allotment Act, and for him ghost-dancing Lakotas signified the failure of this policy. Lakotas, to Dawes, were slipping back to savagery. Senator Pierce, on the other hand, represented people who, as Senator Voorhees of Indiana pointed out, lived close to Lakota lands and were hungrily eyeing the remaining reservation acreage. A nice little war for these constituents might open up these lands for settlement as had happened many times previously in North America.[17]

A third reaction in the Congress came from the hypocritical majority who pretended that they had never heard about any problems among the Lakotas and who were astonished by the news that the Indians were starving. In the end, the Congress was more worried about other policies it was pursuing and their legality, rather than resolving the issues of the Lakotas. Congress, however, was unanimous about one thing: The ghost dance was a serious phenomenon, and it had to be stopped, even by using armed force.[18]

The decision to use force against the ghost-dancing Lakotas was made in November 1890. The U.S. Army under the command of Major-General Nelson A. Miles was sent to western Nebraska. The general opinion held by many of the Army officers at that time was that there was nothing warlike happening on the Lakota reservations. Most officers on location did not even understand why they were sent there in the first place. Brigadier General John R. Brooke, in command of the troops on the field, noted several times that the ghost dancers planned no uprising, and the best way to deal with the Indians was to feed them and wait for a peaceful end to the ghost dancing.[19] In fact, only General Miles was of the opinion that a major Indian war was at hand.

Why General Miles dismissed all the information from his fellow officers cannot be fully explained, but political ambitions might have played a role. He contradicted all the reports indicating that a peaceful solution could occur, and instead he explained to the media that the Indians were planning an uprising far greater than those led previously by Pontiac or Tecumseh. At least once he told reporters that there could be up to 27,000 Indians preparing for war.[20] Interestingly, already during the campaign of 1890–1891, accusations had been made by some army officers and by the public that General Miles was using the Indian troubles to boost his political aspirations.[21] Whether his reasons were political, whether he wanted more power for the Army, or whether he really believed that an Indian uprising of extreme proportions was going to occur is a question without a definitive answer. The fact, however, is that following these "alarmist" reports, the military was put in full control of the Lakota reservations, and Indian agents were ordered to follow military officers' orders.[22]

Unfortunately for the Lakotas, misinformation and fear of the ghost dance were widespread among whites. Newspapers published stories of demonic activities, congressmen speculated about the tolls of starvation and the Lakotas' penchant for "savagery," and the Army fretted about another pan-Indian uprising. In such a climate, drastic and unfortunate events were sure to transpire.

FIRST BLOOD AND SURRENDER

The first major casualty of the ghost dance was Hunkpapa medicine man Sitting Bull. The facts surrounding Sitting Bull's death have been told many times. Generally, historians have concluded that the Indian police and the U.S. Army tried to arrest Sitting Bull and when he resisted, he was killed. Two important considerations, however, have been ignored. First, Indian accounts at the time recall that Sitting Bull was not really interested in the ghost dance and never planned an outbreak. Indian views, reported by Indian Agent James McLaughlin, state that Sitting Bull did not actually believe in the ghost dance, but he had nothing against it either. He simply wanted to let his people dance. For most whites, he was the most ardent supporter of the ghost dance, and thus he had to be planning to lead a major attack in the near future. He had to be arrested.

Second, according to other Indian versions, a few days before the attempted arrest, Sitting Bull received a special message, which told him that his own people were planning to kill him. This message was brought to him by a bird. What does this mean? It does not necessarily mean anything, but it has to be taken into account that Sitting Bull was a Lakota and a medicine man. *He* believed in the bird's message. So, when the Indian police entered his cabin on the morning of December 15, 1890, he perhaps recalled the bird and its message. Whether he thought that this was the day the bird was talking about cannot be determined. Did it affect his actions? We do not know, but when the facts are considered carefully, it has to be taken into account that Sitting Bull first wanted to go with the police, and then for some reason he refused and was then killed by his own people.[23]

The murder of Sitting Bull was a prelude to the Massacre at Wounded Knee. After Wounded Knee, the ghost dancers were concentrated in a single camp near the

Pine Ridge Agency. The Indians faced a decision of whether to fight the U.S. Army or to surrender. Eventually they surrendered without much resistance. The credit for their surrender was immediately given to General Nelson A. Miles and his so-called brilliant tactics of "combining force and diplomacy in just the right proportions," as one historian has noted.[24] However, contemporary whites as well as historians have neglected to consider the power of Lakota traditions during these final phases of the Miles campaign.

On January 13, 1891, Chief Standing Bear rode into the ghost dancers' camp where tensions were extremely high. It was only two weeks after the massacre of many of their relatives. The chief sat down on the ground without knowing if the angry ghost dancers would kill him right there because he was considered a traitor for working with the U.S. Army. He sat there for a while listening to the threats the ghost dancers made against him. Standing Bear remained calm and finally offered the pipe to the ghost dancers. After much hesitation, the ghost dancers accepted the offered pipe and along with the pipe they accepted the offer to surrender peacefully.[25]

CONCLUSION

The final event of surrender after Wounded Knee is remarkable because it shows how strong Lakota traditions remained even after the murders of Crazy Horse, Spotted Tail, and Sitting Bull, and the assignments to reservations of Red Cloud and Sitting Bull's peoples. Not only did Lakota men smoke before "considering any matter of importance," they also used it as a ceremony to "make Indians kin."[26] These extended kinship networks were essential for maintaining domestic harmony and in creating a Siouan identity.[27]

The pipe, then, solidified intertribal relationships. While the new religion was both vital and attractive to many Lakotas, the ghost dancers could not neglect the power of kinship and the power of the sacred pipe. Had they refused the pipe, they would have refused one of their relatives and acted against one of their most sacred principles, the respect for the pipe.[28] Not even a tragedy the magnitude of Wounded Knee could separate Lakotas from their most important traditions, traditions that strongly influenced the Lakota ghost dance of 1890.

ABBREVIATIONS

AAG—Army Adjutant General
AIWKSC—Reports and Correspondence Relating to the Army Investigations of the Battle at Wounded Knee and to the Sioux Campaign of 1890–1891, M

983, vol. I, roll 1–2, RG 94, Records of the Adjutant General's Office, 1780–1917 (Washington, DC: General Services Administration, 1974)

ARSOW—Annual Report of the Secretary of War, 52nd Cong., 1st sess., House Executive Document, vol. 2, no. 1, part 2, vol. 1, serial 2921 (Washington, DC: Government Printing Office, 1892)

CIA—U.S. Senate Committee on Indian Affairs

LSASPR—Letters Sent by the Agents or Superintendents at the Pine Ridge Agency, 1875–1914, M 1282, vol. 9, roll 10, RG 75, Records of the Bureau of Indian Affairs, The National Archives and Records Service (Washington, DC: General Services Administration, 1985)

M—Microfilm

NARS—National Archives Reference Section, Washington, DC

RG—record group

SC—special case 188

WMCP—Walter Mason Camp Papers, Indiana University, Lilly Library, Bloomington

NOTES

1. James Mooney, *The Ghost Dance Religion and the Sioux Outbreak of 1890* (Lincoln: University of Nebraska Press, [1893] 1991).

2. See Patricia N. Limerick, *The Legacy of Conquest: The Unbroken Past of the American West* (New York: Norton, 1987); and Robert F. Berkhofer, *Beyond the Great Story: History as Text and Discourse* (Cambridge, MA: Harvard University Press, 1995).

3. My larger study seeks to go beyond simply collecting the views of these groups to explore and analyze the political, cultural, and economic linkages between their collective viewpoints in order to gain a fuller understanding of what the Ghost Dance represented. Rani-Henrik Andersson, *The Lakota Ghost Dance of 1890* (Lincoln: University of Nebraska Press, 2009,).

4. It must be understood that Lakota concepts of religion differ from Western, or European American, concepts. Words such as "religion" and "doctrine" used in this chapter are references in European American cultures.

5. This category includes such examples as James P. Boyd, *Recent Indian Wars, Under the Lead of Sitting Bull and Other Chiefs; With Full Account of the Messiah Craze and Ghost Dances* (Philadelphia: Publishers Union, 1891); Willis Fletcher Johnson, *The Red Record of the Sioux. Life of Sitting Bull and History of the Indian War of 1890–1891* (Philadelphia: Edgewood, 1891); George E. Hyde, *A Sioux Chronicle* (Norman: University of Oklahoma Press, 1956); Robert M. Utley, *The Last Days of the Sioux Nation* (New Haven, CT: Yale University Press, 1963); and Frank McCann, Jr., "The Ghost Dance, Last Hope of the Western Tribes, Unleashed the Final Tragedy," *Montana, the Magazine of Western History* 16, no. 1 (1966): 25–34. But for a broader, more recent treatment, see Todd M. Kerstetter, "Spin Doctors at Santee: Missionaries and the Dakota-Language Reporting of the Ghost

Dance," *Western Historical Quarterly* 28 (Spring 1997): 45–67; and Todd M. Kerstetter, "God's Country, Uncle Sam's Land: Religious Exceptionalism, the Myth of the West, and Federal Force," PhD diss. (University of Nebraska, Lincoln, 1997).

6. Raymond J. DeMallie, "'These Have No Ears': Narrative and Ethnohistorical Method," *Ethnohistory* 40 (Fall 1993): 532.

7. Captain George Sword, "The Story of the Ghost Dance, Written in the Indian Tongue by Major George Sword," *The Folk-Lorist* 1 (1892): 28–36; James Mooney, *The Ghost-Dance Religion and the Sioux Outbreak of 1890* (Lincoln: University of Nebraska Press, [1896] 1991), 820–22. Mooney got the story from Emma C. Sickles who at the time was the superintendent of Indian schools at Pine Ridge. See Raymond J. DeMallie's introduction in Mooney, *Ghost-Dance Religion,* xxiii.

Other versions of the delegates' journey can be found in Short Bull Manuscript, Eugene Buechel Manuscript Collection, Holy Rosary Mission, Special Collections and Archives, Marquette University Libraries, Milwaukee, Wisconsin, 1–2 [This text has been translated to English by Professor Raymond J. DeMallie, Dennis M. Christafferson and Rani-Henrik Andersson, American Indian Studies Research Institute, Indiana University, Bloomington, Indiana, spring 2005, from Father Buechel's original Lakota manuscript. Another English version of the text has been published in Eugene Buechel S.J., *Lakota Tales and Texts: Wisdom Stories, Customs, Lives, and Instruction of the Dakota People*, ed. Paul Manhardt, S.J. (Pine Ridge, South Dakota: Red Cloud Indian School, Holy Rosary Mission, 1978), but unfortunately the text differs somewhat from the original manuscript and also contains some errors. A retranslation was therefore essential]; Short Bull Document, recorded by George C. Crager, "As Narrated by Short Bull," Buffalo Bill Museum and Grave, Golden, Colorado, 1–2; Short Bull in Wolfgang Haberland, *Die Oglala Sammlung Weygold* (Hamburg, Germany: Mitteilungen aus dem Museum fur Völkerkunde, 1977), 37–38; Selwyn to Foster, November 25, 1890, NARS, RG 75, SC 188, M 4728, Roll 1, 2/97–3/2. See also William S. E. Coleman, *Voices of Wounded Knee* (Lincoln: University of Nebraska Press, 2000), 25–32.

8. See *Omaha* [NE] *Daily Bee,* April 6, 1890, April 12, 1890, April 27, 1890, May 2, 1890, May 14, 1890, and May 29, 1890; *Washington* [DC] *Post,* April 6, 1890, and April 16, 1890; *New York Times,* April 6, 1890; and *Chicago Tribune,* April 7, 1890, and May 28, 1890.

9. For Lakota concepts of spirits held by Little Wound, Good Seat, James R. Walker, George Sword, Bad Wound, No Flesh, Short Feather, Ringing Shield, Finger, John Blunt Horn, William Garnett, Thomas Tyon, and Thunder Bear, see James R. Walker, *Lakota Belief and Ritual,* ed. Raymond J. DeMallie and Elaine A. Jahner (Lincoln: University of Nebraska Press, 1991), 68–124. See also Raymond J. DeMallie, Jr., and Robert H. Lavenda, "Wakan: Plains Siouan Concepts of Power," in *The Anthropology of Power: Ethnographic Studies from Asia, Oceania, and the New World,* ed. Richard Adams and Raymond D. Fogelson (New York: Academic Press, 1977), 153–59, 163–64; Raymond J. DeMallie, "Lakota Belief and Ritual in the Nineteenth Century," in *Sioux Indian Religion: Tradition and Innovation,* ed. Raymond J. DeMallie and Douglas R. Parks (Norman: University of Oklahoma Press, 1987), 29–31.

10. Mooney, *Ghost-Dance Religion,* 822; Utley, *The Last Days of the Sioux Nation,* 72–73, 87; Robert W. Larson, *Red Cloud, Warrior Statesman of the Oglala Lakota* (Norman: University of Oklahoma Press, 1997), 266. Similar ideas were also expressed by for example, Boyd, *The Last Days of the Sioux Nation;* Johnson, *The Red Record,* 171; Robert H. Lowie, *Indians of the Plains* (New York: McGraw-Hill, 1954), 181; Dorothy M. Johnson, "Ghost Dance, Last Hope of the Sioux," *Mon-*

tana, The Magazine of Western History 3 (July 1956): 45–46; Robert M. Utley and Wilcomb E. Washburn, *The American Heritage History of the Indian Wars* (New York: American Heritage Publishing Co., 1977), 294–95; Rex Alan Smith, *Moon of the Popping Trees: The Tragedy at Wounded Knee and the End of the Indian Wars* (Lincoln: University of Nebraska Press, 1975), 75; and Jack Utter, *Wounded Knee and the Ghost Dance Tragedy: A Chronicle of Events Leading to and Including the Massacre at Wounded Knee, South Dakota, on December 29, 1890* (Lake Ann, MI: National Woodlands Publishing Company, 1991), 1–13.

11. Raymond J. DeMallie, "The Lakota Ghost Dance: An Ethnohistorical Account," *Pacific Historical Review* 51 (November 1982): 390–91; Walker, *Lakota Belief and Ritual,* 124, 144. For comparison see, for example, Utley, *Last Days of Sioux Nation,* 71–75.

12. DeMallie, "Lakota Belief and Ritual," 34.

13. DeMallie, "Lakota Ghost Dance," 387–88.

14. Good descriptions of the Lakota Ghost Dance ceremony can be found in Elisha B. Reynolds to CIA, September 25, 1890, NARS, RG 75, SC 188, M 4728, reel 1, 1/22–26; and Elaine Goodale Eastman, "The Ghost Dance War and Wounded Knee Massacre of 1890–1891," *Nebraska History* 26 (January–March 1945): 26–42.

15. *The Illustrated American,* 17 (January 1891): 329; *New York Times,* November 22, 1890. The same eyewitness account was also published in the *Chicago Tribune,* November 22, 1890. For a comparison, see Thomas Tyon, William Garnett, George Sword, and John Blunt Horn, in Walker, *Lakota Belief and Ritual,* 108; John G. Neihardt and Black Elk, *Black Elk Speaks, Being the Life Story of a Holy Man of the Oglala Sioux* (Lincoln: University of Nebraska Press, [1932] 1961), 241; Black Elk and Joseph Epes Brown, eds., *The Sacred Pipe: Black Elk's Account of the Seven Rites of the Oglala Sioux* (Norman: University of Oklahoma Press, 1953), 78–79; Raymond J. DeMallie, ed., *The Sixth Grandfather: Black Elk's Teachings Given to John G. Neihardt* (Lincoln: University of Nebraska Press, 1985), 258–60; Mooney, "The Ghost Dance Religion," 788, 823–24.

For additional commentary by non-Natives, see Agent Hugh D. Gallagher to the Commissioner of Indian Affairs, August 28, 1890, NARS, RG 75, LSASPR, roll 10, 387–88; Special Agent Elisha B. Reynolds to CIA, September 25, 1890, NARS, RG 75, SC 188, M 4728, reel 1, 1/22–26; Agent James McLaughlin to CIA, October 17, 1890, NARS, RG 75, SC 188, M 4728, reel 1, 1/31–43; and Agent Daniel F. Royer to the Acting Commissioner of Indian Affairs, October 30, 1890, NARS, RG 75, SC 188, M 4728, reel 1, 1/47–50.

16. *Congressional Record,* 51st Cong., 1st sess., vol. 21, part 14, December 3, 1890, 48, and December 4, 1890, 68; Senator Gilbert A. Pierce to Secretary of War Redfield Proctor (telegram), November 18, 1890, NARS, RG 94, AIWKSC, M 983, roll 1, vol. 1, 109.

17. Ibid.

18. *Congressional Record,* 51st Cong., 1st sess., vol. 21, part 14, December 4, 1890, 68–69, 70–74, and December 8, 1890, 197–98.

19. Report of Lieutenant Colonel J.S. Poland to the Assistant Adjutant General (AAG) (telegram), November 29, 1890, NARS, RG 94, AIWKSC, M 983, roll 1, vol. 1, 288–92; Brigadier General John R. Brooke to AAG (telegram), November 30, 1890, NARS, RG 94, AIWKSC, M 983, roll 1, vol. 1, 296–301; Report of Captain F.A. Whitney, November 27, 1890, NARS, RG 94, AIWKSC, M 983, roll 1, vol. 1, 307–11; ARSOW 1891, "List of Causes of Disaffection on Different Reservations," November 27, November 30, and

December 7, 1890, 52nd Cong., 1st sess., House Executive Document, no. 1, part 2, vol. 1, serial 2921, vol. 2, 134–39; and Report of Brigadier General John R. Brooke in Brooke to AAG, March 2, 1891, NARS, RG 94, AIWKSC, M 983, roll 2, vol. 2, 1679–82.

20. The actual number of Lakota ghost dancers might have been as low as 4,000 people, or approximately 28 percent of all Lakotas. Even that might have been an exaggeration, since there was a lot of movement between the ghost dancers' and non–ghost dancers' camps. The question is whether people who went to a ghost dance camp to watch the ceremony or perhaps to participate in it a few times can be counted as true ghost dancer believers. Much evidence indicates that this kind of movement was actually quite extensive, and it is therefore extremely difficult to make a clear distinction between who was a ghost dancer and who was not. Furthermore, after the arrival of the U.S. military, many of those who fled to the ghost dance camps were not ghost dancers at all. However, additional evidence suggests the number of Lakota ghost dancers was much lower than contemporary non-Native estimates led people to believe, and the numbers are lower than scholars have generally estimated. See Rani-Henrik Andersson, "Wanagi Wachipi Kin: The Ghost Dance among the Lakota Indians in 1890: A Multidimensional Interpretation," *Acta Universitatis Tempersis,* no. 983 (2003) (Tempere, Finland: University of Tempere Press), 88–89.

21. *Omaha Daily Bee,* November 19, 1890; *Chicago Tribune,* November 19, 1890.

22. Secretary of the Interior John W. Noble to CIA, December 1, 1890, NARS, RG 94, AIWKSC, M 983, roll 1, vol. 1, 392; Redfield Proctor to Major General Nelson A. Miles, December 1, 1890, NARS, RG 94, AIWKSC, M 983, roll 1, vol. 1, 401; *Congressional Record,* 51st Cong., 2nd sess., vol. 12, part I, December 3–8, 1890, 44–48 and 68–74; U.S. ARSOW 1891, Report of the Major General Commanding the Army, September 24, 1891, in 52nd Cong., 1st sess., House Executive Document, no. 1, part 2, vol. 1, serial 2921, vol. 2, 144. See also Nelson A. Miles, *Serving the Republic: Memoirs of the Civil and Military Life of Nelson A. Miles* (New York: Harper & Brothers Publishers, 1911), 238; Utley, *Last Days of Sioux Nation,* 127; Forrest W. Seymour, *Sitanka: The Full Story of Wounded Knee* (West Hanover, MA: Christopher Publishing House, 1981), 143–47; Coleman, *Voices of Wounded Knee,* 97–98, 145–46. A good analysis of Miles appears in Stephen D. Youngkin, "Prelude to Wounded Knee: The Military Point of View," *South Dakota History* 4 (Summer 1974): 333–51.

23. Four Blanket Woman, One Bull, Mrs. One Bull, Indian policemen Lone Man and Grey Eagle, WMCP, box 5, folder 1, envelope 41. The events surrounding the arrest and death of Sitting Bull are documented in ARSOW 1891, 52nd Cong., 1st sess., House Executive Document, no. 1, part 2, vol. 1, serial 2921, vol. 2, 146–47. For Indian accounts of the arrest, see WMCP, box 5, folder 1, envelope 41. See also David Humphreys Miller, *Ghost Dance* (Lincoln: University of Nebraska Press, 1985), 182–90, 303; and Stanley Vestal, *Sitting Bull: The Champion of the Sioux* (Norman: University of Oklahoma Press, [1932] 1989), 286–302. Miller's informants were policemen White Bull and Little Soldier, One Bull's wife, John Sitting Bull, and Henry Sitting Bull. See also James McLaughlin to CIA, November 19, 1890, NARS, RG 75, SC 188, M 4728, reel 1, pp. 2/18–25; McLaughlin, *My Friend,* 201–8.

24. Robert M. Utley, *The Indian Frontier of the American West, 1846–1890* (Albuquerque: University of New Mexico Press, 1984), 257.

25. See Neihardt and Black Elk, *Black Elk Speaks,* 269; Luther Standing Bear, *My People the Sioux* (Lincoln: University of Nebraska Press, [1928] 1975), 228–29; Miller, *Ghost Dance,* 264–65.

26. George Sword, in Walker, *Lakota Belief and Ritual,* 83, 198; and "Lakota Words Index," http://www.lakotawritings.com/lakota_words_Index.htm.

27. Gary Clayton Anderson, *Kinsmen of Another Kind: Dakota-White Relations in the Upper Mississippi Valley, 1650–1862* (Lincoln: University of Nebraska Press, 1984), xi, xii.

28. A similar incident occurred previously during the war of 1876–1877, when a pipe was offered to Crazy Horse's people during the aftermath of the battle of the Little Big Horn. The symbolism of this occasion is explained in great detail in Raymond DeMallie, "'These Have No Ears,'" 515–38.

CHAPTER 9

Force and Possibility: Hopis' Views of the Internet

RITVA LEVO-HENRIKSSON

MODERN NATIVE AMERICAN experiences are frequently characterized as "two-world" approaches. Writers, among them non-Natives and Natives alike, depict Native American lives as conflicted. These conflicts feature struggles for indigenous peoples between the non-Native worlds and the Native traditional worlds they encounter. Interviews with indigenous people often reveal the traits and dynamics of the "two worlds."

This essay seeks to identify attitudes of Native Americans toward the media and, in particular, the Internet through a case study of the Hopi nation in Arizona. Twenty-four Hopis on their reservation were interviewed in the spring of 1996. Information was also obtained through interviews to check on the newest media developments on the Hopi Reservation conducted in the Hopi villages during the early summer of 2002. The subject of the interviews covered a wide range of questions concerning Hopi cultural change and the media.

The interviewees and interview formats varied. Interviewees' ages ranged from fifteen to fifty-nine, with an equal number (twelve) of females and males. All were from the three mesas on the Hopi Reservation in northeastern Arizona, including nine villages and the Keams Canyon area. Four of the twenty-four interviewees were students at Hopi High School, and they were interviewed as a group there. Twenty of the interviews were individual, qualitative, and in-depth, lasting from sixty to ninety minutes each. Interviews were conducted in English. Some of the interviews were administered in offices and some in interviewees' homes.[1]

The frame of reference used for examining these data involved intercultural communication between Hopis and mainstream culture. On the basis of this framework, the data were coded under seven different themes, including attitudes toward the Internet, the topic of this essay. The methodology used was qualitative content analysis. Four different views on the Internet were identified. These views as well as concerns about the influence of the Internet on other indigenous nations are also examined to gain an understanding of the current place of the Internet in indigenous people's media experiences.

RECENT RESEARCH ON INDIGENOUS COMMUNITIES AND THE INTERNET

Generally speaking, Native Americans started claiming territory in cyberspace in the first part of the 1990s. The Oneidas were the first Native American nation to create a web page in May 1994. According to interviews of OIN (Oneida Indian Nation) employees by Jean Armour Polly, the Oneidas were not only the first Indian nation to create a web page, but were perhaps among the first of all nations in the world to do so.[2] At the time, the OIN web page was one of only approximately 5,000 web pages in existence.[3] The Hopis received their official website (www.hopi.nsn.us) in the summer of 1999, when they constructed an important "ramp" onto the information superhighway.[4]

Given the relatively recent extension of the Internet to Native communities, research on the impact and reception of the Internet among indigenous peoples has been minimal. What has been observed, however, offers a number of interesting issues and challenges for Native nations. Some research regarding the influence of electronic information on indigenous communities has been accomplished. For example, in the Northwest Territories of Canada, Barry Zellen found both a positive reception and concerns among Native peoples toward the possibilities of the Internet. James Hrynyshyn, a communication consultant with West Hawk Associates of Ottawa operating out of Yellowknife, sees the Internet as an ideal match for indigenous tribes. Virtual communities, according to Hrynyshyn, maintain coherent group identities and resist assimilating into a larger society. He also believes that because the Internet can support mixtures of audio, video, and text, it suits the oral storytelling traditions of indigenous communities very well. In addition, Hrynyshyn predicts that the Internet will help preserve artifacts of indigenous cultures, which again will make Native societies stronger. He admits, however, that the Internet can also induce pressures to "merge, interact, and standardize."[5]

Jim Bell, editor of *Nunatsiaq News* (Iqaluit, Nunavik), a bilingual Inuit newspaper in the Canadian Arctic, is not quite as sanguine about the Internet's potential for preserving indigenous cultures or languages. Although the Internet increases the ability to store information, he does not see that as helpful, particularly if an elder's grandchildren do not speak their indigenous language. According to Bell, "If you want to keep a culture alive, you have to use it. The medium does not really matter." He thinks, however, that other tools like CD-ROMs, digital video discs, and other multimedia technologies might be more suitable as information storage tools than the Internet.[6]

Fred Lepine, a Metis writer, holds a more ominous view. He believes that the Internet has "the ability to completely dismantle even strong cultures." On the basis of television's impact, he argues that learning about other cultures weakens traditional interpersonal relations. According to Lepine, the Internet has an overwhelming assimilating power that comes from its accessibility. On the other hand, Lepine believes that the risk of assimilation is balanced by many potential benefits of the Internet, including the ability to network among indigenous peoples.[7]

Perhaps the most complex part in Lepine's pondering over the impact of the Internet is his worry about the loss of traditional ways of thinking. According to Lepine, the digital age requires people to think in a more goal-oriented, logical, and linear way. Traditional indigenous thinking, meanwhile, involves "a more interconnected, abstract, and circular sense that is often based on intuition." Lepine calls this kind of thinking "round thinking." According to him, that kind of thinking has kept indigenous peoples alive for thousands of years and has also kept the planet flourishing. To be able to survive in the virtual world, Lepine sees the necessity of combining traditional ways of thinking with "acceptable Western technology."[8]

David Maybury-Lewis, founder and president of the magazine *Cultural Survival*, believes the Internet represents a "two-edged sword."[9] The Internet, according to Maybury-Lewis, may be useful to indigenous peoples in their external political struggles, but it may cause internal problems in their own societies. The intensification of communication with the wider world can undermine distinctive cultures and traditions that indigenous peoples cherish and try to protect. Maybury-Lewis does recognize, however, that Native American and First Nation social problems are not peculiar challenges caused solely by the Internet. More often than not, the Internet exacerbates the problems or makes them more noticeable. The issue becomes then "how to balance [indigenous groups'] interaction with, and participation in the wider society with their desire to maintain a vibrant and separate culture."[10]

CYBERSPACE ACCESS IN HOPILAND

The 1990s brought the Internet to Hopis on their reservation. Hopis were suddenly faced with new uses of new information and communication technology,[11] including the Internet. At first this new information and media were a part of everyday life only for a limited number of Hopis. Before the millennium, it was not possible on the Hopi Reservation to take full advantage of this technology because its buildings lacked an electronic infrastructure. Most Hopis still have no access to e-mail or other online services. It is difficult to provide precise numbers, but a Hopi Reservation survey of media availability showed that 16 percent of Hopi High School students had web access.[12] The great majority of these students were from First Mesa and mostly from Polacca. Some homes with e-mail access pay the long distance access fee to the nearby city of Flagstaff in order to obtain on-line services. This has also been the case with Hopi radio station KUYI, founded in 2000, which pays $300–$500 monthly to be online. Several major organizations on the Hopi Reservation have access to e-mail or other online services via the Internet, including the U.S. Bureau of Indian Affairs, the Hopi Health Care Center, Hopi High School, and the Hopi tribal offices.

Opinions expressed by Hopis living on the Hopi Reservation about new information and communication technologies reveal four different attitudes toward the Internet. Hopis expressed *outside pressure, possibility, critical acceptance,* and *unproblematic attitude* views.

Generally, Hopis were mainly positive, although people generally harbor some qualifications and qualms about these electronic changes. One of the doubts expressed by some interviewees was the ability of Hopis to control unwanted information. They mentioned primarily the issue of new information and communication technology that they would not necessarily like to have. They recognized, however, that Hopis have to utilize it, because other people already use it. They worried about its use against Hopis, particularly by distributing false information about Hopis via the Internet. According to this view, Hopis are "forced" to use this same technology themselves. This outside "force" element represents a kind of argumentation emanating from *outside pressure* views held by some Hopis.

Not only do forces exist outside the Hopi community, but in addition the presenters of these kinds of Hopi viewpoints also spoke of "other people" or "them," referring to the white world or to the mainstream culture. An example of these kinds of views is the comment of a woman in her forties who observed that "we [Hopis] really have no choice in order to keep up with the progress of the world. You know, I think we have also to communicate better with them. I think we really have no choice, I think it is an important way of communication." She speaks about the new communication technology as an issue of inevitability, of "no choice," even while she also believes that there are some positive sides to the new communication technologies.

The positive features of new technologies, which are apparent in the comment of this interviewee, were presented without qualifications by many other interviewees. They saw technology primarily as a positive option within their own *possibility* views. When new communication technologies are seen by Hopis as a possibility, they see it as opening new means of being able to communicate worldwide, access information, educate, progress, and advance Hopi language and culture. When expressing possibility views, young interviewees in particular emphasized the worldwide communication possibilities via the Internet.

Those adults who expressed *possibility* views focused on the meaning of new communication technologies for the youth. Children would be enabled by easy access to information, education, and most importantly competition in the job market. One reason why some parents would like to have computers for their children is that it would provide easy connections with library information, which would be very important as there are no libraries on the Hopi Reservation. Emphasizing computers as a tool for the youth and the Hopi future clearly came up in the comment of this 52-year-old woman:

> I think, most of the time out here, the parents are quite supportive of new things that their children learn. . . . I think we are very supportive of our children learning on the computer, and hope they will be as competitive in the job market if they have to go outside for college or employment.

In summary, while Internet access is both limited and expensive, it appears to have found a place in Hopiland. Not surprisingly, the new medium is perceived in a variety of ways. Many express concern about the Internet because Hopis do not control how they are portrayed. Others, especially those interested in education and job opportunities, see this technology as vital for tribal development.

INTERNET ACCEPTANCE AND CRITIQUE

In most cases, acceptance or rejection of the Internet is not absolute. Some Hopi interviewees hold both positive and negative complicated viewpoints about the Internet. Although they admitted that there were some advantages to the new communication technology, they also expressed some criticism, often relating their negative impressions to possible attacks on Hopi culture and tradition. This combination of criticism and admittance of advantages constitutes *critical acceptance* views. As one forty-five-year-old man put it:

> [I]n some positive ways, in terms of modern involvement, it will help the tribe to become more in line with the world in terms of what's going on. But on the other hand, it can also have negative impacts on the culture and tradition, because the more modern convenience technology that you get into that also has a direct impact upon culture and, you know, the retention of those. And then at the same time, they can also be used to our advantage, like, language and culture has been taught. . . . Well, in particular language has been taught on computers.

According to this interviewee, new communication technologies provide the possibility of monitoring more closely his environment, or as the interviewee puts it, "to become more in line with the world in terms of what's going on." In addition, he noted that the Internet provides a channel for teaching indigenous languages and cultures.

Unfortunately, this "convenience technology" also has negative impacts on language and culture. Some *critical acceptance* interviewees worried about the time that a computer, if it were brought into the home, would take away from interfamily communications. Still others stated that a person could learn much via the Internet, but they also wondered if it was necessary or even possible for people to deal with all of the worldwide information that the Internet makes available.

Among those who hold *critical acceptance* views, some Hopis worry that children who become computer literate at school may become communication disabled at home or in the neighborhood in the absence of computers. Representatives of these kinds of views emphasized the ability to know many kinds of communication and stressed the importance of good communication skills rather than technology skills. According to these views, users of any medium, such as the Internet, should remember that computers must play only an assisting role in communication.

Those who espoused *critical acceptance* views also perceived of present-day computer users as "cipherers," whose lifelong process is to go through oceans of information. These Hopis were uncertain as to the cultural value of deciphering. This critical acceptance view is also present in the words of Loren Sekayumptewa, supervisor of web development for the Hopi Tribal Council on the Hopi Reservation. He said that Hopis "must review this new technology, so that we utilize it effectively, and assure that it does not interfere and intrude into our Hopi values and principles."[13]

For those who are comfortable, the effective utilizing of this new technology means paying attention to how the Hopis are portrayed on Internet releases. Hopis have seen much exploitation of their cultural properties over the Internet.[14] Similar worries over Internet use of incorrect information on Hopis written by non-Hopis also appeared in these discussions with Hopis. The possibility for tribal and individual websites to correct this exploitation was commonly relayed as one of the strongest reasons for having a presence on the Internet for indigenous groups and peoples from various cultures.[15]

Some Hopi interviewees who hold *unproblematic attitude* views see the new communication technologies only positively. These interviewees emphasized the character of technology as a changing continuum, which to them is not a serious problem as compared to a real problem, such as the preservation of Native American languages, including the Hopi language. These interviewees are represented by a 51-year-old man who said, "I am concerned with language, not technique per se. In my youth we had a small radio." He did not care what communication form was used to preserve the Hopi tongue as long as it was preserved. Those espousing *unproblematic attitude* views might also associate the new communication technologies with "anything else" that may be useful. Of course, they reflected, it could be abused. According to these interviewees, the technologies themselves are not the problem, but rather what the users of these technologies do with information.

Clearly, the Internet is imagined by some Hopis as a medium to preserve and advance their own culture. Such *unproblematic attitude* views are certainly not universal, however. Many express disdain for information found on the Internet and do not see the need to include it when educating their children. To them, communications technologies present a potential cultural danger to Hopi traditions. Other Hopis, while similarly inclined, feel forced to contend with the Internet. More proactively, still other Hopis choose to use the medium as a tool to monitor how their culture is portrayed to the outside world.

SOME CONCLUDING THOUGHTS

If these four different Hopi groups who hold diverse views concerning new information and communication technology are returned to the "two-world" framework mentioned at the beginning of this essay, they comprise a case of intercultural communication. It can be understood as a communication in which a message produced in one culture must be processed in another culture.[16] In this "two-worlds" framework or in the context of intercultural communication, these four perspectives tell us about negotiations between cultures. Hopi negotiations between cultures in the context of new communication technologies cover accessibility, use, and possible impacts. But in this discussion, the technology becomes part of a larger global discussion by cyberphilosophers and users.

In this sense, then, the Internet is nothing more than an additional product of mainstream culture, albeit a strong acculturative or culturally useful tool. On the more optimistic side, Hopis and other indigenous groups, such as the Inuits in the Northwest Territories mentioned previously, have a long history of managing media cultural intrusions. The Internet represents just another in a long list of cultural challenges inherent to surviving in two worlds.

NOTES

Author's Note: The issues covered in this article are discussed more extensively in Ritva Levo-Henriksson, *Media and Ethnic Identity: Hopi Views on Media, Identity, and Communication* (New York and London: Routledge, 2007). 1. Taped interviews were transcribed in Finland by a research assistant whose mother tongue is English. All transcripts are held by the author.

2. Jean Armour Polly, "Standing Stones in Cyber Space: The Oneida Indian Nation's

Territory on the Web," *Cultural Survival Quarterly: World Report on the Rights of Indigenous Peoples and Ethnic Minorities* 21 (Winter 1998): 39.

3. Ibid., 37, 39.

4. The Hopi Tribe, Office of Public Relations, "Official Hopi Website Goes On-line," *The Hopi Tutuveni* 9 (July 20, 1999): 3.

5. Barry Zellen, "'Surf's Up!' NWT's Indigenous Communities Await a Tidal Wave of Electronic Information," *Cultural Survival Quarterly: World Report on the Rights of Indigenous Peoples and Ethnic Minorities* 21 (Winter 1998): 51–52.

6. Ibid., 52.

7. Ibid.

8. Ibid., 53.

9. David Maybury-Lewis, "Editorial: The Internet and Indigenous Groups," *Cultural Survival Quarterly: World Report on the Rights of Indigenous Peoples and Ethnic Minorities* 21 (Winter 1998): 3.

10. Ibid.

11. The term that is often used with Hopis when discussing new information and communication technology generally is shortened to "new communication technology" or "telecommunications technology." The term "telecommunications technology" appeared in a report published by the U.S. Congress Office of Technology Assessment, before the interviews were conducted. This report focused on issues for Native Americans in the context of new information and communication technology. Native Americans participated in this project that concentrated on utilizing this technology and planning policy. Telecommunications technology, or new information and communication technology, includes computer networking, videoconferencing, multimedia, and digital and wireless technologies. See Office of Technology Assessment, *Telecommunications Technology and Native Americans: Opportunities and Challenges* (Washington, DC: Government Printing Office, 1995), iii.

12. Ritva Levo-Henriksson, "Media Use and Media Attitudes in Hopiland," Report for the Vice Chairman's Office of the Hopi Tribe, 1997.

13. "Official Hopi Website Goes On-line," 3.

14. Ibid.

15. Steve Cissler, "Introduction: The Internet and Indigenous Groups," *Cultural Survival Quarterly: World Report on the Rights of Indigenous Peoples and Ethnic Minorities* 21 (Winter 1998): 20.

16. Richard E. Porter and Larry A. Samovar, "An Introduction to Intercultural Communication," in *Intercultural Communication: A Reader,* 8th ed., ed. Porter and Samovar (Belmont, CA: Wadsworth, 1997), 8.

CHAPTER 10

Indian Gaming, Sovereignty, and the Courts: The Case of the Miccosukee Tribe of Florida

MIIA HALME

THE FIRST Indian-owned bingo parlor was opened in the United States by the Seminole Tribe in 1979. The venture soon became so successful that it encouraged a great number of other Native American nations to follow their example. As a consequence, by 1997, 142 tribes in 24 states had Las Vegas–style casinos. The success of Indian gaming derives from the sovereign status of tribes guaranteed by numerous treaties and the granting of special title to Indian lands that allows for gambling in states where it otherwise may be prohibited.[1]

In a short period, Indian gaming has grown to account for a considerable proportion of gambling in the United States. In 1998 it constituted 15 percent of the estimated $100 billion annual turnover of the gaming business.[2] Gambling revenues grew rapidly throughout the 1990s, and the trend to the present shows no signs of slowing down as the number of casinos increases and the establishments become more luxurious. Indian gaming has become an important employer, supporting, for example, an estimated 16,000 jobs directly and 34,000 jobs indirectly in California. Gaming has also reduced the state of California's welfare payments by $50 million.[3] As becomes immediately evident from such figures, the influence of casinos is dramatic, particularly on the tribes that possess them, as they have attained an income prosperity that they have never before enjoyed. The effect of casinos becomes even more salient considering that only one of ten tribes without a casino is economically independent.[4]

This chapter examines the effects of Indian gaming on the indigenous peoples of the United States, focusing in particular on the role of courts in this development. Attention is first devoted to federal Indian policies of the past decades and sovereignty developments up to the present. These themes are elaborated through an analysis of the gaming experiences of the Miccosukee Tribe of Florida. The Miccosukees adopted gaming but not without controversy arising from impacts upon tribal sovereignty and new issues related to gambling economic success.

THE COURTS AND INDIAN GAMING

Casinos have induced dramatic changes in the relationship of tribes with the predominant American society. In some ways, they appear to have restarted the old war between Indians and whites, although in a more sophisticated form. In the mid-nineteenth century, as the U.S. Army and settlers fought against Native Americans, whites began to realize how expensive this mode of warfare was, both in terms of money and loss of life. Thus, they began to seek alternatives to outright war through the legal system. As Sidney Harring has argued, history shows law to be a far more effective tool of domination than outright war had ever been: It

Seminole Sovereignty over Two Centuries: Diplomatic Landmarks, 1820–1845, and Gaming on the Miccosukee Reservations, 1970–2000

involved minimal costs, and—as Indians were not allowed to participate in law-making or legal proceedings—it was virtually impossible for them to fight against legal applications.[5] What followed was the creation of one-sided and unfair laws depriving Indians of their collective and individual rights, the most notorious of which was the General Allotment Act, also known as the Dawes Severalty Act, of 1887.

Today, following the money brought in by casinos, Indians have for the first time real chances of fighting back against this unfair legal warfare. Recent years have shown tribes actively challenging anti-Indian laws in courts and lobbying for pro-Indian treatment in legislatures. Evidence of this is found in the number of cases brought to the U.S. Supreme Court concerning Indians and states, which in 1997 through 2000 amounted to a total of 102, of which 16 resulted in high court decisions.[6] The multiplicity of cases is important in two respects. First, it offers a demonstration of the societal power gaming money has granted tribes; over the past four years Indian governments have had the means to pursue their rights in all levels of the American legal system. In other words, tribes today have the financial means to transform themselves into effective proponents of their rights.[7]

However, an even greater impact is created by a second aspect of importance. The abundance of cases demonstrates that the benefits of casinos are making Indian nations into serious collective adversaries for the first time in history. Consequently, although only a small percentage of tribes possess casinos, these cases extend the benefits of gambling revenues to those tribes not owning them and thus lacking the necessary funds to pursue their cases beyond the lower courts. In other words, the fights undertaken by wealthy tribes improve the position of their less wealthy counterparts in the form of precedent.[8] The importance of precedent is well demonstrated by a U.S. Supreme Court ruling from 1974 that declared matters relating to Indian land rights to fall under the exclusive jurisdiction of the federal government, a judgment that has brought enormous benefits to tribal communities as a whole. As a consequence of this ruling, tribes have been free to initiate proceedings in federal courts to correct past violations of their land rights by a state; previously tribes would have required permission from that same state to begin proceedings.[9]

The positive effects of such rulings in part contributed to changes in tribal communities during the 1980s, and particularly the 1990s, that have been termed "revitalization" movements. Combined, these changes brought an end to the isolation of American Indians, which had limited much indigenous political and economic unity among the 1.2 million tribal members.[10] Such recent unity is demonstrated, for example, by annual sovereignty symposiums held since 1994, which have become an important forum for discussions about Indian culture, spirituality, social issues, and tribal law.[11] Revitalization caused the emergence of a new pan-Indian identity, accompanied by growing tribal populations. Out of the many interconnected reasons for this positive development, new leadership and adoption of more favorable federal Indian policies rise above all others in importance.

New and revitalized leadership has been attributed in particular to Indian participation in World War II, where the use of war rituals revived traditions and strengthened Indian collective identity, and decorated war veterans offered leaders who had acquired recognition and experiences outside reservations and who were better equipped to guide Indian peoples in the postwar era.[12] In the 1960s and 1970s, the fruits of these changes produced Native American leaders who became active opponents of government termination policies. Another important development was the founding of NARF, the Native American Rights Fund, originally operated under the Office of Economic Opportunity in California and directed at combating poverty. Behind the creation of NARF was the realization that for effective improvement of Indian political and economic circumstances, a national organization staffed with Indian advocates who specialized in Indian law was needed. Today, after almost three decades of actively pursuing their goals, the NARF has forty full-time staff members and is called the most important advocate organization with expertise in Indian law in the United States.[13]

These internal developments were accompanied by three decades of favorable federal Indian policies dominated by the ideology of self-governance. The explicit goal of the policy was to strengthen tribal communities by giving them more power over their own affairs to make them independent of the Bureau of Indian Affairs.[14] Self-determination was also emphasized during the presidencies of Richard Nixon, Jimmy Carter, and Bill Clinton. Clinton issued two presidential statements during his terms, enforced a government-to-government relationship between the federal government and tribes,[15] and introduced the bill in 2000 permitting land consolidation to reverse the disastrous effects of the 1887 Dawes Act and to begin "real Indian trust management."[16] In addition, the Clinton administration also increased federal funds for Native Americans considerably, which had been significantly reduced since Reagan's presidency, a decline "masked by budget numbers."[17] These changes, however, did not occur entirely without controversy; and before moving to the troublesome aspects of these developments, closer attention will be devoted to a case study of the Miccosukee Tribe of Florida and how it adjusted to changing federal policies.

THE MICCOSUKEES

The Miccosukees are a small tribe of 490 members living in the Everglades of South Florida. With a history of warfare with European colonial powers and subsequently the United States, the Miccosukees hold a special status for being the only Indian nation never to have made official peace with the United States after the Seminole–United States wars of the nineteenth century. The Miccosukees still refer to themselves as "undefeated." Today Miccosukees inhabit three reservations and a large area leased from the State of Florida *in perpetuity*. The tribe has operated a high-stakes bingo parlor located on the Krome Avenue Reservation near Miami since 1990. This bingo operation currently attracts thousands of gamblers daily with aspirations of instant fortune.[18] Its popularity has grown continually, making it a primary source of revenue for the Miccosukees. Annual returns—a closely guarded secret by the tribe—are estimated to be several million. In 1998, the tribe expanded its operations with the opening of the Miccosukee Resort and Convention Center, a 302-room luxury resort and casino, which in addition to gambling has become an important venue for boxing matches.[19]

The casino has had a dramatic impact on the life of the Miccosukees. Previously poverty stricken, the tribe is now affluent, enabling it to offer scholarships to all adult members. Whether this new wealth has helped to alleviate the social problems plaguing the community remains unclear as Miccosukees are still are affected by high rates of alcoholism and other problems previously associated with poverty.[20] Whatever the internal situation, on a societal level the tribe is prospering, as it works actively to preserve and strengthen its culture and operates its own police department and court, education system, and various social programs. All apply both traditional Indian and modern ways to solve tribal problems.

The success of the tribe has been reflected in its population, which jumped from 369 to 492 between 1994 and 2001.[21] Since 1987, Billy Cypress has led the Miccosukees. In addition to campaigning vigorously for the Miccosukees, he has held leadership roles in various Indian organizations since the 1970s, serving on the board of directors of the U.S. South and Eastern Tribes and the Florida Governor's Council on Indian Affairs. Since 2000, he has been a member of the NARF board of directors. Under Cypress's management, the Miccosukees have also become involved in the Florida Governor's Commission for a Sustainable South Florida and the South Florida Ecosystem Restoration Task Force.[22] In 2002, the achievements of Billy Cypress brought him recognition as Indian Leader of the Year by the National Indian Business Association.[23]

LAND RIGHTS AND COURT CASES

Reflecting the national trend, their new prosperity allowed Miccosukees to become active litigators. The cases they resolved to fight are almost all the result of a stormy relationship between the State of Florida and the tribe.

Miccosukee history in Florida is instructive. By 1845 the Miccosukees lived in central and northern Florida on lands they thought would be theirs forever. However, by 1860, following the atrocities of the Third Seminole–United States War, they had to abandon this area to take refuge in the swamps of the Everglades. There, shielded from their adversaries, they reassembled their community and continued their traditional life that had been disrupted by war. Tribal members grew to consider the Everglades their homeland, referring to it as "Our Mother," and lived there relatively undisturbed until the early twentieth century when Miami grew to metropolis proportions.[24] Southern Florida became flooded with immigrants, which gave rise to tremendous housing, resource, and infrastructure needs. These demands were satisfied by drying out large portions of the Everglades swamp and building the Tamiami Trail, actions that made Miccosukee lands for the first time easily accessible to outsiders. The Miccosukees once more found their homelands under siege. By World War I, the State of Florida was "virtually" ignoring the "historic land rights of the Seminole and the Miccosukee people and . . . the State . . . without Congressional authority or approval, removed the Miccosukees . . . from their lands (driving) them deeper into the Everglades."[25]

These events set the background for the ongoing legal battles between Miccosukees and the State of Florida. Between 1995 and 2001, the tribe became involved in a total of eight lawsuits against the State of Florida,[26] of which at least two were triggered by environmental concerns. One of these involved an Everglades restoration plan, a billion-dollar project hailed by President Clinton but called by environmentalists a "license to pollute."[27] As a consequence of a Miccosukee lawsuit, the entire plan was subjected to review.[28] Another case initiated in spring 2000 resulted from tribal opposition to the State of Florida's decision to dry out more of the Everglades wetlands.[29]

The majority of lawsuits relate to Miccosukee land rights, as the tribe aims both to expand its area and to gain more control over lands on which they reside. Both goals have been achieved by the Miccosukees. The tribe also undertook a long struggle with the U.S. government to enforce their right to live in their traditional homelands. As a result, in 1998 after four years of "Congressional pressure and years of litigation," the tribe acquired an additional 300 acres from federal lands for their Tamiami Trail Reservation. The same year also saw the passing of the Miccosukee Reserved Area Act by Congress. Since the passage of this federal legislation, the government entered into a contract with the Miccosukees, promising to preserve the land in its natural state *in perpetuity* for the use and benefit of the tribe. What should further be noted is that the State of Florida was not invited to participate in these negotiations. Understandably, the affair generated great controversy, which was further intensified by the tribe's desires to gain total control over the area, a plan fiercely opposed by state officials who argued that such action would set a "dangerous precedent" to the restoration plans of the area[30]—a curious concern considering the dedication the Miccosukees have demonstrated toward environmental preservation. In addition, following years of litigation, the tribe gained a permit to build additional housing to alleviate a chronic shortage,[31] and a Miccosukee plan to facilitate the purchase of an additional forty-six acres for $1.8 million has been realized.

In sum, the relationship of the State of Florida and the Miccosukees is less than amicable. Another reflection of this state of affairs is the communication allegedly sent by the tribe to the Florida attorney general in 1997 requesting a meeting between the tribe and representatives of the office to outline the "general legal principles limiting the State's authority over the Miccosukee Tribe and its territories." The State failed to respond to this request, and the meeting has yet to materialize.[32] The tribe's increased influence has also resulted in greater exposure in the local print media, generating such newspaper headlines as "Miccosukees' clout is shaping Glades restoration," and "Miccosukees on a roll in the Everglades."[33] In sum, the money brought to the tribe by its casino has transformed it into an important political actor that can no longer be overlooked or belittled by the State of Florida.

GAMING CONTROVERSIES

The increased influence and prosperity of the Miccosukees have, however, not been treated with universal rejoicing, as the arrival of "Las Vegas on the Miccosukee Reservation" has become a sore spot for many Floridians. Although the Miccosukees have thus far been spared lawsuits relating to their casino, general opposition to Indian gaming affected their operations, including attempts by Florida's congressional delegation to tax Indian casinos. This controversy also led to repeated denials of the tribe's requests to expand its casino into a full-scale operation.[34] Attitudes changed gradually over the years since the mid-1990s as tourism supported by gambling has become an important source of revenue and employment for Florida, including floating casinos that, under the pretense of sailing to international waters for a few hours, were free to offer full-scale gaming.[35] This conflict was debated until 2007 when the state of Florida finally reached a gambling accord with the Miccosukee Nation. In a matter of months, the Miccosukee Casino boasted 1,700 video pull-tab machines and 58 poker tables, as well as high-stakes bingo.[36]

Prospective attitudinal changes surrounding gambling, however, have not muffled the ongoing battle between the State of Florida and the Seminoles, Florida's other Indian tribe, as they have been fighting in the courts for years for the right to operate electronic slot machines and video gambling machines. The legal battle has been further complicated by a 1997 U.S. Supreme Court ruling that tribes are, due to their sovereign status, immune to lawsuits brought by states. In other words, despite being physically within their borders, the operation of casinos is outside the regulatory powers of states—yet another fact making states unhappy with the emergence of Indian casinos. This immunity could, however, be in jeopardy in the future, following recent attempts by states to gain more control over Indian casinos, but at present it appears that the controversy and litigation do not pose a threat to the success of Indian gaming. In July 2000, the Seminoles announced to media sources that they were planning a new $300 million, Hard Rock Cafe–theme resort with 750 rooms.[37]

Overall, this situation in Florida reflects national developments surrounding Indian gaming, which has from its instigation been greeted with great controversy. Although Indian gaming has supporters among policymakers, who consider it beneficial as it gives tribes more of "a shot at economic independence,"[38] the voices of these proponents have been muted by opponents who have been creating a racket with their complaints and overshadowing or delaying the opening of new establishments with lawsuits. In 1988, such controversies led to the adoption of the Indian Gaming Regulatory Act (IGRA), a twenty-five-page federal law purported to extinguish the quarrels. IGRA renders Indian gambling the most strictly regulated business in the United States. It defines the percentages of ownership required for tribes for their gambling establishments to be called "Indian casinos" and specifies the purposes for which the proceeds of Indian gaming can be used. The law also classifies Indian gaming into three categories, each meticulously described in detail. However, despite all legal precautions, Indian gaming is far from a resolved issue. This is demonstrated, for example, by the cases continuing to be brought before the U.S. Supreme Court. For instance, in the 1997–2000 period alone, the Court heard twelve new disputes involving matters relating to IGRA. Gaming has become the fourth-ranking source of federal disputes relating to Indians.[39]

On the surface, controversies surrounding Indian casinos appear to derive from the long-standing dislike of Americans for gambling, even though it is a huge business in the United States. Gambling in the 1990s grew at almost twice the annual rate of most other industries. The business is also subject to some of the strictest regulations applied to any business in a country opposed to most forms of governmental regulation. The primary reasons for the opposition stem from the undesired side effects of gambling, including gaming and substance addictions, increased crime, and prostitution. The opposition has also recognized the potential negative corollaries for tribes, such as embezzlement and fraud.[40] Concerns have also been expressed about the effects of casinos on Indian social structures and consequences to cultural preservation caused by exposure to social phenomena tribal members do not traditionally encounter. This matter is of particular importance, considering the extent to which casinos tie tribes to foreign values, capitalism being the most predominant among them. How are tribes to prevent individual prosperity from destroying their social systems? Questions have also been posed inside tribes as to the extent to which the new prosperity should be accompanied by cultural change and to what extent traditions should be preserved. These questions have caused some tribes to vote against opening a casino.[41]

In sum, such arguments generally ignore modern constructions of indigenous sovereignty. First, tribes are informed and able to decide on the issue of gaming themselves, making the patronizing tone of protective concerns unnecessary. Second, considering the kinds and levels of adversity that Indians have experienced and survived in the past—centuries of genocide, plunder, and overall persecution—the argument that mere money could abolish Indian cultures appears unconvincing. Thus, one cannot but observe that the roots of the opposition are embedded elsewhere. A closer inspection of the current relationship between tribes and the dominant society reveals a fierce dispute over money and Indian sovereignty. This is reflected both in initiatives to extend outside regulatory authority over Indian casinos, as well as court cases seeking to address the question of whether revenue provided by casinos should enjoy the same tax exemption of other Indian economic ventures.

The concept of sovereignty plays an important role in Supreme Court cases. On the surface, the main source of friction in cases between tribes and states appears to be land, as ten of the total of sixteen cases decided by the Supreme Court between 1997 and 2000 were connected to issues of control over land. However, a closer examination covering an additional eighty-six cases in which petitions for certiorari were refused by the Supreme Court alters this picture as four major categories emerge: land, Indian gaming, taxation, and Indian sovereign immunity. The latter group—in other words, tribal sovereignty—alone accounted for a total of forty cases.[42]

Kirk Douglas Billie v. State of Florida (2001)

Tension over tribal sovereignty frequently colors the relationship of the Miccosukees with the State of Florida, and it was especially present in the case of *Kirk Douglas Billie v. State of Florida,* a high-profile homicide case tried at the Miami–Dade County Circuit Court in January 2001.[43] The aftermath of this case is still being fought. The events date back to June 26, 1997, when Kirk Douglas Billie, a 31-year-old Miccosukee, went to the home of Sheila Tiger, who at the time was his girlfriend, and seized her truck. Billie drove the vehicle into a canal near the Everglades reservation. What he claims not to have known was that their two small sons were asleep in the backseat, and as the vehicle sank into the water, the boys drowned.

Despite the rather clear-cut facts, the proceedings differed greatly from those of an ordinary trial, and it developed from a manslaughter case into a battle over the historical treatment of indigenous people by the United States, the sovereign rights of Indians, and tribal justice. The incident took place in the Tamiami Canal outside the Everglades Miccosukee Reserved Area, forty miles west of Miami. The heart of the controversy related to the tribe's claims that the incident in question was an "accident" occurring on "historic Indian land," and the Miccosukees therefore should be allowed to decide how best to deal with it. This jurisdictional demand received no sympathy from the State of Florida, which instead sought to convict Billie of first-degree murder with capital punishment. In the end, Billie was convicted of second-degree murder and sentenced in a state court to life imprisonment in April 2001.[44]

The land on which the incident occurred was, despite the objections of the Miccosukees, not considered Indian land by the court, rendering it under the jurisdiction of the State of Florida.[45] Tribal rights did create, however, considerable barriers to the proceedings as State of Florida prosecutors could not, for example, serve subpoenas to potential Miccosukee witnesses residing on the reservation. The prosecution was frustrated by this and attempted to overcome the impediment through a motion to a U.S. District Court judge to obtain permission to use federal agents, who do have access to the reservation, to serve the subpoenas.[46] This generated considerable criticism from the Miccosukees, who stated that "the public should be outraged by the government's attempt to bully the Miccosukee Tribe."[47] Conversely, the exercise of tribal sovereignty generated great criticism from the Florida media. Such headlines as "Tribal Rights Frustrate Trial" and "First-Degree Murder Case Is in Danger of Crumbling" represented biased media coverage.[48] The *Miami Herald* urged that the case should not end when a verdict is reached, but instead that "state officials should press the Miccosukees to develop procedures for granting access to tribal members who are needed for court proceedings."[49]

The significance of the *Kirk Douglas Billie* case and the controversy surrounding its treatment parallels an 1881 dispute. In late summer of that year Crow Dog, a Lakota, killed the Lakota leader Spotted Tail on the Rosebud Reservation in South Dakota. The matter was dealt with by the tribe in their traditional manner, but when whites discovered that the killer had not been executed, they intervened: Crow Dog was taken to a local court, charged with murder, and sentenced to death. The decision was first upheld by the Supreme Court of Dakota Territory, but then reversed by the U.S. Supreme Court, which recognized Crow Dog's claim that the federal courts lacked jurisdiction over the matter and released him. This decision caused Congress to seek immediate action to alter existing legislation, and the outcome—the Major Crimes Act, which was enacted in 1885—granted the federal government jurisdiction over seven crimes, (murder, manslaughter, rape, assault with intent to kill, arson, burglary, and larceny) that involve Indians on Indian land. The importance of *In re Crow Dog* and the Major Crimes Act cannot be overemphasized, and for good reason both have been called a "revolution" in relations between Indians and whites. Not only did Congress clearly override a decision of the U.S. Supreme Court, but it also extended federal jurisdiction for the first time into the strictly internal affairs of tribes occurring on Indian land. Legal scholar Sidney Harring further describes the *Crow Dog* case as a bridge in

Indian law, moving it from the era of ineffective sovereignty language of *Worcester* to the subjugation of tribal sovereignty during the nineteenth century.[50]

The reasons behind the Major Crimes Act appear obscure. Why exactly was it drafted? An interesting explanation is offered by Harring, who argues that the reasons were embedded in the forces that prevailed in contemporary American society then and reflected in the desires of the Bureau of Indian Affairs to extend federal criminal jurisdiction over Indians. Harring states that since 1874, the BIA had been involved in at least six parallel murder cases, each time attempting to extend some form of criminal law, either federal or state, over tribal members. Thus, the *Crow Dog* decision proved to be the appropriate "test case" that could produce the desired legislative modifications. Had the attempt failed, the BIA already had other cases ready to pursue for the desired legal alterations.[51] Harring ascribes the acts of the BIA to a broad national movement toward the policy of assimilation and allotment. The new federal jurisdiction served these purposes in two respects: (1) the extension of criminal law increased direct white control over Indians, and (2) it undermined tribal law and traditional mechanisms of social control, thereby weakening tribal relationships, including clan structures and power hierarchies.[52]

ARM-TWISTING OVER SOVEREIGNTY

Dramatic as a comparison between the *Crow Dog* and *Billie* cases may initially appear, the recent trends in federal Indian affairs make the parallel to the 1880s appropriate, because as a consequence of gambling revenues, the status of tribal sovereignty has again become a source of fierce dispute. By the mid-1990s, even though favorable Indian policies had been implemented during the Clinton administration, the threat to tribal sovereignty was an appropriate concern. This is demonstrated, for example, by several speeches given by Attorney General Janet Reno, previously a Florida attorney, who emphasized the importance of strengthening tribal sovereignty.[53] Concern for tribal sovereignty was also present in the hearings of the U.S. Senate Committee on Indian Affairs, as issues relating to Indian sovereignty in 1998 were raised in a total of eight different discussions of the committee and subsequently led to the introduction of two bills directed at protecting tribal immunity.[54]

Since then concerns over tribal sovereignty issues have been pushed to the sidelines, and concern over Indian gaming has regained center stage, a tendency that appears only to have intensified during the presidency of George W. Bush. This is visible in recent discussions of the Senate Indian Affairs Committee and sessions of the 107th Congress, where Indian immunity and sovereignty issues have been replaced by hearings on the IGRA and taxing gambling. An analysis of some of the 2001 bills discussed by Congress shows a pattern of tighter regulation and increased sovereignty limitations, as demonstrated by a bill labeled "Tribal and

Local Community Relationship Improvement Act," that mainly imposed further regulations on Indian gaming. The same year also produced a six-page amendment to the already lengthy IGRA. Initiatives to increase the maximum yearly fee collected by the Indian Gambling Commission in charge of monitoring Indian casinos, from $1.8 million of 1997 to $8 million, and to require state approval to new Indian gambling facilities were made. This proposed law implies the elimination of tribal sovereignty.[55] Recent years have also witnessed gross violations of tribal sovereignty on the part of states, including the imposition of unauthorized labor agreements on tribes in California,[56] and a bill called S. 1691, introduced first in 1998 by Senator Slade Gorton of Washington State that forces Indians to collect state retail taxes from non-Indians in casinos. This proposed law implies the elimination of tribal sovereignty.[57]

Thus, tribal sovereignty is under attack by serious political pressure. The U.S. Supreme Court is responding to these pressures by restricting Indian rights. In 2001, the question of tribal casino taxing was brought before the Supreme Court in two cases: *Chickasaw Nation v. United States* and *United States v. Little Six Inc.,* both of which involved the federal excise tax and its applicability to "pull-tab" games at Indian casinos. To complicate matters, the cases had received opposite decisions from lower courts. In *Little Six,* the revenue was exempted from federal taxation, whereas in *Chickasaw Nation* it was not. Before these cases, the Supreme Court had been quite unequivocal about the issue and had systematically upheld tribes and their commercial activities as enjoying exemption. These two cases, however, reversed that tendency. *Chickasaw Nation* was resolved first, causing the *Little Six* case to be sent back to the Court of Appeals without a verdict. In *Chickasaw Nation,* the Court held that the pertinent section of 2719(d)(i) of the IGRA does not exempt tribes from paying gambling-related taxes as defined in Chapter 35 of the Internal Revenue Code.[58] The Supreme Court sided with the Court of Appeal's reasoning that pull-tab games are considered a "lottery" and are taxable wagers and that the Chickasaw Nation was considered a "person" and subject to taxes.[59] The Court also ruled that the IGRA does not preclude the imposition of federal wagering excise taxes and that the self-government guarantee of the 1855 treaty between the United States and the Chickasaw Nation did not prevent the imposition of the taxes in question.[60] The significance of this decision is undisputed; it significantly undermines tribal sovereignty in favor of external authority.

CONCLUSION

It appears, therefore, that yet another era may be dawning in the relationships of Native Americans and the United States, one which could bring an end to the expressed policy of self-determination. One cannot help but be reminded of the grim history of Indian-U.S. relations, as it has at least twice before shown how favorable policies abruptly turn into efforts to abolish tribes, first in the 1880s through the policies of assimilation and allotment and in the 1950s and 1960s through termination and relocation policies.[61] This time around something is notably different. Indians are in a position never before experienced in their history. They have the legal ability to fight back. This is evident from the ongoing relationships of the Miccosukees and the State of Florida, particularly after the case of Kirk Douglas Billie. Despite the wishes of Florida, the tribe's sovereign rights "surfaced with a vengeance in the Florida Legislature" during the spring of 2002.[62] A bill was introduced that would cause the State of Florida to lose its jurisdiction to investigate crimes on Miccosukee tribal land, rendering authority solely to Miccosukee tribal courts and federal courts.[63] The State of Florida was anything but happy with this proposal, and Governor Jeb Bush stated that he leaned toward vetoing the bill if it passed.[64] Similar bills were introduced in 2004, 2005, and 2006, but they failed to pass. The issue was reintroduced in 2008.[65] Regardless of this bill's ultimate fate, it remains certain that the relationship of the State of Florida and the Miccosukees is far from being settled, with neither side showing signs of giving in.

Over 200 years ago, the new American nation declared "legal" war on Indians, and now, for the first time in history, Indians have the weapons needed to succeed in this war—meaning access to courts and lawyers—thanks to the money brought to them by casinos and three decades of more favorable Indian policies and federal legislation. Thus, it appears that the war government authorities hoped to use to extinguish treaty rights will not be an easy one to fight. Indians have a real chance to prevail.

NOTES

1. The status of land under Indian law is greatly confusing, following decades of inconsistent legislation. For an introduction, see Stephen L. Pevar, *The Rights of Indians and Tribes*, 2nd ed. (Carbondale: Southern Illinois University Press, 1992), and in particular 16–22. The law governing Indian gaming is the *Indian Gaming Regulatory Act* (IGRA), *U.S. Code*, Chapter 25, Title 29: Indian Gaming Regulatory Act, http://www4.law.cornell.edu/uscode/.

2. Pauliina Raento, "Paheesta perheviihteeksi. Peliteollisuuden leviäminen ja kasvu Yhdysvalloissa [From Vice to Family Entertainment. The Expansion and Growth of the Gaming Industry in the United States]," in *Yhdysvallat—näkökulmia jälkiteolliseen yhteiskuntaan* [The United States—Perspectives on Postindustrial Society], ed. Paulinna Raento and Ilkka K. Lakaniemi (Gaudeamus: University Press of Finland, 1999), 144–58.

3. U.S. Senate, *Tribal Government Tax-Exempt Bond Authority Amendments Act of 2001*, January 3, 2001, http://www.senate.gov.

4. Many of the tribes have gained a measure of economic independence from ventures such as opening dumps on their reservations. Although some commentators view

such ventures favorably, caution is appropriate. It is difficult to imagine how accepting the refuse of the dominant society could, despite new economic possibilities, help disadvantaged tribes to achieve a truly egalitarian position. See Richard J. Perry, *From Time Immemorial: Indigenous Peoples and State Systems* (Austin: University of Texas Press, 1996), 18. The creation of open dumps has also been found to cause serious health and environmental hazards, as the impoverished tribes lack the means to implement proper refuse treatment, a concern that led to the drafting of a proposed statute, "Indian Open Dumps Cleanup," *U.S. Code,* Title 25, Chapter 41, http://www4.law.cornell.edu/uscode.

5. Sidney L. Harring, *Crow Dog's Case: American Indian Sovereignty, Tribal Law, and United States Law in the Nineteenth Century* (New York: Cambridge University Press, 1994), 13–15.

6. U.S. Supreme Court cases involving or affecting Native Americans are available at http://thorpe.ou.edu/supreme.html.

7. It should, however, be noted that the potency of current discussions for offering generalizations is limited by the fact that the cases of the Supreme Court regarding Indians are not available after this year. Thus, it is difficult to make comparisons and establish exactly how numbers have changed over years. To assume that the number has increased as a sign of the Indians' new social activism is, however, supported by the other initiatives taken in recent years.

8. *Encyclopaedia Juridica Fennica VI: Kansainväliset suhteet* (Jyväskylä, Finland: Gummerus Kirjapaino Oy, 1998), 1,028.

9. Riitta Laitinen, "Vahvistuvan itsemääräämisen haasteet—intiaanien aseman kehittyminenYhdysvalloissa," in ed. Raento and Lakaniemi, 86.

10. For a discussion on isolation, see Russel Lawrence Barsh, "The Challenge of Indigenous Self-Determination," in *Native American Sovereignty,* vol. 6, ed. John R. Wunder (New York: Garland Publishing, 1996), 143–78.

11. The symposiums both increased tribal interaction and raised public awareness about the current stage of Indian affairs. The 1997 symposium held in Miami made headlines in the local media. See "Indian Leaders Discuss Sovereignty Issues at Symposium," *Miami Herald Tribune,* March 14, 1997, http://www.miami.com/herald/newslibrary/. The news media also played an important role as demonstrated by the proliferation of websites such as the one providing access to the Constitution, tribal codes, and other legal documents. See http://thorpe.ou.edu. The media have been called an important factor as well in the overall revival of Indian cultures through such films as *The Last of the Mohicans* and *Dances with Wolves.* For a discussion, see Laitinen, "Vahvistuvan itsemääräämisen haasteet," 82–83.

12. Laitinen, "Vahvistuvan itsemääräämisen haasteet," 84.

13. Native American Rights Fund home page, http://www.narf.org.

14. Francis Paul Prucha, *The Great Father,* abridged ed. (Lincoln: University of Nebraska Press, 1986), 379.

15. U.S. Department of Justice, Presidential Documents, "Government to Government Relations with Native American Tribal Governments," April 29, 1994; and Presidential Documents, "Consultation and Coordination with Indian Tribal Governments," May 14, 1998, http://www.usdoj.gov/archive/.

16. The bill was passed by the U.S. House of Representatives in October 2000 and

subsequently forwarded to the White House. Clinton did not approve the bill during his presidency. U.S. Senate Press Release, "Campbell's Land Consolidation, Business, Development Bills Sent to the President," October 23, 2000, http://www.senate.gov.

17. U.S. Senate Press Release, "Campbell: Budget Numbers Mask Quiet Decline in Federal Spending for Indians," February 26, 1997; and Campbell Committee Approves Increased Funding for Indian Programs," February 29, 2000, http://www.senate.gov.

18. "When Your Number—and Letter—Is Up: Answering the Call of the Bingo Game," *Miami Herald*, September 8, 1996. It should, however, be noted that the opening of the casino has not been without controversy among the Miccosukees. A group of tribal members, calling itself "The Governing Body of the Unconquered Seminole Nation," renounces any contact with the casino, while simultaneously the current chairman of the Miccosukee General Council, Billy Cypress, poses on the casino's website. See http://www.miccosukeeseminolenation.com.

19. "Miccosukees Now Sanction Own Bouts: Chairman Promises Cards Will Have High Profile and Club Fights," *Miami Herald*, February 1, 1999; and http://www.miccosukee.com.

20. Diane Ward, attorney for Kirk Douglas Billie, in personal communication relating to the murder trial of *State of Florida v. Kirk Douglas Billie*, March 14, 2001.

21. "A Glimpse at the Miccosukee Tribe of Indians of Florida," Miccosukee Tribe of Indians Press Release, January 29, 2001, http://miccosukeeTribe.com/business.html. Documents obtained from the Office of Lehtinen, Vargas & Reiner, attorneys for the Miccosukee Tribe.

22. Native American Rights Fund, http://www.narf.org.

23. "Success of Miccosukees Hailed," *Miami Herald*, April 9, 2002.

24. "Miccosukee Tribe: Communication from Miccosukee Council Chairman Billy Cypress to State Attorney Katherine Fernandez-Rundle regarding *State v. Kirk Billie,* Case No. F97–21004," August 31, 2000, http://miccosukeeTribe.com/business.html.

25. Ibid.

26. The number derives from the lawsuits reported in the *Miami Herald* from 1995 to 2001. It is, however, unlikely that the number is mistaken, as court proceedings between Indian tribes and states are always cause for headlines. See http://www.miami.com/herald/newslibrary.

27. "Miccosukees Challenge Everglades Plan," *Miami Herald*, September 17, 1997; and "Everglades Plan Called Hazard," *Miami Herald*, November 20, 1997.

28. The final outcome of the situation remains to be seen. The plan was controversial, such as the opposition of conservationists to certain nominations to the plan steering panel by Governor Jeb Bush. See "Biologist's Allegiance Questioned," *Miami Herald*, September 20, 1999.

29. "Tribe Council's Aide Sues Dade," *Miami Herald*, May 20, 2000.

30. "Glades Plans Split Tribe," *Miami Herald*, July 22, 1998. The issue was finally decided on July 8, 1998, by Congress, but no information is available on the status of the land and whether the Miccosukees obtained total control over it. Senate, Hearings of the Committee on Indian Affairs for the 105th Congress, http://www.senate.gov/~scia/105.

31. "Miccosukees Win Some Breathing Room: Tribe Can Build 30 New Houses," *Miami Herald*, October 26, 1996.

32. Miccosukee Tribe, http://miccosukeeTribe.com/business.html.

33. *Miami Herald*, June 12, 1999.

34. As gambling is outlawed in Florida, casinos are only entitled to "class II" gaming, which according to Section 2703(7) (7)(A) means the following:

"(i) the game of chance commonly known as bingo (whether or not electronic, computer, or other technologic aids are used in connection therewith)—

(I) which is played for prizes, including monetary prizes, with cards bearing numbers or other designations,

(II) in which the holder of the card covers such numbers or designations when objects, similarly numbered or designated, are drawn or electronically determined, and

(III) in which the game is won by the first person covering a previously designated arrangement of numbers or designations on such cards, including (if played in the same location) pull-tabs, lotto, punch boards, tip jars, instant bingo, and other games similar to bingo." See IGRA.

In reality, this categorization appears difficult to follow, as traditional bingo games are assisted by computerized scanning devices, multiplying the number of sheets played simultaneously and escalating the amounts to be gambled. See "Indian Leaders Discuss Sovereignty Issues at Symposium," *Miami Herald Tribune*, March 14, 1997. Considering the speed at which the gaming and computer technologies develop, the categorization will undoubtedly have to be modified. This fact has also been recognized by policymakers, who issued the Indian Gaming Regulatory Act of 2001, another six-page addition to IGRA.

35. "New Hotels to Deliver 6,000 Jobs in Miami-Dade," *Miami Herald*, March 3, 2000; "It's Time Florida Legalized Casinos," *Miami Herald*, February 8, 2000; "In Florida, Another Roll of the Dice? Casino Fans, Foes for Battle," *Miami Herald*, November 3, 1996.

36. Robert M. Jarvis, "The 2007 Seminole-Florida Gambling Compact," *Gaming Law Review* 12 (February 2008): 13; "Gaming Action," *Miccosukee Tribe of Indians of Florida*, http://www.miccosukee.com/entertainment_gaming.htm.

37. "Tribal Gaming Grows Despite Fight with State," *Miami Herald*, July 9, 2000.

38. U.S. Senate Press Release, "Campbell Introduces Bill to Preserve Integrity of Indian Gaming," July 31, 1997, http://www.senate.gov.

39. The number refers to both tried cases and denied petitions for certiorari, with the subsequent numbers being 2 and 10. Indian gaming has also encouraged states to exert their rights to tax tribes; in the same years, a total of 24 petitions for certiorari relating to IGRA and taxation were delivered, of which two led to a decision. See http://thorpe.ou.edu/supreme.html.

40. This primary concern is also expressed in the IGRA. One of its explicit purposes is stated to be providing a statutory basis to shield tribes from organized crime and other corrupting influences. To address this concern, the IGRA initiated the establishment of the National Indian Gaming Commission, stated to be essential to meet "congressional concerns regarding gaming and to protect such gaming as a means of generating tribal revenue." The concern is in practice reflected as monitoring the hiring of primary management

officials and key employees and the supervision of gaming revenues to ensure that they are used for the purposes set forth in the IGRA. *U.S. Code,* Chapter 25, Title 29, Section 2702.2 and 3; and 2710 (F)(ii)(II).

41. Laitinen, "Vahvistuvan itsemääräämisen haasteet," 81.

42. U.S. Supreme Court, http://thorpe.ou.edu/supreme.html.

43. Case No. F97–21004, document obtained from the Office of Lehtinen, Vargas and Reiner, attorneys for the Miccosukee Tribe.

44. "Billie Gets Maximum—Life Sentence," *Miami Herald,* April 20, 2001.

45. Jurisdiction over Indian crimes is a confusing matter, governed, in part, by the Major Crimes Act. For an introduction, see Pevar, *Rights of Indians and Tribes,* 129–53.

46. At the end, the prosecution lawyers solved their dilemma by serving subpoenas on witnesses as they left the reservation. Miami-Dade police officers were reported to have waited for Sheila Tiger to leave the reservation and then taken her into custody to get her to testify in the case. Wayne and Margaret Billie, Kirk's parents, were served subpoenas in the hallway of the courthouse when they arrived at the courtroom to support their son. See "Mom of Drowned Boys Compelled to Testify," *Miami Herald,* January 9, 2001.

47. "Miccosukee Tribe responds to attempt to subvert tribal sovereignty by State of Florida. Statement issued by Billy Cypress," Miccosukee Tribe, September 26, 2000.

48. "Tribe Rejects Subpoenas in Murder Inquiry," *Miami Herald,* September 28, 2000; and "Tribal Rights Frustrate Trial," *Miami Herald,* January 16, 2001. These sentiments are echoed in the statements of the prosecution attorneys who argued that "Congress never intended when it created Indian reservations to make them safe havens for murderers." See "American Indian on trial for killing two children," Reuters Internet edition available through "FindLaw Legal News," http://news.findlaw.com/legalnews/s/20010215/crimemiccosukee.html.

49. "To the Point: Respect US Law," *Miami Herald,* January 12, 2001.

50. Harring, *Crow Dog's Case,* 101.

51. Ibid., 115, 134.

52. Ibid., 101–2.

53. U.S. Department of Justice, "Report of the Executive Committee for Indian Country Law Enforcement Improvements," *Final Report to the Attorney General and the Secretary of the Interior,* http://www.usdoj.gov/otj/icredact.htm.

54. U.S. Senate, "Hearings of the Committee on Indian Affairs for the 105th Congress," http://www.senate.gov.

55. "Campbell Introduces Bill to Preserve Integrity of Indian Gaming"; and U.S. Senate, "Tribal Government Tax-Exempt Bond Authority Amendments Act of 2001" (Introduced in the House), January 3, 2001, "Indian Gaming Regulatory Improvement Act of 2001" (Introduced in the Senate), May 3, 2001, "Tribal and Local Communities Relationship Improvement Act" (Introduced in the House), June 19, 2001, and "Internet Gambling Payments Prohibition Act" (Introduced in the House), July 20, 2001, http://www.senate.gov.

56. U.S. Senate, "Tribal Sovereign Protection Act" (Introduced in the House), January 3, 2001, http://www.senate.gov.

57. See "Campbell Introduces Tribal Conflict Resolution Bill," http://www.senate.gov.

58. U.S. Code, Title 2, http://www4.law.cornell.edu/uscode/.

59. *Chickasaw Nation v. United States,* Docket No. 00–50, decided on November 27, 2001, http://thorpe.ou.edu/supreme.html.

60. "Miccosukee Power Play to Remove State Jurisdiction," *Miami Herald,* March 7, 2002.

61. For a brief description of Indian policies, see Pevar, *Rights of Indians and Tribes,* 1–9.

62. "Miccosukee Power Play," *Miami Herald,* March 7, 2002.

63. "Law Would Keep Cops Off Reservation," *Miami Herald,* March 2, 2002.

64. "Governor May Veto Bill on Tribal Land Crimes," *Miami Herald,* March 14, 2002.

65. See HB 231—Reservations of the Miccosukee Tribe of Indians of Florida, Florida House of Representatives. http://www.myfloridahouse.gov/Sections/Bills/billsdetail.aspx ?BillId=31762.

CHAPTER 11

Teaching and Learning about Native North
America: An Analysis of Educational Standards for
Schools in the United States and Canada

SUSAN A. WUNDER

TEACHING AND LEARNING about the indigenous peoples of North America is an important aspect of K–12 education in the United States and Canada. This chapter is focused on how these were addressed in the curricula of the various states, provinces, and territories at the beginning of the twenty-first century.

Specifically, I analyze content related to Native North Americans in available state, provincial, and territorial social studies standards adopted between 1967 and 2002. The focus is on the standards for national history courses at the high school level, because national history is the most commonly taught social studies content in both the United States and Canada. The vast majority of states and other local American education bodies also have legislation or rules requiring the teaching of U.S. history, and this is likely the last formal course many students in both American and Canadian high schools take that addresses national history.

The study used state, provincial, and territorial standards available on Internet websites,[1] as they are official educational sources readily available to citizens, parents, students, and teachers. Relevant standards for all states in the United States were available, except three: Rhode Island and Nebraska (under development); and Iowa (not developing standards in any subject). High school social studies standards and/or curriculum for all Canadian jurisdictions were identified except for Nunavut where educational policies are in development; the Northwest Territories, which with Manitoba, Saskatchewan, Alberta, British Columbia, and Yukon Territory, is part of the Western Canadian Protocol that is in the process of developing a K–12 social studies curriculum; and Prince Edward Island, Nova Scotia, and New

Brunswick, all participants in the Atlantic Canada Education Foundation with Newfoundland and Labrador that have a regional social studies curriculum for eighth-graders. In all, fifty-five state, provincial, and territorial standards for high school–level American and Canadian history comprise the data set for this study.

A BRIEF CONTEXT FOR NORTH AMERICAN SOCIAL STUDIES STANDARDS

In the United States and Canada, most decisions about education traditionally have been reserved to the states, provinces, and territories. Teacher and administrator certification, student requirements, curricular content, and other policies and procedures are determined by legislatures, parliaments, boards of education, departments or ministries of education, school districts, and schools at levels of smaller scope than the national. Indeed, local control of education is not considered an oversight in the national constitutions, but rather a firm commitment to the belief that those closest to the schools can and should best decide how their educational programs should be conducted.

This is not to say that the national governments of the United States and Canada have no interest in or influence on education. Indeed, national governments pass legislation, contribute funding, and organize programs that have important implications at the state, provincial, territorial, and local levels. In Canada, each province and/or territory has a minister of education, and in 1967 they formed the Council of Ministers of Education (CMEC) to serve as "the national voice for education in Canada."[2] Through this organization, the ministers consult and collaborate on initiatives among themselves and with the federal government.

The United States established the federal Department of Education in 1979 (which became effective in 1980, and was preceded by the Department of Health, Education, and Welfare established in 1953) as the national agency that "establishes policy for, administers, and coordinates most federal assistance to education," executes the president's policies and congressional laws, and ensures "that all have equal access to education and to promote excellence in our nation's schools."[3] One of the Department's stated purposes is to supplement and complement state and other educational and related institutions and organizations.[4]

During the 1980s and 1990s, most states in the United States wrote and implemented standards-based reforms. The intent was to "anchor key aspects of policy— curriculum, assessment, teacher education, and professional development—around policy level statements of what students should know and be able to do."[5] This effort was in large part due to a period of increased attention to and demands in the public sphere for "world-class" standards for students in the United States to keep pace with perceived economic advances as well as scholastic testing accomplishments of students in other countries. By 2001, forty-nine states (all but Iowa) had adopted standards in at least most of the core subject areas, and most have some form of assessing student attainment of standards content.[6] In Canada, many of the provinces and territories have also prepared curriculum standards for various grade levels and laid out examination procedures as well.

No one argues against setting high expectations of students. Likewise, there is widespread support for ensuring that all students have equitable access to an education with a substantive curriculum well-taught by a qualified teacher. Whether local education agencies must and/or should adopt standards to ensure these outcomes has been debated, and two aspects—assessment and content—of the standards movement have been and continue to be especially controversial.

The issues related to assessment focus primarily on the type known as "high stakes." In these situations, students may be denied promotion or graduation and/or teachers may be penalized and/or whole districts may be put into receivership in some locations based on students' performances. Proponents of standardized testing of students argue that such procedures are in place in other countries and provide objective views of student learning of a core set of knowledge and skills.[7] Critics have raised important questions about the fairness, utility, redundancy, bias, and expense of such standardized testing. A paradox between standardization and interest in and commitment to diversity is also seen to exist.[8]

A second standards controversy has revolved around the curricular content within standards. This has been the case with both state standards and those developed by professional educational organizations. The latter were created to guide and assist various levels, of curricula decision makers, parents, students, and the wider public at about the same time as the states were writing their own standards. Leading the way was the National Council for the Teaching of Mathematics, which developed widely accepted standards for students at all grade levels, and similar efforts were undertaken in science, language arts, and other disciplines. The field of social studies proved to be the most complex and controversial.

In the mid-1990s, at least five different professional educational groups in broadly defined social studies areas wrote standards. These included documents in civics and government,[9] geography,[10] social studies,[11] history,[12] and economics.[13] Of these five, four were U.S. based and focused, while social studies standards were developed by an international organization, the National Council for the Social Studies. One might ask: Why so many? This question addresses a fundamental and ongoing debate within the field: the purpose and content of social studies education. For many, social studies comprise the fields of history plus all social science disciplines (geography, government, sociology, psychology, anthropology, psychology, and economics) as well as related fields in the humanities. For others, social studies comprise a history-centered and history-based subject area that is informed to a lesser degree by content from related social science fields. For still others, each social science field merits and requires curriculum that is discipline based. The differences in opinion and thrust are long-standing and important but beyond the scope of this essay.

Of the various sets of national standards, those in the area of history were the most unique, complex, controversial, and germane to the topic of the study of Native North American history. In 1991, the National Endowment for the Humanities and the U.S. Department of Education decided to provide funding for national standards for history. Over the next nearly three years, panels of teachers, historians, educators, and interested others debated and formulated standards in U.S. and world history. While the standards were always considered to be voluntary, they were also intended to be a model of excellence for history content. The story of their development has been chronicled elsewhere,[14] but it is important to note that fundamental debates throughout the process centered around questions of content related to significant questions: Who were the players in history? What do decisions about who is included in the national story mean for the nation's students and ultimately their views of history as a subject and of their country as a home? What is the importance of including multiple perspectives on individuals, events, and policies? Is history a sequence of facts and/or is it an interpretive activity?

Arguments against the initial history standards centered on the interpretation that they minimized, and even omitted, heroes and positive events, and instead emphasized aberrant, unpleasant episodes and not-so-important figures in world and U.S. history. After months of high-profile public appearances and op-ed pieces prepared by promoters and detractors of the history standards, the U.S. Senate supported by a 99–1 vote a resolution not to adopt the standards, and furthermore, "that any new project supported by federal funds should show 'a decent respect for the contributions of Western civilization.'"[15] After a period of revisions, the world and U.S. history standards were made available without federal funding to schools and districts throughout the country, and they are cited as sources in a number of existing state standards documents.

A similar debate erupted in Canada as seen in the publication of J.L. Granatstein's *Who Killed Canadian History?* in 1998. Noting the importance of high standards for schoolchildren and youth, Granatstein bemoaned the "parochial regionalism," "antielitist education," "political correctness," and "the ethnic communities that have been conned by Canada's multiculturalism policy into demanding an offense-free education for all Canadian children, so that the idea that Canada has a past and a culture has been all but lost."[16] Countering this view of Canadian history is Daniel Francis, who wrote,

Many people seem to believe that the problem is that our kids are not being taught the old myths. I say, thank God they are not. The story of Canada I learned from my schoolbooks is totally inadequate for understanding Canadian society as it is today.[17]

From this passionate debate over Canadian history content and standards for students, Peter Seixas of the University of British Columbia identified three fundamental views of teaching history and of dealing with such conflicting views of national history.[18] He calls the first "enhancing collective memory," in which the best story of the past is conveyed. With this approach, group identity and social cohesion are developed. The second approach is a "disciplinary" one in which students read and evaluate positions of various sides of issues and draw informed conclusions, a hallmark of informed citizens. The third approach Seixas calls "postmodern," wherein students figure out how various individuals and groups approach their pasts and how these interpretations influence the present. The "history wars" revolved around support for and discomfort with standards and curriculum that seemed to support one of these approaches to teaching and learning history to the exclusion of others and to the overall perceived betterment of students and citizens.

The development of standards for history and general social studies at the various state, provincial, and territorial levels has also been long and sometimes contentious. While none of these entities has adopted any of the subject-area standards of the professional associations in a wholesale manner, certain concepts and even phrases are evident. Here several important extant conflicts intersect:

1. Should students study social studies and/or history? Which discipline(s) contribute to students' necessary knowledge, skills, and dispositions for citizenship, the oft-stated goal of the field?
2. What is history? Is it a chronological detailing of individuals, groups, events, and dates and/or a more disciplinary, inquiry-based approach to the study of the past in which ideas, analyses, and theories are developed?
3. Who should be included in a national history? As "the new history" seeks to include individuals and groups once omitted from the great leaders approach, what should be done in the way of inclusion of women, minority groups, and the poor? What is the place of multiculturalism?

INDIGENOUS HISTORY CONTENT IN SOCIAL STUDIES STANDARDS

In a survey regarding the status of multicultural education in the United States administered in 1998, Bruce M. Mitchell and Robert E. Salsbury asked if Native American history was a part of each state curriculum. Of the forty-eight states that responded, twenty-four replied that they do include Native content, typically within the social studies curriculum. Five additional states responded "no," and nineteen states were unclear, had no state curriculum, or explained that local districts can or must include Native and/or pluralistic content in the curriculum.[19]

A detailed analysis of specific standards helps to define the Mitchell-Salsbury survey findings. For this purpose, standards of states, provinces, and territories were grouped by their discipline stance as "social studies," "history," or "national history." This helped to determine whether these standards offered broader views of social studies content, general history content, or specifically national (American or Canadian) history content.

Examination of the following table suggests interesting findings on the importance of social studies versus history content. While four states have curriculum at the high school level blended into social studies, the remaining locales in the study specifically identified history content and/or themes such as "time, continuity and change" (which included both world and national history) or, in the majority, further categorized the curriculum into Canadian or American history (although many of these also referred to their overall standards document as "social studies standards").

STATES, PROVINCES, AND TERRITORIES BY TYPE OF SUBJECT STANDARDS

Social Studies Standards	History Standards	History of U.S. or Canadian Standards
Arkansas	Alaska	Alabama
Missouri	Colorado	Arizona
Minnesota	Connecticut	California
Montana	Delaware	District of Columbia
	Florida	Georgia
	Hawaii	Idaho
	Kentucky	Illinois
	Louisiana	Indiana
	Maine	Kansas
	Massachusetts	Maryland
	Michigan	Mississippi
	Nevada	New Hampshire
	New Jersey	New York
	New Mexico	North Carolina
	North Dakota	Ohio
	South Carolina	Oklahoma
	South Dakota	Oregon
	Vermont	Pennsylvania
	Wisconsin	Tennessee
	Wyoming	Texas
		Utah
		Virginia

Social Studies Standards	History Standards	History of U.S. or Canadian Standards
		Washington
		West Virginia
		Alberta
		British Columbia and Yukon Territory
		Newfoundland and Labrador
		Ontario
		Québec
		Saskatchewan

In the next stage of this study, state, provincial, and territorial standards were analyzed for their level of specified curriculum detail. Standards were described as "high" if they identified particular individuals, dates, and/or events as required detailed content for students. For example, in their U.S. colonial history units, Alabama students must "analyze the colonists' relationship with Native Americans," including the exchange of goods and services, hostilities such as King Phillip's War and Bacon's Rebellion, expansion into Native American lands, and alliances of the French and the Hurons and the British and Iroquois Confederation.[20]

"Medium" standards included historical themes, concepts, and skills, and gave specific examples for performance indicators. For example, eleventh-graders in Virginia "will analyze and explain the contacts between American Indians and European settlers during the Age of Discovery, in terms of economic and cultural characteristics of the groups; motives and strategies of the explorers and settlers; impacts of European settlement on the American Indians; and legacies of contact, cooperation, and conflict from that period."[21]

"Low" specification standards offered historical themes and concepts but provided no required knowledge of specific historical details. For example, by graduation, students in Montana must "analyze the significance of important people, events, and ideas (e.g., political and intellectual leadership, inventions, discoveries, the arts) in the major eras/civilizations in the history of Montana, American Indian tribes, the United States, and the world."[22]

Using these categories, the states, provinces, and territories may be grouped as having standards with high, medium, or low specifications of detailed curricular content. A look at the next table shows that only two jurisdictions had prepared standards with "high" levels of specified content, while twenty-one of the fifty-five sets of standards under consideration had written curricula "low" in specifics. The majority had expectations for student learning that fall somewhere in between in the "medium" range where broader statements about learning history are made and then exemplified by more particular examples. These three approaches roughly correlate to views of history in terms of whether it is a collection of detailed, factual information ("high"), and/or a study of disciplinary scholarly approaches ("low"), or some combination of the two ("medium") in which identified historical information comprises a basis on which historical analysis and interpretation are related.

STATES, PROVINCES, AND TERRITORIES BY LEVEL OF
CURRICULAR CONTENT

High	Medium	Low
Alabama	Arizona	Alaska
Nevada	California	Arkansas
	Colorado	Connecticut
	Florida	Delaware
	Georgia	District of Columbia
	Idaho	Hawaii
	Illinois	Kentucky
	Indiana	Louisiana
	Kansas	Maine
	Maryland	Michigan
	Massachusetts	Missouri
	Minnesota	New Jersey
	Mississippi	North Carolina
	Montana	Oregon
	New Hampshire	South Dakota
	New Mexico	Vermont
	New York	Washington
	North Dakota	West Virginia
	Ohio	Wisconsin
	Oklahoma	Wyoming
	Pennsylvania	British Columbia & Yukon
	South Carolina	Territory
	Tennessee	Québec
	Texas	
	Utah	
	Virginia	
	Alberta	
	Manitoba	
	Newfoundland & Labrador	
	Ontario	
	Saskatchewan	

INCLUSION OF INDIGENOUS HISTORY IN
SCHOOL CURRICULA

What, then, do these social studies/history/American or Canadian history standards, be they of high, medium, or low specificity of content, suggest for teaching and learning about Native North America? This study developed criteria from a collection of recommendations from various agencies committed to accurate and appropriate representation and inclusion of indigenous peoples in school curricula. These include recommendations for assigning reading materials, often for school-aged children;[23] visiting museums with Native collections;[24] including contacts and information from organizations of and for Native peoples;[25] and using suggestions from national academic organizations.[26]

Using these action plans, a set of guidelines for teaching and learning about Native North America can be drawn to avoid stereotyping and to ensure the inclusion of accurate knowledge and skills for students. This may include avoiding unrealistic yet popular images of what Native peoples do; how, where, and when they live; and what they believe.

Three specific guidelines emerged. First, use the names of tribes and Native individuals whenever possible. While indigenous peoples accept and apply various terms for themselves, using only terms such as "Native Americans" or "Aboriginals" suggests a uniformity that is inaccurate. Second, include the study of Native peoples in discussions and curricula of the present day. Often the indigenous presence is portrayed as having disappeared with the "closing of the western frontier" or as relevant in the United States only at Thanksgiving in November. Finally, embrace Native voices and perspectives. Explain the rich oral traditions of many Native peoples, and include their views of events through written forms in part to provide multiple and accurate perspectives on the past and present.

Of those states, provinces, and territories with standards for national history courses, several meet this first guideline—inclusion of specific Native American/First Nations individuals and tribes. Alabama standards,[27] for example, include the Seminoles and Black Hawk; Arizona[28] and California[29] standards specify learning about the Navajo code talkers; and Newfoundland and Labrador[30] give attention to the Metis people and Buffy Sainte-Marie, among others. These states and provinces are in the categories of high- and middle-level specification of content.

Many standards include content specifying the study of indigenous peoples in the modern era (for purposes here considered to be after the nineteenth century), relative to the second guideline. They include Alabama,[31] Arizona,[32] California,[33] Maryland,[34] New York,[35] Ohio,[36] Pennsylvania,[37] Utah,[38] Alberta,[39] British Columbia and Yukon Territory,[40] Manitoba,[41] Newfoundland and Labrador,[42] and Ontario.[43] These locales range across the three levels of high, moderate, and low specificity of standards content.

An example of such content comes from the Maryland standards in which students:

Analyze how the advances in the African American civil rights movement influenced the agendas and strategies in the quest of Native Americans, Asian Americans, and Hispanic Americans for civil rights and equality of opportunities.[44]

Similarly, students in Ontario will "demonstrate an understanding of the contributions of various social and political movements in Canadian history during the twentieth century" and

describe the contributions of Aboriginal peoples in forming national Organizations (e.g., National Indian Advisory Council, National Indian Brotherhood, Assembly of First Nations) to gain recognition and rights for Aboriginal peoples.[45]

The third guideline, inclusion of Native voices and perspectives, is perhaps the most complex to identify in the standards because it can be developed a number of ways. Ohio standards are quite direct, for example, in stating that "students analyze the impact of commonality and diversity among perspectives, practices and products of cultural, ethnic and social groups within local, national, regional and global settings," including the American Indian Movement (AIM).[46] Likewise, students of Canadian history in Saskatchewan should approach their studies with three views of history, Native studies, and social studies.[47] In other locales, usually with low specificity of detailed content, standards are included that can and should incorporate Native voices and perspectives. Washington state standards, for example, "compare and evaluate competing historical narratives, analyze multiple perspectives, and challenge arguments for historical inevitability."[48]

CONCLUSION

In viewing the existing state, provincial, and territorial standards for students studying national history, there is obviously a broad range of approaches to and inclusion of Native North American content. Those states with the highest levels of specified content may include details, such as names of tribes and Native individuals. The states with moderate levels of specificity may also do so and sometimes also lead toward more complex understandings, such as Native perspectives. However, it is the standards with the lowest level of specified content that seem to encourage and open the possibility for the highest level of thinking in terms of Native perspectives and historical interpretation.

Of course, high school national history courses are not the only times and places where students in the United States and Canada do or should learn about Native North America. Such study should begin early in the child's educational program and should occur in courses in language, literature, science, music, and art. Several organizations in Canada and the United States have developed standards, guidelines, and/or recommendations that supplement history/social studies and all subject area standards to ensure the overall inclusion of Native content. Alaska, for example, has "Standards for Culturally-Responsive Schools" that are intended as "a complement to [and] not as a replacement for" other state standards.[49] In New Brunswick, the Department of Education has an Aboriginal Education division,[50] and the Northwest Territories provides resources for culture-based education.[51] Students in British Columbia have a choice between Social Studies 11 or BC First Nations Studies to meet graduation requirements,[52] and Alberta offers an optional course in Aboriginal studies for high school students.[53]

Initiatives such as these are likely to heighten awareness of the need and desirability of including Native North American content in history, social studies, and all subject areas. It is important to remember that education in each state, province, and territory is influenced to various extents by the adopted standards. Some are considered voluntary guidelines. Others have statewide testing of their content with varying provisions for support, remediation, and/or accountability. For the most part, standards identify the minimum expectations for the teaching and learning of academic content.

The most important consideration, however, is what happens between the teacher and his or her students in the classroom every day. Teachers must retain professional responsibility in making curricular and instructional decisions about national history for Native and non-Native students. In so doing, they make an important contribution to what James Banks has described has "multicultural citizenship," which helps students and the society maintain a balance of local, national, and global identities. As Banks wrote,

> Citizens should be able to maintain attachments to their cultural communities as well as participate effectively in the shared national culture. Cultural and ethnic communities need to be respected and given legitimacy not only because they provide safe spaces for ethnic, cultural, and language groups on the margins of society, but also because they serve as a conscience for the nation-state.[54]

NOTES

1. For links to all Canadian standards, see the Council of Ministers of Education, Canada, http://www.cmec.ca/educmin.en.stm. For links to all United States standards, see http://www.indiana.edu?-ssdc/stand.htm.

2. Canada, Council of Ministers of Education, http://www.cmec.ca/abouteng.stm.

3. U.S. Department of Education, "Mission," http://www.ed.gov/about/overview /mission/mission.html?src'ln.

4. Ibid.

5. Susan H. Fuhrman, "From the Capitol to the Classroom: Standards-Based Reform in States," in *One Hundredth Yearbook of the National Society for the Study of Education,* Part II (Chicago: National Society for the Study of Education, 2001), 1–12.

6. "Quality Counts, 2002: Standards and Accountability," *Education Week,* http:// www.edweek.org.

7. Stephen Buckles, Mark C. Schug, and Michael Watts, "A National Survey of State Assessment Practices in the Social Studies," *The Social Studies* 92, no. 4 (2001): 141–46.

8. Kevin D. Vinson and Wayne E. Ross, "In Search of the Social Studies Curriculum: Standardization, Diversity, and a Conflict of Appearances," in *Critical Issues in Social Studies Research for the 21st Century,* ed. W.B. Stanley (Greenwich, CT: Information Age Publishing, 2001), 39–72.

9. Center for Civic Education, *National Standards for Civics and Government* (Calabus, CA: Center for Civic Education, 1994).

10. Geography Education Standards Project, *Geography for Life: National Geography Standards* (Washington, DC: National Geographic, 1994).

11. National Council for the Social Studies, *Expectations of Excellence: National Curriculum Standards for Social Studies* (Washington, DC: National Council for the Social Studies).

12. National Center for History in the Schools, *National Standards for History: Basic Education* (Los Angeles: National Center for History in the Schools, 1996).

13. National Council on Economic Education, *Voluntary National Content Standards in Economics* (New York: National Council on Economic Education, 1997).

14. See, for example, Gary B. Nash, Charlotte Crabtree, and Ross E. Dunn, *History on Trial: Culture Wars and the Teaching of the Past* (New York: Vintage Books, 2000); and Linda Symcox, *Whose History? The Struggle for National Standards in American Classrooms* (New York: Teachers College Press, 2002).

15. Nash et al., *History on Trial,* 235.

16. J.L. Granatstein, *Who Killed Canadian History?* (Toronto: Harper Collins, 1998), 140.

17. Daniel Francis, *National Dreams: Myth, Memory, and Canadian History* (Vancouver: Arsenal Pulp Press, 1997), 174.

18. Peter Seixas, "Schweigen! Die Kinder!" in *Knowing, Teaching and Learning History: National and International Perspectives,* ed. Peter N. Stearns, Peter Seixas, and Sam Wineburg (New York: New York University Press, 2000), 19–37.

19. Bruce M. Mitchell and Robert E. Salsbury, *Multicultural Education in the U.S.: A Guide to Policies and Programs in the 50 States* (Westport, CT: Greenwood Press, 2000).

20. Alabama Department of Education, http://www.alsde/html/sections/documents.asp ?section'54&sort'8&footer'section.

21. Virginia Commonwealth Board of Education, http://www.pen.k12.va.us/go/Sols /history.html-GradeEleven.

22. Montana Office of Public Instruction, http://www.opi.state.mt.us/Standards /Index.html.

23. Naomi Caldwell-Wood and Lisa A. Mitten, "Selected Bibliography and Guide for 'I' Is Not for Indian: The Portrayal of Native American Books for Young People," Program of the ALA/OLOS Subcommittee for Library Services to American Indian People, American Indian Library Association, June 29, 1991, http://www.nativeculture.com/lisamitten /ailbib.htm.

24. "Use Your Classroom to Change Common Misconceptions about Native Americans, National Museum of the American Indian," http://www.nmai.si.edu.

25. "About Us," Oyate, http://www.oyate.org/aboutus.html.

26. Debbie Reese, "Teaching Young Children about Native Americans," *ERIC Digest,* ED394744, http://www.ed.ov/databases/ERIC_Digest/ed.394744.html; and Karen D. Harvey, Lisa D. Harjo, and Jane K. Jackson, *Teaching about Native Americans,* Bulletin 84 (Washington, DC: National Council for the Social Studies, 1990), 20. For links to all U.S. standards, see http://www.indiana.edu?~ssdc/stand.htm.

27. Alabama Department of Education.

28. Arizona Department of Education, http://www.ade.state.az.us/standards/sstudies /default.asp.

29. California Department of Education, http://www.score.rims.k12.va.us/go/Sols /history.html-GradeEleven.

30. Newfoundland and Labrador Department of Education and Training, http:// www.gov.nf.ca/edu.

31. Alabama Department of Education.

32. Arizona Department of Education.

33. California Department of Education.

34. Maryland State Department of Education, http://www.mdk12.org/mspp/high_ school/what_will/socialstudies/text.html.

35. New York State Education Department, http://www.emsc.nysed.gov/ciai/pub /pubss.html.

36. Ohio Department of Education, http://www.ode.state.oh.us/academic_content_ standards/.acssocialstudies.asp.

37. Pennsylvania Department of Education, http://www.pde.state.pa.us/stateboard_ed /cwp?view.asp?A+3&Q'7671&stateboard_edNav'154671&pde_internetNav'1.

38. Utah State Office of Education, http://www.usoe.k12.ut.us/curr/soc.st/secondary /newcore/newcore.htm.

39. Alberta Learning, http://www.learning.gov.ab.ca/k_12/curriculum/.

40. British Columbia Ministry of Education, http://www.gov.bc.ca/bced/.

41. Manitoba Ministry of Education, Citizenship and Youth, http://edu.gov.mb.ca/.

42. Newfoundland and Labrador Department of Education and Training.

43. Ontario Ministry of Education, http://www.edu.gov.on.ca.

44. Maryland State Department of Education, 25.

45. Ontario Ministry of Education.

46. Ohio Department of Education.

47. Saskatchewan Ministry of Learning, http://www.sasked.gov.sk.ca/docs/history30 /index.html.

48. Washington State Office of Superintendent of Public Instruction, http:// www.k12.wa.us/curriculumInstruct/SocStudies/historyEALRs.aspx, 2.

49. Alaska Department of Education and Early Development, http://www.educ .state.ak.us/tls/frameworks/sstudies/part2a2.htm.

50. New Brunswick Department of Education, http://www.gnb.ca/0000/about-e.asp.

51. Northwest Territories Ministry of Education, Culture and Employment, http://siksik .learnnet.nt.ca/02%20k_12/02%20k-12.html.

52. British Columbia Ministry of Education.

53. Alberta Learning.

54. James A. Banks, "Citizenship, Education, and Diversity: Implications for Teacher Education," *Journal of Teacher Education* 52, no. 1 (2001): 7.

PART IV

Nation and Identity

*Aboriginal people look back to a time when oral traditions and colonial records
agree that communities and nations were self-regulating, self-reliant, and in
remarkably good health. They examine the forces that disrupted the equilibrium—
new diseases, loss of lands and livelihood, relocations that tore the fabric of
community relations, the imposition of alien forms of government, and assaults on
spirituality and family life. They reclaim the history that for a long period was
systematically erased from the story of Canada.* [1]

MARLENE BRANT CASTELLANO, Tyendinaga Mohawk

*American Indians are unique in the world in that they represent the only aboriginal
peoples still practicing a form of self-government in the midst of a wholly new and
modern civilization that has been transported to their lands.* [2]

VINE DELORIA, JR., Standing Rock Lakota

THE EVOLUTION OF NATIONHOOD among Native North Americans is not a new phenomenon. It is not a process unknown to indigenous peoples and tribal historians. Instead, it is a process that has not been the subject of much scholarly scrutiny because recognition of national consciousness is not a desirable trait for colonial settler societies to consider among Native peoples, nor is it a likely topic found among national histories of aggressive colonial powers. Any reconfiguration of Native North America must explore the nuances and issues of nationhood—such as identity formation, geopolitical unities, nation building, decolonization, diplomatic discourse, and legal maneuvering among myriad colonial laws. Four such chapters in this section offer detailed and pointed ways to understand the meanings of indigenous nationhood.

First, Sami Lakomäki shows how the Shawnee peoples of what would become the Middle Colonies of British North America embraced various sophisticated forms of nationhood and constructed a national unity. This process for the Shawnees has not been clearly understood by either anthropologists or historians, as it takes place during a very complex and confusing time of conflicts, diasporas, and migrations, not only for various Shawnee village-states ranging from Pennsylvania and Ohio to Georgia and Alabama, but for the Shawnees' indigenous neighbors and various colonial settlers in their homelands. Demonstrating an impressive command of archaeological and ethnographical literatures as well as British colonial archival records, Lakomäki traces how Shawnees, under early clan decisions of the sixteenth and seventeenth centuries and later in the 1730s with the leadership of the young visionary and skilled orator Nuchneconner, sought to overcome intertribal and intervillage barriers to achieve national unity. As is recorded by a British governor, Nuchneconner explained his goal as to "Gether [the Shawnees] two Gather."[3] These developments in Shawnee cosmology from three to six centuries ago, Lakomäki concludes, continue to influence the Shawnee peoples who were forced to remove to Oklahoma.

Susan A. Miller (Seminole) next explains how one particular incident in her own tribe's past can be elucidated in ways that assist Seminoles in the decolonization of their own tribal history and provide a greater and more thorough understanding of diplomatic discourse that occurred between nations of indigenous North Americans and colonial states. She tells how Seminoles conducted diplomacy and how American agents and military leaders who came to negotiate ignorantly breached protocol after protocol, and what Seminole law required for these egregious actions. At a council at Silver Spring, when the American Indian agent Wiley Thompson attempted to coerce Seminoles into accepting removal from Florida to Oklahoma, he posed various issues to discuss in order to accomplish the ultimate American aim—that of Seminoles living among the Creek Confederacy, moving west to Oklahoma, abandoning their cattle with compensation, traveling by water or land, and requesting annuities in goods or cash. Charley Emathla, *micco* or principal chief of an Apalachee Seminole town, it is recorded, answered, "If we intended to go, then it would be proper the points [h]e proposed to us should be decided upon. But why quarrel about dividing the hind quarter, when we are not going to hunt[?],"[4] a most significant diplomatic concept that Miller highlights in the title to her chapter.

The last two chapters consider past and present identity and sovereignty issues among the Metis and First Nations of Canada. Gerhard Ens chronicles how Canadian government policy in the nineteenth century displaced indigenous First Nations identity, first through the Manitoba Act of 1870 and then through the various Indian Acts passed by Parliament and a 1901 government interpretation. What was created at first was a new Metis aboriginal identity for those peoples who were the progeny of First Nations and Europeans west of the province of Ontario. Euro-Canadians in power wanted to create a society that embraced what was called "hybridity," the absorption of indigenous peoples into an Anglo-Canadian nation, and doing that, they falsely reasoned, required creating policies legally classifying Metis as First Nations. These acts did not please many Metis communities or First Nations, and in part this led to Metis unrest, rebellion, and searches for their own mixed-blood identity.

Joe Sawchuck takes the evolution of sovereignty and identity politics a step further in his thoughtful reconstruction of how Ontario Metis in the twentieth century evolved into a distinct nationhood. Few historians and sociologists recognize the Metis of Ontario because they have not generally been connected to the concentrated Metis populations of Red River and its environs in Manitoba, Saskatchewan, and Alberta. Ontario Metis constitute a mixed-blood society of modern Ontario who found themselves having to make choices about their own identity under various national Canadian laws. They did so through several social and political organizations that had to pursue the divisive choices that were presented: Accept a classification from Canadian courts and legislatures as Aboriginal or opt for an identity tied to that of the Red River Metis. Neither seemed comfortable to Ontario's Metis, although representative organizations attempted to rationalize the various options, and thus identity politics continues to exert its pull even today among the Metis of eastern Canada.

These essays, therefore, search through "the fabric of community relations" to discover how indigenous North Americans have engaged in the processes central to nationhood. Each of these chapters, from evolving Shawnee national unity and Seminole diplomatic discourse to Metis mixed-blood identities, contributes to a greater understanding of First Nations and Native American forms of sovereignty and the highly complex and multilayered nationalism that accompanies nation-hood.

NOTES

1. Marlene Brant Castellano, "Renewing the Relationship: A Perspective on the Impact of the Royal Commission on Aboriginal Peoples," in *Aboriginal Self-Government in Canada,* ed. John H. Hylton (Saskatoon, SK: Purich Publishing, Ltd., 1999), 95.

2. Vine Deloria, Jr., and Clifford M. Lytle, *The Nations Within: The Past and Future of American Indian Sovereignty* (New York: Pantheon Books, 1984), 2.

3. "Indians' Letter to Gov. Gordon, [March 20] 1738," in *Pennsylvania Archives,* 1st ser., vol. 1, ed. Samuel Hazard, 551, as cited in Lakomäki chapter.

4. Myer M. Cohen, *Notices of Florida and the Campaigns* (Charleston, SC: Burges & Honour, 1836), 60, as cited in Miller chapter.

CHAPTER 12

Building a Shawnee Nation: Indigenous Identity, Tribal Structure, and Sociopolitical Organization, 1400–1770

SAMI LAKOMÄKI

IN A RECENT ARTICLE, TITLED "Wanted: More Histories of Indian Identity," Alexandra Harmon called for more studies on American Indian self-identification. She stated that although we know rather well how Europeans and European Americans have at different times seen, identified, and defined Indians—indeed, the very term "Indian" was of course originally a European identification—we know much less about how different Native groups have identified and defined *themselves* through time, especially during earlier phases of their history. Harmon points out, for example, that many modern tribal names were originally given by European explorers or colonial officials to Indian groups with little or no ethnic or political unity, sometimes for the very purpose of colonizing and controlling these groups. Therefore, she cautions us against reifying these names into timeless social units, unchanging survivals of an unknown past, and urges us instead to look at the ever-continuing processes of ethnogenesis and self-identification along with the creation and maintenance of ethnic boundaries in Native communities, both before and after European colonization. In a word, according to Harmon, we should "consciously and consistently *historicize* Indian and tribal identities."[1]

As Harmon herself notes, this kind of historicization of Native American identities has already been a prevalent theme in recent historical and anthropological scholarship. Especially during the past two decades, scholars such as Patricia Galloway, Gregory Evans Dowd, Bruce Bourque, Morris Foster, Michael McConnell, and others have repeatedly and persuasively shown that Indian peoples were never ethnically or politically static and unchanging "primordial groups." Instead, both the ethnic composition and political organization, and thereby the self-identification, of many Native groups have changed time and again through history, as epidemics, wars, environmental changes, population movements, colonization, and other factors have led people to amalgamate, disperse, ally, or fall apart in different and complex ways. As in every part of the globe, tribes, confederacies, chiefdoms, and states have been born and shattered, created, and re-created countless times all over the Americas, and throughout these processes the peoples involved, like all peoples everywhere, have had to invent and re-invent their identity time after time.[2]

Much of the recent research on the changing ethnic composition, political structure, and self-identification of Native groups has dealt with the peoples of the Eastern Woodlands of North America. Thanks to several excellent studies, we have gained new and better understandings of the ethnogenesis, identity, and organization of such Eastern nations as the Choctaws, Delawares, Catawbas, Creeks, and Seminoles, especially during their crucially important late pre-Contact and colonial times (i.e., roughly between 1400 and 1800), when various historical trends like the Mississippian decline, the spread of Eurasian epidemics, a flourishing long-distance trade, and European colonization contributed to make the Woodland societies ethnically and socially highly unstable and dynamic. This was a period of intense change and invention but also of remarkable cultural and social persistence and survival, and it is now rightly considered one of the most important eras in Native North American history.

However, despite the growing number of studies, many aspects of the ethnic and political structure of some Woodland societies in this period remain unclear. In this chapter, the ethnic and political organization of one such poorly understood Indian nation, the Shawnees of the Ohio Valley and adjacent areas from the 1400s to the 1770s, will be examined. This was a crucial period in the history of the Shawnees, since it was during this era that the Shawnee tribe seems to have been originally formed, and then re-formed several times, as a response to changing political and economic circumstances. However, these processes are far from adequately known. It has often been suggested that the Shawnees as a distinct political and ethnic nation was formed some time in the late pre-Contact period, but this process has been difficult to prove or illustrate in any detail.[3] On the other hand, later, numerous, and seemingly random migrations, extensive dispersals, and temporary coalescences of various Shawnee bands have made it hard to understand the inner organization, composition, and functioning of the tribe even up to the early nineteenth century. Greater clarity of this early Shawnee history can be achieved by asking and answering such fundamental questions as who were these people called the Shawnees—indeed, who called them by this name, when, and why? How did they identify themselves? And what kind of a political and ethnic group did they form?

But before the early history, ethnogenesis, and organization of the Shawnees is considered, the difficult theoretical problem of the very concept of *tribe* itself must be tackled. Shawnees, like most of their Native neighbors in late pre-Contact— early colonial era Eastern Woodlands, are usually labeled "a tribe" by modern researchers. Yet what does this actually mean? What indeed is a tribe and what do we mean when we categorize a group of people as such? These are well-known, even time-worn, questions in anthropology and should surprise no one. They might even seem a bit old-fashioned. Yet they must be asked in order to study ethnicity and political organization in tribal societies.

The word "tribe" is notorious in anthropology for stubbornly resisting clear, useful, and generally accepted definitions. It has even frustrated some researchers to the point that they have banished the very term from their vocabulary and replaced it with new ones, such as "segmentary society."[4] However, this might be somewhat too drastic a response, since there seems to be quite extensive consensus about the essential features of tribal societies. The most important of these is, according to most anthropologists, the lack of a central political power. Unlike politically centralized societies, such as chiefdoms and states, tribes seldom have a clearly centralized leadership or power elite. Rather, political power is diffuse and widely distributed among many local and roughly equal leaders, many or most of whom do not necessarily even occupy any kind of formal political office. Therefore, tribes are held together more by social ties (e.g., kinship), ritual, "ethnic feelings," and common language than by political power. Marshall Sahlin's classic term "segmentary tribe" is still very useful for describing these societies, since it nicely underlines this key feature of their organization: Tribes consist of more or less equal, loosely allied "segments," such as neighboring villages and kin groups, without many unifying institutions or officials.[5]

Hand in hand with this lack of political centralization goes another common feature of tribal societies: their ethnic looseness. As ethnographically known tribes are most often rather loose alliances among neighboring settlements, their external, ethnic-political boundaries tend to be quite hazy, permeable, and volatile, especially when compared to those of more centralized societies.[6]

These characteristics pose more than a few serious problems to any consideration of the early history of the Woodland tribes. If tribes are really so loose, both politically and ethnically, how can it be determined—often on the basis of meager written records and ambiguous archaeological data—which groups formed a tribe at a particular time? Can scholars see behind collective tribal names such as Shawnee in colonial documents to recognize the meanings that different people attached to these names at different times? What did tribal identity mean to Natives themselves? What were the sociopolitical and economic processes and forces behind ethnic and political group formation and fission? And finally, since it is known that locality and kin groups, rather than larger tribal entities, usually

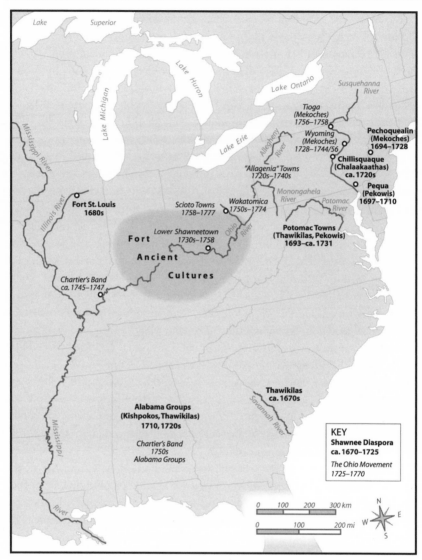

Shawnee Culturescapes: The Diaspora, 1670–1725,
and the Ohio Valley Nation, 1725–1770

constituted the central focus of life for most Woodland people, it is imperative to ask, how did tribes function in the political field and what was their role in the creation of local and individual identities?[7]

There is one more important thread in this tangled web of the "tribe" concept. Although tribes are generally thought to constitute rather loose political and ethnic groups, a number of historians have recently argued that especially during the

eighteenth century, many of these older segmentary tribes of the Eastern Woodlands were transformed into much more centralized political and ethnic units.
Many groups experienced a highly complex process in which a new kind of central
power rose trying to replace local kin groups and villages as the focal point of the
society. New leaders came forth, attempting to concentrate political power into
their own hands and maybe those of their lineage or clan; at the same time, new
kinds of national identities were created. This kind of "nation-building" process
has been documented, for example, among the Delawares.[8] It has also been suggested for the Shawnees, but so far it has not really been discussed in detail.[9]
Therefore, this constitutes one further question in the present chapter: Did this
political and ethnic centralization process indeed take place among the Shawnees
and, if so, what was it like?

ARCHAEOLOGY, ORAL TRADITIONS, AND PRE-CONTACT SHAWNEES

What is known about the early Shawnee tribe, that is, its political and ethnic
organization and formation? By the eighteenth century, the tribe consisted of five
patrilineal subtribes, or divisions, as they are usually called: the Chalaakaathas,
Mekoches, Pekowis, Kishpokos, and Thawikilas.[10] Prior to this time, there may
have existed at least one more division, as several early Shawnee oral histories mention a sixth group, which later became extinct.[11] In addition, some of the obscure
tribal groups and names, such as the Chaskpé, Cisca, and Moseopela, mentioned
in passing in very early European documents have been interpreted by some as
Shawnee-related groups or even former divisions.[12] However, by the early 1700s,
only five divisions remained.

The five Shawnee divisions apparently spoke closely related dialects of a single
Central Algonquian language. Although the differences between these dialects are
not known, it seems they were quite insignificant, and therefore the Shawnees can
be characterized as linguistically unified.[13] Culturally, the divisions were exceedingly similar, too, although there may have been some minor differences in religion
and sociopolitical organization.[14]

The big—and to a large extent unanswered—question concerns the relationships between these five divisions. How were they bound together into a tribal
whole and what were their roles within it? The famous and oft-quoted passages by
the early-twentieth-century Shawnee historian Thomas Alford, stating that each
division had specific duties and functions in the tribe, has been interpreted in various ways, none of which completely agree with the actual historical data. This has
led John Sugden to dismiss Alford's account as apocryphal, whereas James Howard
considered it as some sort of an ideal image of Shawnee society, which was realized
only very rarely during most of the tribe's history. If the five Shawnee divisions

really did have special duties and roles within the tribe—whether those assigned to them by Alford or others—they could probably be best understood as relating to tribal ritual rather than to everyday life or politics, as hinted by Charles Callender.[15] A system of ritual roles and functions could have been created to bind the formerly separate divisions together and maintain their unity, although it must be emphasized that there is little evidence of such a system in the meager documentary record.

Regardless, the cultural and linguistic similarity of the five Shawnee divisions is so great that it would seem reasonable to attribute it to a common background and ancestry. Although it is not the standard interpretation of the Shawnee ethnogenesis, it is possible that the separate Shawnee divisions originally formed a single tribe, which then split into smaller groups, which, in their turn, eventually evolved into the semiautonomous divisions we know from the eighteenth century.[16] However, the more common interpretation sees the closely related, yet basically independent and separate divisions uniting into a new tribe or confederacy at some point in late pre-Contact times.[17] In other words, at that time a new Shawnee polity and a related new tribal identity were created. This tentative view is mostly based on archaeological data and early written sources, but it also gains support from Shawnee oral histories which include separate creation stories for each division and describe how these groups came together and joined to form a single political and ethnic whole.[18]

Even though this view has gained acceptance as a standard interpretation of the Shawnee ethnogenesis, there have been few attempts to document it in closer detail. This is more than understandable, since the paucity of available sources make this kind of study exceedingly difficult, if not impossible. With practically no written records of the location and organization of different Shawnee groups before the 1670s, only ambiguous archaeological materials—open to conflicting interpretations—discern something of the earliest history of the Shawnees.

Nowadays, it is generally accepted that the late pre-Contact Shawnees most likely occupied the Ohio Valley region.[19] Although a more precise location is open to question, most archaeologists and historians tend to associate the tribe at least tentatively with the Fort Ancient cultural complex, which in about 1000–1700 spanned from southwestern Indiana through southern Ohio and northern Kentucky all the way to western West Virginia. However, not all researchers agree with this interpretation. Most of all, it should be emphasized that the Fort Ancient Culture was both spatially and temporally a wide-ranging archaeological complex that probably never constituted a single ethnic, cultural, or political unit.

Bearing such reservations in mind, the majority of researchers conclude that *some* part of the Fort Ancient Culture was most likely ancestral to Shawnees. This association is strongest during late Fort Ancient times, that is, during the Madisonville

Horizon (ca. 1400–1700). It seems reasonable to assume that at least part of the Madisonville Horizon settlements were occupied by different Shawnee groups and divisions, although we will probably never be able to pinpoint exactly which late Fort Ancient sites might represent ancestral Shawnees and which some other populations.[20]

If one accepts this continuum between the late pre-Contact Fort Ancient Culture and the historically known Shawnees, an extremely interesting question arises: Is there any evidence in the Fort Ancient archaeological material that could be interpreted as a sign of a presumed late pre-Contact formation of the Shawnee confederacy out of the previously separate divisions? And if so, what does the evidence tell us about this process or the early ethnic and political structure of the tribe?

There are indeed some findings in the archaeological data that could be interpreted as signs of some sort of an ethnogenesis process. First of all, beginning from about 1450, the material culture, especially ceramics, started to grow more and more similar, even unified, all over the Fort Ancient territory—in startling contrast to earlier Fort Ancient times that were characterized by much more localized material cultures. Obviously, everything did not become suddenly uniform after 1450—indeed, important local differences continued to exist especially between eastern and western areas—but the unification of the material culture has been considered important and noticeable enough to merit the name "Madisonville Phenomenon."[21]

It is hard to say what the Madisonville Phenomenon meant in terms of social life, ethnicity, or politics of the Fort Ancient peoples. Penelope Drooker has interpreted it as a sign of increased social interaction, including visiting and intermarriage, between the different settlements and regions.[22] It would be tempting to push this reasonable view a bit further and see the unification of the material culture as also marking a new ethnic unification of the people involved.[23] This might, however, be difficult to prove, for although there is some ethnoarchaeological evidence on the role of material culture as an ethnic symbol, we simply know too little about the Fort Ancient peoples to make simple equations between ceramics and ethnicity.[24]

The second archaeological sign of a new ethnic and/or political unification process in the Fort Ancient area during the Madisonville Horizon concerns settlement patterns. Formerly, most Fort Ancient occupations were rather small villages widely dispersed all over the drainages of the Ohio River and its major tributaries. However, starting again around the early to middle fifteenth century, the population became much more concentrated into clearly larger villages, which in turn concentrated into a much smaller area along the Ohio and the lower reaches of its largest tributaries. Once again, the sociopolitical implications of this process are anything but easy to understand, but it would appear that new, larger polities were created during this time and that the interaction between these polities increased considerably.[25]

The changes in the material culture and settlement patterns might indicate, if nothing else, increasing social interaction between separate Fort Ancient communities. The result of these processes was the development of quite large, apparently politically and economically independent and self-sufficient villages,[26] whose inhabitants were frequently involved in several kinds of social interaction, including visiting and marrying people from other settlements. Although we cannot recognize them from the archaeological material, there were probably several "interaction spheres" within the Fort Ancient territory whose constituent villages were closely tied to each other through marriage, friendship, and kinship. This picture comes very close to our image of typical segmentary tribes, and it appears likely that such loose groups constituted the major ethnic-political units during the Madisonville Horizon. Although impossible to prove at this point, one might also hypothesize that these archaeologically known changes in the material culture, settlements, and interaction patterns also represent the social process of the gradual coalescence of related, yet independent, Shawnee divisions into a single tribe, or rather a confederacy.

There is still one further piece of archaeological data that has been linked to the problem of Shawnee origins. This is the appearance of large, similarly shaped copper pendants in a few Madisonville Horizon graves in four different villages. These pendants can be dated to the late sixteenth and early seventeenth centuries, to the time most often associated with the formation of tribal unity among Shawnees. As they are usually found in rather prestigious male burials, the pendants have been associated with high sociopolitical status and even interpreted as badges of an important political office. Penelope Drooker has suggested that the copper pendants may have functioned as emblems of equal local leaders representing their settlement in a larger inter-village or inter-regional alliance system or confederacy.[27] The intriguing question here is, of course, could these pendants have been symbols of the first tribal or confederacy chiefs of the Shawnees?

This is again impossible to answer, as there simply is not enough evidence for or against this kind of suggestion. One cannot know, for example, whether the sites where these pendants have been found were inhabited by groups ancestral to the Shawnees or to some other groups. Indeed, one of these sites has been tentatively linked to the Illinois, rather than to the Shawnees. Be this as it may, the copper pendants are just about the only widely distributed Fort Ancient artifact type that can be interpreted as a symbol of high political status or even office.[28] This means that whether the early Shawnee chiefs used these metal pendants as their symbol or not, their power was still very limited and probably did not affect everyday life of most of their fellow tribespeople. They definitely did not constitute any kind of effective central power in society, nor can they be seen as an upper class.[29] All Fort Ancient villages were, after all, politically independent and economically self-sufficient. Therefore, the Shawnee tribe of this period can best be characterized as a segmentary tribe consisting of five or more semiautonomous divisions which probably shared a strong feeling of common ethnicity but lacked a clear or strong political central power. Politically speaking, the tribe was probably very loose.

DIASPORA, 1670–1720

During the second half of the seventeenth century something dramatic happened, and the sociopolitical and even geographical unity of the Shawnees was seriously shattered. This development is witnessed by the earliest European documents, which from the late 1600s begin to make scanty references to Shawnees in amazingly widely scattered locations. Indeed, the picture emerging from these documents is quite bewildering: Some Shawnee groups were in Carolina along the Savannah River, other bands congregated near the French Fort St. Louis on the Illinois River, and still others were identified residing in Pennsylvania and Alabama. Clearly, Shawnees were suddenly dispersed almost all over the Eastern Woodlands region in astonishing, complex, and often seemingly random ways.[30]

This extensive dispersal has for a long time puzzled researchers. What happened? Why did the Shawnees leave their homelands and migrate into almost every possible direction? The standard answer has usually been that the Shawnees were shattered by a series of Iroquois attacks beginning in the 1670s and had to flee from the Ohio region to save themselves. While there is evidence that such attacks did indeed take place—and while it is definitely known that these Iroquois Beaver or Mourning Wars certainly played an important role in the depopulation of other areas around the Great Lakes[31]—it is not likely that they were the *sole* cause for the Shawnees' dispersal. As Penelope Drooker has noted,[32] an extensive and complex population movement process like this one should not be attributed to single monolithic factors, such as the Iroquoian aggression. Judging from the available evidence, it is indeed more probable that the Shawnees left the Ohio Country not only because of the Iroquois threat but also because of the lure of the European fur trade. It is certainly no accident that most of the dispersed Shawnee groups made their first appearance into the written records at or near some trading center, like the English Charles Town and Albany, French Fort St. Louis, or Spanish St. Augustine. Of course, there may have been even more causes behind the Shawnee migrations of the late 1600s, but Iroquois warfare coupled with the pull of European trade do seem to have been the strongest ones.[33]

As important as the factors behind the Shawnee migrations are, the consequences of this process may be even far more puzzling and interesting. What happened, for example, to tribal unity, when the loose segmentary tribe broke up into smaller parts that scattered all over the East? What did this kind of extensive dispersal mean in terms of sociopolitical organization, tribal identity, and ethnicity?

Once again, there are few definitive answers. Unknown, for example, is how the Shawnee tribe broke up in the late 1600s. It would, of course, seem reasonable to assume that dispersal took place along kin group or divisional lines and that the divisions were the main migrating units, but there is little evidence for or against this assumption due to the paucity of the early historical record. Later in the eighteenth century, there are references to Shawnee divisions moving as a whole, but it is debatable whether on this ground it can be presumed that *all* earlier migrations have been division based as well. Nevertheless, it appears highly likely that in at least some cases this was true.[34]

It is quite certain that to the people involved, the migrations were not as random and bewildering as they appear three centuries later. Their complex and seemingly unplanned nature has frustrated some historians into considering them as more or less haphazard and aimless wanderings, but the minimal evidence suggests the opposite. Usually migrations were not begun suddenly but only after careful deliberations, extensive scouting expeditions, and contact with the inhabitants of the intended destination. All this agrees perfectly with what is known of later Shawnee migrations.[35] Also crucially important is that the planning, preparation, and actual moving were not handled on a tribal level; rather, these decisions were made on a much more local level, perhaps within the divisions or villages. This local decision making was certainly the most important to most Shawnees during this period. Communities or settlement clusters migrated based on their own interests and motives, probably into areas to which they already had former social and/or economic connections. Political and trading alliances and kinship ties with distant regions and peoples were important factors when removal was considered.[36] These local concerns and sociopolitical ties, not tribal policy or leaders, apparently determined where any particular Shawnee group migrated during these tumultuous times. These migrations should be considered an orderly diaspora rather than a hasty retreat.

What does all this tell us about tribal organization and ethnic identity of the late-seventeenth-century Shawnees? First and foremost, the tribe does not appear to have constituted the primary basis for the identity or sociopolitical life of most Shawnees. Second, the period of dispersal must have badly shattered whatever tribal unity the Shawnees may have had during the Madisonville Horizon.

Shattered—but not destroyed. The remarkable thing about the Shawnee dispersal of the late 1600s is not the diaspora itself. Similar processes of tribes falling apart and scattering over wide areas due to wars, epidemics, colonization, and new trading opportunities were going on at the same time all over the Eastern Woodlands. However, many of these broken groups had a fate quite unlike that of the Shawnees. Their dispersal proved to be final, as the scattered splinter bands never again re-united but rather joined and eventually acculturated into other, larger tribes or confederacies, finally losing their own identity. This seems to have happened, for example, to other late pre-Contact peoples of the Ohio Valley, of whom very little is known besides some obscure tribal names, which simply vanish from the written sources sometime around 1700.[37] Similar processes were even more evident in the South, where numerous small splinter groups from different regions gradually merged with new multiethnic nations, such as the Catawbas or the Creek Confederacy.[38]

The Shawnees, however, were different. Even though some of their dispersed bands did travel all the way to Alabama and joined the Creek Confederacy,[39] this does not characterize the subsequent history of most Shawnee groups. Instead of scattering permanently and amalgamating into other nations, most Shawnee bands began to gather together anew from the 1690s onward, this time into eastern and central Pennsylvania and adjacent areas, with whose Native inhabitants, such as the Conestogas (Susquehannocks), they may have had earlier ties.[40] Compared to the fate of many other contemporary Woodlands tribes, this is actually quite surprising. More than anything else, it shows us very persuasively that despite the tribe's apparently uncontrolled dispersal and the lack of political or even geographical unity during the same, the Shawnees continued to share strong social ties and a sense of identity.

The Shawnees' migration to and eventual coalescence in Pennsylvania was definitely not a result of planned tribal policy. Rather, different Shawnee groups came in from different regions, motivated by different factors—some seeking cultivatable land, others desiring fur trade with Europeans, and still more wanting protection from the Iroquois—over a long period of time, all the way up to the 1730s. They settled in different and widely separated areas, mostly along the Susquehanna, Delaware, and Potomac Rivers, establishing social and political ties and even common settlements with local Natives. Shawnees were given permission to settle in these areas by the Conestogas and Delawares, who also promised the Pennsylvania colonial government to watch over the newcomers and guarantee their good behavior.[41]

The result of these gradual migrations was not initially a new coalescence of Shawnees into a wholly unified political or ethnic unit. Some Shawnee groups, such as an Alabama band, failed to travel to the Pennsylvania region at all, and others, as noted above, established towns not in close proximity of one another but over wide areas and among settlements of local groups, like Conestogas, Delawares, and Conoys.[42] In fact, the Pennsylvania migrations seem to have resulted in the formation of at least four distinct and politically independent Shawnee centers, most of which were probably to a large degree division based: the

Pekowis on the Lower Susquehanna in and around the town of Pequa, the Cha-laakaathas on the Upper Susquehanna, the Mekoches on the Delaware River at Pechoquealin, and other groups—at least a part of them Thawikilas—along the north branch of the Potomac. The locations of the Kishpokos is unclear, but it is possible that although some of them may have resided in the South in the Caroli-nas and/or Alabama, part of them may have eventually ended up in one or another of the Pennsylvania centers.[43]

In any case, all of these four Shawnee centers—basically clusters of neighboring villages—were politically distinct and independent. They were also acknowledged as such by colonial officials, who usually maintained separate diplomatic connec-tions to each center, organizing, for example, separate treaties with each of them and recognizing that every village cluster was headed by its own local leadership, not by any kind of tribal chief or council. A further evidence of the colonists' view is that they did not, at least in practice, hold Shawnees of one center accountable for the actions of those from others.[44]

There were evidently no overarching political institutions that would have effi-ciently bound all Shawnees together, nor any leader who tried to act as some sort of a tribal head-chief. In fact, most Shawnee leaders were usually quite reluctant to interfere in the political affairs of another village, and even if some had harbored such ambitions, they would have lacked the power to implement such an agenda. Indeed, Shawnee society at this time was so decentralized even at the local level that most village chiefs were little more than spokesmen and arbitrators whose authority was often successfully challenged by kin group leaders and the young men who formed a highly independent social group in quest of higher individual status through military exploits. Therefore, the lack of political unity at the tribal level can hardly be surprising.[45]

The clearest sign of the political disunity of the Shawnee nation in the first decades of the eighteenth century is the fact that separate Shawnee groups rarely embarked on common political action. One possible exception was the bewilder-ing and poorly recorded chain of events of May 1728. This episode started with some lower Susquehanna Shawnees murdering a few Conestogas, which brought the two groups to the brink of open conflict. Soon after this, Pennsylvania colonists witnessed a war party from Pechoquealin on the move, possibly on its way to help the Susquehanna Shawnees. Even this rare example of Shawnee coop-eration, however, was of very limited scope, short duration, and also seemingly ill-planned, ending in an accidental skirmish between the Pechoquealin warriors and some colonists.[46]

This is not to say that Shawnee centers simply minded their own business in local and regional politics; they did not. On the contrary, they cooperated extensively and took common action with neighboring non-Shawnee Native communities, especially when it came to dealing with colonial governments. Indeed, each Shawnee group allied itself politically most closely with its immediate neighbors, commonly the inhabitants of the same river valley, regardless of their tribal affiliation, ethnicity, or language. Therefore, the most important allies of the Pekowis of the Lower Susquehanna, for example, were the local Conestogas, Conoys, and Delawares, whose villages dotted the valley all around Pekowi settlements. Cooperation among these groups became so close that they occasionally called themselves "the four nations" of Susquehanna and were usually represented by a single speaker in treaties with the colonists.[47]

Ties between Shawnee village clusters and neighboring Native settlements were not only political. People often married into other villages and ethnic groups, and it was also quite normal for members of different tribal and even linguistic groups to establish common multiethnic towns together, prompting one Pennsylvanian official to describe how: "They [the Shawnees] had two or three towns of their own but they scattered into divers places as well on the upper parts of Delaware as on Susquehannah living promiscuously & intermarrying with our Indians."[48]

Given all these numerous and complex ties that bound local Shawnee communities both socially and politically to their Conestoga, Delaware, Conoy, and Nanticoke neighbors, how could Shawnees still manage to retain their own distinct identity and remain *Shawnees*? If the Pekowis counted themselves as one of the "four nations" of Susquehanna and interacted more with local Conestogas than with Mekoches from Pechoqualin, what became of their Shawnee identity? If the Mekoches counseled with the Pennsylvania government together with Delaware bands at the same time as the Upper Shawnees, probably Chalaakaathas, were entertained by the French in Montréal, how and why were both groups still called "Shawnees," by themselves and by outsiders?

Yet this is exactly what happened. Despite the lack of political unity on the tribal level and despite the close sociopolitical webs binding Shawnee centers to numerous other Native groups, the Shawnees did, in fact, remain Shawnees. This is evidenced by several facts. First of all, it seems that however infrequent and inefficient the political cooperation among the four main Shawnee clusters was, other forms of social interaction were much more common. Intermarriage, probably very frequent, meant that most individual Shawnees in any community certainly had relatives and kin in others. These webs of kinship and marriage came into play during the annual winter hunts, when most Susquehanna Shawnees traveled to or through the Potomac region to hunt deer and fish, probably visiting and lodging with their local Shawnee tribespeople there, renewing old social bonds and binding new ones. These same ties made it also rather easy for people to move more permanently between different Shawnee centers, for example, to escape intragroup conflicts, as did the Pekowi leader Opessa who around 1711 left his town of Pequa and settled in one of the Potomac villages.[49]

These social ties helped maintain and re-create the old Shawnee identity. The continuing strength of this feeling of belonging and togetherness is shown very concretely by the fact that the widely dispersed Shawnee bands from the South kept migrating to Pennsylvania to settle near or among their relatives and tribespeople. Even though the arriving Shawnees did not coalesce into one big geographical cluster, the latest newcomers usually settled at least initially and temporarily in or near one of the established Shawnee centers, whose inhabitants, in their turn, helped the immigrants organize their everyday life in their new home and intervened both with the Pennsylvania government and the local Natives to acquire for the newcomers permission to settle in the area.[50]

Finally, the name—Shawnee—bound peoples. It is this term of identification, not the divisional names, that appears in almost all of the colonial documents of this era. Although this might be partially attributed to the colonists' indifference or sheer ignorance of Native sociopolitical organization, it also shows how Shawnees themselves chose to call and identify themselves. Hence, despite all their seeming disunity and complex ties to other groups, to the outsiders they were always primarily "Shawnees."[51]

"GETHER TWO GATHER": NATION BUILDING, 1720–1770

A new period began in Shawnee history around the mid-1720s, a time that was to see an unprecedented ethnic and political unification of the tribe. Until then, Shawnees had remained more or less dispersed geographically as well as socially, but now began an ambitious and complex political process that can be best characterized as true nation building. Several rising leaders strove to organize a new kind of central power within the tribe, and at the same time, helped to create stronger ethnic unity between the separate divisions and village clusters.

The main feature and starting point of this period was the gradual migration of most Shawnees back to the Ohio Valley region. This slow population movement, begun around 1725, evolved partly because Shawnees were induced and encouraged to leave east-central Pennsylvania and re-settle along the Ohio by colonial officials of New France. The French eagerly sought strategically located allies against the combined threat of the British colonies and the Six Nations Iroquois Confederacy. More importantly, several Shawnee bands were drawn toward their old homelands by populous deer herds and other game of the region, which offered a considerable contrast to the overhunted and depleted areas in the East. Third, many Shawnees left Pennsylvania to escape the growing land claims of the Iroquois, but even more pressing than this was the insatiable land hunger of Commonwealth settlers who had started to pour onto Shawnee lands as early as the 1710s. It was this loss of land, more than anything else, that forced the tribe to leave Pennsylvania.[52]

The migration started modestly enough, with hunting bands wintering and settling more or less temporarily in the Ohio Valley. However, before long they were followed by diplomats, who carried out long and complex negotiations with local Natives in order to obtain permission for the Shawnees to move permanently to the area. Eventually, Miamis, Weas, and Hurons assented to this, and the migration gained in force.[53] There is some, if very tenuous, evidence that the first immigrants may have been Chalaakaathas from the Upper Susquehanna,[54] but they were soon followed and joined by groups from most of the other divisions. Following the West Branch of the Susquehanna River or the tributaries of the Ohio, they gradually made their way across the Allegheny Mountains to the new land, establishing towns along or near the Ohio, Connumach Creek, Juniata, French Creek, and other rivers.[55]

This was by no means a simple, quick, or unified process. All Shawnees did not follow the migrants, and even some of those who did, did not stay in Ohio permanently. For example, the majority of the Thawikilas, who had arrived at the Ohio Valley from Carolina via the Potomac in 1731, escaped hastily back to the South in 1735 after an Iroquois diplomat had been murdered in one of their towns.[56] Nevertheless, within a decade or so from its beginning, the Ohio migration had totally changed the distribution of Shawnee settlements. In effect, it had created two new Shawnee centers in place of four old ones: one in the Ohio Country and the other in the Wyoming Valley along the Susquehanna. The Ohio group was bigger and consisted apparently of Chalaakaathas, Pekowis, and at least some Thawikilas and possibly Kishpokos, whereas the Wyoming center was mainly made up of Mekoches from Pechoquealin.

Both of these settlement clusters developed into independent political centers. In the Ohio Country, some smaller Shawnee villages continued to be scattered over wide areas, but most of the major towns were established near one another.[57] Even though each village and town had its own local headmen, there was an increasing amount of cooperation among them. For example, in large international treaties and diplomatic relationships, they were often represented by a single spokesman who stated the views and opinions arrived at in inter-village councils. This did not mean an end to political factionalism or quibbling among Ohio Shawnees, but it definitely marked a conscious attempt to achieve a new level of supralocal cooperation and unity. The Wyoming center of Mekoches also usually spoke through a single person in diplomatic affairs, and therefore it is no wonder that the Pennsylvania colonial government, who still remained the Shawnees' most important European ally both in trade and in politics, de facto acknowledged both Shawnee centers as politically independent by maintaining separate diplomatic relations to each of them.[58] This was a view shared by the Indians themselves, since even if representatives from Ohio and Wyoming might travel to Philadelphia together to treat with the Pennsylvanians, they still spoke only for their own group. In fact, in a 1739 council the Wyoming spokesman, Kakowatchiky, apparently did not even take part in the sessions where only concerns of the Ohio group were addressed.[59]

There was, of course, some measure of cooperation between the two groups.

Older social ties also continued to bind the Ohioans and the Wyoming peoples together, as did the numerous small villages which dotted the landscape from the Susquehanna to the Ohio Valley. Tribal unity increased even more—both geographically and sociopolitically—in 1744, when most of the Mekoches left Wyoming to escape persistent rumors of imminent war and migrated across the mountains, establishing Logstown on the Ohio River in westernmost Pennsylvania.[60]

All in all, the growing tribal unity of the Shawnees comes across rather clearly from contemporary colonial documents. But what were the causes and motives behind this unification process? What persuaded Shawnees to strive for this new kind of political cooperation?

One obvious reason was outside threats, which induced Shawnees to seek security from each other. At first, in the 1720s and 1730s, the main military threat to Shawnees was constituted by their long-standing southern Indian enemies, especially the Catawbas, whose raids into Shawnee country became more and more regular and destructive during the 1730s.[61] However, an even more serious threat arose in the 1740s and 1750s, as the competition between the British colonies and New France over ownership of the Ohio Country intensified and turned both European powers into potential—and, at times, very real—enemies of the Shawnees. The threat of colonial aggression reached its peak during the Seven Years' War (1756–1763) and the subsequent "Pontiac's War" (1763–1765). Even though there was a considerable amount of factionalism and political disagreement among the Shawnees during these conflicts, the end of these wars saw them geographically, socially, and politically more unified than ever. By 1764, most had sought safety with one another and concentrated in two nearby settlement clusters in present-day Ohio, one on the Scioto Plains and the other on the Muskingum River.[62]

However, this gradual geographical and simultaneous sociopolitical coalescence of Shawnees was by no means solely a reaction to outside threats and stimuli. It must be understood also as the result of a conscious political centralization process that went hand in hand with the creation of a new, more centralized tribal identity. The political centralization can be partially attributed to colonial Indian policies. British officials had for a long time been interested in creating a more centralized leadership in Indian communities—basically because they calculated that this would be the ideal way to establish easily controlled puppet regimes among the potentially dangerous Natives and to govern the Indians through their leaders. Hence, Natives had often been admonished to select "your King, with whom Publick Business shall be transacted."[63] By the 1760s, this had become a major trend in official British Indian policy, culminating in the 1764 Plan for the Imperial Control of Indian

Affairs, which called for the creation of a very centralized and hierarchical leadership structure in Indian societies allied with the English.[64]

Regardless of British ambitions, their policy did not result in the rise of European-controlled puppet "kings" among the Shawnees. Instead, it helped to create a new and powerful elite in the tribe, an elite most interested in uniting their people both politically and ethnically and creating a strong nation out of the separate communities and village clusters. Several leaders were instrumental in this process, but probably the most important of them was the early leader of the Ohio Shawnees, Nuchneconner. Nuchneconner first appears in European documents around 1730 as one of the more important local head-men of the Ohio region. He was variously called a chief, deputy king, and eventually, as a mark of his growing influence, the king of the Shawnees.[65] He was, of course, no European king. Like all successful politicians in tribal contexts, he relied on his skills as an orator, on generous gift-giving rituals, and on an extensive network of kin and other influential allies. Nuchneconner was indeed a man of exceptional connections, as his immediate allies included Layapareawah, the son of a widely known former Shawnee chief Opessa; Coyeacolinne, the leading orator of the Ohio council; and also several powerful Pennsylvanian fur traders, like the mixed-blood Peter Chartier, who apparently provided his Shawnee friend with a steady supply of valuable European trade goods to be used for political purposes.[66]

Although research is once again hampered by inadequate data, it seems that Nuchneconner had quite ambitious visions about the future of his people. He apparently dreamed of bringing the entire tribe together in the Ohio Country as a politically and ethnically unified, strong nation. At one point he even planned to build one great town for all Shawnees, to "Gether [the Shawnees] two Gather and make a strong Town."[67] Indeed, the establishment of Lower Shawnee Town, an exceptionally large Shawnee center of 1,200 or so inhabitants at the junction of the Ohio and Scioto Rivers sometime between 1734 and 1739, may have been the result of his vision and effort.[68]

The Shawnee unification process continued and even intensified during the following decades so that by the late 1760s most of the tribe resided near the Scioto and Muskingum Rivers. At least the political elite of this time tried repeatedly to organize tribal political, diplomatic, and military cooperation—and often with considerable success. For the first time, some written documents hint at the existence of an effective tribal council that tried to formulate common policy for the separate divisions and towns. At this time, most Ohio Shawnees also acknowledged, at least nominally, a tribal head-chief, although it should be emphasized that his authority was far from steady or all-encompassing and was often challenged by kin group leaders and the young men. Despite the obvious limits of both the head-chief's and tribal council's power, ambitious individuals and groups were clearly trying to establish a new kind of central government for the Shawnees on the tribal level. This was a conscious nation-building process, aimed at replacing the older segmentary tribe with a more centralized ethnic and political unit.[69]

This effort was, however, far from smooth, simple, and harmonious, and it was never entirely fulfilled. It had many opponents, such as kin groups, which were in danger of losing their power to a rising central government, and the young men, who felt their independence was being trampled by a new political elite. In addition to these conflicts, various Shawnee divisions and aspiring head-men frequently argued bitterly among themselves over which of them should have the right to the highest political offices and power on a tribal level. For example, Mekoches usually claimed a divine right to tribal leadership on the basis of oral tradition, but their allegations were often challenged by chiefs from other divisions, sometimes even on the same grounds.[70] In addition, all Shawnees never did coalesce into the Ohio center. Already in the 1740s, Chartier had led one band first to the Wabash region and then eventually to Alabama.[71] Other groups stayed on the Susquehanna, and even though some of them kept migrating to the Scioto and Muskingum throughout the 1760s, others remained behind and finally retreated with the other splinter groups to Iroquois lands during the American Revolutionary War.[72] In addition, most Thawikilas and some Kishpokos evidently stayed in the South, mostly with the Creeks, throughout the eighteenth century. Indeed, the separation of the majority of the Thawikilas from the rest of the tribe was so obvious that they were not even listed among Shawnee divisions in the late 1700s or early 1800s.[73]

CONCLUSION

Eventually, the unification of the Shawnees was cut short by serious new conflicts with Anglo-Americans in the 1770s, namely Lord Dunmore's War of 1774 and the subsequent American Revolution. During these wars, the tribe split into several factions, each of which adopted a different policy to deal with the conflicts and problems created by them. At worst, the relations between some factions soured temporarily to the brink of violence, and even though open conflict was finally evaded, factionalism led to a new tribal dispersal, as some bands migrated to the Creeks and others west to Spanish Missouri to escape the wars and intratribal antagonisms. To date, this new period of dispersal has never fully ended.[74]

However, in the nineteenth century most of the widely scattered Shawnee groups began once again to coalesce gradually into roughly neighboring areas and locations in Indian Territory in Oklahoma. Although they formed three settlements that remained both geographically separate and politically independent, the Shawnees began once again to renew their social networks and kin ties, and once again visited each other's homes and took part in each other's ceremonies, just like they had done 150 years earlier on the Pennsylvania and Ohio frontiers.[75] And despite the lack of the kind of political unification dreamed of by Nuchneconner and his successors, the Shawnees survived and continued to be *Shawnees.*

The persistence of Shawnee tribal identity during the colonial period was remarkable, as was the Shawnees' ability to reinvent and reconstruct their nation creatively in changing circumstances. It also shows that although the everyday life, politics, and personal identity of most late pre-Contact and colonial period Shawnees and other Eastern Woodlands peoples revolved largely around local communities and kin groups, supra-local formations such as tribes and confederacies also played an important part in their lives. Locality and supralocality may perhaps best be viewed as partially contrasting forces in shaping the politics, ethnicity, and identity of Shawnees and other eastern groups. Their complex interrelationships as well as the various economic, political, and ecological factors behind them warrant additional studies.

ABBREVIATIONS

HP—Halimand Papers, British Library, London

NAC—National Archives of Canada, Ottawa, Ontario

OVGLEA—Ohio Valley—Great Lakes Ethnohistory Archive, Bloomington, IN

PA—Hazard, Samuel, ed. *Pennsylvania Archives,* 1st ser., 138 vols. (Philadelphia: N.p., 1852)

PCM—Hazard, Samuel, ed. *Minutes of the Provincial Council of Pennsylvania from the Organization to the Termination of Proprietary Government,* 16 vols. (Harrisburg, PA: N.p., 1838–1853)

NOTES

1. Alexandra Harmon, "Wanted: More Histories on Indian Identity," in *A Companion to American Indian History,* ed. Philip J. Deloria and Neal Salisbury (Oxford: Blackwell Publishers, 2002), 248, my italics.

2. See generally Bruce Bourque, "Ethnicity on the Maritime Peninsula, 1650–1759," *Ethnohistory* 36 (Summer 1989): 257–84; Gregory Evans Dowd, *A Spirited Resistance: The North American Indian Struggle for Unity, 1745–1812* (Baltimore: Johns Hopkins University Press, 1992); Morris W. Foster, *Being a Comanche: A Social History of an American Indian Community* (Tucson: University of Arizona Press, 1991); Patricia Galloway, *The Choctaw Genesis, 1500–1700* (Lincoln: University of Nebraska Press, 1995); and Michael N. McConnell, *A Country Between: The Upper Ohio Valley and Its Peoples, 1724–1774* (Lincoln: University of Nebraska Press, 1992).

3. Charles Callender, "Shawnee," in *Handbook of the North American Indians,* Vol. 15, *Northeast,* ed. Bruce G. Trigger (Washington, DC: Smithsonian, 1978), 624; and A. Gwynn Henderson and David Pollack, "Toward a Model of Fort Ancient Society," in *Fort Ancient*

Cultural Dynamics in the Middle Ohio Valley, ed. A. Gwynn Henderson (Madison, WI: Prehistory Press, 1992), 291–92.

4. Ted C. Lewellen, *Political Anthropology: An Introduction* (Boston: Bergin and Garvey, 1983), 25; and Colin Renfrew and Paul Bahn, *Archaeology—Theories, Methods, and Practice,* 2nd ed. (London: Thames and Hudson, 1996), 169.

5. Lewellen, *Political Anthropology,* 24–26; and Marshall Sahlins, *Tribesmen* (Englewood Cliffs, NJ: Prentice-Hall, 1968), 15–22.

6. The permeable nature of ethnic and political boundaries in the East is evidenced by the prevalence or multiethnic, even multilingual towns and confederacies and cultural practices such as the adoption of outsiders and frequent intermarriage between tribes.

7. Of the interplay and importance of localism and supralocalism in colonial-period Indian life and politics, see, for example, Dowd, *A Spirited Resistance,* xix–xxi; and Colin G. Calloway, *The American Revolution in Indian Country: Crisis and Diversity in Native American Communities* (Cambridge: Cambridge University Press, 1995), 8–11.

8. Dowd, *A Spirited Resistance,* xx–xxi; William A. Hunter, "History of the Ohio Valley," in *Handbook: Northeast,* 592; and McConnell, *A Country Between,* 3, 12–14, 20.

9. McConnell, *A Country Between,* 12–14, 20.

10. James H. Howard, *Shawnee! The Ceremonialism of a Native American Tribe and Its Cultural Background* (Athens: Ohio University Press, 1981), 24–25. For Shawnee words, I have used the transcription conventions employed by Howard (1981). Several other orthographies are also in use among modern researchers, not to mention earlier writers whose renderings of Shawnee words differ considerably and are even internally inconsistent.

11. C.C. Trowbridge, *Shawnee Traditions: C.C. Trowbridge's Account,* ed. Vernon Kinietz and Erminie W. Voegelin (Ann Arbor: University of Michigan Press, 1939), 7, 62.

12. Callender, "Shawnee," 624; Hunter, "History of the Ohio Valley," 589; and Howard, *Shawnee!* 5. There may also have been poorly recorded and little understood dynamism in the divisional structure of the Shawnees throughout the eighteenth century. In the last decades of the century, the Thawikilas, most of whom resided in the South at the time, were sometimes omitted in the listings of Shawnee divisions in the Ohio Region. As a result, the Shawnee nation was often described as consisting of four, rather than five divisions. See Trowbridge, *Shawnee Traditions,* 8; and Jasper Yeates, "Indian Treaty at Fort Pitt in 1776," *Pennsylvania Magazine in History and Biography* 5 (1884): 485. On the other hand, especially during the 1770s and 1780s, the town of Wakatomica and its inhabitants seem to have achieved a distinct indentity to such a degree that they were sometimes specified as their own group among the Shawnees and termed "Wakitumikée Indians" or "Wakitamikie tribe" by the British. The possibility that the town was for some reason acquiring some features of a division needs more detailed research. For Wakatomica, see Henry Bird, "Letter to Arent de Peyster, June 3, 1780," HP, Additional Manuscripts, 21 760, folio 325; Alexander McKee, "Letter to Arent de Peyster, June 4, 1780," HP, 21 760, folio 326; and Alexander McKee, "Letter to Arent de Peyster, May 24, 1783," HP, 21 763, folio 125.

13. Ives Goddard, "Central Algonquian Languages," in *Handbook: Northeast,* 585. The linguistic history of the Shawnees is practically unknown in many respects, especially in regards to the original divisional dialects, because the old Shawnee divisions merged in new

and complex ways in the nineteenth century creating three new groupings whose minor dialectical differences may, to some extent, reflect earlier patterns.

14. Jerry E. Clark, *The Shawnee* (Lexington: University of Kentucky Press, 1977), 33; Lewis Henry Morgan, in *The Indian Journal, 1859–1862,* ed. Leslie A. White (New York: Dover Publications, 1993), 52; and William A. Galloway, *Old Chillicothe: Shawnee and Pioneer History: Conflicts and Romances in the Northwest Territory* (Xenia, OH: Buckeye Press, 1934), 128.

15. Thomas Wildcat Alford, *Civilization* (Norman: University of Oklahoma Press, 1936), 44–45; Thomas Wildcat Alford, "The Shawnee Indians," in Galloway, *Old Chillicothe,* 21; Charles Callender, "Great Lakes-Riverine Sociopolitical Organization," in *Handbook: Northeast,* 618–19; Howard, *Shawnee!* 108; and John Sugden, *Blue Jacket, Warrior of the Shawnees* (Lincoln: University of Nebraska Press, 2000), 269. Of Alford's statement, the claim that the tribal head-chief of the Shawnees came either from the Chalaakaatha or Thawikila division seems incompatible with eighteenth-century documents. On the basis of these records, it would appear that most of the leaders more or less recognized as *tribal* chiefs were actually Mekoches. Confederacies such as the Shawnees were of course by no means uncommon in the Eastern Woodlands. The structure of the Shawnee confederacy may have had its closest parallels among its linguistic and cultural relatives, the Illinois and Miamis, but other notable confederacies include the Six Nations Iroquois, Hurons, and Creeks. A comparison of political and ethnic structure of these confederacies might shed more light on the Shawnee sociopolitical order.

16. Clark, *The Shawnee,* 8–9.

17. Callender, "Shawnee," 624; Penelope Ballard Drooker, *The View from Madisonville: Protohistoric Western Fort Interaction Patterns* (Ann Arbor: University of Michigan Press, 1997), 272–73, 282, 292–93; and John Witthoft and William A. Hunter, "The Seventeenth-Century Origins of the Shawnee," *Ethnohistory* 2 (Winter 1955): 42–57.

18. Trowbridge, *Shawnee Traditions,* 1–10, 61–63.

19. See generally Witthoft and Hunter, "Seventeenth-Century Origins"; and Penelope Ballard Drooker, "The Ohio Valley, 1550–1750: Patterns of Sociopolitical Coalescence and Dispersal," in *The Transformation of the Southeastern Indians, 1540–1760,* ed. Robbie Ethridge and Charles Hudson (Oxford: University of Mississippi Press, 2002), 115–34.

20. On the relationship between Fort Ancient and Shawnees, see Callender, "Shawnee," 630; Drooker, *Madisonville,* 103–5; Drooker, "The Ohio Valley, 1550–1750"; James B. Griffin, "Late Prehistory of the Ohio Valley," in *Handbook of the North American Indians,* Vol. 15, *Northeast,* 557; Henderson and Pollack, "Toward a Model of Fort Ancient Society," 291; A. Gwynn Henderson, David Pollack, and Christopher A. Turnbow, "Chronology and Cultural Patterns," in *Fort Ancient Cultural Dynamics in the Middle Ohio Valley,* ed. A. Gwynn Henderson, 277–79; and David Pollack and A. Gwynn Henderson, "A Mid-Eighteenth Century Historic Indian Occupation in Greenup County, Kentucky," in *Late Prehistoric Research in Kentucky,* ed. David Pollack, Charles D. Hockensmith, and Thomas N. Sanders (Frankfort: Kentucky Heritage Council, 1984), 1.

21. Drooker, *Madisonville,* 327–29; Henderson and Pollack, "Toward a Model of Fort

Ancient Society," 286, 289; and Henderson, et al., "Chronology and Cultural Patterns," 266–68, 278.

22. Drooker, *Madisonville,* 327–28; and Henderson et al., "Chronology and Cultural Patterns," 267.

23. Henderson and Pollack, "Toward a Model of Fort Ancient Society," 291–92.

24. On material culture as an ethnic symbol, see generally Ian Hodder, *Symbols in Action: Ethnoarchaeological Studies of Material Culture* (Cambridge: Cambridge University Press, 1982).

25. Drooker, *Madisonville,* 3, 48, 69–70, 282; Henderson and Pollack, "Toward a Model of Fort Ancient Society," 286; Henderson et al., "Chronology and Cultural Patterns," 269, 273.

26. Drooker, *Madisonville,* 2–3, 282; James B. Griffin, "Fort Ancient Has No Class: The Absence of an Elite Group in Mississippian Societies in the Central Ohio Valley," in *Lords of the Southeast: Social Inequality and the Native Elites of Southeastern North America,* ed. Alex W. Barker and Timothy R. Pauketat (Washington, DC: Archaeological Papers of the American Anthropological Association, 1992), 55; Richard W. Yerkes, "The Woodland and Mississippian Traditions in the Prehistory of Midwestern North America," *Journal of World Prehistory* 3 (June 1989): 344–45.

27. Drooker, *Madisonville,* 272–73, 282, 292–93; Drooker, "The Ohio Valley, 1550–1750," 121.

28. Drooker, *Madisonville,* 3, 75, 88, 104, 269, 292.

29. See generally Griffin, "Late Prehistory of the Ohio Valley."

30. Callender, "Shawnee," 623, 630.

31. Dean R. Snow, *The Iroquois* (Oxford and Cambridge: Blackwell, 1994), 110–11, 114–18; Richard White, *The Middle Ground: Indians, Empires, and Republics in the Great Lakes Region, 1650–1815* (Cambridge: Cambridge University Press, 1991), 1–49.

32. See generally Drooker, "The Ohio Valley, 1550–1750."

33. Callender, "Shawnee," 630; Drooker, "The Ohio Valley, 1550–1750."

34. Most of the early references on divisional migrations pertain to the Thawikilas. See "Number of Indians, 1731," PA, 1:302, and PCM, 608–9; and Callender, "Shawnee," 624.

In the 1770s, there is also information on the Mekoches migrating as a group. See, for example, Reuben Gold Thwaites and Louise Phelps Kellogg, eds., "David Zeisberger to Edward Hand, March 6, 1777," *Frontier Defence on the Upper Ohio, 1770–1778* (Madison: State Historical Society of Wisconsin, 1912), 166; "Diary of the Indian Congregation in Gnadenhütten on the Muskingum River for the Months of January, February, March, April, to May 25, 1777," *Records of the Moravian Mission among the Indians of North America* (New Haven, CT: Research Publications, Inc., 1978) (microfilm), State Library of New York, Albany, reel 9, box 144, folder 13, item 1; Kishanatathe et al., "Shawnee Message to George Morgan, February 28, 1777," George Morgan Letterbook I (microfilm), drawer XIX, OVGLEA; and White Eyes and Killbuck, "Message to Col. George Morgan, March 14, 1778," and White Eyes et al., "Speech to George Morgan, April 26, 1778," both in George Morgan Letterbook III (microfilm), drawer XIX, OVGLEA. That at least some of the late-seventeenth-century migrations were at least partially division based is evidenced by the fact that the Shawnee towns that were established in new homelands sometimes bore divisional names, such as Pequa (i.e., Pekowi) on the lower Susquehanna River.

35. See Reuben Gold Thwaites, ed., "1732: The King's Memoir," *Collections of the State Historical Society of Wisconsin, XVII: The French Regime in Wisconsin II, 1727–1748* (Madison: State Historical Society of Wisconsin, 1906), 156; "Memoir of the King, May 12, 1733," *Collections*, 178; and "The Marquis de Beauharnois to the Minister, October 15, 1732," in *Wilderness Chronicles of Northwestern Pennylvania,* ed. Sylvester K. Stevens and Donald H. Kent (Harrisburg: Pennsylvania Historical Commission, 1941), 5.

36. See generally Drooker, "The Ohio Valley, 1550–1750."

37. Hunter, "History of the Ohio Valley," 588–90.

38. Harmon, "Wanted: More Histories on Indian Identity," 253; James H. Merrell, "The Indians' New World: The Catawba Experience," in *The American Indians: Past and Present,* 3rd ed., ed. Roger L. Nichols (New York: Alfred A. Knopf, 1986), 16–17.

39. Callender, "Shawnee," 623–24, 630.

40. Drooker, "The Ohio Valley, 1550–1750."

41. James Logan, "Letter to Governor Clarke," August 4, 1737, Logan Papers (microfilm), drawer XIX, OVGLEA; Logan, "Letter to Governor Gooch," May 11, 1738, Logan Papers, drawer XIX, OVGLEA; Edmund B. O'Callaghan and Berthold Fernow, eds., "Propositions of the Schagticoke and Five Nations of Indians, &c [July 4, 1693]," *Documents Relative to the Colonial History of the State of New York,* vol. 4 (Albany: Weed and Parsons, 1856–1887), 43; O'Callaghan and Fernow, "Journal of Captain Arent Schuyler's Visit to the Minisinck Country," PCM, 4:99; and PCM, 3:97. See also Drooker, "The Ohio Valley, 1550–1750."

42. For an excellent summary of the settlement locations, see Barry C. Kent, Janet Rice, and Kakuko Ota, "A Map of 18th Century Indian Towns in Pennsylvania," *Pennsylvania Archaeologist* 4, no. 1 (1981): 1–18.

43. To some extent, the divisions inhabiting each center can be deduced from known village names (such as Pequa, that is, Pekowi, and Chillisquaque, that is, Chalaakaatha). A riskier way to study the divisional composition of the Shawnee settlements is to trace back the family history of those late-eighteenth-century Shawnee leaders whose division is known, to see from which of the Pennsylvania centers their families came. Neither method can provide definite answers, since it is questionable whether any center would have been inhabited solely by a single division. In the 1770s, at least part of the Kishpokos lived in the Scioto Valley next to several Shawnee groups who had migrated from Pennsylvania. However, this does not necessarily mean that the Kishpokos had arrived from the same direction. Of the Kishpoko town on the Scioto, see Peter Force, ed., "Commissioners for Indian Affairs to Committee of Congress, September 25, 1776," *American Archives,* 5th ser. (Washington, DC: M. St. Clair Clarke and Peter Force, 1837–1853), vol. 1; and Reuben Gold Thwaites and Louise Phelps Kellogg, eds., "Facsimile of Map in Crèvecoeur's 'Lettres d'un Cultivateaur Américain,'" *Revolution in the Upper Ohio, 1775–1777* (Madison: State Historical Society of Wisconsin, 1908), frontispiece.

44. See PCM, 2:557; and PCM, 3:22.

45. PCM, 2:22; PCM, 3:80–81, 97.

46. Of this somewhat ambiguous episode, see "Letter from John Wright to James

Logan, May 2, 1728," PA, 1:213; "Message from James Le Tort to Gov., May 12, 1728," PA, 1:216; "Instruction to Smith and Skolehoven, 1728," PA, 1:223–24; PCM, 3:303, 309. The sources make it possible to interpret this episode in various ways; the interpretation presented here is derived from Charles A. Hanna, *The Wilderness Trail or the Ventures and Adventures of the Pennsylvania Traders of the Alleghany Path with Some New Annals of the Old West, and the Records of Some Strong Men and Some Bad Ones,* vol. 1 (New York: G.P. Putnam's Sons, 1911), 185–86.

47. PCM, 3:45, 102–3, 149–55, 216, 310–14.

48. Logan, "Letter to Governor Clarke, August 4, 1737," drawer XIX, OVGLEA. Multitribal, even multilingual, settlements like these were by no means rare in the colonial Eastern Woodlands; rather they appeared everywhere where displaced peoples with varied ethnic and political backgrounds came together seeking security and friends from one another. See generally, Merrell, "The Indians' New World"; White, *Middle Ground,* 1–49.

49. Hanna, *Wilderness Trail,* 153, 156–57; PCM, 2:600, 630–31, 637; PCM, 3:97, 116.

50. James Logan, "Letter to Governor Gooch, May 11, 1738," drawer XIX, OVGLEA; and PCM, 2:404, 406.

51. Before the 1770s, the only Shawnee division whose name appears often in the colonial documents is Thawikila. Other divisional names appear rarely if ever in contexts other than town names.

52. McConnell, *A Country Between,* 5–20. See also James Logan, "Letter to Governor Clarke, Aug 4, 1737," drawer XIX, OVGLEA; "Message [of] Shawnee Chiefs to Gov. Gordon, [June 7] 1732," PA, 1:329; PCM, 4:324–25; and "Messrs. De Beauharnois and D'Aigremont to the Minister, October 1, 1728," in *Wilderness Chronicles,* 3–4.

53. "The Marquis de Beauharnois to the Minister, Oct 15, 1732," in *Wilderness Chronicles,* 5–6; "1733: Memoir of the King, May 12, 1733," Thwaites, *Collections,* 17:178.

54. Chief Ocowellos of the Upper Shawnees was probably the first to ally himself with the French. See PCM, 3:219. See also "Message [of] Shawnee Chiefs to Gov. Gordon, [June 7] 1732," PA, 1:329; and PCM, 4:324–25.

55. "The Examination of Jonah Davenport" [October 29, 1731], PA, 1:299–300; "The Examination of James Letort," PA, 1:300–301; "Number of Indians in 1731," PA, 1:302; "Messrs. de Beauharnois and d'Aigrement to Minister, October 1, 1728," in *Wilderness Chronicles,* 3–4; "The Marquis de Beauharnois to the Minister, October 15, 1732," in ibid., 5–6; "Speeches at an Indian Council, 1732," in ibid., 9.

56. "Number of Indians 1731," PA, 1:302; and PCM, 3:608–9.

57. "The Marquis de Beauharnois to the Minister, October 15, 1732," in *Wilderness Chronicles,* 5–6.

58. This is evidenced by the correspondence between the Pennsylvania government and Shawnee leaders. The Pennsylvanians usually addressed the Ohio and Wyoming head-men separately in these letters, even though letters were usually intended for the Shawnees as a whole. See "Newcheconner and Cacowacheco chiefs of the Shawanese Indians [July 12, 1739]" and "George Thomas Esqu. Govn. Of the Province of Pennsylvania &c to his friends & Brethen Cacowachico & Nochiconna [August 16, 1742]," Logan Papers, drawer XIX, OVGLEA. It is extremely important to note that the Ohio and Wyoming chiefs, on the other hand, sent their own messages to the Pennsylvanians separately.

59. See PCM, 3:459–63; and PCM, 4:336–47.

60. PCM, 4:747; and McConnell, *A Country Between,* 22, 62.

61. See "Capt. Civility to Governor, June 10, 1729," PA, 1:241; PCM, 4:234–35; and "Message of King of Shawnees to Governor Gooch [August 4, 1738]," in *Virginia Treaties, 1723–1775,* ed. W. Stitt Robinson (Frederick, MD: University Publications of America, 1983), 23–24.

62. Thomas Hutchins, "A Description of the Country Westward of the Ohio River, with the Distances Computed from Fort Pitt to the several Indian Towns by Land & Water," in *The Wilderness Trail or the Ventures and Adventures of the Pennsylvania Traders on the Allegheny Path with Some of the New Annals of the Old West, and the Records of Some Strong Men and Some Bad Ones,* ed. Charles A. Hanna (New York: G.P. Putman's Sons, 1911), 194–95.

63. PCM, 5:588.

64. "Plan for the Imperial Control of Indian Affairs, July 10, 1764," in *Collections of the Illinois State Historical Library,* vol. 10, ed. Clarence Walworth Alvord and Clarence Edwin Carter (Springfield: Illinois State Historical Library, 1915), 276–77.

65. For example, see "To Newcheconner & Cacowacheco chiefs of the Shawanese Indians [July 12, 1739]," Logan Papers, drawer XIX, OVGLEA; "Indians at Allagheney to Governor, [March 20, 1738]," PA, 1:552; and "Message of King of Shawnees to Governor Gooch [August 4, 1738]," *Virginia Treaties,* ed. Robinson, 24.

66. "Anonymous Diary of a Trip from Detroit to the Ohio River, May 22 to August 24, 1745," English translation, Indians Claims Collection, Royce Area 11, Docket No. 13-G, ox 3, Defendant's Exhibit 155, OVGLEA; "A True Account of all the Men in the Three Towns in Allagania of the Shawnise Nation by Geo. Miranda, [September 27, 1737]," *Logan Papers,* drawer XIX, OVGLEA; "Indians' Letter to Gov. Gordon, [April 24, 1733], PA, 1:394–95; "Indian Resolution Respecting Rum, 1738," PA, 1:549–50; "Indians at Allagheney to Governor, [March 20 1738]," PA, 1:552; PCM, 5:311; "William Trent's Account of Proceedings with the Iroquois and their Allies at Logstown," *Virginia Treaties,* Robinson, 173; and "The Marquis de Beauharnois to the French Minister, October 9, 1739," in *Wilderness Chronicles,* 19. Of Chartier, see White, *Middle Ground,* 189–92. Of the Shawnee unification and Nuchneconner, see McConnell, *A Country Between,* 27–31. Nuchneconner's own divisional background is impossible to attest to definitively. However, he was occasionally styled the deputy king, with Layapaeawah termed as the king. As Layapaeawah was the son of Opessa, former chief of the Pequa town, it is probable that both he and his father were Pekowis. Nuchneconner's role as Layapaeawah's "deputy" (in reality perhaps some kind of mentor and ally) may indicate that he was Pekowi, too.

67. "Indians' Letter to Gov. Gordon, [March 20,] 1738," PA, 1:551.

68. Of Lower Shawnee Town's population, see Christopher Gist, "Christopher Gist's First and Second Journals, September 11, 1750–March 29, 1752, For the Honorable Robert Dinwiddie Esquire Governor & Commande of Virginia," in *George Mercer Papers—Relating to the Ohio Company of Virginia,* ed. Louis Mulkearn (Pittsburgh: University of Pittsburgh Press, 1954), 16; Callender, "Shawnee," 625. Regarding the date of the town's establishment, see A. Gwynn Henderson, Cynthia E. Jobe, and Christopher A. Turnbow, *Indian Occupation and Land Use in Northern and Eastern Kentucky during the Contact Period (1540–1795): An Initial Investigation* (Lexington: University of Kentucky Press, 1986), 24,

55. It should be noted that my interpretation of the town's origins is not the only possible one.

69. The existence of the Tribal Council or at least extensive negotiations among different Shawnee towns comes across clearly in the proceedings of the Shawnees with both the English and French at the close of Pontiac's War in 1764. The same documents also point to a growing role of a small group of leaders, such as Hardman, Nimwha, and Red Hawk. See, for example, PCM, 9:212–33, 250. Of these men, Hardman was apparently recognized as some sort of tribal chief for the next decade or so.

70. "George Ironside to Alexander McKee, Feb 6, 1795," NAC, Ottawa, Record Group 10: Indian Affairs, vol. 9, reel C-10, 999; Sugden, *Blue Jacket*, 27, 269; Trowbridge, *Shawnee Traditions*, 2–8.

.71. Hanna, *Wilderness Trail*, vol. 2, 134; PCM, 5:311–12; Dunbar Rowland and A.G. Sanders, eds., "Vaudreuil to Mauerpas, February 12, 1744," *Mississippi Provincial Archives*, Vol. 4: *French Dominion, 1729–1748*, rev. and ed. Patricia Kay Galloway (Baton Rouge: Louisiana State University Press, 1984), 222; Rowland and Sanders, eds., "Vaudreuil to Rouillé, June 24, 1750," *Mississippi Provincial Archives*, Vol. 5, *French Dominion, 1729–1748*, rev. and ed. Patricia Kay Galloway (Baton Rouge: Louisiana State University Press, 1984), 48; "Beauharnois to French Minister, 25 October 1744," Thwaites, *Collections*, vol. 17, 448; and Reuben Gold Thwaites, ed., "French Minister to La Jonguière," May 4, 1749, *Collections of the State Historical Society of Wisconsin*, Vol. 18, *The French Regime in Wisconsin, 1743–1760* (Madison: State Historical Society of Wisconsin, 1908), 4, 12, 20–21.

72. K.G. Davies, ed., "George Croghan to Thomas Gage, January 1, 1770," *Documents of the American Revolution, 1770–1783*, vol. 2 (Shannon: Irish University Press, 1972), 22–23; Thomas Gage, "Letter from Thomas Gage to Henry Gladwin, April 23, 1764," Gage Papers (microfilm), drawer XIX, reel 11, OVGLEA; PCM, 4:234; "Return of Indians of Colonel Johnson's Department gone to Plant at Buffaloe Creek, May 13, 1781," HP, Folio 181; John Burch, "Return of Indian," "Present State of Officers, Men and Indians, November 4, 1779," "Return of Officers and ca., March 24, 1781," "Return of Indians, May 26, 1780," "Return of Indian War Parties, April 1781," "Distribution of Corn and Hoes, May 13, 1781," and "General State of the Corps of Indians," all in HP, 21 769, folios 16, 34, 46, 62, 118, 120, 122; and James Sullivan et al., eds. "Journal of Alexander McKee," *The Papers of Sir William Johnson*, vol. 7 (Albany: University of the State of New York, 1921), 185.

73. Trowbridge, *Shawnee Traditions*, 8; Yeates, "Indian Treaty," 485. Given the previous history of this division, including long periods of separation from the main group of the tribe, one may wonder if the Thawikilas might have originally been less closely bound to the Shawnee confederacy than its other divisions. More research is needed to clarify this issue.

74. Callender, "Shawnee," 624, 631–34.

75. For a summary, see ibid., 622, 632–33.

CHAPTER 13

"Why Quarrel about Dividing the Hind Quarter When We Are Not Going to Hunt?": Seminole Diplomatic Discourse before the Comet

SUSAN A. MILLER

THIS CHAPTER EXAMINES a nineteenth-century episode in the history of my people, the Seminole Nation. My purpose is to illuminate the cosmos framing Seminole diplomacy at that time using the diplomatic discourse of Seminole leaders. A secondary purpose is to illustrate the method of decolonizing tribal histories that is in use by the present generation of scholars from the tribes.

People in my family four and five generations back were alive during a terrible time when people of the United States invaded our homeland in present-day Florida. They made war on our communities, killing many of us and interning and forcibly relocating others to a place far to the west. The relocation was a genocidal policy, an atrocity as destructive as the war. In the relocation, American governmental officials destroyed lives by starvation, disease, exposure to harsh weather and unsanitary conditions, and by torture of the old, the sick, and the weak.[1] According to one estimate, they killed half the Seminole people in the war and the relocation.[2] Seminoles are eerily quiet about the brutal nature of the relocation, and scholars have made little of it, but I have heard older Seminoles tell disturbing stories about that time. In one story, Americans throw people from a steamboat during the crossing of the Gulf of Mexico. In another, Seminole women hid their boys under their full skirts so that American soldiers would not find and kill them.

American historians date the war for the Seminole homeland to a day in December 1835, when a party of Seminoles executed an American agent. American historians say that Seminoles murdered him, but the incident was really an execution carried out in the Seminole country by Seminole officials under Seminole law.[3] The war for the Seminole homeland had been under way for a long time before the attack that American historians view as the start date. It is certain, however, that the destructive effects of the American invasion intensified after that day.

Our Seminole forebears had a warning in the form of a large comet that had appeared in the sky the previous summer. *Hutkes*—white people—call the comet after one of their men, whose name was Halley. A comet warns of imminent conflict or hard times, as one Seminole later told the American anthropologist John R. Swanton.[4]

THE EPISODE AT SILVER SPRING

In the autumn before the comet appeared, the Seminole Council met on Seminole land with the American agent Wiley Thompson, who was soon to be executed. The meeting took place at a spring that I know only by its American name, Silver Spring, although Seminoles of Florida may yet recall its Seminole name, and the spirit of that spring may yet reside there. The Americans had planted a military base, Fort King, nearby. By the time of the meeting at the spring, American officials had secured two treaties with Seminole leaders, the Treaty on Moultrie Creek in 1823 and the Treaty at Payne's Landing in 1832, and were claiming that those treaties encoded the Seminoles' consent to leave their homeland and be hauled away to the west. Seminole leaders denied that they had agreed to move, and by my reading of the treaties, the relevant passages bear them out.

During the meeting at Silver Spring, Seminole leaders put forth their history and interpretation of the treaties, but the agent Thompson merely insisted that his people intended to force them to move anyway. He grumbled when the Seminole Council was still arguing against their dispossession on the second day. He spoke so intemperately[5] that on the third day, Holata Micco, leader of the Redstick town of Tallassee,[6] prefaced the Seminoles' statements by explaining to the American agent of Andrew Jackson's administration how diplomacy is conducted:

> We are brothers, and should not quarrel and say hard things. . . . Our way of doing business is to proceed coolly and deliberately, and in a friendly manner. We have to represent in our talk a great many people, for which reason we must proceed with care and thoughtfulness. The people differ in their opinions, and they must be indulged with time to reflect. Time makes out of many little branching creeks that run different ways, one large river, the waters of which then flow smoothly all in one direction.[7]

"[Y]our talk of today is the foolish talk of a child," the American agent asserted insultingly at the end of that day.[8]

Since before the signing of the Moultrie treaty, the leaders of the Seminole communities had been divided over whether to comply with the invaders' exorbitant demands or to resist at a cost that might prove to be greater. The speakers at this council represented those recent interests on the one hand and, on the other, the ancient, shifting interests of the multiple ethnic groupings that made up the Seminole Nation.

Among the Seminole people, three clear groups were represented at the Moultrie treaty discussions and the meeting at Silver Spring: the towns centered in the Alachua Prairie, the towns from the Apalachee region, and the towns from the Apalachicola River region.[9] Each of the three sets of towns was organized as a chiefdom, rather than simply an alliance of towns. As described by the anthropologist Richard A. Sattler,

> Each had an established, permanent leadership with regular rules of succession and regulatory power over all of the member bands. These regional chiefdoms also showed considerable cohesion and stability in the face of repeated assaults and forced unification during the period 1815–1835.[10]

Communities that carried the label "Redsticks" were among both the Apalachee and Alachua towns. They had been with the Muscogees, but had fled American aggression on Muscogee lands.[11] The Redsticks were among the most adamant towns for resisting removal.

Micco Nuppa was there, the senior man of the elite lineage of the Okonis, the core ethnic group that had founded the Seminoles in the eighteenth century. The micco led the "Seminoles proper"—those towns from the Alachua Prairie—and also the combined groupings that made up the complete Seminole Nation. His town was the capital and the keeper of the Seminole Fire.

Huithli Emathla, the Seminole Tuski Heniha, whom Americans called "Jumper," was there, too. He was extremely influential in council, "an orator, and what is better, a man of sense, and [a] brave warrior."[12] Although he had come from a Redstick town, one of the cores of the resistance, and his micco opted for resistance, and Huithli articulated that position, his personal preference was for accommodation.[13]

Holata Emathla, the Ocese micco, represented one segment of the Apalachee Seminoles. The towns that had formed that grouping along the Apalachee River were crowded by then onto a reservation in central Florida along with the Alachua towns. The Apalachees had polarized around the issue of removal, and Holata Emathla spoke for those Apalachee towns that favored compliance with the Americans' demands. His "brother" Charley Emathla, micco of the Apalachee town Totolosi, also favored compliance.[14]

Apalachee towns committed to resistance were represented by a contingent from the main Redstick community of Tallassee: Micco Holata was their principal chief,[15] and Asin Yahola[16] was *tustenuggee thlacco,* the community's top military leader. Asin Yahola's importance emerges from the accounts of the council. An outsider to hereditary Seminole authority, he appears influential beyond his station and his years, seated beside Micco Nuppa and exhorting him while the agent spoke. During those three days, Asin Yahola became known to American officials for his hostility to their designs and his charismatic influence among his people.[17]

Finally, the white-haired medicine man and prophet Abayaca (Arpeika, Abiaca, or Sam Jones) made a rare appearance in the written record.[18] Because a medicine man does not speak for his people, Abayaca was always in the background during discussions with Americans, but his relations with spirits gave him great influence among the Seminoles. He maintained the spiritual center of the Seminoles' resistance to relocation, and his descendants still carry his tradition today.

The Seminoles' statements were translated into English by a man from a *maroon* community (a community of free Africans) that was associated with the Seminoles. Given that the maroons' interests did not coincide entirely with the Seminoles, his translations may reflect some bias. We have rather detailed English-language records of what was said at that conference, because various Americans made transcripts. In 1836, two Americans, neither of whom appear to have been present, published accounts of the conference, each account quoting transcripts at length.[19] Somebody appeared to have rephrased the translator's words, presumably for what publishers call the "felicity of language." The multiple transcriptions provide some comparisons of the Seminoles' statements, while the translations and rephrasings probably tend to obscure them. The transcripts from Silver Spring show how Seminole diplomatic discourse illuminates an indigenous cosmos and the viable diplomacy that can go on within it. That cosmos survives in Seminole communities, both western and eastern, and this chapter systematically gives it priority over the other cosmos that came from Europe.

The meeting lasted three days. (In accordance with Seminole cosmology and practice, it should have been four.) One of the authors describes "[t]he Council House and the conference within—the excited agent on one side, the calm chiefs on the other." He goes on to note the children playing outside, the Seminole women and men crowding into the council house and around the door "with the most intense, yet subdued interest, catching every look as it gleamed from the countenance, and hanging on every word as it fell from the lip of the headmen who spoke."[20]

For three days, the American agent pressed the Seminole leaders to accommodate his plans for their removal: Would the Seminoles accept the Muscogees' invitation to scatter their dwellings among the Muscogees?[21] Would they rather take their cattle with them or be compensated for their abandoned cattle when they arrived in the west? Did they want to go by water or by land? Did they want their next annuity in goods or in money?[22] Later, Charley Emathla, the micco (principal chief) of the Apalachee town Totolosi, would comment, "If we intended to go, then it would be proper the points [h]e proposed to us should be decided upon. But why quarrel about dividing the hind quarter, when we are not going to hunt[?]"[23]

What the Seminole leaders did want to discuss with the agent was their inability to separate themselves from their homeland. Again and again, they referred to a cosmos in which landscape connects with the spirit world and diplomatic relations are embedded in that landscape. In that reality, a network of sacred obligations binds the Seminole people to the land. "The agent tells us we must go away from the lands which we live on, our homes, and the graves of our fathers," said Asin Yahola at Silver Spring.[24] The graves of the fathers is a recurring theme in the Seminoles' resistance to removal. The graves of a community link the dead forever to the landscape, for the spirits of the deceased either stay at the grave sites or return to them after an initial absence. The spirits of Seminole relatives remain involved with their families and their communities. They attend the sacred ceremonies[25] and are also present more generally in the community. "[T]he moon brings back the spirits of our warriors, our fathers, wives, and children," said Coacoochee, a Wind Clan leader, circa 1841.[26] The living members of Seminole communities were obligated to remain in Florida, because the dead members were bound there to their graves.

Seminole leaders understood diplomacy in terms of family relations. Micco Holata, the Redstick micco of Tallassee, told the agent,

> We were all made by the same great Father, and are all alike[,] his children. We all came from the same mother, and were suckled at the same breast. Therefore we are brothers, and as brothers, should treat together in an amicable way, and should not quarrel and let our blood rise up against each other. If the blood of one of us, by each other's blow, should fall on the lap of the earth, it would stain it, and cry aloud for vengeance, from the land wherein it had sunk, and call down the frown and thunder of the Great Spirit.[27]

Here, the Father is a being in the sky who directs thunder. He wants amicable relations among all his children and will be displeased if those children fall into conflict. The Mother is the Earth, who nurtures the children; she will punish them if they shed each other's blood onto her lap. The Mother and the Father here are not metaphors. The Earth is our Mother and the Sky or the Sun or a Creator Above is our Father, and that is literal. The American scribe, however, believed that *Father,* but not *Mother, Earth,* or *Thunder,* warranted capitalizing.

Talking among themselves, the Seminole leaders considered accommodation. "If we don't go," said Huithli Emathla, "the father will send his men to make us go, and we will lose many of our tribe, because the wrath of the Great Spirit will come upon us."[28] In this instance, "the father" refers to the American president. If this translation and transcription are faithful, Huithli envisioned the state-sponsored violence of the United States as a punishment to be hurled at the Seminoles by the "Great Spirit."

Huithli Emathla employed the metaphor of the Tree that is common in the discourse of the eastern tribes. He said,

> At the [T]reaty of Moultrie it was engaged that we should rest in peace upon the land allotted to us for twenty years. All difficulties were buried, and we were assured that if we died, it should not be by the violence of the white man, but in the course of nature. The lightning should not rive and blast the tree, but the cold of old age should dry up the sap, and the leaves should wither and fall, and the branches drop, and the trunk decay and die.[29]

Here, the tree appears to represent the individual, who should not be destroyed by hutke violence but should be left unmolested to live out the natural life span.

Charley Emathla added, "When a man has a country in which he was born and has there his house and home, where his children have always played about his yard, it becomes sacred to his heart and it is hard to leave it."[30] Having visited the proposed new home in the west, he pointed out, "The country is very distant. It was with difficulty that we, with firm health, reached it. How then would it be with the sickly and infirm? If the sound tree is unrooted by the spirit of the storm, can the decayed branches stand upright?" He concluded, "May the Great Spirit smile and the [S]un shine on us."[31]

Here, the tree represents the people. The threatened relocations are a gathering storm. If the people were uprooted, their weakest members would suffer most. Note how this metaphor roots the human community into the land, and how reasonable the huithli's point is:

> "Our present habitation is *poor*," said Huithli on the final day of the council, "but still we *prefer* it. We are used to it, and habit has made it dear to us. It was our home when the game was plenty, and the corn high. If the deer have departed, and the corn tassels not, it is still our home, and therefore we love, we prefer it."[32]

Note the huithli's contribution to the environmental history of Florida. Game had become scarce during the American occupation. The corn did not tassel because American soldiers were destroying the Seminoles' food base systematically.

Said Charley Emathla,

> The Indians and the whites have spilt no blood. They stole things from each other. At Payne's Landing the tomahawk was buried, and peace was to prevail as long as agreed on between whites and Indians. They agreed that if blood was seen in the path, to think that it was because a person had snagged his foot.[33]

In other words, the Seminoles had not violated the relevant treaty, and so the Americans had no cause to violate it either. Accordingly, and because the American plan threatened the safety of old and weak Seminoles, the Seminole leaders refused to cooperate in their relocation.

ON SEMINOLE DIPLOMATIC DISCOURSE

In the cosmos described by Seminole leaders at Silver Spring, a supreme being holds the paramount power. Thunder, a powerful god throughout the Southeast and Mexico, serves the will of the supreme, and the state-sponsored violence of the United States also appears to serve that higher will. Presumably, the Seminole communities—or some member or members of the communities—had failed to perform their obligations to the supreme being, who responded in kind to punish them. The invasion of Seminole lands was punishment for somebody's failure of virtue. Traditional Seminoles still attribute (post)modern social ills to the failure to maintain the ancient customs.

Seminoles' obligations are many. They include protecting the Sacred Fire, adhering to taboos, performing the necessary ceremonies, and behaving as good relatives in the gendered world in which Earth is Mother and a Great Spirit in the sky is Father. Humans are children of this gendered cosmos. No child would willingly leave a beloved mother, even if she could no longer provide, or "if the deer have departed and the corn tassels not" in Huithli Emathla's image. The parents demand that the children live together harmoniously and refrain from spilling each other's blood. If the children violate the rule, the father, angered, will send lightning or *hutkes* to punish them.

The tree occurs as a metaphor for a people in the Seminole Council of 1834 and in political discourse throughout eastern North America. The Iroquoian Great Tree of Life is the best-known example. (Huithli Emathla's use of the tree as a metaphor for the individual is at variance with the main trunk of the tradition.) The tree may be uprooted by the storm that the angry Father may send, but if the people appease that deity, he will smile, and the Sun will shine.

As in the indigenous diplomatic discourse of eastern North America generally, the Seminole discourse in this episode envisions a peaceful landscape. The people of the human communities all belong to a single family. Paths of white, the color of peace, connect even the most alien communities. Nevertheless, relations between communities are a path that may be chosen. Peace is a white path, as the peace clans are white. The warpath is red. Should blood appear on the white path, nations committed to peace will assume peaceful intentions all around: The blood must connote an accident. To declare peaceful intentions, the weapons of war are buried in the earth where troublemakers cannot get at them. Thus, relations between nations are represented in two geographical images: Peace or war winds through the landscape, and war is buried in the earth and may be dug up.

Thus, international relations, like human communities, are bound to the land.[34] This diplomatic discourse prescribes peaceful resolution of disputes and encodes human rights. People are to be left in peace on their land. At Silver Spring, the American agent called this discourse "the foolish talk of a child."[35] He must have been motivated by the psychological mechanism known as "projection."

May Our Father smile and the Sun shine on us all.

NOTES

1. In American historiography, words such as "invasion," "interning," "genocide," "atrocity," and "torture" are taboo in this context. Those taboos mask inconsistencies between colonial beliefs and historical realities, such as the belief that the United States behaves legally and humanely despite the reality of its behavior toward the Seminole nation. The decolonizing method ignores those taboos and instead selects words that would be used in comparable cases outside the United States. I use the word "torture" in light of the following definition from the United Nations Convention against Torture and Other Cruel, Inhuman or Degrading Treatment or Punishment, to which the United States is a signatory:
"For the purposes of this Convention, the term 'torture' means any act by which severe pain or suffering, whether physical or mental, is intentionally inflicted on a person for such purposes as . . . intimidating or coercing him or a third person, or for any reason based on discrimination of any kind, when such pain or suffering is inflicted by or at the instigation of or with the consent or acquiescence of a public official or other person acting in an official capacity. It does not include pain or suffering arising only from, inherent in or incidental to lawful sanctions." United Nations, Convention against Torture and Other Cruel, Inhuman or Degrading Treatment or Punishment, part I, article 1, sec. 1; U.N. Doc. A/39/51 (1984).
Apologists for Indian removal might argue that the pain and suffering incurred by the discriminatory coercion of Indian people under the Indian removal policy "[arose] from [or were] inherent in or incidental to lawful sanctions," and therefore do not meet the definition of torture. Ibid. Indian removal was never sanctioned under Seminole law, which was the law of the land when and where the Americans invaded. Apologists might also argue that the Convention against Torture did not exist in the 1830s and 1840s when the forced relocation occurred, as though absence of a formal injunction makes torture acceptable.

2. Michael F. Doran, "Population Statistics of Nineteenth Century Indian Territory," *Chronicles of Oklahoma* 53 (no. 4 1975–1976): 498, as cited in Russell Thornton, "Cherokee Losses during the Trail of Tears: A New Perspective and a New Estimate," *Ethnohistory* 31 (no. 4, 1984): 293.

3. Decolonizing scholarship upholds indigenous governments and legal systems. Wiley Thompson had violated a Seminole law against alienating the Seminoles from their land, a crime that carried a death sentence.

4. *Army and Navy Chronicle*, 13 vols. (Washington, DC), August 31, 1835, 1:295; John R. Swanton, "Religious Beliefs and Medical Practices of the Creek Indians," *Forty-Second Annual Report of the Bureau of American Ethnology* (Washington, DC: Goverment Printing Office, 1928), 478. A central principle of decolonizing scholarship is not merely to respect, but actively to assert indigenous realities, even when people of colonizing nation-states believe them unreal, as in this affirmation of the occurrence of signs. Indigenous ancestors knew what they were doing, and the task of indigenous scholars is to recover their ancestral knowledge and figure out how to use it for the well-being of their descendants.

5. T. Frederick Davis, "The Seminole Council, October 23–25, 1834," *Florida Historical Quarterly* 7 (1928): 342–43.

6. The identities of Seminole towns and their leaders is a matter of much discussion and little consensus among scholars. The names and locations of Seminole polities have changed often. The records of those polities in Spanish and English language documents are extremely confused. I follow the interpretation of the anthropologist Richard A. Sattler.

7. Myer M. Cohen, *Notices of Florida and the Campaigns* (Charleston, SC: Burges & Honour, 1836), 59–60.

8. [Woodburne Potter], *The War in Florida, by a Late Staff Officer* (Baltimore: Lewis & Coleman, 1836), 61. Cohen writes that Thompson exhibited "excited feelings" and that his address might have struck the Seminole Council as exhibiting more "violence of passion than, in *their* minds, and according to *their* habits, comported with a deliberative occasion." Cohen, *Notices*, 59.

9. Richard A. Sattler, "Seminoli Italwa: Socio-Political Change among the Oklahoma Seminoles between Removal and Allotment, 1836–1905" (PhD diss., University of Oklahoma, 1987), 96–97.

10. Ibid.

11. Ibid., 97.

12. Cohen, *Notices*, 239; Grant Foreman, *Indian Removal: The Emigration of the Five Civilized Tribes of Indians* (Norman: University of Oklahoma Press, [1932] 1953), 329.

13. Sattler, "Seminoli Italwa," 114, 141.

14. Ibid., 88–89, 112. "Brother" here could refer to either a male sibling or a parallel cousin. John Lee Williams says that Holata Emathla was acting at this council as speaker for the Seminoles. John Lee Williams, *The Territory of Florida* (Gainesville: University of Florida Press, [1837] 1962), 238–39.

15. Sattler, "Seminoli Italwa," 111.

16. Indigenous scholars are decolonizing the language with which they discuss their peoples. Much work is now being done in indigenous languages. In English language works, decolonization includes privileging indigenous names as I have done by referring to the

famous Seminole leader as Asin Yahola, the name used by my Seminole elders, and rejecting the English language form "Osceola."

17. Davis, "Seminole Council," 338, 348; [Potter], *War in Florida,* 66; Sattler, "Seminoli Italwa," 111; Cohen, *Notices,* 234; and see Patricia R. Wickman, *Osceola's Legacy* (Tuscaloosa: University of Alabama Press, 1991), 23–31, on the nature of Asin Yahola's leadership.

18. *Army and Navy Chronicle* (December 14, 1837), 5:382, regarding white hair.

19. T. Frederick Davis has compiled a narrative of that meeting, drawn from the two accounts. One was by M.M. Cohen, a lawyer of Charleston, South Carolina, who later served as a representative in the state legislature from that district, and entitled *Notices of Florida and the Campaigns*; and the other was by Woodburne Potter, *The War in Florida.* Both had served as officers in the opening campaigns against the Seminoles.

Cohen apparently derived the greater part of his information from David Levy, of St. Augustine, who was present at the council and made extensive notes of the proceedings on the spot. See Cohen, *Notices,* 62 n. Potter evidently had access to official memoranda, some of which seem never to have been published officially. Davis, "Seminole Council," 334.

20. Cohen, *Notices,* 62.

21. [Potter], *War in Florida,* 51.

22. Ibid., 52–53.

23. Cohen, *Notices,* 60.

24. [Potter], *War in Florida,* 54.

25. John T. Sprague, *The Origin, Progress and Conclusion of the Florida War* (New York: Appleton and Co., 1848), 251.

26. Ibid., 260.

27. Cohen, *Notices,* 57.

28. [Potter], *War in Florida,* 55.

29. Cohen, 57–58.

30. Ibid., 58.

31. Ibid., 59. Note that the storm has life (spirit).

32. Ibid., 60. But compare to [Potter], *War in Florida,* 60.

33. [Potter], *War in Florida,* 60. But compare to Cohen, *Notices,* 61: "The disorderly among us may have committed some depredations, but we have spilled no blood. . . . At Moultrie, my head men and yours agreed that all ill feeling should be buried, and a lasting peace take place between us. The tomahawk was to be under ground, and the smoke of the calumet was to rest forever above it." Davis substitutes "Moultrie" for "Payne's Landing" in Potter's version. "Moultrie" is correct.

34. Decolonizing scholarship seeks to develop literatures free of colonial distortions. Toward that end, indigenous scholars privilege the works of indigenous scholars and regard warily any influence from colonial peoples. My discussion of Seminole diplomatic discourse draws from my reading of statements by nineteenth-century Seminole leaders and recent works by indigenous authors and from my understanding of remarks by contemporary indigenous leaders from Seminole and other communities. I rely on these sources not to slight works on related topics that contribute to the literature of American history, such as *A Spirited Resistance* by Gregory Evans Dowd (Baltimore: Johns Hopkins University Press,

1992) and *Cultivating a Landscape of Peace* by Matthew Dennis (Ithaca, NY: Cornell University Press, 1993). I am not even claiming that those works might not be useful in a decolonized historiography; I am merely demonstrating the mechanics of developing a decolonized literature.

35. [Potter], *War in Florida*, 61.

CHAPTER 14

Hybridity, Canadian Indian Policy, and the Construction and "Extinguishment" of Metis Aboriginal Rights in the Nineteenth Century

GERHARD J. ENS

THROUGHOUT NORTH AMERICA, racial mixing or *metissage* between Indians and Europeans accompanied the fur trade. It was virtually assured by the presence of adult European males isolated from European women and the hospitality of many Indian bands. This metissage, however, was not only a result of the scarcity of European women, but also an integral part of the fur trade. Based, as the trade was, on a commodity exchange between two culturally distinct groups of people, it engendered a mutually dependent economic relationship. Many fur trade practices, including intermarriage, took place within the structure of Indian social and political customs.

Although frequent intermarriage and its attendant metissage between fur traders and Indians did not lead inevitably to separate, identifiable Metis[1] communities,[2] Metis communities did emerge in various localities in both Canada and the United States, including the Great Lakes region, on the northwestern Plains, on the Missouri, and in the Canadian North.[3] Only in western Canada, however, did there emerge a concept of Metis aboriginality and rights separate from recognized treaties. This chapter does not purport to examine the process of the "ethnogenesis" of various Metis communities, but focuses instead on how and why only the Metis of western Canada were accorded aboriginal rights separate from specific Indian treaties. This recognition, or construction of a new category of aboriginality in western Canada and its extinguishment, it is argued, occurred for several rea-

[236]

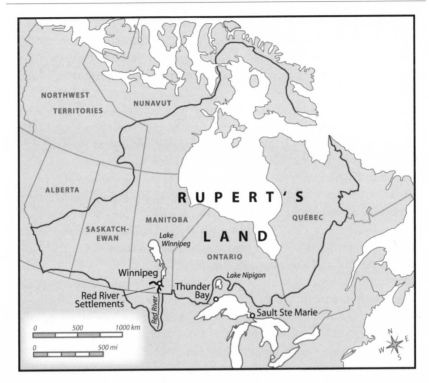

Metis Country, 1860–2000

sons: (1) the differing ideas of hybridity or metissage in Canada in comparison to the United States in the mid- to late nineteenth century, and their incorporation into the Indian policy of Canada; (2) the political exigencies of the transfer of Rupert's Land to Canada in 1869–1870; and (3) the confusing policies of the Canadian government in allowing Metis of the Northwest to enter Indian treaties or take extinguishment by way of Metis scrip. This confusion took thirty years to clarify, at the end of which the categories of treaty status and Metis status had hardened into distinct identities with different meanings.

HYBRIDITY AND PERCEPTIONS OF METIS

The widespread intermarriage and mixing of Indian and European populations in North America was recognized at a very early date and became the subject of considerable debate within the scientific community in both the United States and British North America from the late eighteenth century onward. This discussion was framed by both the policies of various governments and philanthropists seeking new approaches for "civilizing" Indians, and the larger debate over the origins of humans and the question of the racial origins of North American Indians. As Robert E. Bieder has noted, the debate over mixed-bloods turned on changing white assumptions about Indians and their future, and "polarized over the issue of whether the mixed-blood was a new race, a 'mongrel' more Indian than White, or the hybrid offspring of two separate species."[4]

In general, the various views of Indians' origins fell into two camps or schools of thought: monogenism and polygenism. On the one hand, the monogenists saw humankind as one species derived from a single pair, and argued that Indians had originally come from the Middle East or Asia. This theory produced a positive evaluation of the capabilities and potential of Indians for civilization. The polygenists, on the other hand, maintained that each of the major human races had been created separately and differed radically not only in appearance but also intellectually and emotionally. This theory was used to oppose the emancipation of blacks and to provide a scientific gloss for the widespread conviction that Indians were incapable of adopting European culture.[5]

From the American Revolution to the late 1820s, the monogenists dominated the ethnological scene in North America and their views were shared by the government and public. The optimistic belief in humankind's progressive nature was a product of enlightenment belief and led to the view that Indians could be incorporated into the new order not on a "separate but equal" basis, but rather through an ideal of genetic unification—the genetic blending of white and red races that would result in a unified North American people. These views never became the official government policy in the United States, but Thomas Jefferson advocated miscegenation in regard to Indians. It was a view that also mirrored early French practices in North America.[6]

As Robert Bieder has written, "[T]o government officials and philanthropists the physical characteristics resulting from such unions were less important than the effect of intermarriage on 'civilizing' the Indian." Observers noted that wherever there were "half-breeds," there were factions created within Indian communities that espoused the interests of civilization and Christianity. Thus, "education, Christianization and miscegenation became the means by which the early nineteenth century sought a solution to the problem of how best to 'civilize' Indians and incorporate them into American society."[7]

By the late 1820s, however, American attitudes toward Indians and mixed-bloods shifted from a positive belief in their capabilities and potential for civilization to one of doubt and finally to discouragement over the lack of progress. Mixed marriages or unions acceptable in the Great Lakes region in the 1820s were by the 1830s no longer officially viewed favorably. As settler societies replaced the fur trade in this region, mixed marriages were no longer economically advantageous but instead were socially condemned. These changing attitudes led to an ascendancy of the polygenists' assumptions, at least in the United States, and ethnologists increasingly demonstrated a growing preoccupation with questions of race. The decline of Indian populations and Indian intransigence in the face of change, despite efforts of missionaries to "civilize" them, convinced many members of the public, government, and the scientific community of the inferiority of the Indian race—an inferiority now deemed innate rather than due to a lack of education. This view was reflected in the United States by the government policy to remove Indians west of the Mississippi.[8]

This new attitude had ominous implications for the public perception of the Metis. If Indians and Europeans were separate species, the offspring of the unions of the two were hybrids and were "faulty stock" that resulted from a violation of nature's laws. Metissage, in this view, became not a part of the progress of man, but a degeneracy that portended the demise of civilization. In the minds of some, metissage entailed a "pollution" of America, the end result of which would be the death of Anglo-Saxon civilization.[9] By the mid-nineteenth century, the views of the polygenists were ascendant in the United States, and mixed-bloods were no longer perceived as the agents of civilization. Robert Bieder has argued that the prevailing belief among most Americans by 1850s was that,

> If a person possessed some Indian blood, he was an Indian. Blood not only gave a person his identity but served to shape the public's expectations of his destiny. . . . Not only were mixed-bloods considered "faulty stock," but they were believed to prefer Indian life and to have cast their lot with the Indian. Like the Indian, the mixed-blood was viewed as headed for extinction.[10]

The polygenist argument, however, did not convince everyone, and in the United States its success was due in part to the fact that it closely reflected the fears of the time. Its ascendancy over monogenism did not derive from good evidence; indeed, very little data supported it.[11] Monogenists continued to believe that mixed-bloods were not only catalysts for the civilization of the Indians, but also offered proof, through their fertility, that Indians and Whites were one species. There is ample evidence that in Canada monogenism held sway and was crucial to the formation of Indian policy in British North America. The policy of Indian removal, a policy in force in the United States and advocated in Canada by Francis Bond Head in 1836 was in fact rejected by both missionaries and British colonial administrators.

DANIEL WILSON AND MONOGENISM

The most influential proponent of monogenism and the salutary effects of metissage in Canada in the period from the 1850s through the 1880s was Daniel Wilson.[12] Prior to his arrival in Canada in 1853, Wilson's research in Scotland had already aroused his interest in a variety of anthropological issues, but his residence in Canada stimulated his interests in archaeology. Wilson came to believe that a study of contemporary changes in North America would result in a more general understanding of the nature of cultural contact, racial mixing, and adaptation to the environment. The publication of *Prehistoric Man: Researches into the Origin of Civilization in the Old and New World* in 1863 represented the culmination of not only his past European training, but eight years of research in Canada.[13]

His views on metissage were much colored by what he observed in and around Native communities and reserves in Canada. The "extinction" of Indians in North America was for him inextricably tied to the absorption of Indian races into the Anglo-American population by way of intermarriage and racial mixing—a process which he regarded as "progress."

These ideas, fully worked out and published by 1862, form the backdrop for Wilson's most detailed analysis of the Canadian Metis in his article, "Hybridity and Absorption in Relation to the Red Indian Race," published in 1875.[14] For Wilson, the Metis were a transitory and intermediate race portending progress and the eventual absorption of the Indian races within the Anglo-Canadian nation. While the numbers of Indians were increasing by the 1860s bespeaking any extinction of their race, Wilson argued that at the same time the "pure race" was being largely replaced by younger generations of "mixed-blood," and that "at best the results point rather to such a process of absorption as appears to be the inevitable result wherever a race, alike inferior in numbers and in progressive energy, escapes extirpation at the hands of the intruders."[15]

Wilson observed that "half-breeds" could be members of various tribes, a separate ethnological, ethnic or racial category, or fully merged with the Anglo-Canadian population. The trend, however, was absorption. Those who were still affiliated with various tribal entities did so to share in the Indian funds granted by the government; otherwise, they "would long since have merged in the common stock."[16] He noted that in frontier areas, where the mingling of European and Indian races was the natural result of the shortage of European women, a distinct "half-breed" population arose and was maintained in this border land. Some of these offspring, he argued, "cling to the fortunes of the mother's race, and are involved in its fate; but more adhere to those of the white father, share with him the vicissitudes of border life, and cast in their lot with the first nucleus of a settled community."[17]

The history of the Canadian Northwest, Wilson argued, offered proof of this progression and the salutary result of metissage. Here intermarriage between fur traders and Indian women produced a Metis population greatly outnumbering the whites. This "race of half-breeds" was divided into two classes according to their Scottish or French paternity, who had kept themselves distinct in manners, habits, and allegiance from both whites and Indians.

Within the larger "hybrid" population in the West, Wilson noted several categories. He acknowledged racial "hybridity" did not preclude an Indian identity, but the general trend was toward an intermediate identity that would eventually merge with the European population. According to Wilson, the Metis of the Canadian Northwest, although existing in larger numbers and in isolation, could no more hope to perpetuate themselves as a distinct race than those of the older provinces. Already the change had begun that involved their disappearance. For Wilson, Metis occupied an intermediate or transitional stage in the path to civilization and would eventually be absorbed into the dominant European population but not without leaving some traces on the predominant race and perhaps helping it to adapt it to its new home.[18]

Wilson noted that it could not but excite regret that any race with unmistakable aptitudes for civilization should utterly perish, but that the progress of colonization entailed expatriation, extermination, or the absorption of the races as an ethnological element of the young nation that was supplanting them.

The influence of these ideas on policymakers in Canada is difficult to judge in any hard and fast way, but the Indian "civilization" policy pursued by successive Canadian governments after 1830 certainly paralleled Daniel Wilson's ideas regarding the progress of nations and races. Wilson, from his arrival in Canada in 1853, was conversant with policymakers and had a deep interest in the fate of the Native peoples of British North America. By the 1870s, he was writing articles for Toronto newspapers on Canadian Indian policy and the present state and future prospects of Indians in British North America.[19] He was, without doubt, the preeminent ethnologist writing about Metis and racial mixing in pre-confederation Canada.

METIS AND CANADIAN POLICY

Central to Canadian Indian policy, from the inauguration of the "civilization" policy in the 1830s, was the absorption of Indians within the Canadian population. Daniel Wilson's ideas regarding metissage and the intermediary role that the Metis played in this incorporation certainly fit in well with the policy of the day. As a rule, Canadian legislators did not accord Metis any separate legal status or recognition. While they used the term "half-breed," it was purely as a biological distinction. Persons of "mixed-blood" could under certain circumstances be recognized as Indians or whites—"half-breeds" or "metis" carried no separate legal or constitutional rights.

This new "civilization" policy was conceived to facilitate the full incorporation of Indians into Canadian society, and land reserves were to be the instrument to achieve this. Reserves were thought to be halfway houses on the route to civilization as the ideal of full citizenship was not seen as immediately possible or desirable.[20] Within this conceptual and policy framework of incorporation there was no room for a separate Metis category. Thus, "half-breeds" were to be regarded as Indians if adopted by tribes and living as Indians, but where the difference was "clearly marked" and they were not a member of a "tribe," they still had no separate status.

Until the 1860s then, the colonial government of Canada admitted persons of mixed ancestry into treaties and defined them as "Indians," but they did so only when these "half-breeds" lived with Indians and were considered members of a tribe or band. Those Metis that assumed an identity separate from Indian or white, and who lived away from Indian bands were not considered as Indians. By law, they were ordinary citizens with no special privileges. This was similar to the way the U.S. government viewed persons of mixed Indian-European ancestry with regard to treaty rights and status—the difference was that in Canada, hybridity or metissage was still viewed in a positive light as a transitional stage that would further the goals of civilizing and incorporating Native peoples of Canada into the general population. This positive view of metissage would even play an important role in the political events related to the transfer of Rupert's Land (the Canadian Prairie West) from Great Britain to Canada in 1869–1870.

When Canada began negotiations with Great Britain to transfer Rupert's Land from the control of the Hudson's Bay Company to the government of Canada, none of the inhabitants of the Canadian West were consulted on the transfer. Fearing for their rights (language, religion, and property), some Metis from the Red River settlement, led by Louis Riel, took over the government of the settlement in 1869 and forced the Canadian government to negotiate their acceptance of confederation and entry into Canada.

Interestingly, neither Riel, the provisional government, nor the various conventions convened to discuss the Red River settlement's terms of entry into the confederation ever officially dealt with Metis claims to aboriginal status or rights.[21] Those rights that were considered included linguistic and religious rights, provincial status, the respect for lands already settled (preemption), and local control of public lands.[22] N.J. Ritchot, one of the negotiators for the Metis, noted that they did not claim any of the privileges granted to Canadian Indians and wanted only to be treated like the settlers of other provinces.[23]

The issue of Metis claims to any kind of aboriginal status and the need to extinguish these rights arose only when it became clear that the Canadian federal government would not surrender control of lands and resources to the newly created province. Discussion then shifted to compensation for the loss of control over public lands. From this point on, discussion centered on a land grant for the Metis population as compensation. The prime minister of Canada, John A. Macdonald, told the Metis delegates that the only way to obtain this large a land grant through Parliament was to justify it for the extinguishment of Indian land title for the

Metis.[24] The legitimacy of this concern was more than justified by the Liberal opposition to the Manitoba Act in the House of Commons. Alexander Mackenzie, leader of the Liberal opposition, noted that in relation to what would become Section 31 of the Manitoba Act (Metis Land Grant), he could find no reasonable explanation for this reservation. It was unasked for by the people of Manitoba, and no one in the Commons had "vouchsafed an explanation as to who this demand for reservations came from."[25]

This Metis extinguishment clause in the Manitoba Act produced some confusion and outrage. Liberals in Parliament regarded the entire bill as one of the "most preposterous schemes" ever submitted to the Parliament. In relation to the Metis land clause, Alexander McKenzie noted:

> A certain portion to be set aside to settle Indian claims and another portion to settle Indian claims that the half-breeds have. But these half-breeds were either Indian or not. . . . They were not looked upon as Indians, some had been to Ottawa, and given evidence, and did not consider themselves Indians. They were regularly settled upon farms, and what the object could be in making some special provision for them that was not made for other inhabitants was more than he could understand.[26]

Despite strenuous Liberal opposition, the Manitoba Act passed final reading in the House of Commons on May 10, 1870, and received royal assent on May 12.

As this land grant was interpreted after 1870, a total of 240 acres of land were to be given to each Metis child.[27] Having justified this land grant to quiet land claims of Metis children, the government faced the problem of how to quiet land claims of Metis parents as they were not included in the land grant.[28] To do this, the Canadian Parliament passed yet another bill in 1874 "for extinguishing the Indian title to such lands as respects the said half-breed heads of family residing in the Province at the period named." To achieve this purpose, each half-breed head of a family resident in Manitoba on the fifteenth day of July 1870 was entitled to a scrip certificate for $160 receivable in payment for the purchase of Dominion land.[29]

Born of the political exigencies of the Riel Resistance of 1869–1870 and the difficulties of approving a Metis land grant in Parliament, neither the 1.4-million-acre grant nor the issue of scrip in extinguishment of Indian title was well thought out or consistent. As Adams Archibald, the first lieutenant governor of Manitoba, and as such the official in charge of implementing the grant, noted in late 1870, "I presume the intention was not so much to create the extinguishment of any hereditary claims (as the language of the Act would seem to imply) as to confer a boon upon the mixed race inhabiting this province."[30] The seeming lack of concern in granting the Metis of the Northwest a claim to aboriginal status was connected to the belief that the Metis were a transitional people en route to civilization and absorption into the general population.

Ironically, this newly coined "Metis" status, almost an afterthought on the part of the government and not requested by the Metis, would in succeeding years become almost an article of faith with those Metis further west who had not been granted land or scrip under the Manitoba Act. They would in succeeding years demand that they be treated exactly like their brethren in Manitoba. In their memorials and petitions to the government, Metis demonstrated not only that they wanted a scrip program, but also that they understood that this was the compensation due them in extinguishment of their aboriginal title.[31]

THE CONFUSION OVER TREATY, SCRIP, AND EXTINGUISHMENT

The government for its part tried to back away from any extension of Metis rights farther west. Having let the genie of Metis aboriginal rights out of the bottle in the Manitoba Act, the Canadian government would try valiantly to at least partially stuff it back in after 1870. Prime Minister Macdonald noted that the grant of land and scrip to the Metis in Manitoba had been made to secure peace and bring the West into Canada. The justification of this grant by the use of the phrase "extinguishment of Indian title," he argued, was an incorrect one, because the "half-breeds" did not allow themselves to be Indians. If they are Indians, they go with the tribe; if they are "half-breeds," they are white.

The growing scale of Metis agitation in the early 1880s, the return of Louis Riel from the United States in 1884, and the outbreak of the North-West Rebellion in 1885, however, pushed the government to repeat what they had done in Manitoba.[32] Every Metis child in the Northwest Territories was to be granted scrip either for $240 receivable in payment for Dominion land, or scrip entitling the bearer to locate 240 acres of land, and every Metis head of family was to be granted scrip for $160 or 160 acres. Even those Metis who had died or moved to the United States after 1870 were eligible for Canadian scrip. These grants were again rationalized by reference to Metis claims to Indian title. This new program and series of scrip commissions that began in 1885 would continue well into the twentieth century, ending finally in the 1920s.

A further problem the government encountered in administering these Metis scrip commissions after 1885, the solution to which further entrenched the concepts of a separate Metis aboriginal status, had to do with mixed-bloods who wished to abandon treaty rights to take scrip. A large number of scrip applications that were received in the period 1885–1900 dealt with mixed-bloods leaving treaty lands to take scrip. As a result, scrip policy involved not only the Department of the Interior but also the Department of Indian Affairs, and this more closely tied scrip policy to Indian policy—particularly in the area of civilization and enfranchisement.

Many Metis had entered into treaties from the early 1870s on, not only because of their close relationship with some Indian bands, but also because their economic base, the buffalo, was disappearing and the Canadian government had not yet formulated any policy of scrip for the Metis west of Manitoba. By 1878 some Metis covered under treaties were attempting to withdraw, but no mechanism existed to allow them to do so. It was in response to these questions that amendments were passed to the Indian Act (1880 and 1884) allowing Metis to leave treaties and take scrip with no penalty.[33] Many mixed-bloods under treaties perceived the offering of scrip, which could be sold and converted into a large sum of money, as preferable to a long-term relationship with the federal government and small treaty payments on a yearly basis. As the *Edmonton Bulletin* noted in October 1885,

> When the Indians in this neighbourhood were first paid treaty money a large number of persons who were actually half-breeds classed themselves as Indian for the purpose of securing the $5 a year payment. Many of these now see the disadvantages accruing from their condition as Indians and desire to abandon it. This desire is to be facilitated by the Indian department as much as possible by securing for those parties scrip as half-breeds.[34]

Thus, in 1885 when "North-West half-breed scrip" became available, many of the treaty mixed-bloods chose officially to change their status to Metis or "half-breeds" and take scrip.

This new policy relating to mixed-bloods leaving treaties to take scrip initiated a long debate in both the Departments of the Interior and Indian Affairs, and between departments, as to who would be allowed to leave treaties to take scrip as the Departments were deluged after 1885 with leave applications. These withdrawals from treaties to take Metis scrip fit in with the Departments' program of enfranchisement. The intention of the revisions to the Indian Act permitting Metis to withdraw from treaties and allowing them to apply for scrip had been to allow those Metis who might otherwise cease to be Indians to become self-supporting citizens to do so without penalty. However, having once withdrawn from treaties and accepted scrip they became for all official intents and purposes "whites," and as such they could not be permitted to reside on an Indian reserve. Their names would be erased from the treaty pay lists, and this would prevent the likelihood of their ever again receiving annuity money as Indians.[35] Metis scrip and Metis status were thus again seen by the Canadian government as a step on the way to civilization and incorporation.

Some officials in the Indian Department, however, warned that many who were withdrawing would not be self-supporting, and the government would be obligated to care for them.[36] In an effort to forestall this problem, the government initiated new procedures stipulating that only those treaty Metis who could clearly show that they were Metis, that they did not lead the same mode of life as Indians, and who could support themselves would be allowed to withdraw from treaties. As well, every person accepting discharge was informed that he forfeited all Indian rights, and that he must leave the reserve and give up a house and all other improvements without compensation.

The door, however, was still fairly open for Metis to withdraw from treaties in large numbers. The Indian Department, given its policy of civilization and enfranchisement, did not want to close any door that would bar the withdrawal of enterprising "treaty half-breeds" who might otherwise cease to be Indians and become self-supporting citizens; the Interior Department also did not want to slow down the process of the final extinguishment of "Metis claims," and both were being pressured by Metis to be allowed to forsake treaties. Given this situation, the various scrip commissions continued to grant large numbers of scrip certificates to Metis who had withdrawn from treaties.[37]

At the same time that the Department of the Interior was trying to clarify these problems, the Department of Indian Affairs was also trying to formulate a policy in regard to those "Metis" who had been discharged from treaties and had taken scrip but who did not want to leave the reserves or even wanted readmission to treaty status. On the question of readmission, the Department advised its agents that they could allow a few treaty re-admissions but cases should not be considered precedents for "wholesale re-admissions." Any application for readmission to treaty rights had to be forwarded to the Indian Department, and the agent had to provide full particulars regarding each case. Only then was action to be taken. A measure of leniency might be extended to those who were incapable of providing for themselves, but each individual case had to be investigated, a time-consuming process.[38]

From the foregoing, it should be obvious that the Departments of the Interior and Indian Affairs did not have a hard and fast policy regarding whether people of mixed Indian and white ancestry should be classed as Indians or Metis. Consequently, persons of mixed ancestry could take either treaty or scrip and, in many cases, took both. As the only signatories to Indian treaties were the leading chiefs, "half-breeds" could be admitted to treaties as long as they lived with the Indian bands, were accepted by them, and practiced the same lifestyle. In this case, the government considered them as Indians for the purpose of treaty signing.

In 1885, however, when the Canadian government began taking applications for scrip from Metis in the North-West Territories, many of these same "half-breeds" decided to renounce treaty rights to take scrip. They decided, on instrumental grounds, to change their official ethnicity or designation from Indian to

Metis. Many treaty "half-breeds" perceived the offering of money scrip, which could be sold and converted into a large sum of money, as preferable to a long-term relationship with the federal government and small treaty payments on a yearly basis.

This somewhat haphazard policy regarding the choice between treaty and scrip, and the ability to move back and forth between treaty and scrip, was tightened in the years after the 1899 Scrip Commission. The government realized that to continue to allow this movement between treaty and scrip would be to forever leave open the issue of scrip and obviate the entire rationale behind the scrip programs—the extinguishment of Metis claims and the civilization and enfranchisement of Indians. While it was difficult and often impossible to draw a clear line of demarcation between Indian and Metis,[39] if the criteria for allowing withdrawal from treaties was mixed ancestry, government officials argued that it would be difficult to ever close the issue of scrip for the great majority of those with some "white blood" who had treaty status. The government increasingly took the position that at the time a treaty was signed, aboriginal inhabitants had been given the option of having their territorial rights extinguished by the taking of a perpetual annuity as Indians or by taking scrip as "half-breeds." After selecting, they should be bound by the selection, and if any one of them who chose to be an Indian should wish to leave the treaty, and he be considered fit to leave the treaty by the Indian Commissioner, he then became an ordinary citizen of the country having no claim as an aborigine.[40]

Thus, prior to 1900 it had been customary, if otherwise eligible, to grant scrip to Metis who had withdrawn from treaties. In some cases, scrip recipients were also readmitted into treaties if they proved unable to support themselves. After 1901, however, a Metis who had once joined a band of Indians under a treaty and subsequently was discharged from it was debarred from ever receiving scrip as a Metis, it being contended that all such claims had been extinguished by his accepting the benefits of an Indian treaty up to the date at which he voluntarily surrendered them. For this reason the choice of opting to be under treaty or receive scrip became a once and for all decision. Although the Metis were generally given the option of extinguishment by treaty or scrip,[41] once they chose they were bound by their choice.

CONCLUSION

Importantly, the hardening of Canadian policy regarding scrip eligibility put into law by a Canadian federal order-in-council in 1901 produced two separate and different notions of aboriginal status: one was treaty status, and a second and lesser was Metis status. Metis in the Northwest had the choice of becoming treaty Indians or accepting Metis scrip. One entailed an ongoing relationship with the federal government, perpetual annuities, and the right to live on a reserve. Those who chose Metis scrip received a one-time payment in extinguishment of their aboriginal title. Thereafter, their rights and status were the same as other Canadians. Thus, by 1901 the Canadian government believed that they had finally settled the vexing question of Metis aboriginality and its extinguishment. They believed that the concept of Metis aboriginality, invented and unleashed by the Manitoba Act of 1870, had now been contained.

In the 1870s and 1880s, the government had decided that hybridity, Metis status, and scrip might be a path to the incorporation of all Indian people into Canadian society. This policy, however, quickly turned into a quagmire of shifting statuses. As a result, the Canadian government changed its policy at the turn of the twentieth century to end the movement from treaty to scrip. It also hoped to close down the scrip process, which it succeeded in doing by the 1920s. Their confidence that the question of Metis aboriginality had been settled, however, would disappear in the second half of the twentieth century when the institutional memory of the Metis question was lost and an upsurge of Metis political activism forced new political arrangements. By the 1960s, Metis had begun to use the receipt of scrip (seen by the government as the extinguishment of Aboriginal title) as an ethnic marker or badge of identity.

NOTES

1. The term "Metis," originally a French term (*métis*) meaning "mixed," is used by scholars to designate individuals and communities who identify their antecedents with historical fur trade communities and refers to people who possess a distinctive sociocultural heritage and sense of self-identification. These peoples or communities were distinct from indigenous Indian bands and from the European world of the trading posts. Some of these communities used "Metis" to identify themselves, although other terms were used including "Michif," "Bois Brûlé," "Chicot," "Half-breed," "Country-born," and "Mixed-blood," among others.

2. Some "mixed-blood" progeny were raised among their mothers' peoples and assumed Indian cultures, while others were taken to European or American metropolitan centers by their fathers to be educated and assimilated into European society.

3. A significant "mixed-blood" population also arose in the Pacific Northwest, but the late date (1820s) when this population began to coalesce around fur trading posts in the Oregon Territory and the rapid influx of American settlers by the 1840s prevented the development of a distinctive Metis identity.

4. Robert E. Bieder, "Scientific Attitudes towards Indian Mixed-Bloods in Early Nineteenth Century America," *Journal of Ethnic Studies* 8 (Summer 1980): 17. See also his *Science Encounters the Indian, 1820–1880: The Early Years of American Ethnology* (Norman: University of Oklahoma Press, 1986).

5. My account of this debate has been summarized from Robert Bieder's "Scientific Attitudes," 18–27.

6. See Olive Dickason, "From 'One Nation' in the Northeast to 'New Nation' in the Northwest: A Look at the Emergence of the Métis," in *New Peoples: Being and Becoming Métis in North America,* ed. Jacqueline Peterson and Jennifer S.H. Brown (Lincoln: University of Nebraska Press, 1985), 37–72.

7. Bieder, "Scientific Attitudes," 19–20.

8. Ibid., 21–22.

9. Ibid., 23–24.

10. Ibid., 26–27.

11. Ibid., 26.

12. Originally from Scotland, Wilson became a professor of English and history at the University of Toronto in 1854 where he helped found the Royal Society of Canada and was the leading ethnologist in the country in the second half of the nineteenth century. He not only lectured widely and wrote a number of very influential books, but he wrote widely for scientific journals and popular newspapers of the day. In short, he was very influential in shaping opinion regarding Indian policy in Canada.

13. Bruce Trigger, "*Prehistoric Man* and Daniel Wilson's Later Canadian Ethnology," in *Thinking with Both Hands: Sir Daniel Wilson in the Old Word and the New,* ed. Elizabeth Hulse (Toronto: University of Toronto Press, 1999), 82.

14. Daniel Wilson, "Hybridity and Absorption in Relation to the Red Indian Race," *Canadian Journal,* n.s. (July 1875). While this article was published in 1875, it represented an elaboration of the ideas that Wilson had worked out and written about in the 1860s.

15. Ibid., 441.

16. Ibid., 441–42.

17. Ibid., 452.

18. Ibid., 459–63.

19. See bibliography of Wilson's writings in Hulse, 297–315.

20. Robert J. Surtees, "Canadian Indian Policies," in *Handbook of North American Indians,* Vol. 4, *History of Indian-White Relations,* ed. Wilcomb E. Washburn (Washington, DC: Smithsonian, 1988), 88.

21. This in itself is not surprising. Neither the Hudson's Bay Company nor the Council of Assiniboia had recognized Metis as an indigenous population. Like the Canadian and European settlers of the colony, they were regarded as British subjects.

22. See "The Proceedings in the Convention, February 3 to February 5, 1870," in *Manitoba: The Birth of a Province,* ed. W.L. Morton (Winnipeg: Manitoba Record Society, 1965), 5–24; and the Second to Fourth "List of Rights," 242–50. For a more detailed reconstruction of the negotiations leading to the Manitoba Act, see chapter 3 of Thomas Flanagan, *Metis Lands in Manitoba* (Calgary: University of Calgary Press, 1991), 29–50.

23. A microfilm copy of Ritchot's journal is in the Provincial Archives of Manitoba, MG 3, B14–1, no. 12 (M151). The French text was published by George F.G. Stanley as "Le Journal de l'abbé N.-J. Ritchot," *Revue d'Histoire de l'Amérique Française* 17 (1964), 537–64. The translated version used here is found in Morton, 140.

24. *The New Nation,* July 1, 1870. This newspaper reported Ritchot's speech of June 24, 1870, to the Legislative Assembly of Assiniboia. A translation of part of Ritchot's speech can be found in Flanagan, *Metis Lands,* 34.

25. Canada, House of Commons, *Debates,* May 9, 1870, reprinted in Morton, *Manitoba,* 225.

26. Ibid., 172.

27. Until 1874, the only land rights accorded Metis heads of family included the confirmation of title to lands possessed by the inhabitants of Manitoba before the transfer to Canada. This section of the Manitoba Act, however, put Metis heads of family on the same footing as other pre-1870 residents. Section 32 of the Manitoba Act, assented to on May 12, 1870, provided for the granting of land titles to settlers on July 15, 1870, the date of the transfer to Canada of Rupert's Land and the Northwest Territories. Subsections 3 and 4 read as follows:

"For the quieting of titles, and assuring to the settlers in the Province the peaceable possession of the land now held by them, it is enacted as follows:

"3. All titles by occupancy with the sanction and under the license and authority of the Hudson's Bay Company up to the eighth day of March aforesaid, of land in that part of the Province in which the Indian title has been extinguished, shall, if required by the owner, be converted into an estate in freehold by grant from the crown.

"4. All persons in peaceable possession of tracts of land at the time of the transfer to Canada in those parts of the province in which the Indian title has not been extinguished, shall have the right of pre-emption of the same, on such terms and conditions as may be determined by the Governor in Council."

Subsection 4 was enlarged by an Order-in-Council dated November 11, 1872, that put many of these claims under the same category as subsection 3, as Treaty Numbers 1 and 2 had been by then concluded.

28. The Order-in-Council of April 3, 1873, declared that Section 31 applied only to Metis children.

29. Canada, House of Commons, *An Act respecting the appropriation of certain Dominion lands in Manitoba,* Chapter 20, 37. Victoria was assented to on May 26, 1874. The bill also made provisions for the grant of additional scrip for $160 to all non-Metis who had settled in Red River between 1813 and 1835.

30. A.G. Archibald to Joseph Howe, December 27, 1870, Library and Archives of Canada (henceforth LAC), RG 15, vol. 236, file 7220.

31. A number of these petitions can be found in Canada, *Sessional Papers,* "Papers and Correspondence in connection with Half-Breed Claims and other matters relating to the North-West Territories," vol. 13, Third Session of the Fifth Parliament, 48 Victoria 1885 (no. 116).

32. Canada, Debates of the House of Commons of the Dominion, "Speech of John A. Macdonald," July 6, 1885, Third Session—Fifth Parliament, 48–49 Victoria, 1885, 3117–18.

33. In 1880, the Indian agent at Edmonton noted that there were "many half-breed men, who are now taking treaty [who] would like to withdraw were they able to pay back the money they have already received; as they are not likely ever to get this much ahead, I

think it would be better to do so without exacting the return of the money, than to continue paying them and their families year after year." Report of J.G. Stewart, Indian Agent, Edmonton, in "Annual Report of the Department of Indian Affairs for the year ending December 31, 1880" (Ottawa: Government of Canada, 1881), 87.

34. "Local," *Edmonton Bulletin,* October 10, 1885.

35. R. Sinclair (for Deputy of the Superintendent General of Indian Affairs) to John R. Hall, August 31, 1885, LAC, RG 15, D-II-1, vol. 488, file 138133.

36. H.H. Smith, Dominion Lands Commissioner, Winnipeg, to Minister of the Interior, August 4, 1885, LAC, RG 15, D-II-1, vol. 488, file 138133.

37. Goulet noted that after his commission left Edmonton, he had received 469 applications (28 at Victoria, 231 at Lac La Biche, 22 at Fort Pitt, 115 at Battleford, and 73 at Prince Albert). The greater portion of these claims had been preferred by "half-breeds" who had obtained their discharges from the Indian treaties. Progress Report of Roger Goulet to A.M. Burgess, Prince Albert, October 5, 1886, LAC, RG 15, D-II-1, vol. 501, file 140682.

38. Indian Comissioner to Indian Agent, Edmonton Agency, January 10, 1889, LAC, RG 10, vol. 3595, file 1239, pt. 12.

39. For treaty and scrip commissioners, the distinction between Metis and Indians in the region covered by Treaty Number 8 was almost impossible to make on any genetic or genealogical basis. Persons from the same family were given the option of taking either treaty or scrip, and in some case one sibling chose treaty while the other took scrip. The issue was further complicated in the sense that both Indians and Metis followed a similar way of life that involved hunting, trapping, freighting, and fishing. Given this genealogical and occupational convergence, the main basis on which to differentiate between the two populations was self-ascription.

40. Report of J.A.J. McKenna to Clifford Sifton, March 16, 1901, LAC, RG 15, D-II-1, vol. 782, file 55680, pt. 1. J.A.J. McKenna to Clifford Sifton, May 31, 1901. This report constitutes Annex "A" approved by Order in Council, June 6, 1901 (P.C. 1182).

41. Although in theory, the Metis were free to choose treaty or scrip, in practice scrip commissioners could and did disallow some Metis from taking scrip, arguing that they were members of a band society and lived as Indians. In these instances, they could appeal these decisions, but generally they accepted the treaty.

CHAPTER 15

The "Metis Indians" of Ontario

JOE SAWCHUK

THE TERM "Metis" has undergone some fundamental changes in meaning, content, and geographical location in the latter half of the twentieth century. Originally, the term was limited mainly to the western provinces and the Northwest Territories of Canada. But in the 1960s and 1970s, it began to be adopted by other cultural groups in different areas, including Labrador, the Maritime Provinces, and parts of the United States. One of the more interesting examples of this expansion of the term is found in Ontario, where a growing identification with the western or "Red River" Metis has become an important political force, despite the fact that the term was almost unknown in the province before the 1960s. This essay outlines some of the major features in the evolution of the meaning of "Metis" in Ontario.

In order for an ethnic group or an aboriginal group to develop a sense of self-awareness, it must have a sense of opposition to something else. In the case of the Metis, that opposition is not so much between Metis and whites as it is between Metis and other Aboriginal peoples. There are many categories of "Native"[1] recognized in Canada today, thanks to over 100 years of mostly federal legislation. These include status Indians, non-status Indians, registered Indians, nonregistered Indians, treaty Indians, non-treaty Indians, C-31s (non-status Indians who are allowed to become status Indians), on-reserve Indians, off-reserve Indians, Metis, Metis Nation, and Inuit or Eskimo. This can be confusing, and is exacerbated by the fact that many of these terms are neither mutually exclusive nor precisely used. For example, "non-status Indian" can refer to either Metis, nonregistered, or non-treaty Indians, but often the term is used to refer to all of them, treating them as a single unit. "Status" can include both treaty and non-treaty Indians, C-31s, on-reserve Indians, or off-reserve Indians. Although most of these terms are derived from governmental legislation rather than cultural affiliation, some of them, especially the term "status" and "Metis" have become reified for Aboriginal populations, and now bear considerable emotional and cultural significance.

There might not be obvious cultural and phenotypic differences among status Indians, non-status Indians, and Metis, but the legal differences are clear-cut and far-reaching. Status Indians are entitled to an array of services, including social assistance, housing, education, and health care that are not available to Metis or non-status Indians. These legal differences for a time caused the Metis and non-status Indians to band together for political purposes beginning in the mid-1960s in western Canada. What they had in common at the time was a lack of recognition as Native peoples from the government of Canada and exclusion from the special services afforded status Indians.

At that time, the definition of who was a Metis, or who was allowed to join a Metis organization was broadly based. Most Metis organizations defined a Metis as someone of mixed white and Indian ancestry (or of mixed non-Indian and Indian ancestry); and non-status Indians were welcome to join. No distinction was made between Metis with roots in Red River and those Metis whose ancestry was founded in other parts of Canada, and no cultural affiliation or references to historical populations or events were needed for a person to join the political organizations. There was nothing to prevent a non-status Indian from identifying as Metis if he or she wished. Taking on the name Metis was an innovative assumption of identity for "half-breed" and non-status alike. In the prairies, the term was almost unknown—or at least unused—until Metis political organizations began to re-emerge in the 1960s.[2]

So, from the 1960s to the 1980s, a strong political union between non-status Indians and the Metis existed in western Canada. All this changed in 1982, when aboriginal rights were entrenched in the newly structured Canadian Constitution. Section 35(2) of the *Constitution Act, 1982* defined "aboriginal peoples of Canada" as the Indian, Inuit, and Metis peoples of Canada. Conspicuous by its absence from this definition was any mention of the non-status Indians of Canada. This made the legal positions of Metis and non-status Indians quite different, and the political organizations that had housed the two groups began to split apart.[3]

It was at this time that the western Metis began to develop a conscious ethnic identity that excluded non-status Indians, creating the idea of a "historic Red River Metis community," inhabiting a "historic Metis Nation Homeland" (west central North America) on or before December 8, 1869, the date of the proclamation of the Provisional Government of the Metis in the Northwest

Territories.[4] This reification of a Red River Metis identity has become very powerful in the prairies, but it is also becoming visible in Ontario. Ontario is an interesting place to witness this reformulation, because it has a very different group of Native people laying claim to the term "Metis," and the territory is not usually considered part of the historic Metis homeland by many Metis outside of Ontario.

Although I want to discuss some of the ways that ethnic boundaries are being redefined, I should make it clear that I am not in any way suggesting that the claims made in Ontario are counterfeit or "false," or that the motives of the Ontario group are spurious. Developing or adopting a "new" tradition is a typical way an ethnic group or an aboriginal group can create legitimacy for itself. Several scholars, such as David Lowenthal, have commented on this practice. Traditions that are claimed to be ancient frequently turn out to be recent inventions intended to provide continuity with a real or imagined past. They are used to establish group membership in communities and legitimize the group in its own eyes and the eyes of others as well as to inculcate a sense of belonging and self-worth.[5] However, as we shall see in Ontario, creating a past is not easily automatic nor is it without opposition from within.

Although the mixed-blood population of Ontario has come to be identified as "Metis," this group has few historic links to the historic Metis population of the prairies. Its historic presence is centered around Sault Ste. Marie, Ontario. It does have a clear sense of separateness from other Native groups, but this identity in and of itself does not necessarily fit into the political demands of the new millennium.

SELF-IDENTITY STRATEGIES

Currently, two diametrically opposed strategies for self-identification exist in Ontario for the Metis. One approach—attempting to create an exclusive Ontario identity—is exemplified by the Ontario Metis Aboriginal Association (OMAA). It attempts to represent the "Metis Indians" or the "woodland Metis tribe"—the population that regards itself as Ontario Metis. They also claim to represent non-status Indians and off-reserve Indians in Ontario. Its national affiliation is with the Congress of Aboriginal Peoples (CAP), an organization that is attempting to represent Metis, non-status Indians, and off-reserve Indians across Canada.

The other approach is represented by the Metis Nation of Ontario (MNO). This political organization explicitly opts for an alliance or amalgamation with the Red River Metis. This approach stresses ties to Red River and appropriates the cultural symbols of the prairie Metis. The MNO is an affiliate of the Metis National Council, the national organization representing the "historic Metis nation" within Canada.

Both of the major Metis political organizations in Ontario had their beginnings with the Ontario Metis and Non-Status Indian Association (OMNSIA). OMNSIA had its beginnings with the formation of a housing corporation, started in 1962 in the small community of MacDiarmid, situated on the shores of Lake Nipigon in northern Ontario north of Thunder Bay. In 1965, this became the Lake Nipigon Metis Association and eventually the founding chapter of OMNSIA. From its founding, it was recognized as an organization for people who were aboriginal, but who did not have Indian status. For lack of a better term, its members called themselves "Metis." They did not choose this name for cultural or historic reasons—rather it was seen as the widest and most all-encompassing term that could be used. It was almost unknown in Ontario at the time, "half-breed" or "breed" being much more common. The new term became known to the fledgling association because of political activity in another part of Canada—the prairie provinces. Observed Paddy McGuire,

> The Lake Nipigon meetings . . . all started because we had read in the paper about out west where Jim Sinclair and Dr. Howard Adams were doing something about the Metis movement out there. At that time, we didn't know what a Metis was. We thought you had to be half French to be a Metis. We knew we were half-breed but some people called us non-status Indians. According to them two fellows, we were all Metis, so that's how we founded the Lake Nipigon Metis Association, because we heard those guys talking about it.[6]

It is significant that Jim Sinclair, a charismatic Saskatchewan Aboriginal leader, is mentioned in this context, because although he was an important force in the mobilization of AMNSIS, he is a non-status Indian, not a Metis.

On March 27, 1971, OMNSIA, the first province-wide Metis and non-status association, was formed. Again, the word "Metis" was incorporated into the title, not because it was in common use in Ontario, but because it was seen as encompassing the widest possible group of people. Mike McGuire remembers the founding:

> There were different names that they wanted to call it. Some wanted to call it Ontario Metis Association, and others wanted to call it the Ontario Aboriginal Association. But I put a different name on the floor; the Ontario Metis and non-status Indian Association, and that was the name we chose. The reason I put that motion on the floor was because some people were enfranchised, some people considered themselves non-status, some people considered themselves Metis and some other considered themselves half breeds and we had to try to unite these people into one organization. So that name was a good name for a lot of years.[7]

However, this attempt at uniting the "half-breed" population and non-status Indians created the same strains that the prairie Metis political organizations had: Metis is a cultural and racial term (i.e., "half-breed"), while non-status is a legal term based on government legislation.

The partnership was strained to the breaking point in 1985 with the passage of Bill C-31, an act of the federal Parliament. The *Indian Act* was amended to permit many "non-status Indians" to regain their status and become registered Indians. As a result, approximately 20 percent of OMNSIA's members registered under the *Indian Act*. In order to reflect this change in their constituency, OMNSIA dropped the term "non-status Indian" from its name in 1987 and changed to the Ontario Metis Aboriginal Association. OMAA now claims to offer representation to 200,000 Indian and Metis peoples living off-reserve in Ontario.[8]

Although for many years OMNSIA was the only representative of the Ontario Metis, it never suggested an actual link with Red River Metis for its constituency, nor did its successor OMAA, other than borrowing the name "Metis." This changed in 1994 with the formation of the Metis Nation of Ontario. The MNO was founded at a delegates meeting that brought together Metis (mostly OMAA members) from communities around Ontario. In contrast to OMAA, and OMNSIA before it, MNO offered an aggressive identification not only as Metis of Ontario, but as a group having a similar historical background and identity as the Red River Metis. It became affiliated with the Metis National Council as "the only representative body of the Metis in Ontario." In 2001, it claimed that over 380 communities were included in the MNO Registry, the only registry of Metis in Ontario recognized by the historic Metis Nation and the Metis National Council, and that the MNO "offers the most legitimate way in Ontario for Metis people to be recognised."[9] Thus, today there are two Ontario organizations, both purporting to speak for the Metis of Ontario.[10] Both have very different ideas of who their constituents are. To understand why such a situation could come about, one must look at the specifics of Metis and non-status identification in Ontario since the 1980s.

IDENTITY, DIVISION, AND SYMBOLISM

In the 1970s and early 1980s, the situation looked very different in Ontario. The discussions over Metis identity that took place at the time suggested most rank and file members of the association were interested in non-status issues, rather than in developing an identity as Metis, and often they referred to themselves as "Indians," "breeds," or "half-breeds."[11] Most did not even speak to the issue of being Metis, and those who did adopted the term "Metis" for lack of a better one. A typical statement from the time would identify the speaker as a "breed" rather than Metis even if the term "Metis" was simultaneously used:

I personally am not in favor of our people joining together with treaty Indians in forming one organization. I am also not prepared to risk losing the pride and independency that is mine because I am a breed. We have always owned our own homes, and always made a respectable attempt to survive as a breed. We have always did things our own way without any handouts. In other words, we and our ancestors have always paddled our own canoes. Our ancestors were a proud and independent breed, capable of living in harmony with the land, the Indian and the whites. We stand our ground for special rights and the recognition of ourselves as half-breed. Joining the treaty Indians would be a total loss of our own identity. I strongly believe that we can work together with our treaty brothers to achieve common goals, to better our land which is rightfully ours. We should endeavour to obtain official recognition by all levels of governments throughout this land, and not only as another ethic group or as another native organization. We should be recognized for what we are, and we are Metis.[12]

There is some indication that OMNSIA began to discourage the use of the term "breed" in the early 1980s. The organization held two surveys, one in 1981 and one in 1985, to gather data on a variety of policy matters.[13] Some of the most interesting questions involved self-identity. Both surveys were close-ended; they gave a number of choices for self-identity, including Metis, non-status, status, Canadian-born and naturalized citizen, but neither offered "breed" or "half-breed" as an option, even though both terms were in common use in Ontario at the time. Nor was there a space to write in another identity not listed.

The surveys had other shortcomings. Respondents were free to choose more than one of the identities offered, and many did so. While 40.9 percent of the respondents identified as non-status, and 36 percent identified as Metis, there was nothing in the survey to indicate why the respondent would choose to identify one way or another. Both surveys also failed to allow for a distinction between "Red River" Metis and "Ontario" Metis. The surveys do seem to show that there was a feeling of separateness from Indians on the part of many of the respondents. The sociologists who collated the data concluded that the Ontario Metis "represent a group distinct from the Metis who trace their heritage and identity to their experiences at Red River."[14] This is a reasonable conclusion, but other than referring to some historical authorities, they could offer no internal evidence to support or refute this claim, because nothing in the survey was designed to elicit such information.

The eventual split between OMAA and MNO probably proceeded along the lines hinted at in these surveys. For example, the 1985 survey revealed a division in attitudes about heritage; those who identified as non-status Indians tended to identify more closely with Indian heritage in terms of language and spirituality than those identifying as Metis. The split between the two organizations may reflect this cultural differentiation—with the OMAA more closely supporting non-status Indian and "Native" values, and with the MNO more closely supporting Red River Metis values. An examination of the symbolism used by each organization would seem to bear this out.

The original OMNSIA logo (1971–1987) had an equal number of Indian and white symbols and is indicative of who OMNSIA considered its constituents. It had an outer circle that symbolized infinity, and the fact that Native peoples "have been here since time immemorial." White symbols included the trillium (official flower of the government of Ontario), maple leaf (government of Canada), the scales of justice (white man's justice), and a book (white man's "book learning"). Native symbols included the lynx, the feather, and the bow and arrow. Interestingly, there were no explicit Metis symbols—no Metis flag, sash, or image of Louis Riel.

That symbolism has changed drastically in the new OMAA logo. There are six North American Indian symbols used: tribe, the sacred number four (four races, four seasons, four stages of life), arrows, tipis, sun ("father sun"), and the eagle. There is one Metis symbol used; the "infinity" symbol from the Red River Metis flag. About the only "white" symbols are the color white itself (the "white race" is part of the four colors) and the anthropological term "woodland." When speaking to members of OMAA today, it is obvious that many Native values—particularly Cree and Ojibwa—are still a major influence. For example, there is an origin story about the early days of organizing which recounts that at the Lake Nipigon Metis Association's inaugural meeting, a baby's cry was heard from the wilderness, symbolizing the birth of a "new people." Furthermore, a special "fire ceremony" was designed for the organization, and it is common practice for the leaders of the organization to go to the Native community for spiritual guidance.[15]

While the MNO does not have an official logo, their website calls on four specific historical symbols to help define its constituency.[16] Three of these are derived from the prairie Metis: the Metis flag, sash, and Louis Riel. The only truly Ontario historical element in this litany is the mention of the adhesion of Metis to Treaty Number 3 (which until recently had been referred to typically as the adhesion of "half-breeds" to the treaty process).

In 1978, Duke Redbird, who was president of OMNSIA in the early 1980s, wrote a master's thesis (published in 1980) suggesting that "half-breeds" and non-status Indians might wish to look to the western Metis to find an identity.[17] The MNO seems to have borrowed Redbird's thesis and turned to Red River as the source for their Metis identity. This is a recent innovation and even their own website alludes to the fact that the term "Metis" (in terms of Red River Metis) was not always known in Ontario. The statement stops just short of admitting that they are "inventing" the Ontario Metis. They make the case that the Metis were always in Ontario but just not recognized as such:

> The Metis Nation of Ontario (MNO) evolved, members believe, from the rich and dynamic history of an Aboriginal people *long thought to be non-existent in Ontario.* The MNO has drawn Metis people together in ever-increasing numbers, encouraging them to claim their inheritance and to establish their identity within the Province of Ontario.[18]

CONCLUSION

Who are the Ontario Metis? It is obvious that there is a split identity at work in Ontario. Both provincial organizations claim to represent the Metis of Ontario, but both have very different ideas of who their constituents are and what constitutes a Metis. It is still not clear whether the imported western values and culture posited by the MNO can actually take root. Mike McGuire, one of the founding fathers of OMNSIA and current president of OMAA, has this to say about the creation of Ontario "Metis" culture:

> Well, Tony Belcourt (president of the MNO) wanted to go more with the Red River things, eh? Maybe they wanted to say to be Metis, you have to come from the Red River in order to have that identity. But in Ontario we don't identify with that. The Metis people of Ontario; they are the Ontario Metis people. They're not from the west. Tony comes from Alberta. He comes into Ontario and says well, here are the values of the Metis people. Well, maybe in the west they do have a different set of values. But in Ontario we're a different being. . . . So that's how the split (between OMAA and MNO) began. I think it was more of the Western Metis concept, I think that they wanted to put the Western Metis values here.[19]

Despite OMAA's skepticism over the Red River link, it may well be that a new Metis identity based on those criteria is developing in Ontario through the activities of the MNO. The desire to do so is understandable. The idea of "Metis" in the Red River sense is itself an attractive one. The portrayal of the "new Nation," the creators of western Canada, and Louis Riel as culture hero are parts of this tradition. These are all positive images, which give people a sense of pride in an actual ethnoaboriginal identity as opposed to an "anti-identity" based on rejections from other groups.

The one thing that can be predicted with some certainty about ethnic or aboriginal boundaries is that they change with the times. The times today may demand a Metis identity in Ontario far different from the one envisioned by activists who started the Ontario Metis and Non-Status Indian Association in 1965. Despite the fact that the "Metis of Ontario" as presented by the MNO is at least a partial construction affected by outside influences and national politics, it also seems to be becoming the accepted reality for many Metis in the province. Probably, it is inevitable that a change in identity of this magnitude and quality should happen at this time, as the Metis begin to assert their unique place in Canadian and Ontario society and in relation to other aboriginal peoples.

NOTES

Acknowledgments: The Canada Social Science and Humanities Research Council and the Brandon University Research Council provided financial support for gathering some of the data and interviews.

1. The terms "Native" and "Aboriginal" are more or less interchangeable when referring to Canada's indigenous population. Neither has a precise meaning, but "Aboriginal" is defined in Section 35(2) of the Canadian *Constitution Act, 1982,* as comprising the Indian, Inuit, and Metis peoples of Canada.

2. In a survey undertaken by the Manitoba provincial government in 1958, it was found that less than 1 percent, or three out of 295 people who identified themselves or were identified by others as Metis or "half-breed," said they would give "Metis" in answer to the question, "What is your nationality?" "Half-breed" was a more common answer—42 percent or 123 stated that they would claim "half-breed" as their nationality, while 68 or 23 percent would answer that they were Indian. Jean H. Lagasse, *A Study of the Population of Indian Ancestry Living in Manitoba* (Winnipeg: Department of Agriculture and Immigration, 1959), 54–56.

3. This is not to suggest that non-status Indians are not covered by the Constitution, but that is a complex issue deserving further consideration at length.

4. Metis National Council provisional definitions, http://www.metisnation.ca/.

5. See David Lowenthal, *Possessed by the Past: The Heritage Crusade and the Spoils of History* (New York: Free Press, 1996).

6. Paddy McGuire, "Mr. Paddy McGuire," *Dimensions Special Editions* 8 (no. 5, 1980): 12–15; Individual Questionnaire of the OMNSIA Commission of Inquiry, in *Dimensions Special Editions* 9 (no. 4, 1981): 47–53.

7. Mike McGuire, president of OMAA, interview by author, June 17, 1997, Thunder Bay, Ontario (tape recording).

8. Ontario Metis Aboriginal Association, http://www.omaa.org.

9. Metis Nation of Ontario, http://www.metisnation.org.

10. There are other smaller special-interest Ontario Metis organizations, such as the Red Sky Metis Independent Nation, not included in this discussion.

11. At least three sources reveal the thoughts and conflicts surrounding the idea of Metis identification at that time. One is a series of meetings that discussed the merits of a "special

status" for Metis and non-status in Ontario, a policy briefly pursued by OMNSIA under Duke Redbird's leadership. See *Dimensions Special Editions* 8 (August/September 1980). The second is a series of debates that OMNSIA held to discuss issues surrounding the repatriation of the Canadian Constitution, including the definition of Metis and Aboriginal Rights. See *Dimensions Special Editions* 9 (no. 4, 1981): And finally, OMNSIA conducted two different surveys polling its members on issues of policy and self-identification. See Robert Chilton, "Moose Factory," *Dimensions Special Editions* 8 (August/September 1980).

12. See Chilton, "Moose Factory."

13. The 1981 survey had 73 respondents, and the 1985 survey, 2,004 respondents. The 1981 survey is reported in *Dimensions Special Editions* (1981) (see n. 6), and the 1985 survey in Evelyn Peters, Mark Rosenberg, and Greg Halseth, *The Ontario Metis: Characteristics and Identity* (Winnipeg: Institute of Urban Studies, University of Winnipeg, 1991).

14. Peters et al., *Ontario Metis*, 13.

15. McGuire interview.

16. See Metis Nation of Ontario, http://www.metisnation.org.

17. Duke Redbird, "We Are Metis: A Metis Perspective of the Evolution of an Indigenous Canadian People" (master's thesis, York University, 1978), published as *We Are Metis* (Toronto: Ontario Metis and Non-Status Indian Association, 1980).

18. Metis Nation of Ontario, http://www.metisnation.org, emphasis added.

19. McGuire interview.

PART V

The People

Traditionally, this is the land of the Eskimo—the Inuit, that is, the People *(par excellence)—and from time immemorial they have lived by hunting and fishing. Historically, in accord with the equitable principles of the British Crown, they have been assured of their right to follow their vocations of hunting and fishing. In the early days the Eskimos were considered as a tribe or nation of Indians.*[1]

Regina v. Kogogolak, SUPREME COURT OF THE NORTHWEST
TERRITORIES, CANADA (1959)

To do what they called civilizing us . . . was to destroy us. You know they thought that changing us, getting rid of our old wars and language and names would make us like white men. But why should we want to be like them, cheaters and greedy? Why should we change and abandon the ways that made us men and not the beggars we became?[2]

OVERTAKES THE ENEMY, Pawnee

O N THE FORT APACHE RESERVATION in east central Arizona, tourists visit the Apache Cultural Center and Museum daily to learn about the Apache past. They take tours of Fort Apache from Apache guides and witness first-hand the renovations and reclamation of the Apache past on the very grounds of the U.S. Army's nineteenth-century occupation. In the museum gift shop, visitors may purchase a variety of books and crafts and curios, and some of these items have important decolonization messages. Perhaps the most relevant to today's world is a T-shirt that has a famous picture stamped on the front; it is a portrait of Geronimo, Apache patriot, holding a rifle with three of his fellow armed Apaches. The words on the T-shirt convey a serious modern meaning "Homeland Security: 'Fighting Terrorism Since 1492.'"

In the twenty-first century, significant issues confront *The People*. Many challenges have their origins in the distant past, but many others are the result of events and policies shaped in the twentieth century. Interestingly, few scholars have researched the indigenous twentieth century, but that is of course changing, and this scholarship has the added advantage of greater Native American and First Nations first-person participation and commentary.

"The People" is a term that each indigenous nation has asserted. Oftentimes, it is a direct translation of nationality from their own languages. For example, the term non-Indians and some Indians use, Apaches, is an inaccurate term, most likely written down by Spanish scribes when they heard Zunis call Navajos *Ápachu*, meaning "the enemy" in Zuni. Apaches call themselves *N'de, Dinî, Tinde,* or *Inde,* meaning The People.[3] Similarly, their relatives, the Navajos, call themselves *Diné,* The People, and they live in *Dinetah,* the land of The People, not in Navajoland.[4] Other Athapaskan-speaking relatives in Canada, the Sarcees, call themselves the Tsuu T'ina Nation. Their name translated means "a great number of people."[5]

The last two chapters of this collection describe modern indigenous life of The People of Native North America. Each considers the twentieth century as a backdrop to twenty-first-century issues. Both show this to be a time of renewal and strength, and of the challenges afforded by urbanization, retention of language and traditions, education, and economic sustenance.

Patricia Burke Wood starts an initial discussion that is important for any reconfigurations of Native North America. She explains how postcolonial methodologies do not work for assessments of First Nations and other indigenous people's experiences. Virtually all Native peoples continue, in varying degrees, to be under colonial rule. They do not control their geopolitical destiny, and they often have problems with colonial societies over the most fundamental questions of sovereignty. As a case study, Wood tells of the continuing problems the Tsuu T'ina Nation has with the city of Calgary, its neighbor. The Tsuu T'ina are signatories of Treaty 7 (1877), and as such, they eventually obtained a reserve near Calgary in central Alberta.[6] With the massive expansion of Calgary beyond its original environs in the last half of the twentieth century, the Tsuu T'ina found their reserve lands surrounded, both geographically and culturally. That the city of Calgary would prefer to ignore the Tsuu T'ina is not possible in twenty-first-century Canada, and thus a kind of aboriginal citizenship at the local level is in the process of transforming urban relationships.

In the last chapter, Peter Iverson, one of the early writers of twentieth-century Native American history, offers us a personal memoir of his experiences in forcing the academy to take modern indigenous history seriously. It has not been an easy struggle, but all of the evidence suggests that he and his compatriots have been very successful. A brief look at the abundance of dissertations being written on twentieth-century Indian topics and the publication of Native American modern history monographs easily confirms this assessment. Well-known for his seminal work on the Navajos, Iverson explains the dos and don'ts for writing modern Indian studies, and he offers potential topics on the recent challenges to the Diné as new avenues for research. All of this raises, as Iverson reflects, "poignant questions about what it means to be Navajo in the twenty-first century."

Yes, The People and their scholars have much to say about their past, present, and future. It is a time of reclamation and decolonization, an exciting time in which The People recognize the struggles of their pasts while forging a future. As Overtakes the Enemy observed in 1859 about European Americans who sought to take Pawnee lands and alter Pawnee culture, today's Native North Americans seek The People's way. And they also rhetorically ask, "Why should we want to be like them?"

NOTES

1. Quoted from *Regina v. Kogogolak* (1959), emphasis added, a decision rendered in the Supreme Court of the Northwest Territories by Judge J.H. Sessions, in Dorothy Harley Eber, *Images of Justice: A Legal History of the Northwest Territories as Traced Through the Yellowknife Courthouse Collection of Inuit Sculpture* (Montreal: McGill-Queen's University Press, 1997), 85.

2. Martha Royce Blaine, *Pawnee Passage, 1870–1875* (Norman: University of Oklahoma Press, 1990), 143, quoted in Roger C. Echo-Hawk and Walter R. Echo-Hawk, *Battlefields and Burial Grounds: The Indian Struggle to Protect Ancestral Graves* (Minneapolis, MN: Lerner Publications, 1994), 47.

3. Michael E. Melody, *The Apaches: A Critical Bibliography* (Bloomington: Indiana University Press, 1977), 2–3.

4. John R. Wunder, *"Retained by The People": A History of American Indians and the Bill of Rights* (New York: Oxford University Press, 1994), vii–viii. See generally Peter Iverson, *Diné: A History of the Navajos* (Albuquerque: University of New Mexico Press, 2002); and Peter Iverson, ed., and Monty Roessel, photo ed., *"For Our Navajo People": Diné Letters, Speeches & Petitions, 1900–1960* (Albuquerque: University of New Mexico Press, 2002).

5. "Tsuu T'ina Nation," www.treaty7.org/Article.Asp?ArticleID'36, March 16, 2005.

6. See Jill St. Germain, *Indian Treaty-Making Policy in the United States and Canada, 1867–1877* (Lincoln: University of Nebraska Press, 2001), 41, 55–57, 65–66, 74–75, 94, 109, 117, 137, 160; "Treaty 7 Nations," www.treaty7.org/Article.asp?Article ID'2. The Tsuu T'ina Nation describes Treaty 7 as "a peace treaty made between two nations—the tribes of the Blackfoot Confederacy . . . and Her Most Gracious Majesty the Queen of Great Britain and Ireland. . . ." The Confederacy is further defined as including the Blackfoot nations of the Siksika, Piikani (Peigan), and Kainaiwa (Blood) and the Stoney nations of the Bearspaw, Chiniki, and Wesley/Goodstoney, and the Tsuu T'ina Nation.

CHAPTER 16

Scales of Aboriginal Citizenship in Canada: Postcolonial Problems and Progress

PATRICIA BURKE WOOD

To ACHIEVE a truly *post*colonial nation, that is, one that has successfully exited its colonial stage of history, one must create postcolonial citizens. As many frustrated writers have observed, there is often too little "post" in postcolonial societies, as they remain mired in swamps of colonial legacies. Moving beyond the hegemony, inequality, violence, and silences of colonial societies requires more than the passage of time or the occurrence of a watershed event. Networks of power and authority must be reconstructed through active decolonization. Postcolonial citizens of the nation-state must have rights that do not place them in a subservient, colonized position, and some structure must be in place that prevents them from being placed in or returning to such a state.

In Canada, the achievement of this postcolonial state faces challenges that many other countries do not. As Alan Cairns has noted, in Canada (as in much of the Americas) the colonized have not thrown out their colonizers.[1] Instead, the parties of colonizer and colonized have had to construct a nation-state that includes both of them. Building the postcolonial nation is not a small task, particularly in the absence of the inspirational event of reclaiming indigenous territory from the conquerors. To make colonized and colonizers equal citizens of the same state necessitates a thoroughly inclusive process. It is necessary to have a relationship between Natives and non-Natives that is respectful, peaceful, cooperative, and collaborative.

Determining how such a relationship might be achieved requires the recognition of two key elements of the postcolonial project. First, this process is profoundly material and spatial, despite symbolic gestures and representations that

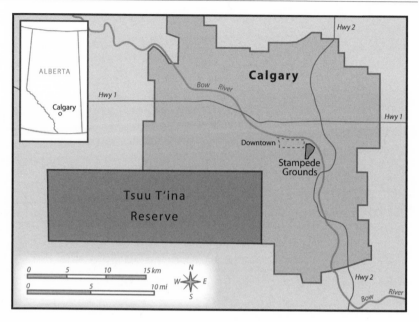

First Nations Country Today: The Tsuu T'ina Reserve

gloss over these realities; and second, that Aboriginal citizenship operates at multiple scales, although it is commonly presented in a more narrow fashion. This chapter will discuss the challenges of Aboriginal citizenship in Canada in a broad postcolonial context and through the lens of a specific relationship between a city and a First Nation. It concludes by suggesting how these parties might make some progress in their relationship by addressing the spatial and scalar complexities of their interactions through more participatory and inclusive practices at the local level.

ORIGINS OF MODERN ABORIGINAL CITIZENSHIP

In Canada, one key source of the foundations of Aboriginal citizenship was the negotiation of treaties. Although there are many instances of profound misunderstanding between the parties as to what was decided,[2] the treaties were, roughly speaking, an attempt to establish the basic contract through which colonized and colonizers would inhabit the same nation, if not precisely the same space. Treaties normally provided reserve land for indigenous groups, as well as delineated particular rights and responsibilities, such as hunting and fishing, annual payments, and education. The overall structure for governance of and within Native bands was delineated by the Indian Act, which made its first appearance in 1876 and in many ways represents a consolidation of various smaller pieces of legislation. The Indian

Act, which has been revised several times, last in 1985, does not apply to the Inuit. Despite the overarching framework provided by the Act, it is these treaties, where they exist, that establish the specifics of exactly which lands may be occupied or used by whom. Treaties ascertain the spatial and social practices of Native/non-Native coexistence in a given place in Canada. The complexity of Aboriginal citizenship derives from this and is addressed by treaties. Citizenship established through treaties is different from that of non-Natives; the basis of the contract with the state is unique for each particular treaty relationship.

Prior to 1867, representatives of the British Crown dealt with First Nations in what would become Canada; following Confederation, the Canadian federal government negotiated on behalf of the Crown. This intergovernmental relationship with Aboriginals was affirmed through the British North America Act of 1867 whereby, in the division of jurisdictions, authority to address Native concerns and to manage their property, education, and social welfare was allocated to the federal government and not to the provinces or territories. Provincial governments have become increasingly involved in recent land claim negotiations and other policy discussions regarding Aboriginals, largely out of recognition that the land involved, particularly in off-reserve situations, is often provincially owned.

Particularly since 1982, when the Canadian Charter of Rights and Freedoms was added to a newly patriated Canadian Constitution, the rights of citizens have been and are seen to be articulated and protected at the national level. One is, therefore, a citizen of Canada, whereas one is a resident (or, to some governments, merely a taxpayer) of a province. The provincial government is frequently regarded as a level of administration rather than the holder of the power of governance on central concerns of citizenship, such as immigration and health care. From time to time, some provinces, most notably Québec, have sought to increase their executive powers in the administration of federal dollars, and they have occasionally been successful in reaching new arrangements with Ottawa. Despite their authority, however, provinces are rarely understood as a locational basis for citizenship. Québec is a distinct exception, although there may be similar, lingering ideas in Newfoundland, a province that only joined Canada in 1949. The lack of a sense of provincial citizenship, with rights specific to that scale of political jurisdiction may also be due to the political strategies of some provincial governments to position themselves as accountable to residents in a narrow, economic vein, rather than a more holistic fashion.

ABORIGINAL CITIZENSHIP AT THE LOCAL LEVEL

Scale is a way of seeing. Like any way of framing, scale creates the object of observation as much as it presents a view of it. As Neil Brenner has argued, "scale operates simultaneously as a presupposition, a medium and an outcome of social relations,"[3] and different objects and patterns are visible at varying distances and angles. Simply put, we see differently at different scales. Although this chapter stresses the importance of the local scale, my primary interest in Aboriginal citizenship does not concern any particular scale in and of itself, but instead focuses on the process of creating scales and in the strategic use of scales and discourses of scale. It is akin to Pierre Bourdieu's rhetorical emphasis that it is not the class, but the process of classification that should interest us and concern us.[4] And we should be particularly interested in those who want us to see certain things exclusively in a certain way, whether they want us to keep a great distance or keep things right in our face. There is no ideal distance: The problem is the compulsion to keep a singular distance.

Aboriginal citizenship has been framed by the Canadian state (like others) at a national scale that distorts and delegitimizes both the particular postcolonial citizenship claims that Natives make *and* the way in which they make those claims. Even the use of the word "Native" or "Aboriginal" invokes this scale, or one even larger. The state's view lumps together a great diversity of peoples and cultural practices, as well as a diversity of its own legal agreements, implying a commonality that is rarely the case. This encourages non-Natives to see Aboriginal peoples and their concerns at the national scale, in the context of a grand swath of national history, in simplistic terms of "us" and "them" where "we" won and "they" lost. Addressing their citizenship claims follows from that superficial understanding of history and reduces their claims to a choice of "fitting in" (accepting the victory) or "living in the past." Such universalizing (and yet divisive) language and policy masks the differentiated history of state/Native relations in Canada, and blinds us to the opportunities that might be found at other scales.

The national state's assertion of jurisdictional authority to create citizenship, and to define its terms, is not applied only to Native peoples. It makes this assertion for all citizens and noncitizens within its borders, and to some extent, beyond them. However, there is no equivalent, for any group, to the Indian Act. The Indian Act defined who an "Indian" is according to race, gender, and culture; it has defined how "Indians" are to organize themselves politically, where they are to live, where else they can go, what they are and are not to do, and the conditions through which they may or may not challenge the situation.

Similarly, citizenship is rarely conceptualized, at least by the state, as a local issue. While both federal and provincial governments have developed programs that encourage the individual citizen to enact his or her citizenship at the local level, by cleaning local parks, for example, or volunteering in the community, the Canadian state has not invested municipalities with much authority.[5] Cities are entirely subject to provincial jurisdiction, with no power (with few exceptions) over the creation or dissolution of their borders and no other capacity to raise funds except property taxes and user fees. Some new urban social movements have explicitly challenged this local lack of power. With such notable examples as the creation of Citizens for Local Democracy in Toronto, and other organizations that have challenged the amalgamation of municipalities, these movements have identified neighborhoods and communities as centers and foundations of democracy and citizenship.[6] It is in these locales, such activists insist, that rights must be embedded and practiced for citizenship to be meaningful.

The question of citizenship for Aboriginals is not an abstract idea that lives in words alone. It is a matter of geography. Colonial and postcolonial states are spatially manifested, and the consequences of their spatial allocation, and restriction and representation of space are real. By and large, Natives and non-Natives in Canada do not share the same space. They live in profoundly different landscapes. Presently, about 50 percent of "Status Indian" Aboriginals in Canada live on reserves,[7] spaces designated for them by the federal government, usually through the treaty process. Large portions of these reserved spaces have also been taken away from the First Nations living on them, often through policies and practices that were irresponsible, unethical, and illegal. Much of the other 50 percent who reside off-reserve live in cities, often in circumstances of social danger where their well-being and even their lives are severely compromised. If the figures for individuals self-identifying as having any Aboriginal origin are considered, almost five times as many in this group live off-reserve than on-reserve.[8] This is not a past or a present for equality, participatory democracy, or full citizenship. The situation stands as both a legacy of colonialism and as evidence of a vacuum of policy toward Aboriginals who implicitly (and sometimes explicitly) challenged the colonial geographical order by moving off reserves.

The question of Native/non-Native relationships, then, whose success is fundamental to building a postcolonial Canada, is not only a matter of bridging personal and cultural differences. It is also a relationship of landscapes. On a reserve, land and some other property are held collectively, not individually. Moreover, through the policies established by Ottawa, First Nations possess property rights over reserve land, which are in some instances stronger than others' rights. In addition, Native identities are rooted more clearly in and articulated through the community rather than the individual. The connection between the community and the land (including, but not limited to, reserves) is more spiritual, more complex, and more important to Native groups than to most non-Natives.[9] The strong connection to the land by Native peoples is fundamental. These lands and identities are also interrelated in important and complicated legal and social ways to the Natives who live off-reserve.

CALGARY AND THE TSUU T'INA NATION

As urban social movements for local democracy make clear, what makes citizenship meaningful and stable is how nationally established citizenship is practiced at the local level in ordinary ways, where people live their daily lives. This is no less true for Aboriginals, whose rights are almost entirely vested at the federal level. As for non-Natives, the community needs to be a center of a set of practices that secures the well-being of the collective and the individuals within it. Thus, it is insufficient for Ottawa to make guarantees through social policy or law if, in practice, Natives' rights are eroded or neglected every day in their encounters with non-Natives.

The city of Calgary, Alberta, and the Tsuu T'ina Nation have begun to grapple with the questions involved in local Aboriginal citizenship. Calgary is a city with a metropolitan population of about 1 million people, located to the immediate north and east of the Tsuu T'ina Nation, which is a reserve of three townships, or approximately 70,000 acres. Not only are this city and this reserve neighbors, but the city has begun to wrap itself around the reserve. In 1877 when the Tsuu T'ina signed Treaty Number 7, they were settled initially with the Blackfoot community (Siksika) east of Calgary. But the Tsuu T'ina considered the Bow and Elbow Rivers traditional territory, and preferred to be near the emerging white settlement with which they had established some trading relationships. Led by their chief, Bull Head, the Tsuu T'ina successfully negotiated a separate reserve within that territory. Calgary and the Tsuu T'ina Reserve were formally established at approximately the same time, in the early 1880s, but they have had far different fates. In the late nineteenth and early twentieth centuries, Calgary's economy and population grew at a continent-leading pace, while the Tsuu T'ina Nation declined in health and numbers.

There are and have been a variety of points of contact between Calgary and the Tsuu T'ina, in addition to that early trading relationship. For example, Anglican and Catholic churches established a presence on the reserve; Tsuu T'ina children have been bused to Calgary schools; the Tsuu T'ina have built a middle-class housing development on the reserve in which non-Native Calgary workers also live; a large portion of the former Canadian Armed Forces Base-Calgary was located on reserve lands, and a larger area of it was leased by the military for training; local utility companies have constructed substations on the territory; and the Calgary Police Force has a cooperative program with the reserve tribal police. With few shops and services on the reserve itself, many Tsuu T'ina come to Calgary on a regular basis for everything from groceries to health care. The most visible point of contact is Tsuu T'ina participation (along with other Treaty Number 7 Nations) in Calgary's annual Exhibition and Stampede, a week-long festival and rodeo that stands at the center of the city's image and tourist economy.

Rather than discuss any one of these interactions in detail here, a summary is afforded briefly along two lines. On the one hand, Calgarians have frequently excluded the Tsuu T'ina from actual participation in the city. During the late nineteenth and early twentieth centuries, the City of Calgary attempted to contain the Tsuu T'ina on their reserve and even to remove them to a greater distance from the city.[10] Since then, Calgarians have rarely sought to involve or consult them in the day-to-day activities of the city, and their exchanges and interactions with Tsuu T'ina have declined in quantity and quality in the past twenty years or so. By and large, most Calgarians are oblivious to the presence of the reserve on the city's western edge, except when traffic woes activate the debate about putting a road through the reserve.[11]

On the other hand, Calgarians have historically insisted on Native participation at their annual civic celebration, the Stampede. Within the grounds of the city's agricultural exposition and fair is the Indian Village, where members of the Treaty Number 7 nations set up tipis and demonstrate culinary practices, traditional crafts, and dancing. When the Canadian federal government did not wish Natives to perform traditional practices of any kind and forbade Native participation in the event, the organizers successfully lobbied against that decision.[12] Everyone involved in the organization of the Indian Village, including Natives, believes that the Native presence is of crucial importance. Alberta Premier Ralph Klein, who is also a former mayor of Calgary, suggests that it would be a disaster if they refused to come.[13]

There have been other efforts to include Natives in Calgary life and society. Calgarian residents hired individual Tsuu T'ina to undertake work around their houses, farms, and ranch properties. The Calgary Industrial School, run by the Catholic Church, had as its goal the education of Native young men and boys and their subsequent integration into non-Native society. The school explicitly separated the children from reserves, actively discouraged visits from their families, and arranged for visits and employment in the city.

What about the Tsuu T'ina? First of all, they are much more aware of their neighbor than their neighbor is of them, some of which is the result of their regular trips into the city. When one remains on the reserve, however, the city has a certain presence: From the main administration building looking east, one is confronted by a dense colony of detached family housing where there was once open prairie. There are members of the band who wish to engage with Calgary, particularly with regard to development on the reserve that could accommodate the road sought by the city, but there are also those who feel self-sufficiency through greater independence is a better goal. The Tsuu T'ina now have their own schools, police, recreational facilities, and court of law.

On both sides, then, there are efforts to include and to exclude, occurring at different times and at various levels. The landscapes are involved in a similar relationship: Calgary's built landscape is predominantly suburban with an urban business core, and its residential development is eating into areas outside the city limits. The reserve, meanwhile, is mostly rural, with a desire by most Tsuu T'ina to leave it as untouched as possible. In addition to other impacts of proximity, the landscapes are linked environmentally in a singularly important way. The river that feeds the city's reservoir runs through the reserve. The pressure and opportunity of the city's development has also blurred the landscapes' distinctions. For example, the Tsuu T'ina have established a middle-class residential/golf course development on the reserve, available for lease to non–Tsuu T'ina.

How are these landscapes discursively related? From Calgary's perspective, the reserve is both in the way of further development *and* a guaranteed beautiful, unhindered view of the mountains that increases the value of existing development. To the Tsuu T'ina Nation, the city's built landscape (and plans for more) and subsequent ecology are a threat to the well-being of the reserve, but they also provide opportunities for economic development to the band. These landscapes challenge and complement each other, simultaneously.

In large part due to the proximity of the city, the Tsuu T'ina are *relatively* successful and less poor than many other Canadian First Nations. Calgarians are no longer actively trying to remove them to another part of the province. There are many points of contact between the communities, and there are windows of positive exchange and common capital that offer promise of a *post*colonial future. And yet, by all accounts, Calgary and Tsuu T'ina do not have a strong relationship. If ever a Native or non-Native community could establish something meaningful, positive, and mutually beneficial, it would be here. But it has not happened.

CONCLUSION

Why not? And what to conclude from this about the local practice of Native/non-Native relations and the prospects for a postcolonial state? Are the practices of inclusion and exclusion contradictory? Is it the case for Calgary that Natives are good enough for show, but not for real, meaningful citizenship inclusion? There may be some of that, but the situation is more complex. There is no contradiction here, only a complexity. What is absent, despite all efforts to bridge the communities, is a local space for interconnections to happen on a regular basis. Even the Stampede, which appears to be a collective celebration, is segregated in practice; the visitors to the Indian Village are more often European or Japanese tourists than Calgary citizens.

It is not clear what a common space should look like or how it might be constructed. No rational person suggests the elimination of reserves, but the residents' poverty in these places must be addressed so that First Nations as collectives and repositories of rights are able to function. Each community also needs private and public spaces. The spaces of the reserve and privately owned property are, for purposes of this argument, the private spaces of each community in their relationship with each other. Natives off-reserve need a similar private space for their community, and Natives and non-Natives need public spaces, at the local level, where their interaction may produce—however informally, for its formality is not important—a common space. Without such a space, different people in different landscapes cannot work together to navigate their way from a relationship of colonizer and colonized.

It would be disingenuous to suggest that the nation-state is the shared space. Segregation within Canada and the absence of a substantial means for Aboriginals to participate in decision-making processes that affect them speaks to the lack of common investment in Canada as a shared space. More appropriate would be joint management of the city's reservoir, for example, as a means of explicitly recognizing their environmental interdependence, and providing a forum for building political trust. Such a space would respond to the reality of links between the communities and build a healthier relationship between two peoples and their landscapes, without damaging the integrity of either.

The differences between people, with regard to their cultural practices, need to be respected and protected. Their well-being, which should not depend on their beliefs, should be promoted and secured. Similarly, our landscapes, in which we have inscribed and from which we draw so much of our identities, need to be respected and secured. Their own well-being, in terms of such things as security, sacredness, and environmental health, must also be a priority. Only in these circumstances, where everyone's well-being and rights to participation are secured at the local level, is full citizenship achieved.

None of this discussion of local practice is meant to suggest that the Indian Act or any other action the national government takes is insignificant. Indeed, the Tsuu T'ina Nation is one of several bands with profound concerns about proposals to make changes to the Indian Act. The Nation has taken many opportunities to voice objections, precisely because the Tsuu T'ina recognize the ways in which the Act affects them. But local issues or issues with important local implications, such as the incompleteness of the recent treaty-making renewal process, environmental damage on reserves, and the right to participate in decisions affecting the land or population at the borders of reserves, are equally significant to the practice of Aboriginal citizenship, and thus the achievement of a truly decolonized postcolonial nation-state. The federal government may assist in these objectives, but they will not be achieved in the absence of a positive relationship among local governments, such as the City of Calgary, all its residents, and its indigenous neighbors.

NOTES

1. See Alan C. Cairns, *Citizens Plus: Aboriginal Peoples and the Canadian State* (Vancouver: University of British Columbia Press, 2000).

2. See, for example, Treaty 7 Elders, *The True Spirit of the Original Intent of Treaty 7* (Montreal and Kingston: McGill-Queen's University Press, 1996).

3. Neil Brenner, "The Urban Question as a Scale Question: Reflections on Henri Lefebvre, Urban Theory and the Politics of Scale," *International Journal of Urban and Regional Research* 24 (no. 2, 2000): 367. See also Erik Swyngedouw, "Neither Global Nor Local: 'Glocalization' and the Politics of Scale," in *Spaces of Globalization: Reasserting the Power of the Local,* ed. Kevin R. Cox (New York: Guilford/Longman, 1997), 137–66.

4. Pierre Bourdieu, *Distinction: A Social Critique of the Judgment of Taste,* trans. Richard Nice (Cambridge, MA: Harvard University Press, 1984), 466–84.

5. See Engin F. Isin, *Cities without Citizens: The Modern City as a Corporation* (Montreal: Black Rose Books, 1992).

6. Engin F. Isin, "Governing Toronto without Government: Liberalism and Neo-Liberalism," *Studies in Political Economy* 56 (Summer 1998): 169–91; and Julie-Anne Boudreau, *The Megacity Saga: Democracy and Citizenship in This Global Age* (Montreal: Black Rose Books, 2000).

7. Canada, 2001 Census, "Table of Aboriginal Identity Population, Registered Indian Status and Area of Residence," Statistics Canada, Catalogue No. 97F0011XCB01003, January 21, 2003.

8. Canada, 2001 Census, "Table of Aboriginal Origin and Area of Residence," Statistics Canada, Catalogue No. 97F0011XCB01003, January 21, 2003.

9. J.J. Shute and D.B. Knight, "Obtaining an Understanding of Environmental Knowledge: Wendaban Stewardship Authority," *Canadian Geographer* 39 (no. 2, 1995): 101–11.

10. Patricia K. Wood, "Pressured from All Sides: The February 1913 Surrender of the Northeast Corner of the Tsuu T'ina Nation," *Journal of Historical Geography* 30 (no. 1, 2004): 113–30.

11. Patricia K. Wood, "A Road Runs through It: Aboriginal Citizenship at the Edges of Urban Development," *Citizenship Studies* 7 (December 2003): 371–78.

12. Daniel Francis, *The Imaginary Indian: The Image of the Indian in Canadian Culture* (Vancouver: University of British Columbia Press, 1992).

13. Ralph Klein, interview with author, Calgary, Alberta, June 21, 2002.

CHAPTER 17

The Land Remembers the People, the People Remember the Land: American Indian History as a Continuing Story

PETER IVERSON

IN THE AUTUMN of 1967 when my graduate study at the University of Wisconsin began, the field of twentieth-century American Indian history did not really exist. Scholars examined federal policies, and popular writers kept going over the minute details of Custer's final moments on the Little Bighorn. Perhaps they thought if they persisted in this preoccupation that eventually Custer would somehow reappear. The editor of the *Journal of American History* dismissed Indian history as "the subfield of another subfield (the history of the American West)," and most observers ignored what they termed "prehistory," or any developments before Europeans came to North America. Historians generally portrayed Native peoples as tragic but inevitable victims, with *Bury My Heart at Wounded Knee* exemplifying this perspective. After 1890, the year the frontier supposedly came to a close and the year of the terrible massacre at Wounded Knee, Indians usually became invisible in regional and national contexts.[1]

Because scholars saw "Indian history" as a subset of the history of the westward movement, "Indian history" largely consisted of studying how "they" interacted with "us." We thus learned of "good Indians" who helped whites (e.g., Sacajawea assisting Lewis and Clark or the Crow scouts for George Armstrong Custer) or of "bad Indians" who did not (e.g., those who brought Custer's career to an abrupt close). Native communities, such as the Hualapais who did not fit neatly into this pattern, usually disappeared.[2]

However, a series of events in the late 1960s and early 1970s started to focus public attention on American Indians. Native protestors occupied Alcatraz,

Indian Country Today: The Navajo Reservation

Wounded Knee, and federal offices in Washington, DC. N. Scott Momaday received the Pulitzer Prize for a novel set long after 1890; Vine Deloria, Jr., informed the American public that Custer had died for their sins. Indigenous communities began to establish their own schools, elect new leaders, and build toward the future. These developments stunned a lot of Americans who had been hearing for generations that Native peoples were about to vanish.[3]

Most scholars teaching and writing American Indian history remained unaffected by the turbulent present. They were historians, after all, unconcerned about the turbid and decidedly messy world of today. I remember serving as a teaching assistant for Robert Berkhofer's American Indian history class at the University of Wisconsin in the spring semester of 1973. The occupation of the village at Wounded Knee captured the interest of students in the class. A clamor arose to change the syllabus to spend less time on Red Cloud and more time on Russell Means. Berkhofer proved unmoved by the uproar. "Go talk to Iverson," he counseled. "He has an interest in current events."

WRITING MUDDLED AND STATIC INDIGENOUS HISTORIES

With some noteworthy exceptions, historians accepted assumptions that limited what they could see and what they could say. This approach resembled that of Senator Albert Beveridge of Indiana, the chairman of the U.S. Senate Committee on the Territories in the early 1900s. Traveling west by train in 1902, ostensibly to determine whether the territories of Arizona and New Mexico were worthy of statehood, Beveridge and his associates seemed to have answered the question before they made the journey. They rarely left the security of their known environment, choosing to remain most of the time on the train rather than disembarking and actually talking with local residents who wanted to correct the visitors' mistaken assumptions about the area's past, present, and future. Flagstaff, Arizona's newspaper, the *Coconino Sun,* poetically complained:

> Out in the West, the wild, wild West,
> The private car of the Senators flew
> And the farther they went the thicker the dust
> On the polished pane of the window grew.
> "I'll polish it off," said the Porter man.
> Said the Dignified Senators, "Nay, let it be.
> If the glass were clear and the glass were clean,
> There are many things which we might see."[4]

Most students of the Indian past, not unlike Senator Beveridge's entourage, seemed equally reluctant to abandon comfortable surroundings and conclusions. They generally adhered to approaches that also limited what they might see. These tendencies may be summed up in a list called "Ten Commandments for Unsatisfying American Indian Histories":

1. Do not visit the people or visit their land. Remaining in an air-conditioned library affords one a proper detachment.
2. Do not employ traditional Native accounts. If they are not written, you cannot rely on them.
3. Do not consider developments after 1890. Leave such recent developments to journalists.
4. Do not portray Indians as adaptive, continuing peoples. The best days of Indian life came before 1900.
5. Do not acknowledge the central role played by women in Native societies. Only talk about women when an individual is blessed with a catchy name like Mankiller.

6. Do not pay any attention to Indians who live outside of the West. These are people who think they are Indians, but really are not.

7. Do not recognize Indians as "pioneers" or "settlers." All of the great tribes were nomadic.

8. Do not emphasize the importance Native peoples give to doing something well. This is just a myth created to make Indians look better in retrospect.

9. Do not share the results of your work with Indian nations. They won't be interested in it anyway.

10. Do not encourage Native students to pursue a PhD. If they show potential for graduate study, send them to law school.

These stipulations obviously reinforced each other. Most scholars emphasized federal policy rather than providing what Berkhofer termed "Indian-centered" history.[5] Federal policy, of course, did matter and needed to be included in any overall analysis. But in making it one's primary or exclusive focus, one ran the risk of making federal officials the actors and Native peoples the acted upon. In the same sense, one was more likely to term the first non-Indians to come to an area as "pioneers" or "settlers," with all the attendant privileges those terms implied, rather than appreciating the Indians as the true pioneers and the original settlers. Doing research in federal archives often yielded crucial information. But if one only relied on archival sources, one rarely heard the voices of people who did not speak English or who used nonwritten means to advance their views. Moreover, if one did not go to the land the people treasured, one tended not to appreciate how certain landmarks—mountains, lakes, canyons, trees, and other formations—possessed cultural significance. The written record tended to discount the status of women within Native societies. Historians felt uncomfortable dealing with the recent past. The neglect of this era promoted the misconception that Indian societies were on the verge of disappearance. Indian communities became recognized as fragile entities with problematic futures.

Historians who brought the story up to the present were greeted with an attitude that combined discomfort with disdain. Most scholars felt absolutely no obligation to seek approval for their research from Native communities. They could not imagine letting these entities know what they had found out about them, even though they profited professionally from these investigations. Most historians did not honor the old Indian values of reciprocity and generosity. They believed they had no responsibility to inspire and prepare Indian historians.

WRITING CRISP AND DYNAMIC INDIGENOUS HISTORIES

I knew students of the Native American past had the opportunity to tell a different kind of story. My grandfather had taught in Indian schools in Kansas, Michigan, New Mexico, and Arizona. His stories and those of his daughters, including my mother, informed me in particular about Navajos (or Diné, as they called themselves in their own language) making their own history and continuing on their own land. In 1969, I had the great good fortune of being offered the opportunity to teach at a college Navajos had just started. My years in Diné Bikéyah—the Navajos' country—added to the foundation family stories had furnished. I realized we needed new histories, ones that emphasized indigenous success rather than aboriginal failure. We needed accounts that did not deny racism or discrimination but attested to the ability of Indian nations to hold on to portions of their land, develop viable economies, create viable communities, educate their children in an appropriate way, affirm their rights, govern themselves, and find ways to maintain their heritage while forging a brighter future.

There is no better example of these elements than the Navajos, the largest American Indian community in North America, with a population of nearly 300,000, and with a land base about the size of West Virginia. They are, in Luci Tapahonso's words, a people who "believe in old values and new ideas."[6] Throughout time, the Navajos have demonstrated that it is from contact with others that cultural vitality is encouraged. At the same time, it is through continuing association with a particular place that identity is rooted. Thus, Navajo history does not start in Alaska or northwestern Canada or along the Rocky Mountains or in the Great Basin. Rather it begins in what we now call the Southwest. It begins with Changing Woman, the first cultural hero of the Diné, who helps bring the present Navajo world into being. It begins with other cultural heroes like the twins, Monster Slayer and Born of Water. It begins with sacred mountains. It begins here.

Historians are starting to figure it out. They are starting to understand that some approaches are not only more appropriate but also more accurate. These realizations may be summed up in ten more commandments that illustrate a better way to proceed:

1. Visit the land of the people. Try to understand why this particular place matters so much to members of a particular Indian nation.
2. Make the people themselves the center of your analysis rather than the actions of federal employees. Present Indians as active participants in their own story.
3. Seek the approval of the tribal council or some other appropriate entity to do one's research. Keep the people informed about your progress and

provide copies of your final reports or studies to people in the community.

4. Take full advantage of traditional stories and oral histories.

5. Honor the old values of reciprocity and generosity. Find an appropriate way to pay back individuals and the community for their assistance.

6. Emphasize that women are centrally important in Native societies. Recall the observation that "men are the jawbones of our communities but women are the backbones."

7. Avoid doing "no-fault" histories. There may be silences in our writing, but there are times when mistakes of misconduct must be analyzed.

8. Take advantage of available visual material to provide photographs, illustrations, and maps.

9. Recall that doing something well has always been important in Indian communities.

10. Encourage Native students to complete PhDs in history or related fields.

In *Diné: A History of the Navajos,* Monty Roessel and I have attempted to follow this second list. Roessel, a member of the Navajo Nation and an internationally known photographer, is an educator currently serving as executive director of the Rough Rock Community School. *Diné* is a broad, sweeping narrative history that emphasizes the past century and a half. It takes appropriate advantage of past scholarship, but it also is based on extensive new archival research, Navajo oral and written history, and firsthand observations. There are four major themes: defense and survival, adaptation and incorporation, expansion and prosperity, and identity and continuation. This book is graced by two stunning sixteen-page color photo essays by Monty that illustrate the importance of the land to the people and the central role of women in Navajo culture. The book demonstrates the importance of telling Indian history as a continuing story, even though most historians hesitate about analyzing the recent past.[7]

I can understand such hesitation. A generation ago I was invited to speak at a Native American Studies conference at Dartmouth College about the life and career of Navajo leader Peter MacDonald. No sooner had I accepted this flattering invitation than the trap closed. It turned out that MacDonald had agreed to serve as the keynote speaker at the conference, and he was, of course, looking forward to commenting on my presentation. Naturally, he thought what I praised demonstrated real insight and what I criticized revealed my lack of understanding, but he was glad to be present to set the record straight.[8]

Those historians who work on topics centered in the 1700s may not have such memorable experiences, but ultimately it didn't matter what era we described or which individuals we included. We had a responsibility to get it right. We also needed to present Indian history as a continuing story. Of *Diné*'s eight chapters, one covers the 1940s and 1950s, one extends until the early 1980s, and one takes the story of the Navajo Nation to the present.

NAVAJO RECENT HISTORY

Although analyzing the recent past has its complications, as noted, consideration of this period allows a fuller incorporation of Navajo voices and the employment of a wider array of visual material. It permits us to demonstrate and document that time-honored Navajo quality of adaptation. And it can give us the opportunity to reflect upon how Diné culture has often been strengthened through contact with outside people and forces rather than weakened by it. Contact with other peoples, then, did not automatically lead to doom and gloom, to decay and despair. Of course, it certainly provided its share of difficulties. Throughout Navajo history, the Diné have always been willing to add to or subtract from their cultural repertoire.

Older Navajos hold on to their sheep and goats not for economic gain but for social and cultural reasons. They still like to trade a sheep for firewood or to donate an animal to relatives for food at a healing ceremony. The sheep and the goats remind them of another time, ever more distant, when almost all Navajos owned livestock. The decline of livestock parallels the loss of the Navajo language. Few Diné children grow up with the sheep; few now speak the Navajo language. These transitions raise poignant questions about what it means to be Navajo in the twenty-first century.[9]

In part, it means an individual is likely to live in or near town. The past twenty years have witnessed a dramatic change in where Navajos live and where they work. This change has occurred for essentially the same reasons as elsewhere in the American West. Navajos are drawn to town because the economy today consists almost entirely of town-based wage work. If one lives in or near town, he or she can shop more easily at a Basha's supermarket or some other larger grocery store. One's son or daughter can attend a public school and participate more easily in basketball. And one has access to cable television, Burger King, and the latest lousy movie directed by John Woo.[10]

Living in town can mean that one lives within the boundaries of the reservation, in rapidly growing communities like Shiprock, Tuba City, Chinle, Fort Defiance, Kayenta, Window Rock, and Ganado. Or it may mean that one resides in a town that borders the reservation, such as Farmington, Gallup, Holbrook, Winslow, or Flagstaff. It also could mean that you have decided to live in cities more distant from the Navajo Nation. There are now sizable Navajo enclaves in Albuquerque, Phoenix, Tucson, Los Angeles, Denver, and Salt Lake City.

Anthropologists and sociologists have been writing about Navajo urbanization for decades. However, they have focused their studies almost exclusively on migration into major metropolitan areas. They have failed to appreciate that moving to border towns furnishes a kind of middle-ground compromise. Proximity offers more opportunities to return home to join other family members on weekends and for various special occasions. And not all familiar activities are lost in this transition. Reading the box scores of high school basketball games in Arizona reveals that when Window Rock plays Winslow, Winslow has a significant number of Navajo players. Such continuation generally goes unobserved by anthropologists and sociologists, who in the best social scientific tradition, prefer to stress dysfunction rather than success.[11]

Many Navajos will never reside away from the Navajo Nation. Through the last few decades, though, their degree of contact with off-reservation life has steadily increased. Shiprock, for example, is thirty miles from Farmington. Even in the 1950s, Navajos were making the journey into Farmington to use the clothes washers, buy groceries at a market, and check books out from the public library. Luci Tapahonso has described this kind of day. The younger children drew straws to determine who got to go, but her oldest brother "always went because he drove," another brother "went because he helped carry laundry," her father went "because he was the father," and her mother went "because she had the money and knew where to go and what to buy." When they left Farmington and headed home to Shiprock, she recalls, "we talked about who we saw, what we should have bought instead of what we did buy (maybe we could exchange it next time), then the talking would slow down and by the time we reached the Blue Window gas station, everyone but" her "father was sleepy." He would begin to sing in Navajo and her mother would ask him if he knew a certain song and she would sing a little of it and her dad "would catch it and finish the song" as Luci and her siblings listened, before they drifted off to sleep.[12]

Going to Farmington did not always mean sweetness and light. Farmington High School's athletic teams are called the Scorpions, and Navajo visitors did worry about getting stung. One of the points of tension involved car and truck dealerships. Navajo customers often were persuaded to buy vehicles of somewhat indefinite vintage and pay exorbitant interest rates in the process. Only the establishment of a legal services program in the late 1960s began to curb this form of exploitation. Attorneys employed by Navajo Legal Services established offices in Chinle, Crownpoint, Shiprock, Tuba City, and Window Rock, and tackled such matters as sales contracts, grazing rights, misdemeanors, and pawns. In 1972, representatives from the Federal Trade Commission held hearings about trader practices. Trader Jay Foutz labeled these proceedings a "circus in a circuit tent" and dismissed them as a "total farce."[13] Nevertheless, the new regulations that emerged could not be shrugged off so easily. They essentially brought to an end the old practice of pawning on the reservation. Not unlike rural non-Indians who began to drive past mom-and-pop grocery stores and make longer trips to buy at large chain establishments like Safeway or Wal-Mart, Navajos now had more choices on where they did business. The end result found more and more trading posts going out of business, an outcome as predictable as the demise of the mom-and-pop stores elsewhere.

An Arizona-based supermarket chain, Basha's, built new grocery stores in Chinle, Tuba City, and Window Rock that employed many Navajos and offered some traditional food items. Smaller towns were left with characterless Thriftway "convenience" stores that offered that familiar one-two combination: reduced selection accompanied by higher prices. Thriftway's idea of a good pictorial was Andrew Jackson on a twenty-dollar bill. Operators of these enterprises had as much interest in weaving as the Diné had in learning Finnish.

Urbanization did provide the short list of Navajo entrepreneurs with new opportunities. Richard Mike opened his first Burger King franchise in Kayenta in 1988. In 1992, he opened a second franchise in Chinle, and in 1997 a third in Shiprock. He prefers to hire Navajo women as managers because they "are strong and make the tough decisions." The Shiprock franchise was facilitated by an $870,000 guaranteed loan through the Rural Business–Cooperative Services Program. The franchise created forty new jobs. At the grand opening of Shiprock Burger King, Navajo Nation president Albert Hale stated that economic development on the Navajo Nation "hasn't progressed because of the tremendous bureaucracy we've created." Borrowing a line from Vine Deloria, Jr., Hale blamed "white tape" for much of the problem.[14]

Observers continue to bemoan the outflow of the Navajo dollar off the reservation. The demise of most trading posts decreases the amount of money brought in by weaving and silversmithing, but the Crownpoint rug auction and destinations such as Canyon de Chelly and Monument Valley do bring in some money. Navajos are starting to get involved in the tourist business, either through building places to stay and eat—Richard Mike's Hampton Inn in Kayenta is a recent case in point—or through guiding tourists to scenic spots. Will Tsosie has even introduced a hogan-based bed-and-breakfast operation. Tourist behavior continues to baffle most Diné. They don't understand why visiting Anglo men would not wear a hat when they have little hair on top of their head or why they would decide to wear shorts. They cannot comprehend why these people would insist on driving hours out of their way to visit the Four Corners monument (where the states of Arizona, New Mexico, Utah, and Colorado come together) in order to place their left leg in Arizona, right leg in New Mexico, left arm in Utah, and right arm in Colorado.[15]

For a long time Navajos resisted the siren song of gaming, but the revenues brought in through this means eventually proved too much to resist. In January 2003, the Navajos signed a compact with the state of Arizona that will enable the Diné to build casinos. There is little doubt such enterprises will prove to be enormously lucrative, but their emergence will be accompanied by much debate about location. One can envision the red cliffs of Lukachukai and in the foreground a hotel in the shape of a pyramid with a sphinx in front of it and a green laser shooting miles in the air. The Lukachukai Luxor?

On-reservation urbanization has been accelerated by the essential demise of the old economic and social order, centered on livestock raising. As noted earlier, the decline in this traditional way of life has truly been precipitous. Some Navajos remain on the land, but their numbers appear to be shrinking with each passing year, and a major percentage of those who do remain are elderly. There is more than an economic price associated with this transition. Few Navajo children now have the opportunity to learn key social and cultural lessons from the land. They are much more likely to watch television and to speak English as a first language. In *A Weave of Time,* a documentary film that looks at a Navajo family and weaving through time, one of the most poignant moments comes when a grandfather, who speaks no English, comments about his inability to communicate with his grandchildren. "I live in silence," he sadly, softly murmurs, his face unable to mask his pain.[16]

On the other hand, more Navajo students now enroll in colleges or universities, speaking English as a first language. In part because of greater facility with the English language, in part because of greater familiarity with the larger society, Navajo students generally are doing better at places like Arizona State University, where today approximately seven hundred of them enroll. Former Navajo Nation president, Peterson Zah, has served for a number of years as special advisor to the president of Arizona State University in regard to Indian concerns. He has also given cogent advice to the admissions office. It is not accidental that Arizona State University's Native enrollment has essentially doubled in the last ten years.[17]

Difficulties remain for Navajo university students. Preparation at Navajo Nation high schools remains inadequate. Although more financial aid is possible, financial difficulties persist. Some university instructors, on the other hand, have gone out of their way to provide relevant and supportive classes. Professor Lynn Nelson has offered special sections of first-year English classes to Navajo and other Indian students. The positive experience that Navajo students have in his class sometimes makes all the difference in encouraging them to remain in school.

When we ponder contemporary Navajo identity, language, kinship obligation, and participation in organizations, all are important. Since the language has always been an important marker of the boundaries of Navajo identity, its future is clearly vitally important. There are intriguing examples of this transition. At the Navajos' own radio station, KTNN, for example, the arrival of a new non-Navajo operations manager, Scott Scarsborough, in late 1996 prompted orders for on-air personalities to reduce their "chit-chat" in the Navajo language. Such an edict prompted several staff members to quit. *Diné bizaad* (Navajo language) continues to be heard on KTNN, but an increasingly smaller percentage of the listening audience under the age of thirty can understand it.[18]

Kinship obligations still matter to many young Navajos. Organizations like the Native American Church continue to command the attention and loyalties of many individuals. On the other hand, there are danger signs about the social fabric that are painfully evident in the growth of gang activity in some Navajo towns and an increase in family violence and violence directed toward the Navajo police.

The publication of books relating to Navajo history and culture by the Diné College Press, the University of New Mexico Press, and other publishers, the emphasis on Navajo studies at schools like Rough Rock, the writings in Navajo by Rex Lee Jim and other poets, however, provide more encouraging signs. Navajos have a clear sense of themselves as distinct entities and keen interest in their remarkable past. The stories continue to be told.

CONCLUSION

Many Navajos have gained a university education or training in some vocational-technical area and have gone on to live well outside the boundaries of the Navajo Nation. But Diné Bikéyah remains, and whenever possible most Navajos decide that they want to return to it. The anthropologist Edward Spicer concluded that Navajos and other Indians differed from most other populations in how they see and feel about the land. Rather than perceiving the land in terms of utility and power—a secular, human perspective—Navajos have been more likely to have as part of their identity what he termed "the symbol of roots in the land—supernaturally sanctioned ancient roots regarded as unchangeable."[19]

It is that land and all that accompanies it that provides the real key to the Navajo Nation in this new century. This will always be their center of the world. The sacred mountains, Tapahonso declares, were placed there for us. Accompanying the land are the people who have gone before, are the stories and the teachings, are the memories that all speak to identity, and, indeed, destiny. Northern Arizona University faculty member Evangeline Parsons Yazzie arranged in 1998 for an original copy of the Navajo Treaty of 1868, housed in Washington, DC, in the National Archives, to be put on display for a year in Flagstaff, and she spoke of the Treaty missing the people.[20]

And the land remembers; the land knows, the Diné believe, who is supposed to occupy this particular space. The obligation to and responsibility for the land continues. More Navajos now wait for stoplights in Chinle than herd sheep outside of Chilchinbeto. But the land and sky remain to call the people home. "I have lost my way many times in this world," poet Joy Harjo says, "only to return to these rounded, shimmering hills. . . ." "Stories are our wealth," she emphasizes. "Winter nights we tell them over and over." Harjo fully appreciates that "it is an honor to walk where all around me stands an earth house made of scarlet, of jet, of ochre, of white shell." "Anything that matters is here," she believes. "Anything that will continue to matter in the next several thousand years will continue to be here."[21]

As long as the land remembers the people, as long as the people remember the land, there will be Navajos. There will be Diné.

NOTES

Acknowledgments: I wish to acknowledge my many Navajo and American Indian teachers, the memory of D'Arcy McNickle, Robert Thomas, and Vine Deloria, Jr., and the contributions of Myla Vicenti Carpio, Jane Hafen, Susan Miller, and Kaaren Olsen to the "Reconfigurations of Native North America" conference and this chapter.

1. For a more extensive discussion of these themes, see Peter Iverson, "The Road to Reappearance: Indian History Since 1890," *Montana: The Magazine of Western History* 51 (Winter 2000), 73–75.

2. See D'Arcy McNickle, *Native American Tribalism: Indian Survivals and Renewals* (New York: Oxford University Press, 1974), for a related discussion.

3. See N. Scott Momaday, *House Made of Dawn* (New York: Harper & Row, 1968); and Vine Deloria, Jr., *Custer Died for Your Sins: An Indian Manifesto* (New York: Macmillan, 1969).

4. Karen Underhill Mangelsdorft, "The Beveridge Visit to Arizona in 1902," *Journal of Arizona History* 28 (Autumn 1987): 250.

5. Robert F. Berkhofer, Jr., "The Political Context of a New Indian History," *Pacific Historical Review* 40 (August 1971): 357–82; Luci Tapahonso, "They Were Here for Us," in Tapahonso, *Blue Horses Rush In: Poems & Stories* (Tucson: University of Arizona Press, 1997), 39.

6. Tapahonso, "They Were Here for Us," 39.

7. See Peter Iverson, *Diné: A History of the Navajos* (Albuquerque: University of New Mexico Press, 2002).

8. This event is discussed in greater detail in Peter Iverson, "I May Connect Time," in *The American Indian and the Problem of History*, ed. Calvin Martin (New York: Oxford University Press, 1987), 141–42.

9. See Navajo journalist Betty Reid's essay about her mother and aunt and their livestock, in "Returning to the Flock," *Arizona Republic*, May 9, 1999.

10. Woo produced *The Windtalkers*, a melodramatic film loosely based on the story of Navajo codetalkers.

11. See, for example, several chapters in Jack O. Waddell and O. Michael Watson, eds., *The American Indian in Urban Society* (Boston: Little, Brown, and Company, 1971).

12. Luci Tapahonso, "It Was a Special Treat," *Saanii Dahataal/The Women Are Singing: Poems & Stories* (Tucson: University of Arizona Press, 1995), 15–16.

13. Foutz is quoted in Willow Roberts Powers, *Navajo Trading: The End of an Era* (Albuquerque: University of New Mexico, 2001).

14. Iverson, "The Navajo Nation in the 21st Century," presentation at 11th Annual Navajo Studies Conference, Window Rock, AZ, October 21–24, 1998.

15. Iverson, *Diné,* 223–25.

16. *A Weave of Time* (1987) tells the story of the Burnsides/Myers family of Pine Springs and includes film footage taken by anthropologist John Adair in the late 1930s and the early 1940s.

17. Navajo enrollment and retention have also grown substantially at other area colleges and universities.

18. Iverson, "The Navajo Nation."

19. Edward H. Spicer, "Plural Society in the Southwest," in *Plural Society in the Southwest,* ed. Spicer and Raymond H. Thompson (Albuquerque: University of New Mexico Press, 1975), 25.

20. Iverson, *Diné,* 323.

21. Joy Harjo, *Secrets from the Center of the World* (Tucson: University of Arizona Press, 1989), 24, 32, 52, 60.

Beginnings

KURT E. KINBACHER

Modern technology and the astounding tasks that gadgets can perform have
effectively blinded us to the intelligence of our ancestors. We've become arrogant as a
society and as a nation. And if we look with disdain on one aspect of the past, we
have a strong tendency to assume that our ancestors were somehow lacking across the
board. We then characterize everything about the past as "quaint" or "archaic," and
we forget the value and power of wisdom. Of all the mistakes,
that is arguably the worst.[1]

JOSEPH M. MARSHALL, III, Sicangu/Oglala Lakota

The day will soon come when First Nations people and whites will sit together in
the greatest potlach of all. They will sing about the wonderful world
they will be leaving their children.[2]

ERNIE CREY, Cheam Band of the Sto:lo Nation

INDIGENOUS NORTH AMERICA, when reconfigured, is an exploration of Native peoples' pasts, presents, and futures. These are not necessarily separate entities, as most American Indians and First Nations conceive of time as a circular process rather than a linear one. Such thought patterns and accompanying worldviews encourage traditions and behaviors to be reimagined and reinvented to meet the needs of evolving societies. They also allow core values—including generosity and strong focuses on family and community—to be preserved and revitalized. In the concluding chapter of this volume, Peter Iverson suggests that Navajos "believe in old values and new ideas." Certainly many other nations share these expectations.

Realizing that reconfiguring Native North America will be an ongoing task with wide-ranging implications, the scholars who contributed to this volume have taken great care to present works that favor Native voices and sensibilities.

Although divided into five sections—comparative historical and cultural perspectives, the literary indigenous voice, challenges past and present, nation and identity, and the people—for convenience, their chapters all celebrate the sophistication and complexities of indigenous cultures. These cultures remain vital on reservations and reserves as well as in urban areas scattered across the continent. Indeed, since World War II, Native peoples have established dynamic communities in cities of all sizes; and at the dawn of the twenty-first century the majority of Native Americans and First Nations peoples congregate in relatively new communities. Significantly, their urban enclaves serve not only as outlets for growing populations but as additional repositories of tradition and centers of cultural revitalization. Consequently, this collection begins to accomplish its stated task, but it is by no means the last word on any of the subjects it addresses.

Comparative discussions are powerful tools; the works of John Wunder, David Harding, and Riku Hämäläinen help illustrate the amazing diversity of indigenous peoples in North America and beyond. These narratives of historical and cultural perspectives cross social and ethnic boundaries, international borders, and temporal distances. They also explore unique complexities that emerge as indigenous and mainstream societies interact. Ultimately, for Native peoples, reinvention and reexamination never happen the same way twice. This is true when examining treaty making, economic development and the quest for local control of resources, or rituals that have long-standing tribal histories.

John Wunder traces the development of treaty making and illustrates a transported Western European bias for linear movement. Early agreements with indigenous peoples—often promises of perpetual friendship—started with notions that equality was a possibility. They soon evolved to reflect growing power disparities that ultimately curtailed Native practices. Finally, they became tools of full-scale colonization, and, as power imbalances became severe, treaty making ended altogether. Significantly, colonizers tended not to honor the terms they dictated while the colonized generally did.

The terms of the treaties, however, remained valid to Native peoples, as words spoken and written in circular time rarely lose their meanings. As colonized peoples sought to reclaim their cultures and national agendas in the twentieth century, treaties maintained long-lasting ramifications. Indeed, an important tool of modern revitalization efforts includes legal efforts to force colonizers to accept the terms they once dictated. Still, mainstream government structures deeply influence Native communities, and they must often wade through layers of red tape as they work to move their peoples forward.

Rather than discussing treaty making, David Harding examines resource use and compares the consequences of Canadian and American energy policies on large Native nations. He suggests that conflict over land use will necessarily exist as "dominant political systems" do not share the same values regarding land use as

Native peoples. Living in places that colonizers often deemed undesirable in the nineteenth and early twentieth centuries, Navajo coal and uranium deposits and Eastern Cree water power capabilities drew enormous attention from their respective federal, state, and provincial governments after World War II.

While tapping these resources might benefit Indians and First Peoples economically, their use raises important questions of sovereignty. Ultimately, Harding outlines many of the variances of the modern self-determination process. Navajos, for instance, not only negotiate with the federal government, they also contend with legal claims to the resources from the neighboring Hopi nation. Crees confront both the Canadian national government as well as a distinct Québeçois agenda that insists resource development aids their own quest for self-determination.

Diversity issues, of course, are not new in Native North America, and Hämäläinen's analysis of bear ceremonialism demonstrates that even shared events take on culturally specific meanings. Ritual constructions among Lakotas, Eastern Crees, and beyond necessarily have some similarities, as the bear is a significant presence wherever it is found. In every case, Native constructions of nature place humans and other animals on a more inclusive plane than the European-based cultures that currently dominate the continent. Differences aside, Native economies and experiences dictate a collective understanding of bears and all other creatures.

For many in the mainstream, first contact with Native worldviews comes through the literary indigenous voice. Mark Shackleton, P. Jane Hafen, and Patrice Hollrah demonstrate that the written word is an effective medium both to explain culture to a broad audience and to transmit important values to new generations of Native peoples. This genre has also proven quite popular in the marketplace. A search of "Native American literature" in December 2007 on Amazon.com—a large online bookseller—yielded 4,593 books for sale on the subject. A search for "Native American fiction" yielded 2,642 results. Some are penned by members of indigenous nations, but the majority of these entries were likely written by Americans and Canadians of European stock. Significantly, many authors and readers are drawn to Native images and ideas, but they often fail to recognize their meanings within indigenous societies.

Shackleton, in his discussion of Coyote, confronts the problematic nature of appropriating Native themes. In indigenous space, Coyote is often a complicated trickster who acts for a myriad of reasons. Even when comical, however, he works to "consolidate and define the wisdom and values of the people." Because mainstream appropriators tend to be insensitive to Native values in both form and intent, Coyote is not generally depicted as a culture hero; ultimately, he is incomplete, a mere villain or clown without knowledge or wisdom. Appropriation of Native icons produces additional cultural friction as differing worldviews create differing expectations. In the Native cosmos, characters and art objects in general are communally owned property that is not available on any market. In mainstream views, art is the expression of individuals and can be used for personal profit. While many non-Native writers attempt carefully and respectfully to include Native ideas in their works, appropriation issues make this practice suspect to many.

Not immune from criticism, Native authors, such as Sherman Alexie (Spokane), often challenge mainstream misconceptions about indigenous practices. They also tell intriguing stories rich with meaning. Hollrah suggests that Alexie examines and critiques Native communities in order to bring attention to values that have their origins within colonizing cultures. He is especially concerned with the Spokane nation's acculturation of American sexism, misogyny, and homophobia. These ideas, he avers, did not exist prior to Contact. Gender parity—the traditional norm—was devastated by mainstream patriarchal ideas, and women's roles as creators have been consistently debased and devalued. To battle this tendency, Alexie constructs strong female and homosexual characters as an act of cultural resistance. His ultimate goal is the revitalization of traditional tribal gender roles.

Literature also lets Indian and First Nations peoples address other pressing problems within and beyond their communities. Hafen, in examining the work of Wendy Rose, suggests that literature allows individuals to explore their own "Indianness." Indeed, in a mobile, urbanizing world, identity issues are increasingly important; and due to the complexities of being modern, Rose writes about her own Hopi identity from the "outside in." While her father was Hopi, she has no standing in matrilineal Hopi society as her mother is Scots-Irish and Miwok. Despite her bloodline, she is not recognized as Indian in the mainstream as she carries no blood quantum card.

Significantly, what it means to be a tribal member in the United States is often influenced by outsiders. In Native culturescapes, identity depended on kinship. Individuals belonged first to a family, then to a clan, and then to a nation. Although blood descent may have been desirable, most nations had mechanisms to adopt outsiders into their fold both as individuals and as groups.[3] Tribal membership depended largely on a willingness to practice appropriate cultural behaviors. This sort of self-definition began to dissipate in the United States as Indians reluctantly accepted their status as members of a "domestic dependent nation."[4] During the Indian New Deal, being Indian was refined to include persons of "Indian descent" recognized by a tribe, descendants of an Indian living on a "reservation," or individuals with 50 percent or more Indian blood.[5] From this point on, blood quantum began to work its way into what it meant to be Native, and nations that drew up constitutions in compliance with the Indian Reorganization Act generally included some restrictions in this regard. While First Nations do not define membership by blood only, the complicated array of status and non-status designations makes identity an omnipresent issue for many groups and individuals.

Rose's personal struggle defining her Indianness is just one example of the types of issues that indigenous individuals and groups have faced since European contact. Indeed, Native peoples have confronted and continue to confront a plethora of challenges past and present. Although they are never stagnant, cultures and traditions are continually reconfigured to improve and advance societies. For some nations, transformation is forced upon them. Others cautiously embrace changes including the Internet and Las Vegas–style casino gaming.

For Native peoples, however, the past is alive. By confronting it, they are often able to reclaim and reassert their own national agendas.

For their part, Canadian and American mainstreams have often missed out on many positive aspects of indigenous cultures. Despite some efforts at inclusion, exclusion and marginalization have been the norms. In this vein, Peter Messer and Susan Wunder examine the places of indigenous peoples in mainstream North America in the early 1800s and in the twenty-first century. Messer suggests that at the time of the American Revolution, the rhetoric of reform could have constructed a more inclusive republic. In doing so, the young United States could have atoned for the poor treatment of Native Americans during the colonial era. Instead, the emerging nation limited the scope of its citizenship, painted Indians as savages, and united around a sense of superiority.

Significantly, this decisive turning point and other major hallmarks in American and Canadian histories may or may not be studied by schoolchildren. It appears that new nationwide standards in social studies education work to limit discussions of inclusion and diversity. Susan Wunder documents this trend and suggests that school districts that provide the least amount of direction and specificity in their standards often have the greatest appreciation of cultural inclusion. Conversely, in-depth examination of American Indian and First Peoples histories are declining in the educational environments most concerned with training students to compete in a global economy. While Native nations may no longer be the "other" that defines limited inclusion, cultural diversity and standardization of curricula are most certainly at odds.

The dichotomy between Native ideas and mainstream ones, of course, is not new. Rani-Henrik Andersson avers that the 1890 massacre at Wounded Knee was largely the result of cultural apprehension and misunderstanding in the general American population, especially as Lakotas began practicing a "new" religion. Looking less at the viciousness of the massacre and more to its underlying causes, Andersson argues that Lakotas and Americans necessarily saw the ghost dance of 1890 through different cultural lenses. For Lakotas it was a hopeful religion that emerged as a combination of new ideas and age-old traditions. Mainstream America—already trained to disapprove of all things Native—reacted violently and self-righteously because they were miseducated, thinking that Lakota activities were both barbaric and dangerous.

While the mainstream is frequently not open and willing to understand or accept the Native presence in the body politic, American Indians and First Nations peoples are necessarily adapting to new educational needs and economic conditions. Ritva Levo-Henriksson and Miia Halme document these processes. Computers and cyberspace have remarkable potential to serve dispersed populations. In addition to bringing the outside world onto reservations and reserves, the Internet serves to reunite relatives in distant places. Consequently, as indigenous peoples urbanize, the Internet is a likely tool for addressing many needs. Hopefully, cultural preservation and revitalization will be served. Even traditionalists recognize the benefits of using new technologies as Native peoples often live in two worlds. Acceptance is of course not universal, but even among the famously conservative Hopis, new communication technology is beginning to find its place.

Perhaps even more controversial among some Native peoples, high-stakes gaming was another significant development that emerged in the late twentieth century. Halme argues that such ventures were established by asserting national sovereignty through treaty rights. For Miccosukees and other peoples, gaming serves as a major source of revenue and as a tonic to improve the impoverished conditions caused by confinement, isolation, and land loss. Nations that have implemented gambling have addressed housing and health service concerns, implemented many important tribal services, and, in many cases, provided per-annum payments as a profit-sharing incentive. At its best, Indian gaming encourages economic, political, and cultural revitalization—at least according to its proponents. While she does not address deep divisions in some nations on this subject, Halme suggests that armed with new gaming revenues and legal ability, indigenous peoples have the tools to fight against persistent colonialism.

This is a significant turn of events as Native voices often go unheard throughout much of North America. The Constitution of the United States, for instance, is largely silent about its indigenous population. Indians were omitted from population counts that determined congressional representation, an indication that they were initially barred from the polity. Additionally, for purposes of commercial regulation, they were denoted neither as "foreign Nations" nor as "States," but as a third entity whose status is undefined.[6] Finally, the Bill of Rights was silent on indigenes altogether, an omission that left Indians with little or no "protection from the powers of government."[7] Similarly, the Canadian Indian Act of 1876 recognized First Nations, but it is not any more inclusive. This law created reserves, but did not protect cultural practices. Indeed between 1880 and 1951, aboriginal religious services were illegal. Similarly, voting rights were denied in provincial and federal elections until the middle of the twentieth century.[8]

Despite these legal disadvantages, Native American and First Nations peoples continuously assess multiple meanings of nation and identity. Intriguingly, both concepts are constantly renegotiated; and although traditionalists closely guard nationhood and national identity, these are never stagnant constructions. In concert Sami Lakomäki, Susan Miller, Gerhard Ens, and Joe Sawchuk examine some of the complexities of being Shawnee, Seminole, and Metis.

Lakomäki suggests that "Indian"—or "First Nation"—had no particular meaning in indigenous space. Instead, ethnicity and nationality were specific. He demonstrates that between 1400 and 1800, groups such as Shawnees "amalgamate, disperse, alloy, or fall apart in different and complex ways." Although cultural change is constant, collisions with Eurasian peoples created an era of amazing transformation and reevaluation. Ultimately, among Shawnees contact tended to promote ethnic and political unification, although entire generations dispersed from traditional ranges and economies only to return when conditions warranted it.

Miller—who writes about her relatives and their diplomatic discourse at the dawn of Seminole confederation—likens Contact with the Earth colliding with a comet. This is an apt metaphor as age-old patterns of governance and economy disappeared, and portions of the nation were subjected to "genocidal" relocation policies. The most conservative Seminoles believed that the invasion of their homeland was punishment for failing to obey traditions. Ultimately, Contact forced Seminoles to dig up their weapons of war and turn their backs on peace. In the end, the people remained Seminole, but traditional culturescapes were forever lost.

Contact, however, sometimes created new peoples who in turn struggled and continue to struggle to find senses of nationhood. The development of Metis identities and their quest for recognition in Canada during the nineteenth and twentieth centuries bear witness to this process. Ens and Sawchuk examine two distinct populations of mixed-race peoples. The Red River Metis emerged around 1820 in an era when racial hybridization was still an accepted possibility in Canada. Their settlements of distinctive peoples were actually encouraged by the Hudson's Bay Company—this corporation governed Manitoba and much of Canada West until 1869 when Canada confederated. After Rupert's Land was ceded to Canada, these populations were expected to merge with the Anglo-Canadian mainstream. To ease the transition, old land claims were dissolved and populations dispersed throughout much of the western reaches of the country. Despite dispersal, deep knowledge and a connection to a historical Metis identity remained significant.

The scions of the Red River population are presently recognized by the Canadian government as First Nations peoples. Populations of mixed-race individuals in the rest of Canada did not have this historic land base to claim identity. Consequently, their attempts at gaining recognition in the 1960s and 1970s were more problematic. Metis was a term that evolved among Ontario peoples after "non-status Indian" and "half-breed" identities proved less than satisfactory. Ontario Metis as an identity had its ethnogenesis in the 1980s. From their political headquarters in Sault Ste. Marie, this relatively new identity serves the needs of modern populations still finding their place in Canadian history and law.

Significantly, long-recognized peoples in both Canada and the United States share many of the same identity, nationhood, and inclusion concerns. The volume's final section—The People—comprises chapters about two distantly related Athapaskan peoples by Patricia Burke Wood and Peter Iverson. The Tsuu T'inas comprise a small nation whose home reserve is situated uncomfortably close to sprawling metropolitan Calgary, Alberta. Nearly a thousand miles south, Dinés (Navajos) have a largely rural and remote reservation in the Four Corners region of the United States. While their physical and human geographies are distinct, both peoples face exclusion from mainstream economies, political systems, and—at least in the not-too-distant past—popular imagination and historiographies.

Wood suggests that despite tendencies to address indigenous peoples as part of a postcolonial world, Tsuu T'inas remain embroiled in a colonial system. To advance further would require intercultural relationships to be respectful, peaceful, cooperative, and collaborative. To date, this has not been the case, despite close proximity. With the exception of invitations to participate in the famed Calgary Stampede, local First Nations peoples are excluded from the city as a matter of policy. Tsuu T'inas, Wood argues, are more aware of their mainstream neighbors as they necessarily enter the metropolis as consumers and workers. Ultimately, they are still expected to enter the mainstream as assimilated individuals rather than unique cultural contributors.

Iverson echoes some of Wood's concerns, and he suggests that scholarly disciplines within the humanities can serve as tools to aid decolonization. Still, the field of history, for instance, has only recently evolved from being part of a colonial system. Prior to the 1970s, few writers examined Native perspectives and principles in their works, and some still maintain this old practice into the twenty-first century. Fortunately, more and more scholars are working to reconfigure their disciplines. Iverson suggests that one sure method to begin this task is to meet modern indigenous peoples as human beings—not just subjects—and attempt to learn as much about their worldviews as possible. This is not the easiest prescription for individuals mostly comfortable with archival research, but it still is valuable advice that a scholar has learned from long-standing ties with generations of Dinés.

For Native peoples, such prolonged contact and involvement are natural, as their relationships are durable across time. Scholars, on the other hand, often move on to other projects, and involvement in specific indigenous communities is usually transitory. Reconfiguring Native North America, therefore, is a complicated mission. Certainly the voices of indigenous scholars such as Susan Miller (Seminole), P. Jane Hafen (Taos Pueblo), and Joe Sawchuk (Metis) are significant as they already work from indigenous perspectives. They know that the history is never past, and—as Joseph Marshall suggests—wisdom has deep roots in the ages. Non-Native scholars writing from many different places and biases also have a role to play. In concert, reconfigured Native North America will—as Ernie Crey optimistically hopes—aid cultural understanding across borders real and imagined.

NOTES

1. Joseph M. Marshall III, *Walking with Grandfather: The Wisdom of Lakota Elders* (Boulder, CO: Sounds True, 2005), 6.

2. Ernie Crey, "The Children of Tomorrow's Great Potlach," in *In Celebration of Our Survival: The First Nations of British Columbia,* ed. Doreen Jenson and Cheryl Brooks (Vancouver: University of British Columbia Press, 1991), 150.

3. A. Irving Hallowell, "American Indians, White and Black: The Phenomenon of Transculturalization," *Current Anthropology* 4 (December 1963), 523, 527–28.

4. See David R. Edmunds, "Native American Voices: American Indian History, 1895–1995," *American Historical Review* 100 (June 1995), 733–34; Gary Clayton Anderson, *Kinsman of Another Kind: Dakota-White Relations in the Upper Mississippi Valley, 1650–1862* (Lincoln: University of Nebraska Press, 1984), ix–xi, 30.

5. William T. Hagen, "Full Blood, Mixed Blood, Generic, and Ersatz: The Problem of Indian Identity," *Arizona and the West* 27 (Winter 1985), 317.

6. See U.S. Constitution, Article I, sections 2 and 8.

7. John R. Wunder, *"Retained by the People": A History of American Indians and the Bill of Rights* (New York: Oxford University Press, 1994), 213.

8. Crey, "The Children of Tomorrow's Great Potlach," 150–51.

About the Authors

M ANY HAVE CONTRIBUTED essays and editing to this volume, and collectively they represent a diverse international contingent of scholars. The following includes, in alphabetical order, a compilation of brief biographical sketches of all who participated in the construction of *Reconfigurations of Native North America.*

RANI-HENRIK ANDERSSON holds a PhD from the University of Tampere (2003) and was a research scholar at the American Indian Studies Research Institute at Indiana University in 2004–2005. Currently he is working as an Academy of Finland postdoctoral fellow in the North American Studies Program at the University of Helsinki's Renvall Institute. His recent publications include *Wanagi Wachipi ki: The Ghost Dance among Lakota Indians in 1890: A Multidimensional Interpretation* (Tampere, Finland: University of Tampere Press, 2003); "The Ghost Dance and the Traditional Lakota Belief System," in *North American Indian Religions: Writings about Tradition, Change and Continuity among North American Indians,* ed. Riku Hämäläinen (Helsinki: SKS, 2004); and *The Lakota Ghost Dance of 1890* (Lincoln: University of Nebraska Press, 2008).

GERHARD J. ENS is associate professor of history and classics at the University of Alberta. His recent publications include *Homeland to Hinterland: The Changing Worlds of the Red River Metis in the Nineteenth Century* (Toronto: University of Toronto Press, 1996); *From Rupert's Land to Canada: Essays in Honour of John E. Foster* (Edmonton: University of Alberta Press, 2001); "Fatal Quarrels and Fur Trade Rivalries: A Year of Living Dangerously on the North Saskatchewan, 1806–07," in *Alberta Formed—Alberta Transformed, Alberta 2005 Centennial History Society,* edited by Michael Payne, Donald G. Wetherell, Catherine Cavanaugh (Edmonton: University of Alberta Press; Calgary, Alberta: University of Calgary Press, 2006); and *A Son of the*

Fur Trade: The Memoirs of Johnny Grant (Edmonton: University of Alberta Press, 2008).

P. JANE HAFEN (Taos Pueblo) is associate professor of English at the University of Nevada, Las Vegas. Her most recent publications include *Reading Louise Erdrich's* Love Medicine (Boise, ID: Boise State University, 2003), a volume of the Western Writers Series of Boise State University; editing *Dreams of Thunder: Stories, Poems and The Sundance Opera by Zitkala-Sa* (Lincoln: University of Nebraska Press, 2001); and co-editing, with Diane D. Quantic, *A Great Plains Reader* (Lincoln: University of Nebraska Press, 2003).

MIIA HALME is a research fellow at the Finnish Centre of Excellence in Global Governance. She holds a doctorate in social anthropology and an international law degree from the University of Helsinki. Her research interests include legal anthropology, human rights, legal theory, and Indian tribes in the American context.

RIKU HÄMÄLÄINEN, a coordinator in the Department of Comparative Religion at the University of Helsinki, is currently completing a doctoral dissertation on Plains Indian shields. He is a contributor to volume 16 of the Smithsonian Institution's *Handbook of North American Indians*. His recent publications include "A Forgotten Comanche Shield? Highlight of My Research Work," in *The People of the Buffalo 2: The Plains Indians of North America. The Silent Memorials: Artifacts as Cultural and Historical Documents* (Wyk auf Foehr: Tatanka Press, 2005); "Individualism and Collectivism in the Plains Indians' Visions and Visionary Art," in *Indian Stories, Indian Histories* (Torino: OTTO Editore, 2004); "Mató Tópe's Knife and Crazy Horse's Shield: The Use of Ethnographic Objects as Cultural Documents," in *The Challenges of Native American Studies: Essays in Celebrating the Twenty-fifth American Indian Workshop* (Leuven: Leuven University Press, 2004); and an edited book, *Indian Religions of North America: Essays on Traditions, Change, and Continuity* (Helsinki: SKS, 2004).

DAVID HARDING is lecturer at the Department of English and Institute of Language, Literature and Culture at Aarhus University, Aarhus, Denmark. His major research areas include American studies, Native American/First Nations studies, and the environment. He is currently focused on the field of eco-tourism.

PATRICE HOLLRAH is director of the Writing Center in the Department of English at the University of Nevada, Las Vegas. She has published essays on Native American literature in various journals, and is the author of *"The Old Lady Trill, the Victory Yell": The Power of Women in Native American Literature* (New York: Routledge, 2003).

PETER IVERSON is Regents' Professor of History at Arizona State University. He has published extensively on twentieth-century Native American history. His most recent books include *When Indians Became Cowboys: Native Peoples and Cattle Ranching in the American West* (Norman: University of Oklahoma Press, 1994); *Diné: A History of the Navajos* with photographs by Monty Roessel (Albuquerque: University of New Mexico Press, 2002); and *"For Our Navajo People": Diné Letters, Speeches and Petitions, 1900–1960* with photo editing by Monty Roessel (Albuquerque: University of New Mexico Press, 2002).

KURT E. KINBACHER earned his PhD in history at the University of Nebraska-Lincoln (2006), where he was a postdoctoral researcher. He is a history instructor at Spokane Falls Community College in Spokane, Washington. He is author of "Imagining Place: Nebraska Territory, 1854–1867," in *Regionalism and the Humanities,* ed. Timothy R. Mahoney and Wendy Katz (Lincoln: University of Nebraska Press, forthcoming). His manuscript, "Urban Villages and Local Identities: Germans from Russia, Omaha Indians, and Vietnamese in Lincoln, Nebraska," includes a discussion about the urbanization of Native Americans in the twentieth century.

SAMI LAKOMÄKI is a PhD student of cultural anthropology at the University of Oulu (Finland). He is also a member in the Finnish Graduate School of North and Latin American Studies. He co-edited with Matti Savolainen, *Kojootteja, Sulkapäähinetä, Uraanikaivoksia: Pohjois-Amerikan Intiaanien Kirjallisuuksia ja Kulttuureja* (Oulu: University of Oulu, 2002) and authored "Jumalan Leipää ja Mustakaapuja: Muutos ja Pysyvyys Shawnee-Intiaanien Uskonnossa 1700-Luvulla," in *Pohjois-Amerikan Intiaaniuskonnot: Kirjoituksia Perinteestä, Muutoksesta ja Jatkuvuudesta,* ed. Riku Hämäläinen (Helsinki: SKS, 2004). His dissertation research focuses on the Shawnees.

RITVA LEVO-HENRIKSSON is senior lecturer in the Department of Communication at the University of Helsinki. Interested in intercultural communication, her most recent publications include *Media and Ethnic Identity: Hopi Views on Media, Identity, and Communication* (New York: Routledge, 2007); and "Media as Constructor of Ethnic Minority Identity: A Native American Case Study," in *Community Media: International Perspectives,* ed. Linda K. Fuller (New York: Palgrave Macmillan, 2007). She has also examined culture and media relationships in the context of cross-cultural comparisons. Her publications in this area include *Eyes upon Wings: Culture in Finnish and U.S. Television News* (Helsinki: Finnish Broadcasting Company, 1994), "Television News as Cultural Products: The Cases of Finland and the United States," in *Civic Discourse: Intercultural, International, and Global Media,* ed. K.S. Sitaram and Michael Prosser (Norwood, NJ: Ablex, 1999); and *Archetype and Versions: TV Drama from America to Asia* (published in Finnish, with English summary) (Helsinki: Finnish Broadcasting Company, 1991).

PETER C. MESSER is associate professor of history at Mississippi State University.

He is author of the book, *Stories of Independence: Identity, Ideology, and History in Eighteenth-Century America* (DeKalb: Northern Illinois University Press, 2005), and is currently working on a manuscript entitled "Revolution by Committee: Law, Language, and Ritual in Revolutionary America."

SUSAN A. MILLER, a member of the Seminole Nation, is a historian and freelance writer living in Norman, Oklahoma. Her works include *Coacoochee's Bones* (Lawrence: University of Kansas Press, 2003) and "Seminoles and Africans under Seminole Law: Sources and Discourses of Tribal Sovereignty and 'Black Indian' Entitlement," *Wicazo Sa Review* (Spring 2005).

JOE SAWCHUK is professor and chair of the Department of Anthropology at Brandon University. His research focuses on Aboriginal activist organizations, including Metis in Canada and Chamorros in Guam. His recent publications include "The Metis in the 20th Century," in *Handbook of North American Indians,* Vol. 2, *Indians in Contemporary Society,* Garrick Bailey, vol. ed., W.C. Sturtevant, general ed. (Washington, DC: Smithsonian Institution, 2008); "Negotiating an Identity: Metis Political Organizations, the Canadian Government, and Competing Concepts of Aboriginality," *American Indian Quarterly* 25 (Winter 2001), 73–92; *The Dynamics of Native Politics: The Alberta Metis Experience* (Saskatoon, SK: Purich Publishing Co., 1998); and *The Metis of Manitoba: Reformulation of an Ethnic Identity* (New York: Peter Martin Associates, 1978).

MARK SHACKLETON is currently university lecturer in the English Department, University of Helsinki, and co-director of the University of Helsinki project, "Cross-Cultural Contacts: Diaspora Writing in English." He is the author of *Moving Outward: The Development of Charles Olson's Use of Myth* (English Department Studies, University of Helsinki, 1994), has co-edited *Migration, Preservation and Change* (Helsinki: Renvall Institute Publications, 1999) and *Roots and Renewals: Writings by Bicentennial Fulbright Professors* (Helsinki: Renvall Institute Publications, 2001), and edited *First and Other Nations* (Helsinki: Renvall Institute Publications, 2005), all three volumes relating to North American studies. His main field of publication is postcolonial writing and Native North American literature, including articles on Thomas Highway, Thomas King, Monique Mojica, Louise Erdrich, and Simon J. Ortiz. His most recent publication is the Canada section of the *Routledge Companion to Postcolonial Studies,* ed. John McLeod (New York and London: Routledge, 2007).

PATRICIA BURKE WOOD is associate professor of geography, and a faculty member of the City Institute at York University. Her research focuses on diversity, identity politics, and citizenship, particularly in cities. She does both contemporary and historical work, and conducts research primarily with immigrant groups and First Nations, with an emphasis on participatory, collaborative research practices. Tricia is the author of *Nationalism from the Margins* (Montreal: McGill-Queen's, 2002) and, with Engin F. Isin, *Citizenship and Identity* (Thousand Oaks, CA: Sage, 1999), and has also published in several journals, including *Citizenship Studies, Space and Polity,* and the *International Journal of Urban and Regional Research.*

JOHN R. WUNDER is professor of history and journalism at the University of Nebraska-Lincoln. His most recent publications on Native American history include *"Retained by the People": A History of American Indians and the Bill of Rights* (New York: Oxford University Press, 1994); *Native Americans and the Law: Contemporary and Historical Perspectives on American Indian Rights, Freedoms, and Sovereignty* (New York and London: Routledge, 1996 and 1999), 6 vols.; and "'Looking After the Country Properly': A Comparative History of Indigenous Peoples and Australian and American National Parks," *Indigenous Law Journal* (University of Toronto College of Law) 2 (Fall 2003), 1–42.

SUSAN A. WUNDER is associate professor in the Department of Teaching, Learning and Teacher Education at the University of Nebraska-Lincoln, where she is a secondary social studies educator. She is the coauthor of two texts that feature specific aspects of Native Nebraskan history and culture: *Journey Through Nebraska* (Lincoln: Nebraska Schools Instructional Materials Council, 1997) and *Nebraska Moments* (Lincoln: University of Nebraska Press, 2007).

Index

Abayaca, 228

Abeita, Lucy, 71

Aborigines (Australian), 13–16, 27n1, 96, 127, 131

Acomas, 83–84, 99

Adams, Hannah, 125–26, 137n37

agriculture, 58

Alabama, 183, 184, 186, 195, 209, 216

Alexie, Sherman, v, 73–74, 92, 102–08, 296

Alford, Thomas, 203, 204

Algonquian language, 203

allotment, 45, 144, 162, 172, 233n9

American Indian Movement, 187

American Revolution, 7, 111, 115–39, 216, 238, 297

Anishinaabes, 6 (*see also* Chippewas and Ojibwas)

Apaches, 89n36, 265

Apalachees, 196, 227, 229

Archibale, Adams, 243

Arctic, 28n8, 34, 112, 153

Arizona, 46, 89n36, 92, 97, 103, 112, 152, 184, 185, 186, 265, 281, 283, 286–89

Assiniboines, 60–63, 69n61, 99

Athapaskans, 56, 265, 300

Australia, 14, 27, 27–28n2

bears, 7, 12, 295

bear ceremonialism, v, 54–65

Belcourt, Tony, 259

Belknap, Jeremy, 117–26, 103–31, 133, 133n1, 135nn9–12, 137n, 138n

Bieder, Robert E., 238

Bill of Rights (U.S.), 298

Black Mesa, 43, 46–47, 50

Black Tail, Henry, 61, 62

Blackfoots, 57, 61, 68n45, 267, 274

Blackfeets, 55, 96

Bone Dance, 93, 101nn22–23

Bourassa, Robert, 35–37, 42–43, 51n17, 52n42

Bozeman Trail, 19–20

Brenner, Neil, 271

British Columbia, 26, 78–79, 113n1, 179, 182, 184, 185, 186, 188, 190n40, 191n52

British North America Act (1867), 21

Brown, Joseph Epes, 54, 66n4, 67n19, 149n15

Brulés, 16, 19, 29n21 (*see also* Sicangus)

buffalo, 64, 141–43, 245

Bull Head, 274

Bureau of Indian Affairs, 44, 45, 46, 47, 147, 155, 163, 170

Burkhofer, Robert, 280

Bury My Heart at Wounded Knee, 279

C-31s, 252, 256 (*see also* "No Status Indians")

Cairns, Alan, 269

Calgary, Alberta, 266, 274–77, 300

Calgary Industrial School, 275

California, 36, 92, 95, 97, 99, 160, 163, 171, 183, 184, 186

California Institute of Technology, 47

Canada, vi, 3, 6, 8n, 11, 12, 21, 25, 26, 27, 29n26, 30n45, 32, 34, 36, 37, 38, 39, 40, 43, 49, 50, 52n46, 111, 112, 153, 178, 179, 180, 181, 188, 189n1, 196, 217, 236, 237, 239, 240, 241,242, 244, 250n27, 252,

253, 254, 255, 258, 263, 269, 270, 278n7, 283, 299, 300

Canadian Charter of Rights and Freedoms, 271

Canadian Parliament, 8n1, 21, 196, 242, 243, 250n31, 256

Carter, Jimmy, 163

casinos, 99, 160, 161, 162, 164, 166, 167, 168, 171, 174n18, 287, 297

Castellano, Marlene Brant, 193, 197n1

Catawbas, 200, 209, 214

Catlin, George, 60, 62, 68n37, 69n52, 70n72

Chalaakaathas, 203, 211, 213, 221n43

Cherokees, 23, 30n37, 75

Cherokee Nation v. State of Georgia (1831), 30n37

Chickasaw Nation v. United States (2001), 171

Chief Joseph, 3, 8n2, 16, 28n9

Chippewas, 3 (see also Anishinaabes and Ojibwas)

Choctaws, 200

Civil War, 130

Clinton, William, 108n21, 163, 165, 170, 173–74n16

Coal mining, 12, 43, 50

Coeur d'Alenes, 103, 106

Collier, John, 45

colonial(ism), 11, 40, 85, 95, 98, 99, 273, 298

Conestogas, 209–11

Conoys, 209

Coon Come, Matthew, 37–38, 40

Columbia Plateau, 63

Columbus, Christopher, 96, 119

Congress, U.S., 18, 19, 21, 44, 47, 49, 112, 140, 143, 144, 165, 169, 170, 174n30, 176n48

Constitution, Canada, 179, 253, 260n1, 260–61n11, 271

Constitution, Hopi, 47

constitutions, Indian Reorganization Act, 296

Constitution, U.S., 3, 123, 127, 132, 173n, 179, 298, 301n6

Constitution Act, Canada (1982), 38, 255

Council of Ministers of Education, Canada, 179, 189n1

coyote, v, 73, 75–87, 295

Crazy Horse, 146, 151n28

Crees, v, vii, 3, 11, 12, 21, 22, 32–43, 48, 50, 55–60, 63, 79, 88–89n20, 258, 295

Cree language, 33

Creeks, 98, 200, 216, 219n15

Creek Confederacy, 196, 209

Crey, Ernie, 293

Crow Dog, In re (1883), 169–70

cultural appropriation, 73–74, 75–77, 79–80, 86, 87n3, 88n5, 94, 295–96

cultural imperialism, 76

cultural re-appropriation, 86

cultural survival, 79, 82

Cultural Survival, 154

Custer, George Armstrong, 279–80

Cyberspace, 153, 154, 298

Cypress, Billy, 164, 174n24, 176n47

Dakotas, 19, 25, 61, 147n5, 169

Dances with Wolves, 76, 173n11

Dawes, Henry, 143–44

Dawes Act (General Allotment Act), 162, 163

Delawares, 200, 203, 209, 211

Deloria, Vine, Jr., 193, 197n2, 280, 287, 290, 290n3

Denig, Edwin Thompson, 56, 60

Department of Education, U.S., 179, 180, 181

diplomacy, 19, 21, 146, 225, 226, 228, 229

domestic dependent nations, 50, 296

Drooker, Penelope, 205, 206, 207

Eagle Shield, 62

Emaltha, Holata, 227, 233n14

Emaltha, Charley, 196, 227, 229, 230, 231

ethnogenesis, 199, 200, 201, 204, 205, 299

Everglades, 163–66, 168

Finland, xii, 15, 67n21, 158n1

First Nations, vii, xi, 7, 8n1, 11, 12n1, 13, 22, 24, 25, 26, 29n27, 35, 38, 55, 73, 76, 88n8, 111, 113, 118, 187, 188, 196, 197, 265, 270, 271, 273, 276, 293, 294, 296, 298, 299, 300, 301n2

Florida, vi, 112, 160–77, 183, 184,196, 225–35

Florida Governor's Council for a Sustainable South, 164

Fort Ancient, 204–07, 219n20

Fort Laramie Treaty of 1851, 19

Fort Laramie Treaty of 1868, 11, 19–20, 29n20

gaming, vi, 2, 101n31, 111–12, 160–72, 175n39, 176n55, 287, 297, 298

gays, 74, 103, 105, 106 (see also homosexuality)

genocide, 26, 168, 232n1
Georgia, 183, 185, 195, 207, 212
Geronimo, 265
Ghost Dance, 112, 140–46, 149n14,
    149–50n20, 297
Gitxsans, 109
Going to War with All My Relations, 95
Granatstein, J. L., 181
Grant, Ulysses S., 18
Great Basin, 68n38, 87n1, 283
Great Lakes, 43, 63, 207, 219n15, 236, 238
Great Plains, 19, 60
Great Sioux Reservation, 21
Great Spirit, 3, 17, 55, 229, 230, 231
Gulf of Mexico, 225

half-breeds, 91, 92, 238, 240–47, 250n31,
    253–60, 299
Halfbreed Chronicles, 91
Hallowell, A. Irving, 57
Harjo, Joy, 289
Harper, Elijah, 8, 26
Harring, Sidney, 161
Highway, Thomson, 78, 88–89n20
Hillerman, Tony, 77, 78, 79, 81, 84, 88n9
Hobson, Geary, 75, 76, 87–88n3
homosexuality, 74, 103–06, 296
homophobia, 74, 103–05, 107
Hopis, vi, vii, 12, 45, 47, 73, 74, 91–93, 96–99,
    112, 152–59, 295–96, 298
Hopi High School, 152, 155
Hopi language, 155, 157
Hopi Reservation, 44, 152, 156, 157
Hopi Tribal Council, 46–47, 157
Hudson Bay Company, 299
Hunkpapas, 19, 29n21, 145
hunting rights, 36
hydroelectricity, vii, 33–39, 42–43
Hydro Québec, 34, 37

identity, 7, 32, 34, 35, 73, 74, 76, 92, 93, 98, 99,
    101n27, 106, 116, 134, 146, 162, 163,
    182, 193, 195, 196, 199, 200, 201, 204,
    209, 211, 214, 217, 239, 241, 242, 247,
    248, 253, 254, 256, 257, 258, 259, 260,
    283, 284, 288, 289, 296, 298, 299, 300
Indian Acts (Canada), 196, 245, 256, 270, 272,
    277, 298

Indian blood, 71, 92, 239, 296
Indian Claims Commission, 8n1, 11, 18, 26
Indian Country, vii, 37, 81, 93, 94, 98, 283
Indian Gaming Regulatory Act, 167, 170, 171,
    172n1, 175n34, 176n55
Indian Killer, 104, 107
Indian nations, 18, 43, 140, 141, 162, 283
Indian New Deal, 296
Indian Peace Commission, 19
Indian Reform Act, 45
Indian Reorganization Act, 296
Indian Territory, 216
Inter-American Conference on Human Rights,
    48
internet, vi, 7, 111, 112, 152–58, 178, 297, 298
Inuits, 26, 37, 153, 158, 252, 253, 263, 271
Iowa, 179, 180
Iowa City, 93–94
Iroquois, 184, 207, 209, 212, 213, 216, 219n15
Irving, Washington, 56
Ishi, 80
Itch Like Crazy, 98–99

Jackson, Andrew, 226, 287
James Bay, 34, 35m
James Bay Project, 11, 34–43, 50
Jefferson, Thomas, 120–23, 125–28, 135n17,
    136n21, 238

KTNN, 288, 289
Kenny, Maurice, 97
Kersean language, 83
King Philip's War, 129, 137n36
Kirk Douglas Billie v. State of Florida (2001), 168
Kishpokos, 203, 210, 213, 216, 221n43
Koyukons, 71
Kutchins, 71

Laguna Pueblos, 76, 99
Laguna language, 86
Lake Nipigon Metis Association, 255
Lakotas, vi, 8n8, 9, 11, 19, 21, 55, 57, 62–63,
    65, 70n72, 112, 140–46, 147n4, 148n7,
    150n20, 169, 193, 293, 295, 297 (*see also*
    Brulés, Hunkpapas, Miniconjous, Oglalas,
    and Sicangus)
Lame Deer, 62
Le Guin, Ursula, 80

Lendrum, John, 124–125, 136n29, 137n36
Lepine, Fred, 154
lesbians, 74, 103–04, 105, 106
Lone Ranger and Tonto Fistfights in Heaven, 104
Long Division: A Tribal History, 91
Lowenthal, David, 254

McGuire, Mike, 255
McGuire, Paddy, 255
Macdonald, John A., 106, 242, 244
MacDonald, Peter, 284
Mackenzie, Alexander, 243
Madisonville Horizon, 205, 206, 208
Maine, 125, 128, 137n44, 183, 185
Major Crimes Act, 169–70, 176n45
Manitoba, 8n1, 17, 21, 178, 185, 186, 190n41,
    196, 243–45, 250n27, 260n2, 299
Manitoba Act (1870), 196, 243, 248, 249n22,
    250n27
Marbury-Lewis, David, 154
Marshall, John, 30n, 50
Marshall, Joseph M. III, 8n8, 65n2, 293, 300,
    301n1
Maoris, 13–16
Maracle, Lee, 80
material culture, 54, 205, 206
Mawedopenais, 9
medicine man, 57, 62, 145, 228
Mekoches, 203, 210, 211, 213, 214, 216,
    219n15, 220n34
Mesoamerica, 7, 8n7
Menominee Tribe of Indians v. United States
    (1968), 18
Metis, vi, vii, 80, 154, 186, 196–97, 236–48,
    250n27, 299, 300
    Metis Nation of Ontario, 254–60
    Ontario Metis, vi, 196, 252–60
    Ontario Metis and Non-Status Indian
        Association, 255–60
    Red River Metis, 196, 253, 254, 256, 258,
        299
Mexico, 7, 95, 231
Miami, Florida, 164, 165, 168, 169
Miamis, 213, 219
Miccosukees, vi, vii, 112, 160–72, 298
Miles, Nelson A., 144, 146
Miniconjous, 11, 29n21
Minot, George, 129

Mississippi River, 24
Missouri River, 56
Mitchell, Bruce M., 182
Miwoks, 73, 91, 92, 95, 296
Mohawks, 11, 17, 26, 78, 97, 193
Momaday, Scott, 280
Mormons, 44, 92, 104, 105
Morris, Alexander, 17, 28n12
Moses, Bertha, 78
Moses, Ted, 39, 52n36
Mount Rushmore, 96
multiculturalism, 181–82
Mukash, Matthew, 40
Muscogees, 98, 227–28

Nakotas, 19, 99
Naskapis, 63
National Council for the Social Studies, 180,
    189n11
National Endowment for the Humanities, 181
National Indian Business Association, 164
Native Americans, xi, 7, 11, 13, 16, 18, 24–26,
    30n37, 44, 54, 56, 63, 73, 74, 77, 85,
    89n36, 90n47, 91, 111, 112, 113, 115–24,
    126, 130–33, 135n15, 152–54, 159n11,
    160, 163, 171, 173, 182, 184, 186, 187,
    190n23, 197, 199, 265, 266, 283, 284,
    289, 294, 295, 297, 298
Native American Church, 289
Native American Rights Fund, 26, 163, 173n13
Native language, 6, 8n5, 17, 33, 82, 83, 86, 99,
    147n5, 153, 155–57, 188, 201, 203, 211,
    233n16, 242, 257, 263, 265, 283, 288
Navajos, v, 8, 11, 12, 32, 33–4, 43–48, 50,
    70n70, 77–78, 103, 186, 265, 266, 280,
    283–90
Navajo language, 288
Navajo Reservation, vii, 44, 77, 280m
Navajo Tribal Council, 45–46
Navajo-Hopi Settlement Act (1974), 47
Nebraska, 56, 144, 178
Nelson, Robert M., 85, 86, 87
Nevada, 141, 183, 185
New France, 65n2, 212, 214
New Hampshire, 97, 117, 118, 125, 183, 185
New Mexico, 183, 185, 281, 283, 287, 289
New Zealand, 14, 15, 27
Nez Percés, 3, 11, 16

Nixon, Richard, 163
Non-Status Indians, 252–56
North-West Rebellion, 244
Northwest Territories, 17, 21, 153, 158, 178, 188, 191n51, 244, 250n27, 254, 263, 266n1
Nunatsiaq News, 153
Nuchneconner, 195, 215, 217, 223n66

Ohio, 183, 185–87, 195, 204–05, 212–13, 215, 217
Ohio River, 205, 214, 223n62
Ohio Valley, 200, 202m, 204, 209, 212, 214
Oklahoma, 77, 183, 185, 195, 196, 216
Omahas, 6, 7, 8n5
Omaha language, 6–7
Oglalas, 19, 29n21, 67n20, 293
Ojibwas, 3, 11, 17, 63, 80, 89, 258 (*see also* Chippewas and Anishinaabes)
Oneidas, 153, 158–59n2
Okanagas, 17
Ontario, vi, 184, 185, 186–87, 252, 254–60, 299
Ontario Metis and Non-Status Indian Association, 255, 256, 258, 260
oral tradition, 186, 193, 203
Ortiz, Simon, 80–87, 89m, 99
Osages, 99
Overtakes the Enemy, 263, 266

Paiutes, 141
Pan-Indian, 87, 88–89n20, 97, 145, 162
Parti Québéquios, 38
Pawnees, 56, 263, 266
Peabody Coal, 46
Pekowis, 203, 210, 211, 213, 223n66
Pennsylvania, 183, 185, 186, 207, 209–13, 215, 221n43, 222n58
Pequots, 127
Pit Rivers, 91
Pontiac, 144, 214, 224n69
postcolonial, vi, 101, 265, 269, 272–73, 276–77, 300
Potomac River, 209–11, 213
Pueblo Revolt, 92

Quapaws, 75
Québec, 8n1, 11, 12, 32–43, 184, 185, 271

railroads, 20
Ramsay, David, 117–19, 121 126, 134, 135n13, 137n14
racism, 37, 81, 93, 94, 98, 283
Reagan, Ronald, 163
Red Cloud, 19–21, 143, 146, 280
Red River (of the North), 17, 196, 242, 252, 253, 254, 257, 258, 259, 299
Redsticks, 226–29
Redbird, Duke, 258, 261n17
religion, 3, 7, 9, 54, 55, 56, 64, 117, 118, 123, 125, 126, 132, 136, 141, 142, 147n4, 203, 242, 297
relocation policy, 47, 172, 193
removal policy, 47, 196, 208, 227–29, 232, 299
Reno, Janet, 170
Reservation Blues, 107
Resolution of 1871, 11, 18–19, 29n18
Revitalization, 112, 140, 162, 294, 296, 298
Riel, Louis, 242, 244, 258, 259
Ritchot, N. J., 242
Roessel, Monty, 284
Rose, Wendy, v, 73, 91–101, 296
Rosebud Reservation, 146
Rupert's Land, 21, 34, 37, 39, 237m, 242, 249

S'Klallams, 109
Said, Edward, 82
Salsbury, Robert, 182
Samis, 13, 15–16
Saskatchewan, 21, 178, 184, 185, 187, 196, 255
Scioto River, 215–16
Sekaymptewa, Loren, 157
self-determination, 32–51
Seminoles, vi, vii, 96, 160–72, 186, 195–96, 197, 200, 225–32, 299
Seminole language, 228
Seminole relocation, 225, 228, 230–32, 299
Seven Years War, 214
Shawnees, vi, 195, 197, 199–217, 299
Shoshones, 57
Sicangus, 16, 19, 296 (*see also* Brulés)
Silko, Leslie Marmon, 76, 80–87, 99
Silver Spring, Florida, 196, 226–32
Sinclair, Jim, 255
Sioux, 9, 19–21, 29n21, 95, 146

Sitting Bull, 9, 12, 143, 145, 146, 150n23

Smith, Low Man, 103

sovereignty, 13–15, 18, 23–27, 32, 33, 37–39, 41, 47–50, 98, 111–13, 160–72, 196–97, 266, 295

Spokanes 73, 102, 103, 104, 107, 296

Spotted Tail, 16, 17, 20, 28n11, 146, 169

Standing Bear, 146

Status Indians, 252–58

Sto:los, 293

subarctic, v, 12, 54, 55, 57, 58, 63–64

Sullivan, James, 128, 137n32

Sun Dance, 57, 61, 143

Supreme Court (US), 18, 23, 47, 50, 162, 166–69, 171, 173n6, 176n42

Tallmountain, Mary, 71, 74n1

Tlingits, 17

Taos Pueblos, 73, 300

Tecumseh, 144

Tennessee, 184

termination policy, 163

Texas, 185

Thawikilas, 203, 210, 213, 216, 218

Thompson, Wiley, 236

Treaty 3, 258

Treaty 4, 11, 21, 22

Treaty 5, 11, 12n1

Treaty 7, 266, 267, 274–75, 278n2

Treaty 8, 251n39

Treaty of Moultrie, 230

Trickster, 73, 75–89, 295

Tsuu T'inas, 265–66, 269–78, 300

Tsuu T'ina Reserve, vii, 270m, 274

Turner v. American Baptist Missionary Union (1852), 25

Two Shields, 62

United Nations, 23, 26, 38, 47, 48, 49, 232n1

UN Commission on Human Rights, 48

UN Declaration of Rights of Indigenous Peoples, 14, 27, 49

United States, 7, 11, 12, 16, 18, 19, 20, 21, 22, 24, 25, 27, 32, 33, 43, 46, 47, 49, 50, 75, 85, 102, 111, 112, 115, 116, 117, 118, 124, 127, 130, 132, 140, 144, 160, 163, 164, 167, 168, 171, 178, 179, 182, 184, 186, 188, 225, 230, 232, 236, 237, 238, 239, 244, 252, 296, 297, 298, 300

United States v. Little Six Inc. (2001), 171

United States Army, 20, 112, 140, 144–46, 161, 265

urban Indians, 97, 99, 103, 265, 274, 286–88, 294

Uukw, Delgam, 109

Virginia, 120, 122, 137n41, 183

Wampum, 17

Warren, Mercy Otis, 111, 131, 138n54, 139n56

Warrior, Robert Allen, 99

Washington (territory and state), 16, 103, 171, 184, 185, 187

Washington, D.C., 20, 280, 289

A Weave of Time, 288, 291n16

Welch, James, 96

West Virginia, 184, 185, 204, 283

Western Canadian Protocol, 178

Williams, Samuel, 123, 130, 136n29

Wilson, Daniel, 238–41

Wilson, Darryl Babe, 91, 100n1

Womack, Craig, 98

women, 59, 65n2, 84, 85, 87, 102, 104–07, 127, 182, 225, 228, 236, 240, 281, 282, 284, 287, 296

Worcester v. Georgia (1832), 170

World War I, 165

World War II, 15, 25, 28n5, 34, 163, 294, 295

Wounded Knee, 7, 96, 112, 145–46, 279–80, 297

Wovaka, 141–43

Yahis, 80

Zeller, Barry, 153

Zunis, 265